Schema Therapy
for Children and Adolescents
ST-CA

A Practitioner's Guide

Edited by
**Christof Loose, Peter Graaf,
Gerhard Zarbock and Ruth A. Holt**

Schema Therapy for Children and Adolescents: A Practitioner's Guide

This edition first published in English in 2020
English translation ©2020 Pavilion Publishing and Media Ltd.
This book is a revised and updated edition of the German language book:
Schematherapie mit Kindern und Jugenlichen
edited by Christof Loose, Peter Graaf and Gerhard Zarbock
©2013 Programm PVU Psychologie Verlags Union in the publishing group Beltz –
Weinheim Basel

Published by:
Pavilion Publishing and Media Ltd
Blue Sky Offices
Cecil Pashley Way
Shoreham by Sea
West Sussex
BN43 5FF
Tel: 01273 434 943
Fax: 01273 227 308
Email: info@pavpub.com

Published 2020

A catalogue record for this book is available from the British Library.

ISBN: 978-1-912755-82-0

Pavilion Publishing and Media is a leading publisher of books, training materials and digital content in mental health, social care and allied fields. Pavilion and its imprints offer must-have knowledge and innovative learning solutions underpinned by sound research and professional values.

Edited by: Christof Loose, Peter Graaf, Gerhard Zarbock and Ruth A. Holt
Production editor: Ruth Chalmers, Pavilion Publishing and Media Ltd
Cover design: Phil Morash, Pavilion Publishing and Media Ltd
Page layout and typesetting: Emma Dawe, Pavilion Publishing and Media Ltd
Printing: Ashford Press

Contents

Foreword by Jeffrey E. Young

I was interested in people from a very early age. As a child I would listen to others' problems, absorbing what people were thinking about. In high school I started collecting psychological texts, keeping records of how my friends scored on personality tests – and then, of course, I went on to study psychology. Not everyone starts off with such a high degree of interest in others, but everyone begins life absorbing the environmental cues around them. These experiences develop life themes that tend to repeat themselves from childhood on. When critical emotional needs are unmet, in concert with temperament and biology, early maladaptive schemas and coping modes can become embedded in the brain's survival system, serving to 'protect' us from interpersonal and intra-psychic threats. Without intervention, these patterns keep playing themselves out, often with distressing and debilitating results.

In developing Schema Therapy I have sought to provide an intensely personal therapeutic approach, working cognitively, experientially and behaviourally with patients, bringing together techniques from a variety of therapeutic traditions. Over the past 25 years an evidence base has developed for the effectiveness of Schema Therapy for a variety of adult populations, which is immensely gratifying. With the publication of this work, this powerful therapy will become available to a younger patient group, serving to intervene in the course of schema development.

When a therapist sits with a child or adolescent, the developmental origins of schemas are in the room and are playing out. So what a perfect opportunity to meet the needs of that child and help the family to provide the care and nurture, structure, autonomy and fun needed to flourish. Understanding the interplay between the parent schemas, family patterns and the child's responses provides a rich opportunity to bring healing and early intervention, preventing the development of psychopathology.

So, to my friends and colleagues, Christof Loose, Peter Graaf, Gerhard Zarbock and Ruth Holt, who wrote this book, I want to say thank you for leading the way in bringing Schema Therapy to children and adolescents. Through wonderfully clear examples, the authors bring Schema Therapy to life for the child and adolescent therapy community. The authors' experience and genuine care are evident on every page of this book, displaying years of masterful work as Schema Therapy practitioners and educators.

I enthusiastically recommend this wonderful book to any professional working with children, adolescents, families, and parents, especially those who aim to intervene in the generational patterns of childhood trauma and distress. This work will richly reward those seeking to develop skills and long lasting outcomes in working with children, adolescents and their families.

Jeffrey E. Young, PhD
Honorary President: International Society for Schema Therapy
Director and Founder: Schema Therapy Institute
Adjunct Faculty Member: Columbia University Department of Psychiatry

Foreword by David Edwards

For therapists who work with children and adolescents, there is an exciting and inspiring array of approaches to intervention as well as specific techniques and expressive media. But this diversity can be bewildering. Depending on the theories on which they are based, the various therapy 'brands' often make very different and apparently competing recommendations. All can be right. But they can all be wrong too. It depends on the case: the broader context, the personality of the young person and the dynamics of the family. There is such a wide variation in these factors that there is no simple recipe, no 'one size fits all.'

So, what is the best approach for the case I am presented with in my office this afternoon at 4 o'clock? To answer this, we need an integrative approach – and this is what this book provides. The psychotherapy integration movement has been gaining momentum for three decades. In the introduction to the third edition of the *Handbook of Psychotherapy Integration*, Goldfried and Norcross (2019, p. vii) write that integration is now "the modal orientation of mental health professionals." They refer to increasing research evidence for effectiveness of integrative approaches, and how "integration has developed into a mature and international movement."

Schema therapy provides a framework for integrating a wide range of tried and tested approaches and techniques as well as many original ones. But it is not just eclectic; that is, it is not an excuse to use whatever the therapist feels like on the day. Although there are specific techniques that are a regular part of schema therapy whether we are working with adults or young people, the heart of schema therapy is its approach to case conceptualization. A major focus for this is the needs of infants and young children, familiar to us from decades of research on attachment theory, and how, when these needs are not adequately met, problematic patterns of cognition and emotion result, which we call early maladaptive schemas. Another important perspective is multiplicity: people of all ages move between different recognizable states of schema modes; and understanding these provides important insights and leverage for change. Assessment in terms of these factors allows us to conceptualize how the maladaptive schemas are perpetuated or exacerbated by coping modes and the current stressors that activate them. We then look for appropriate therapeutic strategies to break the cycle.

This book provides insight into the range of approaches that can be used when working within the schema therapy model, whether individually with the young person, with the parents, with the family, and using therapy groups. These can be selected or combined based on the case conceptualization and the therapy tasks that are identified as important. This book provides numerous examples of different kinds of interventions, cognitive and behavioural work, emotion focused experiential work using imagery and chairwork, games, stories, various expressive and play media, and working with the relationships both with the therapist and within the family. We see how these are selected based on how the therapist conceptualizes the case.

Several chapters describe the thorough assessment process on which case conceptualization is based. This normally involves not only the child or adolescent but also significant family members. In addition to clinical interviews, schema therapists are likely to combine traditional tools such as a multigenerational genogram with specialized ways of identifying schemas and modes and the extent to which parents did or did not meet their child's needs. These may be employed with the child or adolescent whose problems are the focus of the initial referral, but the same kind of information about the parents can also be valuable in obtaining a comprehensive understanding.

I warmly welcome publication of this book for an English-speaking audience. It offers an exciting collection of insights, full of practical clinical examples of the schema therapist's way of conducting an assessment, conceptualizing cases, and implementing interventions for a range of clinical problems and across the entire age range from infancy to adolescence. It is a rich resource.

Reference

Norcross, J. C., & Goldfried, M. R. (Eds.). (2019). *Handbook of Psychotherapy Integration* (3rd ed.). New York: Oxford University Press.

David Edwards, PhD
President: International Society of Schema Therapy.
Founding Fellow: Academy of Cognitive and Behavioral Therapies.
Professor (Emeritus): Rhodes University.
Honorary Professor: University of Cape Town.

Preface

This book is not only a joy for us, it is also a risk. For the first time we are completely transferring the concepts of Schema Therapy, as formulated by Jeffrey Young and further developed and evaluated by Arnold Arntz, to the field of child and adolescent psychotherapy.

It is a book by practitioners, for practitioners. We also want to be upfront about the fact that the ideas and concepts are still developing. We are continually adapting ideas and techniques and present our book as a work in progress. At the same time we would like to ask you, our readers, to support and further develop Schema Therapy for children and adolescents not only with constructive criticism and feedback from your own experience in practice, but also with research (e.g. controlled case studies, group studies, RCT studies, etc).

Before we give our grateful thanks to all our supporters, we would like to quickly explain how we came to write *Schema Therapy for Children and Adolescents*. Gerhard Zarbock, an experienced Schema Therapist and head of a training institute which includes Child and Adolescent Behavioral Therapy (IVAH, Hamburg), had the idea for a book about Child and Adolescent Schema Therapy. In outlining ideas for the book, the complexity of the task quickly became obvious. Gerhard then recognised the need for co-authors with clear and long-term experience in Schema Therapy with children. He contacted Petra Baumann-Frankenberger (IST Cologne), who leads a supervision group focusing on Schema Therapy for children and adolescents in Cologne. Christof Loose, an experienced colleague from this group who has his own website about Schema Therapy for children, was also eager to help create the book. Peter Graaf from Hamburg, who has given seminars and workshops Germany-wide for several years on ideas he has developed alongside Heinrich Berbalk (Schema and mode-based behaviour therapy for children, adolescents and parents), was also enthusiastic. An extremely hard working and ambitious trio was now gathered whose creative contributions can be found in this book. The order below reflects the authors' respective fields of work and experience, and the amount of time that they could invest in the book.

Structure of book

Following the Foreword, you can find a general introduction to Schema Therapy with children and adolescents (ST-CA) in Chapters 1 to 3. These chapters sketch the main theories, developmental models and psychopathology, outline the Schema

Therapy model, explain the concept of modes, focus on age-specific issues and give initial insights into ST-CA (Case conceptualization, phases, therapeutic stance, central features). Start with these chapters, as the rest of the book is built upon this foundation. Throughout the book the male pronoun has been used, apart from case studies and examples where relevant, for the sake of simplicity and readability.

Chapters 4 to 8 focus on age-specific issues. Chapter 4 deals with Schema Therapy for infants and young children. An innovative Schema Therapy contribution to the field is suggested, starting with developmental psychology and established treatment considerations. The following chapters deal with preschool age, primary school age and early adolescence (Chapters 5, 6 and 7 respectively). These chapters are focused on implementing Schema Therapy with each age group and provide new perspectives, ideas and methods. Chapter 8 (Schema Therapy in late adolescence and young adults) gives practical and deeper insights into techniques when working at this transitional stage.

Chapters 9 and 10 provide invaluable support in setting the tone for ST-CA and beginning therapy, with Chapter 10 outlining in detail the five key components in ST-CA. Chapters 11 to 14 focus on how to implement those components using creative, child-friendly mediums, including puppets, drawing, chair work and imagery.

Chapters 15 to 17 are especially important because ST-CA is very much grounded in parent work (which is more briefly covered in the other chapters). Chapter 15 also underlines the specific strengths of Schema Therapy for children and adolescents in comparison to other therapies, showing how Schema Therapy techniques and approaches can be integrated with systemic approaches.

The German edition of this book included chapters on formulating expert opinions using Schema Therapy approaches and an overview of the development and spread of ST-CA. However, in updating the book we have replaced these with a chapter on group work with children and adolescents, building on the success of Group Schema Therapy with adults. Chapter 18 discusses practical issues in setting up Schema Therapy groups for children and adolescents, stages of Group Schema Therapy (GST-CA) and group-based interventions, from the wealth of experience of Maria Galimzyanova and Elena Romanova.

Acknowledgments

We also want to draw your attention to the International Society of Schema Therapy (ISST). The ISST's current president, David Edwards, has provided great encouragement on this project and we appreciate his thoughts in his Foreword.

By becoming a member of the ISST, you have access to the most current developments in Schema Therapy research and applications. You can also find the ST-CA working group there. More information can be found at www.schematherapysociety.org.

If you are interested in the latest developments in ST-CA, the website www.schematherapy-for-children.de is where you can also find up-to-date information about the current state of ST-CA.

We would now like to thank lots of people whose engagement and support made this book possible. First and foremost, we thank Jeffrey Young for the foundational concepts of Schema Therapy. Arnoud Arntz is owed gratitude for his untiring striving for empirical evaluation of Schema Therapy concepts and procedures. Schema Therapy can only gain a fixed place as an evidence-based therapy through extensive empirical studies. Heinrich Berbalk is here not only for being the first to spread Schema Therapy, training many heads of Schema Therapy institutes in the German-speaking region, but also for having the initiative to develop Schema Therapy for children and adolescents. We see him as the father of Schema Therapy for children and adolescents – and not just because of his finger puppets in mode work! Eckhard Roediger is another person we cannot thank enough, for his brilliantly thought out, didactically superb books, but especially for his support for ST-CA. We would also like to thank Gitta Jacobs for her excellent books about Schema Therapy, particularly mode work, which have demonstrated the concepts so clearly and practically for a large readership. On top of that, Beltz publishers are also owed our thanks, for their numerous German-speaking publications on this subject. They have – like us – committed themselves to Schema Therapy and have greatly helped it to reach its current level of popularity in Germany, Austria and Switzerland. Also, Bruce Stevens has been very instrumental in bringing this English edition to life, helping find our current publisher.

In addition to the publishers and authors, we have also sought experienced and well-known child therapists like Günter Groen (Hamburg) and Dorothee Verbeek (Lübeck), who gave their opinion on relevant excerpts. They provided very valuable and constructive feedback that we readily took into account before completing the German-speaking manuscript. Note that the current English-speaking manuscript is slightly changed to the German version, containing more information about the main theories, including the attachment theory, Ellis's ABC model, and other significant models and concepts.

We would further like to thank Annekatrin Thies (Werner-Otto Institute, Hamburg) for reviewing the chapter on infants and providing tips on current regulatory disorders guidelines. Ulla Eckardt from Berlin also gave us some lovely suggestions concerning her Schema Therapy work with the family board.

Thank you also, Mrs Schrameyer, who liaised with the editorial office, providing very constructive support for the German publication (Beltz), and Darren Reed, for taking on a large project and bringing ST-CA to the English-speaking world.

We would also like to thank Lucy Goldstein, LMSW, New York City, and Erin Bulluss, an Australian Child and Adolescent Schema Therapist and Trainer, for their assistance in providing helpful feedback and beginning the task of revising Chapters 9 to 14. In addition, Vibeke Vaerum, Astrid von Lojewski-Wilson, Dorothea Anna Carl, Fritz Renner and Pamela Fitzgerald all assisted with early translations of the work and made significant contributions in developing the English language version you have in your hands.

We are extremely thankful for the support of our employers (Christof Loose: HHU Düsseldorf, Institute for Experimental Psychology, Department of Clinical Psychology; Head: R. Pietrowsky; Peter Graaf: Werner-Otto Institute, EKA-Alstersdorf, Hamburg; Gerhard Zarbock: IVAH, Institute for Behavioral Therapy Training, Hamburg).

We – Christof, Peter and Gerhard – also have profound gratitude for Ruth Holt (Schema Therapist/Trainer and Principal at Canberra Clinical and Forensic Psychology, Australia) who reread and revised each of the book's chapters, and brought the book into its final version in English. Her thorough research and dedication to clarity were crucial in bringing our work to an English language audience. We have appreciated her warm and gracious manner throughout the translation work.

Last but not least, we would like to give our families a very special and loving thank you for their consideration during the creation of the manuscript, which saw us disappear behind our computers much too often.

We wish you, our readers, lots of enjoyment in immersing yourself in the book, and hope to inspire as many colleagues as possible. We look forward to hearing feedback, whether positive, complimentary or critical feedback.

Christof Loose, Peter Graaf, Gerhard Zarbock & Ruth A. Holt, January, 2020

Chapter 1: Child and Adolescent Psychology and Psychotherapy

Christof Loose, Gerhard Zarbock, Peter Graaf and Ruth Holt

1.1 Introduction

Schema Therapy for children and adolescents (ST-CA) is a powerful approach that brings the tools and techniques of Schema Therapy (ST) to the field of child and adolescent psychotherapy.

Child and adolescent psychotherapists are dedicated to understanding deeply the complex emotional lives of infants, children, young people, and parents/caregivers. Meanwhile, Schema Therapy aims to look below the surface of problematic emotions, behaviours or relationships in order to help individuals and family systems to understand themselves and their difficulties more clearly. By putting the two together to reveal the deeper layers of a problem affecting a young person or family system, clinicians can create a strong platform from which to design and deliver successful interventions.

This chapter explores the historical underpinnings of Schema Therapy for children and adolescents. When trying to understand the emotions and behaviours of children and adults, we are always standing on the shoulders of giants and it is helpful to have some key theories and concepts in mind. Join us, then, on a whistle stop tour through the history of psychology and psychotherapy.

1.2 Exploring the human psyche

Our first stop is early 20th century Vienna, where a neurologist is beginning to disseminate theories about the development of the human psyche that will prove immensely influential. His name is Sigmund Freud, and he has already begun to use the term *psychoanalysis*. According to Freud, the whole of life is built around tension and pleasure. In particular, he stressed that the first five years of life are primarily unconscious yet crucial – not only to the development of the child but also to the eventual development of the adult personality. Today, implicit systems and memories from these early years are critical to many psychological and psychotherapeutic approaches, including Schema Therapy.

Perhaps Freud's best-known and most important idea was that the human mind has more than one aspect. According to his Personality Theory (1923), the psyche is structured into three component parts or systems: the id, ego and super-ego. The id is the instinctual part, incorporating sexual and aggressive drives, and follows what Freud called the 'pleasure principle' (seeking pleasure and avoiding pain). At the other extreme, the super-ego is our critical compass, incorporating the norms and values of society that are taught by parents and other caregivers. The super-ego develops around age four and follows the 'morality principle' (behaving in socially acceptable, responsible ways). Mediating between the two, the ego balances the desires of the id and the constraints of the super-ego. It is the decision-making part and works by reason, according to the 'reality principle.' The ego takes account of social and emotional rules before deciding how to think, feel and behave.

While the passage of time has seen much of Freud's work superseded, he remains a central figure in the development of psychotherapy and his core ideas have endured. Some of his central theories – for example that the mind can have simultaneous and contradictory perspectives, that early experience is of vital importance to adult personality, and that early memories have an unconscious impact on present behaviour – can be clearly seen in contemporary approaches such as ST-CA.

1.3 Classical conditioning

We now move to St. Petersburg, where a physiologist named Ivan Pavlov is conducting research into learning processes – and in the process becoming a founder of modern behavioural therapy. Pavlov established how physiological responses (including emotional responses) could become associated with specific stimuli or situations. His breakthrough came when he realised that his dogs began to salivate not on being given food, as he expected, but on hearing the footsteps of someone bringing food. Pavlov investigated this further, pairing the expectation of food with sounds such as a bell and a metronome in order to create 'conditioned' responses, and the field of classical (or Pavlovian) conditioning was born.

Later, the South-African born psychologist Joseph Wolpe showed how anxiety could be reduced by pairing events that trigger anxiety in an individual (such as spiders) with an antagonistic response (such as relaxation). He developed a procedure called Systematic Desensitization, involving a graded exposure to a hierarchy of feared situations whilst inducing a relaxed state. This proved to be an effective treatment for many simple phobias. Later evaluative conditioning, an extension of classical conditioning developed in England by Irene Levey and A.B. Martin, showed that a person's response to a conditioned stimulus could be changed simply by pairing the stimulus with a positive (or negative) unconditioned stimulus.

Conditioning and the broader field of associative learning is fascinating in its own right; however its core value to ST-CA lies in its discoveries that behaviour and emotions can be produced by the association of stimuli, and that ideas, experiences and attitudes can reinforce each other.

1.4 Behaviourism and social learning theory

Another powerful learning theory was developed by John Watson in America. Behaviourism is only concerned with observable stimulus-response behaviours and therefore emphasizes the crucial role of environmental factors on human behaviour. Watson's credo was that all behaviour, no matter how complex, is reducible to stimulus-response features. In a further development, B.F. Skinner introduced operant conditioning – a method of learning that occurs through punishments and rewards for behaviour. In operant conditioning, an individual comes to associate a specific behaviour with its consequences. Developing Edward Thorndike's Law of Effect (behaviour followed by pleasant consequences is more likely to be repeated than behaviour followed by unpleasant consequences), Skinner argued that the best way to understand and modify behaviour is to look at the preceding stimuli of an action and what follows after it. He investigated how the provision of rewards and punishments for specific behaviours caused individuals to respond in a range of predictable ways.

In order to cover all the most important learning theories we must also mention the social learning theory of Albert Bandura. Bandura generally agreed with classical and operant conditioning but recognized that there was also a cognitive element that the behaviourists had discounted. This played a huge role in humanising the behavioural approach. Bandura also proposed a critical factor for understanding children's behaviour – that behaviours are acquired through so-called observational learning. When children are with influential models like parents, teachers and friends, they can encode behaviour (good or bad) simply by observing it and later imitate that behaviour. A child may eventually come to identify with the person who originally modelled the behaviour, resulting in a wider adoption of that person's observed behaviours, values, attitudes and beliefs.

1.5 Attachment theory

We now visit London, where a theory was developed that proved immensely important both to child psychology in general and to Schema Therapy in particular. Attachment theory came about through the pioneering work of John Bowlby and later Mary Ainsworth. In the 1930s, Bowlby worked as a psychiatrist in a Child Guidance Clinic, where he treated emotionally disturbed children. During this challenging work he observed and investigated the importance of the relationship between mothers and their children from social, cognitive and particularly emotional points of view. This shaped his basic idea about the link between early separations of mother and child and later maladaptive behaviours.

Bowlby's findings contradicted the dominant behavioural theory of attachment, which stated that a child becomes attached to its mother because of conditional learning processes (for instance via the provision of food). Bowlby defined attachment as a "lasting psychological connectedness between human beings". He argued that attachment can be understood as an evolutionary process, and that infants have a universal need to seek proximity with their caregiver in order to help them survive. Infants display behaviours such as crying and smiling to stimulate caregiving responses, and when caregivers are under stress or feel threatened the security of the infant is compromised too.

Mary Ainsworth was an American developmental psychologist who worked with Bowlby and later independently. She is best known for the Strange Situation Procedure, developed to observe individual differences in attachment behaviour by evoking children's reactions when encountering attachment stress. She categorized different types of attachment, showing that there are different ways of regulating emotions and responding to perceived attachment threats, and demonstrated what can go wrong when a child's needs for secure attachment are not met. Together, Bowlby and Ainsworth argued that attachment is a deep and enduring emotional bond that connects one person to another across time and space, and that the crucial factor in creating a secure attachment relationship is not food but nurturing care, loving warmth and emotional responsiveness.

1.6 Psychosocial development theory

Erik Erikson, a German-American developmental psychologist and psychoanalyst, is best known for a theory he formulated on the psychological development of human beings. Like many other developmental psychologists, Erikson maintained that the personality develops in a predetermined order, with a series of defined stages each building on the previous stage. Erikson defined five stages from birth to the age of 18, and a further three for adulthood. Within each stage every human being experiences a characteristic psychosocial crisis, where their individual psychological needs are pitted against the needs of society. The outcome of each crisis influences the next crisis, and successful completion of each stage is important for the development of a healthy personality and the acquisition of basic virtues. Table 1.1 depicts these stages and their associated virtues.

Table 1.1: Stages of Psychosocial Development by E. Erikson (1950)			
Stage	Psychosocial Crisis	Basic Virtue	Age
1	Trust vs. Mistrust	Hope	0 - 1½
2	Autonomy vs. Shame	Will	1½ - 3
3	Initiative vs. Guilt	Purpose	3 - 5
4	Industry vs. Inferiority	Competency	5 - 12
5	Identity vs. Role Confusion	Fidelity	12 - 18
6	Intimacy vs. Isolation	Love	18 - 40
7	Generativity vs. Stagnation	Care	40 - 65
8	Ego Integrity vs. Despair	Wisdom	65+

Practitioners working therapeutically with children and adolescents are typically faced with at least one issue related to the first five crises in addition to the presenting problem. We may also face typical childhood crises when working with adult clients or parents of clients, who may relive the unresolved crises of their own childhoods (e.g. through their parenting approaches).

The developmental tasks model of Robert Havighurst provides further insights into the roots of maladaptive behaviour and psychopathology. The model asserts that development occurs in stages throughout the lifespan, and individuals proceed from one stage to the next by completing tasks. The tasks may be normative (inevitable challenges such as mastering daily hygiene or separating from parents in order to attend school) or non-normative (atypical challenges such as adjusting to the death of a parent). Successful completion of a task results in pride, satisfaction and approval; failure can lead to unhappiness and other problems. This is a biopsychosocial model: the tasks at each stage are influenced by an individual's biology (genetics and physical state) and psychology (personal values and goals), as well by the society and culture to which he or she belongs.

1.7 Cognitive Behavioural Therapy

After the first generation of behaviour therapy – the application of learning principles in an effort to change human behaviour – and keeping in mind the developmental stages and tasks of Erikson and Havighurst, the next major milestone was the shift to classic Cognitive Behavioural Therapy (CBT). The pioneers of CBT were Albert Ellis and Aaron Beck.

Let's start with Ellis's ABC model (1957). The basic idea behind this model is that external or internal events (A for Activating event) do not in themselves cause emotional, cognitive, somatic and/or behavioural responses in an individual. Rather, it is the way in which these events are cognitively processed and evaluated (B for Beliefs) that produces the result (C for Consequences). The ABC Model can also be referred to as the ABCDE model (Ellis & Dryden, 1987), where D stands for the Disputation of beliefs and E stands for the (new) Effect, meaning the alternative consequence when the irrational belief has become a rational one. The core therapeutic idea behind the ABC Model is that clients do not necessarily have to change their environment (A) to change an outcome; they simply need to recognize and change the processing of events (B->D) and the original response (C) will become a new one (E). An example how to apply this model for children is shown in chapter 9.

Aaron Beck is widely regarded as the father of both Cognitive Therapy and CBT. His pioneering work at the University of Pennsylvania led to approaches that are at the heart of clinical treatment of depression, anxiety disorders and many other mental health problems today. He also supported and influenced many other psychologists who in time became hugely influential in their own right – they include Martin Seligman (who developed Positive Psychology), Mervin Smucker (who developed Imagery Rescripting, a core component of Schema Therapy), Mark Williams (who developed Mindfulness-Based Cognitive Therapy) and Jeffrey Young (the founder of Schema Therapy). Beck's approaches have also been adapted into age-appropriate tools for young people, for instance by Paul Stallard (2018) – a tradition we continue in this book. For anyone approaching ST-CA without prior knowledge of CBT, we recommend further study of Beck and his most influential theories.

1.8 Temperament and personality

The ability to cope with developmental tasks, and with mental well-being challenges more generally, is partly dependent on the temperament of the individual child. One of the best-known descriptions of temperament was formulated by Alexander Thomas, Stella Chess and colleagues, based on an influential New York longitudinal study of young children which they began in 1956. They differentiated nine dimensions of temperament (1963), and subsequently three constellations of childhood temperament (1977). These dimensions and constellations are shown in table 1.2.

Table 1.2 Temperamental Dimensions and Constellations in Children	
Temperamental dimensions (Thomas *et al*, 1963)	Temperamental constellations (Thomas & Chess, 1977)
■ Level of activity ■ Regularity/rhythmicity ■ Initial reaction (approach or avoidance) ■ Adaptability ■ Response intensity ■ Mood ■ Distractibility ■ Attention span and persistence ■ Sensitivity	■ The easy child ■ The difficult child ■ The slow to warm up child

Thomas and Chess argued that it is possible from early infancy to differentiate children with 'easy', 'difficult' and 'slow to warm up' temperaments. Difficult children tend to react negatively to unfamiliar stimuli and irregularities in routine. They cry frequently and find it difficult to adopt regular and predictable rhythms of eating and sleeping. Slow to warm up children have generally low levels of activity and tend to demonstrate avoidance of new situations and of men, though their reactions are less marked than those of difficult children. Easy children, by contract, are generally happy, establish routines easily and adapt to new experiences without significant problems.

More recently, Mary Rothbart and John Bates (2006) reviewed approaches to understanding temperament and concluded that there was general agreement on there being two major dimensions of temperament – *approach* (positivity, extroversion, seeking stimuli, curiosity) and *inhibition* (negativity, shyness, anxiety, irritability). This links to Jeffrey Alan Gray's biopsychosocial theory of personality (1970), which proposed that two systems govern an individual's interactions with their environment – a behavioural inhibition system (sensitivity to punishment, motivation to avoid) and a behavioural activation system (sensitivity to reward, motivation to approach).

1.9 The 'Big Five'

The temperamental factors described above have clear links to the 'Big Five' model of personality. This model was initially proposed by Ernest Tupes and Raymond Christal in 1961 but did not become influential until the 1980s and has been developed by many researchers since. It groups personality traits into five robust overarching domains, which are assumed to represent the basic structure behind all personality. The five domains are openness to experience, conscientiousness, extraversion, agreeableness and neuroticism. The age at which each of these factors occurs is currently being researched, but since they are also found in non-human primates (Weiss *et al*, 2006) we can assume that at least the precursors of these factors can be detected relatively early in development.

Table 1.3 Big Five Personality Factors with Typical Characteristics

Personality Factors	Characteristics
1. Openness to experience	■ Open children have a strong need to explore. New experiences are often intensely sought. There is a high need for variety. Stimulus monotony is difficult to endure. ■ Children who score low on openness may have more blunted affect, find change difficult, prefer familiarity and have limited curiosity.
2. Conscientiousness (organization and perseverance)	■ Children who have a high level of conscientiousness are inclined towards obedience of authority and rules without connection to fear of punishment. ■ Children who score low tend to feel inept, are disorganized, impetuous and have low level of need for achievement. ■ The extent to which this factor is predominantly genetic, and not the result of an internalization of parent-sanctioned standards and regulations, is open for discussion.
3. Extraversion (versus Introversion)	■ An extroverted child is directed outward, sociable, and often on the lookout for new stimuli. ■ An introverted child is rather unsociable, inward, and occupied with his or her own feelings and thoughts.

Personality Factors	Characteristics
4. Agreeableness (trust, honesty and compliance)	■ Agreeable children are able to resolve social conflicts and have a high threshold in terms of aggressive behavior. They are more easily able to empathize with others. ■ Children who score low score on this factor are characterized by irritability, being a loner, and displaying aggressive tendencies and self-interest.
5. Neuroticism (emotional stability versus instability)	■ An emotionally stable child is 'unflappable'; able to calm down quickly, often in a good mood and happy. ■ Emotionally unstable children respond quickly to aversive stimuli, become agitated easily and are slow to calm down.

1.10 Environmental risk factors and transactional stress

When thinking about temperament and personality traits, we are exploring the neurobiological foundation of the individual and their natural proclivity toward psychopathology or mental well-being. However, we must keep in mind that no child exists in a vacuum. There are many socio-environmental risk factors that are associated with the development of mental ill health – including low socio-economic status, dysfunctional family relationships, sexual or physical abuse and the loss of a parent. Conversely, protective factors aid development and can lessen the impact of risk factors. The best-known protective factors are having at least one high quality attachment relationship and a high level of general intelligence, but resilience and even physical attractiveness are also considered protective factors. If an individual has some of these factors, then the impact of a negative environment is likely to be reduced.

How neurobiological factors interact with environmental factors and learning theories is a complex question. One way to answer it is via the Transactional Model of Stress and Coping, first proposed by Richard Lazarus in 1966. This presents stress as the product of a transaction between an individual and their environment. The individual has a set of predispositions of temperament that causes them to experience their environment in a specific way – and respond accordingly. This response then impacts their environment further in an ongoing interaction between nature and nurture.

An alternative way to understand the interactions between a child and its environment is to think of the total environment as representing a fulfilment or a frustration of the child's basic psychological needs. Thinking in this way is, as we shall see in the next chapter, a cornerstone of Schema Therapy.

Literature

Ellis, A. & Dryden, W. (1987). The practice of rational-emotive therapy (RET). Springer Publishing Co.

Ellis, A. (1957) Rational psychotherapy and individual psychology. Journal of Individual Psychology 13 38–44.

Erikson, E. H. (1950). Childhood and society. New York: Norton.

Freud, S. (1923). The ego and the id. SE, 19: 1-66.

Gray, J. A. (1970). The psychophysiological basis of introversion-extraversion. Behav. Res. Ther. 8, 249–266.

Lazarus, R.S. (1991). Emotion and Adaption. New York: Oxford University Press.

Rothbart, M. K., & Bates, J. E. (2006). Temperament. Handbook of Child Psychology

Stallard, P. (2018). Think Good, Feel Good: A Cognitive Behavioural Therapy Workbook for Children and Young People. Wiley-Blackwell

Thomas, A. & Chess, S. (1977). Temperament and Development. New York: Brunner & Mazel.

Thomas, A., Chess, S., Birch, H.G.& Korn, S. (1963). Behavioral Individuality in Early Childhood. New York: University Press.

Tupes, E. C. & Christal, R. E. (1961). Recurrent Personality Factors Based on Trait Ratings. Technical Report ASD-TR-61-97, Lackland Air Force Base, TX: Personnel Laboratory, Air Force Systems Command.

Weiss, A., King, J. E. & Perkins, L. (2006). Personality and subjective well-being in orangutan. Journal of Personality and Social Psychology, 90, 501–511.

Chapter 2: Key theories and concepts in Schema Therapy and ST-CA

Christof Loose, Gerhard Zarbock, Peter Graaf and Ruth Holt

2.1 Introduction

The Schema Therapy model and its associated clinical approach draw to some extent on all the perspectives described in the previous chapter, but give a central place to four aspects in particular:

1. **Basic needs**

Schema therapy considers psychological needs to be the basis of our self-experience and the driving force behind human behaviour. Chronic frustration of needs through absence of nurture, presence of abuse, trauma, or a lack of limits will allow risk factors to unfold their potential to harm mental and emotional well-being.

2. **Schemas**

Schemas (also termed 'Early Maladaptive Schemas') are 'a broad organizing principle for making sense of one's life experience' (Young *et al*, 2003), and are made up of thoughts, feelings, memories and body sensations. They develop when core emotional needs are not met and provide a way of explaining past experiences and setting up future expectations. Schemas express one's view of the self and relationship with others, reflecting the tone of the early environment.

3. **Coping styles**

Each person develops individual responses to adapt to schemas, providing relief from the intense emotional distress that arises from them. From a developmental psychopathology perspective, coping styles can also be the precursors of disorders.

4. **Schema modes**

Schema modes are the 'moment-to-moment emotional states and coping responses – adaptive or maladaptive – that we all experience' (Young *et al*, 2003). There are helpful modes and unhelpful modes. Unhelpful modes are activated when a schema or coping style has taken over. Modes are momentary states rather than longer-term traits.

2.1 Basic needs

The Schema Therapy model proposes that psychopathology symptoms result from toxic frustration of *basic psychological needs*. Various authors, including Klaus Grawe (2017), have postulated core psychological needs grounded in evolution. Their work has informed a more accessible model (Figure 2.1) which helps us to understand the different levels and facets of needs. Note that basic physical needs like nutrition, sleep and safety are not included here, although we acknowledge their importance and in situations where they are absent there will of course be significant impact.

Figure 2.1: Key psychological needs defined by Klaus Grawe (2017)	
1. Attachment	Being part of loving relationships and belonging to supportive communities.
2. Autonomy	Being independent from the influence of others; having self-reliance, self-efficacy and the ability to control one's own environment.
3. Self-esteem	Being able to appreciate and value oneself, and to have self-respect.
4. Play, joy, happiness, stimulation	Being spontaneous and having the freedom to express oneself and gain pleasure.

Grawe also postulated an overarching human need for *consistency*. One could also view this as a need for structure and orientation, in the sense that an individual's environment should be understandable and predictable in order to be controlled. Of great importance here is the basic human need to experience boundaries, structures and rules. Humans strive to find rules and consistency in their personality, in their memories and in their experiences. The same holds true for the significant environment that humans live in – there is a desire for clear rules that define belonging (or not belonging) to key social structures like family, peer group or nation.

A chronic frustration of basic needs, and/or a lack of consistency, leads to the forming of certain dysfunctional schemas and coping patterns. See Figure 2.2, which shows our model of basic needs. The axis from north to south, the autonomy axis, is central for the healthy development of the child. Attempting to meet basic needs in the presence of risk factors and developmental tasks can lead to situations where these needs are frustrated. If this occurs then emotions like anxiety, sadness, anger, and shame result. If these emotions are experienced intensely enough, and for long enough, then it may establish an automatic tendency to cope with such emotions in a stereotypical way.

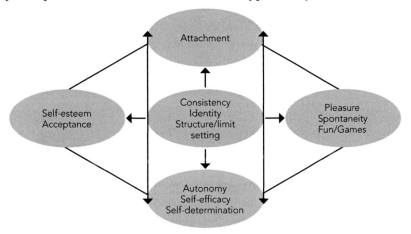

Figure 2.2 Basic Needs Frustration model

2.2 Schemas

As we have seen, Early Maladaptive Schemas, or simply schemas, are 'a broad organizing principle for making sense of one's life experience' (Young *et al*, 2003). A schema can be understood as a system of memories, cognitions, emotions, and bodily sensations. In Schema Therapy, schemas are self-defeating patterns in that they drive behaviour that prevents individuals from overcoming life difficulties and fulfilling their potential. Schemas are self-perpetuating, in that individuals will be drawn to situations and people that confirm their schemas in their search for consistency.

Young defines schemas as being enduring in the sense of *traits*. Such traits develop when an individual temperament has recurrent damaging interactions with close and/or significant others, and forms representations of that experience. These representations can involve negative self-attributions (such as 'I am helpless, weak, and exposed') as well as negative interpretations of the other person (such as 'you are untrustworthy, overpowering, or threatening'). Because they typically develop in childhood, dysfunctional schemas are described within

Schema Therapy as Early Maladaptive Schemas. They persist throughout the lifespan and become familiar ways of thinking – we interpret events through their distorting lens. Sometimes a schema can be dormant, and it will not be evident until it is activated by an event or situation relevant to it.

Schemas can be differentiated as *unconditional* or *conditional*. Unconditional schemas, also known as core schemas (Roediger *et al*, 2018), relate to a child's earliest experiences and encapsulate what was learned in those experiences. For example, an Emotional Deprivation schema develops when significant others do not meet normal emotional needs for nurture, empathy and protection, despite being physically present, and an Abandonment schema develops from the loss of a positive relationship with a significant other (e.g. through the death of a parent) or instability in emotional presence. Conditional schemas, by contrast, develop in order to manage the distress of unconditional schemas. For example, a Subjugation schema (excessive surrendering to others) could develop in order to keep an attachment figure close rather than risk Abandonment through losing that person. Table 2.1 lists both kinds of schemas (note that there is no direct relationship between rows in the table).

Table 2.1 Unconditional and Conditional Schemas; Young, 2003 and Roediger *et al*, 2018

Unconditional (Core) Schemas	Conditional Schemas
■ Abandonment/Instability	■ Subjugation
■ Defectiveness/Shame	■ Unrelenting Standards/Hypocriticalness
■ Social Isolation	■ Self-Sacrifice
■ Emotional Deprivation	■ Approval-Seeking/Recognition-Seeking
■ Mistrust/Abuse	■ Emotional Inhibition
■ Dependence/Incompetence	
■ Vulnerability	
■ Enmeshment/Undeveloped Self	
■ Failure	
■ Insufficient Self-Control/-Discipline	
■ Negativity/Pessimism	
■ Punitiveness	
■ Entitlement/Grandiosity	

It should be noted there are differing points of view regarding which schemas belong to the core and conditional groups. For example, Punitiveness has a primary aspect ('I deserve to be punished') but also a secondary one in terms of self-critical behaviour. For further remarks see Roediger *et al*, 2018, p. 32.

Together, schemas represent a model of basic emotional needs being met or frustrated. Clinically, when seeking to understand a client's schema, it is helpful to ask 'which basic need may have been frustrated during the development of this schema?' and to remember that, no matter how dysfunctional, the schema was originally developed as a strategy for getting needs met.

2.3 Coping styles

The damaging experiences that lead to the development of schemas are typically managed with one or more overall types of unhealthy response, called coping styles. Coping styles are the result of the interaction between modelling, temperamental factors, and operant conditioning. Schema therapy identifies three coping styles, with some parallels to evolutionary 'fight-flight-freeze' responses.

- **Overcompensation** describes behaving in a way that is the opposite of the schema, or at least as different as possible to the schema. This coping style can transform a person from a passive victim to an active perpetrator, with distressing emotions like shame or anxiety being deliberately and determinedly fought in order to suppress the schema threatening to erupt.

- **Avoidance** describes behaving in a way that hinders, blocks or delays activation of the schema. This can involve literally running away from the situation or avoiding the schema in other ways. It can involve detaching to numb emotional distress, or more active avoidance strategies like distraction or substance abuse.

- **Surrender** describes behaving as if the schema is true – surrendering to the situation and being flooded by associated emotions and bodily reactions as a result. This is often accompanied by either stillness or uncontrolled agitation – but it can go far beyond immobility to incorporate active, 'voluntary' compliance with the schema.

The following four tables (2.2-2.5) give an overview of schemas and coping styles. They identify a range of patterns of behaviour by parents and significant others, the accompanying cognitions of the child or adolescent, and the typical responses based on the three coping styles.

Table 2.2: Schemas 1-5 (Young et al, 2003) with examples of parental behaviour, the young person's cognitions and typical responses with coping strategies of surrender, avoidance, and overcompensation

Schema	Parental characteristics	Child's/adolescent's cognition	Surrender	Avoidance	Overcompensation
1. Abandonment/Instability	Unstable connection, inconsistent care and support, frequent change, being or feeling left behind	I often feel neglected and lonely; there are no real friends or stable people in my life	Seeks friends who are not stable or inappropriate (e.g. too young, too old)	Rejection of in-depth relationships; flees serious relationships	High standards with friends; relationships are too close/very intense
2. Mistrust/Abuse	Emotional, physical or sexual abuse	Getting too close is dangerous; I must be careful so that I am not exploited or mistreated	Seeks inappropriately close, exploitative or abusive friendships/ relationships	Fear-laden avoidance of situations in which he/she might be exploited or abused	Chooses friends who can be dominated, exploited or possibly humiliated
3. Emotional Deprivation	Neglect, emotional coldness, rejection	I often get the short end of the stick; nobody supports me/understands me. Others do not accept my feelings	Has friends who are emotionally distant; does not demand satisfaction of his/ her own needs; puts up with rejection	Emotional and social withdrawal; daydreaming	Emotionally demanding behaviour, unpredictable relationship patterns; neglectful of other people's needs
4. Defectiveness/Shame	Humiliation in front of others; lack of regard for the child's boundaries; degradation of child's needs	I feel so defective and bad that I think I am not loveable; because I make so many mistakes, I feel inferior	Having friendships characterized by embarrassment; accepts being a scapegoat	Shows introverted, tense behaviour, conceals his/her own feelings and opinions	Excessive self/ aggrandisement, or harsh criticism and degradation of others
5. Social Isolation/Alienation	Socially isolated family; often pertaining to immigrant status, minority ethnicity, or some other social exclusion (e.g. socioeconomic class)	I am different, my family is different; I don't fit in; no one understands me	Acceptance of exclusion; embraces being a loner	Avoids friendships and group activities	Indiscriminate pursuit of relationships; wants to be everybody's friend; strongly adaptive behaviour without resistance

Table 2.3: Schemas 6-9 (Young et al, 2003) with examples of parental behaviour, the young person's cognitions and typical responses with coping strategies of surrender, avoidance, and overcompensation

Schema	Parental characteristics	Child's/adolescent's cognition	Surrender	Avoidance	Overcompensation
6. Dependence/ Incompetence	Overcautious parents who want to control the child's experiences; possibly parents with anxiety disorders or trauma	I am weak and helpless, I cannot do things without my parents or teacher, making decisions is really hard for me	Asks parents to take care of his/her own interests, such as making connections with other kids or doing homework	Avoids challenges and important tasks; hands over responsibility to others	Does reckless things with overconfidence; looks for "powerful" friends; does not allow help or support when necessary
7. Vulnerability to Harm	Overcautious parents who warn against diseases and accidents with high levels of control and exaggerated precautions	I must be careful wherever I am; the world is dangerous; it is very risky to do anything	Distressed by negative or scary news stories; hyper-vigilant to health and safety issues; always has a cell phone or another means of contact	"Couch potato" existence, avoiding potentially hazardous situations; may use anger/defiance to avoid feared situations	Cocky behaviour; sensation-seeking; behaves carelessly and irresponsibly, sometimes causing accidents or harm
8. Enmeshment/ Undeveloped Self	Children become dependent on their parents (e.g. parentification, partner compensation); when children show bad behaviour, parents' reactions are preachy and sanctimonious, thereby generating feelings of guilt	I need my parents and they need me; I am obliged to tell them everything about my life and to do everything they want me to	Hesitant to abandon dysfunctional friendships; overly supports parents; being a "pseudo-adult" counselor; dismisses own needs	Avoids parental proximity and close friendships, e.g. going abroad, living a socially isolated life	Overly self-sufficient; isolates him/herself; unresponsive to the needs of others; persistent superficiality in relationships
9. Failure	Inadequate support and encouragement in coping with developmental tasks; devaluation of the child's abilities; represent faults as stupidity	I am afraid to fail (for example, in school or sports); I often feel stupid; others are much better than me	Selects tasks and challenges below their own level; defers boring jobs; shows stoic acceptance of lack of stimulation	Avoids interesting, challenging activities; refusal to try new or difficult tasks	Excessive striving for perfection and difficult task selection; pushes him/herself to be successful

Table 2.4: Schemas 10-14 (Young et al, 2003) with examples of parental behaviour, the young person's cognitions and typical responses with coping strategies of surrender, avoidance, and overcompensation

Schema	Parental characteristics	Child's/adolescent's cognition	Surrender	Avoidance	Overcompensation
10. Entitlement/ Grandiosity	Indulgence, lack of structure and limit setting; child is treated like a prince or princess; all of their desires are instantly gratified	I do not need to learn new things' homework is for "stupid people" only; rules that everyone follows do not apply to me because I am special	Lack of self-reflection; doesn't perceive others' needs or consciously ignores them; claims to have his or her own set of rules; brags about his or her own success; wants to impose his or her own will onto others; know-it-all	Avoids situations where they will likely "only" accomplish average success and not be the best	Focuses intensively on the needs of others; does things like completing other students' homework
11. Insufficient Self-control/ - discipline	Undisciplined parents with capricious behaviour driven by the pleasure principle	I can't complete boring tasks; instead I am looking for something else I can do	Breaks rules and promises; indifferent towards performance requirements	Avoidance of conflicts, challenges, social obligations and responsibilities	Extreme ambition to the point of self-flagellation with emphasis on discipline and requirements; high or compulsive self-control
12. Subjugation	Parents with authoritarian education style; if child is submissive, then they will be rewarded with love and care	What I feel and think is not important; others know better than me; they should decide how things have to be done	Selects more assertive and dominant friends; subordination; ingratiating behaviour; anticipatory obedience	Avoidance of situations in which conflicts could arise, e.g. unstructured situations with no clear rules, like the schoolyard	Rebellion against authority; reacts against any regulation in social structures
13. Self-Sacrifice	Parents in need of care or support, who tend towards parentification; oblivious to child's needs	Without me, everything collapses; if I didn't do all the things I do, nothing would work properly	Strives for positions with high responsibility; tendency to be exploited ; doesn't allow his or her own needs to be met	Prefers impersonal situations where give-and-take is not important (e.g. highly structured social situations, such as a gym)	Overemphasized separation from obligations, selfishness

Table 2.5: Schemas 15-18 (Young et al, 2003) with examples of parental behaviour, the young person's cognitions and typical responses with coping strategies of surrender, avoidance, and overcompensation

Schema	Parental characteristics	Child's/adolescent's cognition	Surrender	Avoidance	Overcompensation
14. Approval-Seeking	Recognition and acceptance based on school performance, social adjustment, social concepts	I have to show people how good/excellent I am, otherwise I feel restless and unsatisfied	Tries to impress others with activities and achievements, seeks performance-based situations and relationships with continuous feedback	Avoids close relationships, but still hopes for praise and recognition	Refuses to be the centre of attention, stays in the background
15. Negativity/ Pessimism	Overanxious parents with black-and-white thinking and a tendency to see every situation as a potential disaster	My happiness is temporary; something bad will inevitably happen; things will be worse than I can even imagine	Focuses on negative details and remembers them to use as proof that things always go wrong; always expects the worst	Distracts himself/ herself; evades unpleasant thoughts or experiences	Exaggerated optimism; denies unpleasant facts
16. Emotional Inhibition	Emotionally cool, rational parents, who devalue spontaneity and silly behaviour	It is not acceptable to show any emotions or behave in an irrational, childish, or silly way	Constant effort to be serious, behaves in an overly controlled manner	Avoids situations that trigger emotions, avoids talking about emotions	Makes herself/himself the centre of attention (clown-like), but is being laughed at rather than recognized
17. Unrelenting Standards	Had to work hard for success; believes that someone who has no success must have been lazy	The only way I can be lovable is by achieving something	High-reaching ambitions, perfectionism with constant pressure, spends a lot of time focused on learning and achievement	Avoids performance-related situations; procrastinates; evades assessments or evaluations/ does not take part in competitions	Criticises performance tests; deliberately ignores performance standards; acts intentionally carelessly in performance-focused scenarios
18. Punitiveness	Authoritarian upbringing; harsh consequences for making mistakes; parents maintain power over the child or others	If I make a mistake, I deserve punishment	Punishes himself/herself for human imperfection; treats himself/herself and others severely for making mistakes	Social withdrawal because of fear of making mistakes or being punished	Behaves in an overly indulgent manner, but occasionally shows a tendency towards excessive punishment

2.4 Schema modes

The number of schemas and coping responses can be challenging for the therapist and client alike, even before the fact that multiple schemas can be activated at the same time. Therefore, while it is important for clinicians to understand and assess schemas, the mode model offers a simpler language for treatment. Rather than a trait, a dysfunctional mode can be thought of as a state occurring as the result of schema activation and maladaptive coping. One might picture schemas and coping responses as atoms, and modes as molecules – different schemas and coping responses can combine to create new modes, which may or may not have different characteristics to the constituent parts. Table 2.6 shows an overview of the modes used in ST-CA, which will be explored in detail in the next section.

Table 2.6 Introductory overview of schema modes

Child modes	Dysfunctional parent modes	Competent modes	Maladaptive coping modes
■ Vulnerable Child ■ Angry/Enraged Child ■ Impulsive Child ■ Undisciplined Child ■ Spoiled/Egotistic Child ■ Happy Child	■ Punitive Parent ■ Demanding Parent	■ Clever and Wise Child ■ Caring Parent ■ Good Protector	■ Overcompensation* ■ Avoidance* ■ Surrender* *Each contains a group of relevant modes

Young views dysfunctional modes as dissociated states. 'Schema modes can be characterized by the degree to which a particular schema-driven state has become dissociated, or cut off, from an individual's other modes. A dysfunctional schema mode, therefore, is a part of the self that is cut off to some degree from other aspects of self' (Young et al, 2003, p.40). For Young, modes can be understood and experienced as a continuum of dissociation – from relatively healthy through to the severely pathological splitting processes seen in dissociative personality disorders.

Elements of the mode model show up in daily life experience. Even the concept of dissociation can be understood in an everyday sense as a way of putting aside mental content that is experienced as unimportant or unenjoyable – for example, short episodes of daydreaming can be considered a form of dissociation. However, in a therapeutic context, clinically relevant dissociation is experienced during or after traumatic situations. This kind of dissociation is often described as a 'shutting down' or detachment from experience. In trauma, therefore, dissociation may be seen as an automatic survival mechanism designed to help the individual cope with unbearable emotions of hurt, anxiety or distress. During dissociation, elements of functioning like behaviour, affect, bodily reactions or cognitions can be collectively or individually split off from the normal stream of consciousness.

Modes (and/or schemas) can interact with other people's modes in ways that can be harmful or healing. This interaction can also be reciprocal, in other words the effect on the 'receiver' causes a response that itself impacts back on the 'sender'. For instance, imagine that a child keeps fidgeting at the dinner table, which causes his father to become angry and react with exaggerated sharpness. The sharp rebuke activates an angry mode in the child, which in turn causes a more intense reaction in the father. This is an example of a mode clash causing escalation of a relatively trivial situation that should have been comparatively easy to manage and keep under control.

2.5 Applying the mode model to young people

In ST-CA, we primarily use the mode model as it allows for a simpler language and increased therapeutic versatility. The idea of a schema is often too abstract for children, so focusing on modes allows the therapist to work in a less complex way. Younger school children are usually able to describe their behaviour and experiences in terms of modes. There is only one concept to learn: a mode is a state, not something more permanent. Understanding this new word can immediately reduce identification with maladaptive behaviour. If the child can label their state, then it opens the possibility of gaining verbal control over it – 'if you can name it you can change it.'

Note that it is essential when working with young people to be careful not to label as maladaptive any behaviours that may be within the normal range for the child's developmental age. For example, stubborn and compulsive behaviours happen quite frequently with three-year-old children! On the other hand, the precursors of behavioural disorders can appear surprisingly early in childhood, and the concept of coping modes can be helpful in flagging potential problems early in development.

Many children feel great pride in tracking down and labelling a mode, turning it from something invisible and unacknowledged to something identifiable that can either be approved (reinforced) or disapproved (disempowered). Sometimes the idea of disempowering a mode using a spell, like Harry Potter, is helpful. The 'Mode Magic' game works well with children, and it's great for the therapist if a young client can accurately identify what mode they are in and understand how to manage it. Note that while the client's focus should be entirely on modes, it is still helpful for the therapist to keep in mind which schemas are activating which modes – the ultimate goal remains to understand which basic needs are not being met, so as to maximise the effectiveness of therapy.

In adult schema mode work, therapists seek to reinforce the 'Healthy Adult' mode and to disempower maladaptive modes. In working with children and adolescents, we replace the Healthy Adult mode with a healthy 'Clever and Wise' mode (often called 'Clever and Wise Sally' or 'Clever and Wise Sam', especially for younger children). As we will see, this mode is the 'captain' of the mode team.

Modes also provide a therapeutic vehicle for exploring the inner dynamic of self-devaluing introjects (unhelpful attitudes and mindsets unconsciously adopted from other people). These can otherwise be difficult to access and nearly impossible to work with therapeutically. The source of these introjects is often the dysfunctional parent or significant other, whose sustained criticism is internalized and becomes a critical inner 'voice' within the child. One of the great positives of working with children and adolescents is that introjects can be changed much more easily than in adulthood; however, this is clearly difficult if there is continued exposure to abusive parents. Therefore, in order to create a healthy environment and to make therapeutic change possible, it can be necessary for the therapist to act as an advocate for the safety and welfare of the child, contacting services as appropriate and recommending appropriate interventions in order to limit exposure to one or more people. More broadly, when working therapeutically with young people it is important to assess the impact of the child's environment on an ongoing basis.

The mode model allows us to simplify things to a level that most children can understand; still, they will often need to be supported in a co-regulative way (as developmentally appropriate) to ensure that their Clever and Wise mode is strong and stable enough to meet their needs and enable progress. Note that the goal when including others as co-regulators should always be for them to provide respectful support ('only as much as is necessary') of the child's own autonomous coping efforts.

We must stress again that, while the mode model is central to ST-CA, the 18 schemas are also helpful and important for therapeutic understanding and intervention. Our child client perceives reality through the lens of former negative experiences. When a schema is activated, the traumatic past again becomes a present experience. The schema's activation triggers automatic maladaptive coping responses in the client; this prevents new solutions being developed and perpetuates the trauma. As a result, a different *today* becomes impossible. However, if the child can respond in a new way that reduces their vulnerability to the earlier traumatic experience, the 'emergency solution' that was once the only available option will no longer be necessary. This, in simple terms, is the goal of ST-CA. We aim to enable new possibilities to open up, to weaken the power of perpetrators from the past, and to equip the now older and 'wiser' child to find those new options for taking action, enlisting support and ultimately getting needs met.

2.6 Mode groups, typical presentations and characteristics

The following tables describe the modes used in ST-CA and are adapted from Young *et al.* (2003), Lobbestael *et al.* (2007), Arntz & Jacob (2012), and Roediger *et al.* (2018). They are supplemented by our experiences of working with young people, and they have been slightly reorganized. The modes fall into four groups – child modes, parent modes, competent modes, and dysfunctional coping modes. We have added ideas for age-appropriate names for each mode to use with young clients in therapy.

2.6.1 Child modes

When talking about child modes, we refer to expressions of emotion and behaviour that are innate to a child, prior to any parenting or guidance in life. All children experience times of vulnerability, anger, and impulsivity. They also can be undisciplined, possibly entitled, and happy (at least in the short term, if they get what they want or need). These modes are emotionally intense; they usually display primary emotions. Imagine an excitable preschool or primary school child – they can be a challenge to spend time with due to their impatience, insistence on being entertained or unwillingness to compromise. They might get very angry, but on the other hand they may also be very cheerful. However, when children experience their needs being chronically frustrated the child modes become more intense, holding the emotions and memories connected to the core schemas. The exception is the Happy Child mode, whose needs are currently met.

Table 2.7 covers typical child modes as they present in daily life, including characteristics and how to recognize them. Note that we have combined the Angry Child and Enraged Child modes, since the essence of both is anger and it is only the intensity that is different. The terms in italics are suggestions for simpler and more playful names that can be used with children. Please note that these modes reflect our experience as child and adolescent psychotherapists. They are not the direct result of scientific research; rather, our list comes 'from the practitioner, for the practitioner.' In this respect we do not present the list as exhaustive, and it should be regarded as a work in progress.

Table 2.7 Mode table: Child Modes (*Italics suggest names to be used with the client*)

Child Modes
Vulnerable Child: *'Little Jane, Sad Emma, Lonely Boy, the Hurt Part'* The lonely, isolated or sad, abused or misused child: the scared, unsupported, lost, helpless, powerless, worthless, dependent child: confused, insecure, or overwhelmed by requirements
Angry and Enraged Child: *'Angry Pete, Furious Sally, the Volcano'* The child is frustrated because basic needs are not fulfilled; desires inappropriate limits, outbursts take place. The child screams, goes wild, destroys things, and may hurt themselves or other people. Note: The Angry child is responding to injustice (and needs validation), while the Enraged child has the same response but with the additional aspect of wanting to inflict physical damage.
Impulsive Child: *'Impulsive Jose, Careless Jane, Me First'* The child tends to engage in impulsive, unreflective actions for his own satisfaction, without any regard for other persons or possible negative consequences.
Undisciplined Child: *'the Giver Upper, Slack Jack, Can't Be Bothered Julie'* Routine or boring tasks cannot be completed; difficult tasks or requirements are not even attempted. The child gives up quickly, applies himself reluctantly, and does not persist.
Spoiled or Egotistic Child: *the Prince, the Princess, the Emperor* Unlike the undisciplined or impulsive child, the child is used to all their wishes coming true. Accordingly, the child is demanding and disappointed if others do not fulfil this expectation.
Happy Child: *'Happy Child, Happy Sally, Happy Sam'* The child feels loved, valuable, connected with others and secure. He is spontaneously sociable, happy in play, effective and resistant, because basic needs are fulfilled; may be jolly, amused, giggly.

The Happy Child mode may also be called the Contented Child mode – reinforcing the fact that feelings of belonging, security and safety are present, and all basic needs are met. The Happy Child mode is part of healthy development and is a resource for the whole of the lifespan. For example, the Happy Parent mode (someone able to experience happiness, relaxation and enjoyment in the parenting role, see chapter 4) is ultimately an expression of the Happy Child mode.

2.6.2 Dysfunctional Parent modes

There are two Dysfunctional Parent modes – the Punitive Parent and the Demanding Parent.

The Punitive Parent mode is characterized by overly critical and punishing voices or self-talk that are typically introjects of critical or abusive others, often parents. The Punitive Parent attacks the child's identity, belittles the child, undermines self-worth, and may even attack a child's right to exist.

The Demanding Parent mode is characterized by unrelenting standards and can be distinguished from the Punitive Parent as more achievement-oriented and/or emotionally demanding. Demands may be placed on a child that 'good is never enough', or there may be unhelpful expectations of continuous improvement. This can apply to better school grades, more success at sport, or simply being 'better'. In some cultures, negative gender stereotypes may play a role, for example girls may experience themselves as having fewer rights and less worth than boys. The emotionally demanding parent mode may place age-inappropriate expectations on a child concerning care of siblings, other people, or even the parents themselves. In so doing they leave no room for the child to be childlike, instead forcing them into the role of caretaker, nurse or educator at the cost of spontaneity and normal development.

The term 'Parent Mode' is potentially misleading, since experiences with peers and significant others like schoolteachers or sports coaches can also be a key part of these modes. For this reason, these modes are also referred to as Parent/Peer modes or Inner Critic modes (Farrell & Shaw, 2018).

While there is some ongoing debate, we follow Roediger and colleagues' assertion (2018) that the internalized Demanding or Punitive Parent mode can either be inwardly or outwardly directed. That means that the child experiences the impulse to criticise and or punish not only themselves, but also other people. Similarly, Berbalk and Kempkensteffen (2000) introduced the idea of differentiating between maladaptive parent modes that are directed inward (i.e. toward one's own person) or outward (i.e. toward other persons). In some clients, for instance in adults with Borderline Personality Disorder, the Punitive Parent mode can flip in an instant from outwardly-directed criticisms (toward the therapist, for example) to internally-directed critical language focussing on self-mutilation and self-hatred.

Table 2.8 Mode table: Parent and Peer Modes (italics suggest names to be used with the client)

Dysfunctional Parent (or Peer, or Inner Critic) Modes

Inward: *Punitive Parent: 'the Punisher, the Naughty Little Man'*
Internalized parental or peer voices that punish and depreciate the child. Harsh, depreciative, cold, accusing tone: 'I am worthless'.

Inward: *Demanding Parent: 'the Critic, Pushy Pam, Boot-camp Bob'*
Internalized parent/peer who creates pressure; forms excessively exaggerated standards, never feels good enough, unable to relax. Others often appear more important and better.

Outward: *Punitive Parent: 'the Punisher, the Criticizer, the Terminator, the Bully'*
Resorts to violence and inciting others to violence in service of the survival of the class, the club, the community, the society; accuses others, judges them ethically.

Outward: *Demanding Parent: 'the Critic, the Pusher, the Missionary, the Boss'*
Demands high responsibilities but few rights for everyone, has a long list of do's and don'ts, acts as a 'wise guy' and 'moralizer'; however, when alone, he does not even obey his self-determined rules; he is ruthless towards others; exploits their deficiencies and feels superior.

The Parent modes and the Vulnerable child mode can trigger each other. For example, adolescence is a time when normal developmental tasks provoke conflict with authority, both internal and external 'voices'. As the adolescent seeks to be more autonomous, there is internal conflict with the rules of the Punitive and Demanding Parent modes (which can include school expectations). The parent mode can then attack the Vulnerable Child mode. This mode needs attachment, autonomy, and self-worth – in other words love, support and praise. But at this age the healthy and competent modes are not yet fully developed. This can result in a fundamental instability of self-regulation. A multitude of voices (parents, school, peers, expected paths) placing competing and/or ambiguous demands that can also trigger the Vulnerable Child mode followed by the internalized Demanding Parent mode, which induces enormous tension in the adolescent. In order to cope with this tension, maladaptive coping modes are activated. If these modes are Avoidant, a pattern of withdrawal can appear – including social isolation, shyness, and possibly excessive use of video games or substances. If the modes are Overcompensating, we often see aggressive or antisocial behaviour, bullying of peers, or the adoption of very radical stances concerning ethical, economic, political, or religious issues.

2.6.3 Competent modes

So far, we have looked at the innate Child modes and internalised Dysfunctional Parent modes. Mediating between the two are Competent modes. These modes are needed to lessen tension caused by Dysfunctional Parent modes, and to look after the Child modes in age appropriate ways.

If we think of a child as having an 'inner mode team', then the team's captain is the Clever and Wise mode that we introduced earlier. The Clever and Wise mode is the boss who controls what happens on the outer stage (i.e. at the behavioural level). It is not a Child mode as it does not develop innately; rather, the Clever and Wise mode requires appropriate care and guidance from a caregiver in order to become an internalized 'lawyer for the child's needs.'

If a child experiences distress and shifts into the Vulnerable Child mode, or if there is a clash between a Child mode and a Dysfunctional Parent mode (for example the Angry Child seeks an outlet for frustration, but a Demanding Parent counters that he has no right to be angry), then the child will need internalized competent modes such as the Caring Parent mode. The internalized Caring Parent mode is focused on security and helpful advice. It is modelled not only on parents and other family role models, but also on educators, teachers, coaches and other adults with caregiving responsibility. Note that the Caring Parent mode is a Competent mode, and quite distinct from Dysfunctional Parent modes.

The Caring Parent can play a protective and strengthening role for children. In therapy, it is often useful to explicitly introduce this mode via imagery, inner helpers and heroes. Similarly, the Good Protector mode draws on fantasized protectors who bring in autonomy, protection, friendship and support, and enables the child to draw on 'external' help when needed. These protectors can include religious or spiritual feelings and emotions, if appropriate for the client and their situation.

Table 2.9 Mode table: Competent Modes (italics suggest names to be used with the client)

Child Competent Modes

Clever and Wise Child: *'Clever and Wise Sally, the Clever Kid, Cool Sita, Wise John'*
The child experiences feelings of self-efficacy and self-control. He or she has the capacity for (age-appropriate) self-monitoring, frustration tolerance, verbal self-monitoring, and acceptance of rules, norms, and values.

Child Competent Modes
Caring Parent: *'the Caring One, Inner Helper, the Safe Person'*   The child takes care of himself, like a good parent. However, he does not yet experience this as self-regulation, but still clearly as an internal protector, who has control, enabling comfort. He maintains the memory of a parent, even if attachment figures are absent.
Good Protector: *'the Network Builder, Superman, Confident Kim'*   When the child needs help and support he or she can connect to a 'helper' and therefore achieves autonomy through fantasized supporters who protect, accompany, comfort and defend the child.

2.6.4 Dysfunctional coping modes

Dysfunctional coping modes are responses to distress that are elaborated on and reinforced over time. They are subdivided into Overcompensation modes, Avoidance modes and Surrender modes. In our experience, children as young as two can display precursors to dysfunctional coping modes. If a child has an even temperament and success in psychosocial interactions, they will translate this into a habit and develop a readily accessible healthy mode such as the Clever and Wise Child. However, if those interactions are too complex or difficult for the child to navigate, they will begin to rehearse a response to their distress. They may instinctively retreat (flight), attack the source of their distress (fight) or become overwhelmed by their experience (freeze).

Coping modes can be triggered by relatively minor frustrations and unintentionally reinforced by parents. Often it is overlooked or not taken seriously. How does this happen? First, the Vulnerable Child mode shows up. Ideally the parent (or caregiver) notices this mode, validates and assists. If this does not happen, however, then a rapid shift takes place into a coping mode that can protect the Vulnerable Child's emotions, such as entitled rage or withdrawn watchfulness. Parents can reinforce this mode-flipping if they are too insecure about how to respond, too lenient to provide focused attention or simply dismissive of such rapid, hard-to-manage mood changes. The child himself isn't aware of a shift from the primary emotion (e.g. feeling hurt) to the coping mode (e.g. being offended, or becoming avoidant) and experiences his behaviour as justified and providing safety.

Which coping mode is invoked at any given time depends on many factors – temperament, constitution and bodily state (e.g. tiredness), parental modelling, and momentary physiological directions linked to the autonomic nervous system (with its reactive tendencies directed toward the inner or outer). The coping mode is selected more or less automatically, without conscious thought on the child's part, and becomes increasingly embedded over the course of development. A key part of this embedding process is the repetition of the behaviours that prove most effective in terms of neutralizing or diverting the parent or significant other in a way that feels safe to the child, and thus protecting the Vulnerable Child.

Overcompensation modes

Children using Overcompensating modes (see Table 2.10) are characterized by challenging norms and rules. Bully and Attack mode, for instance, can be quite strong in children, who sometimes display anti-social behaviours such as pyromania or compulsive stealing. Children struggling with disorders such as oppositional defiant disorder are often in an overcompensating mode.

It is important to differentiate between children and adolescents who are using Overcompensation coping modes from those using Impulsive and Undisciplined Child modes. We assume that behind the overcompensation behaviour is a primary feeling of insecurity, anxiety, or frustration, related to the child modes. The overcompensation mode stabilises the child's self-worth or sense of safety. However, if the motivation for the behaviour is simply non-compliance or impulsivity, we would instead focus on the Impulsive and Undisciplined Child modes.

Table 2.10 Mode table: Overcompensation modes *(italics suggest names to be used with the client)*

Dysfunctional Coping Modes: Overcompensation

Defiant-oppositional child: *'the Manipulator, Defiant Daniel, the Stubborn One, Dr No'*
The child acts in a stubborn and resistant manner, and gives the cold shoulder in order to pressure others into pleasing them ('Make me feel good; otherwise you should feel bad')

The dominator: *'the Boss, the Terminator, the Governor, Mr President'*
The child always wants to make decisions, keep his parents under control, and restrain peers; acts in a strong-willed and pleasure-oriented way without compunction, displaying his 'strength' and 'power.'

The perfectionist: *'Mr Perfect, Neat Freak, Mister Worry Pants, Miss Worry Pants'*
The child tries to protect himself from perceived or real dangers in terms of criticism/mistakes, harm, or guilt through a high level of conscientiousness; puts himself under high pressure

---

Dysfunctional Coping Modes: Overcompensation
Excessive Controller: *'Mr. Control, the Policeman'* Everything must be checked, whether a mistake has actually been made or not; the child feels responsible for everything; complains about too much work and grubbiness.
Self-Aggrandizer: *'the Narcissist, the King, Best Bob, Best Bella, the Chief'* Acts like he has special rights; others are inferior to him. He competes, thinks he is great, shows highly developed egocentrism and little empathy for others, brags to get admiration or puffs himself up.
Dramatizer (Histrionic): *'Drama-queen, the Flirt, Stage Sam'* Looks for attention and acceptance; interacts in an exaggerated emotional way, though the message is rather superficial and stagy (for adolescents, possibly flirty and/or sexualized).
Intimidator: *'the Humiliator, the Bully, Hannibal'* This mode scares other children; he wants to subordinate and take advantage of them, partly for his own amusement and partly out of boredom; possibly sadistic features.
Conning Mode: *'the Juggler, the Deceiver, Con Man, Chess Man'* In the conning mode the child plots against other, plans for revenge, and uses others as pawns in a game; tells lies and casts himself in a positive light.
Bully and Attack: *'the Hooligan, the Bully, the Enforcer'* Others are laughed at, humiliated, or threatened; the child attacks others in verbal or physical ways; wants others to feel the same pain the child experienced in the past.
Predator: *'the Killer, the Persecutor, the Predator'* This mode is about destroying, harming, and even killing. It is the mode for psychopaths, and those who show strong antisocial traits.

Avoidance modes

Avoidance modes (see Table 2.11) occur in children who actively or passively withdraw from situations which induce distress, uneasiness, or anxiety. Examples include the child who retreats socially (the classic wallflower), or the child who self-soothes by eating or playing video games to excess. As therapists we know that maladaptive Coping modes develop in order to protect the emotions of the Vulnerable Child, so we can try to detect the Vulnerable Child behind an Avoidant mode. This is often possible by looking for unmet needs, anxieties, and low self-worth in the child's history or current situation. Identifying and naming this threat or distress is often a starting point for therapeutic change. A helpful principle for distinguishing between the Vulnerable Child and Avoidance Modes is to take the 'emotional temperature' of the behaviour. Avoidance modes are 'cool' and detached, while the Vulnerable Child mode feels 'hotter' and readily expresses distress.

Table 2.11 Mode table: Avoidance Modes *(italics suggest names to be used with the client)*

Dysfunctional Coping Modes: Avoidance

Detached Protector: *'the Cool One, Mr Spock, Dr Cool, Shut Down, the Wall'*
Cuts himself off from distress through emotional alienation. Emotions seem to be turned off; the child does not socialize with others and offers of support are rejected; thinking is highly rational, actions seem robotic; internal emptiness and strong sense of boredom.

Dissociated Protector: *'Spacey Sam, the Dreamer, the Distracted Protector'*
The child seems mentally distracted, dreamy, hypnotized; is barely able to 'come back' unaided and has to be approached/addressed loudly and activated energetically; shows low degree of suffering.

Complaining Protector: *'the Complainer, the Blamer, Couch Potato, Mr/Ms Grumpy Pants'*
The child often complains about physical problems, problems with others, injustice at school, at home and in the world; acts depressed and is easily offended ('I'm always blamed for everything!'). Searches actively for the mistakes of others in order to avoid acceptance of his own mistakes.

Angry Protector: *'Annoyed Stacey, Sarcastic Tom, Talk to the Hand'*
The child creates distance from people by showing anger; abuses the counterpart, other people, or outer circumstances when in fact his own problems or difficulties should be addressed. The anger does not seem 'real,' but rather planned (as a convenient means to avoid pressure or alienation).

Self-Soother or -Stimulator: *'the Role-Player (Multi-Player), the Sweet Tooth, TV Tom'*
Turns off feelings by doing things that have a superficial calming or stimulating effect, e.g., addictive behaviour, video games, excessive eating, watching TV (for adolescents this may include substance abuse, excessive consumption of pornography, gambling, high risk sports); isolates himself through weird or otherwise repellent behaviour, provokes exclusion from social connections.

Hyperactive Protector: *'Busy Bee, Social Junkie, Attention-Seeker, the Helicopter, Mr Everywhere'*
The child avoids negative feelings by caring excessively about his environment; seems to be bubbling over with ideas and never tires of showing everyone; desperately looks for stimulation, seems rushed; apparently happy, but also quickly becomes irritable.

Surrender modes

Surrender modes (or Subjugation and Self-Sacrifice schemas) can be seen in children who feel dominated or threatened by parental figures, family systems, or peer groups. Often this is expressed through psychosomatic problems such as stomach aches, nausea and vomiting, or early precursors of depressive disorders such as intense sadness, emotion instability, sleep disorders, or deterioration of achievement. However, it can extend to acute suicidal ideation or even suicidal acts.

Table 2.12 shows the two common Surrender modes in children and adolescents. It is important to note that, in order to understand how dysfunctional a coping mode is, a dimensional understanding of its intensity is helpful. Coping modes are not necessarily dysfunctional at a low level but, as the level of intensity rises, they become more dysfunctional. In the case of Surrender, it can be healthy when deployed as the ability to accept advice and to tolerate frustrations, to allow give and take, to integrate oneself adaptively (Roediger *et al.*, 2018). In some clients a 'healthy subjugation' can even be a therapeutic goal.

Table 2.12 Mode table: Surrender Modes *(italics suggest names to be used with the client)*

Dysfunctional Coping Modes: Surrender

Compliant Surrender: *'the Pleaser, the Yes Man'*
Passive, submissive, obedient, humiliated, laughed at without any resistance. Capitulation or unhesitating subordination.

Currying Favor: *'the Brown-Nose, the Servant, the Follower'*
Integrates actively, even if the 'costs' are high, looks for social contacts in order to be part of a group; seeks to inappropriately connect with the dominant person in a group in order to gain acceptance.

The goal of therapy is to integrate or connect adaptive elements of coping modes with the Clever and Wise mode, and to be able to deploy them appropriately and flexibly.

Literature

Arntz, A., & Jacob, G. (2012). Schema therapy in practice: An introductory guide to the schema mode approach. John Wiley & Sons.

Berbalk, H. & Kempkensteffen, J. (2000). Die Bedeutung des „Momentanen personalen Gesamtzustandes" für die Arbeit in der Depressionstherapie. Psychotherapeuten Forum: Praxis und Wissenschaft, 3.

Farrell, J. M. & Shaw, I. A. (2018). Experiencing Schema Therapy from the Inside Out : A Self-Practice/Self-Reflection Workbook for Therapists. New York: Guilford.

Grawe, K. (2017). Neuropsychotherapy: How the neurosciences inform effective psychotherapy. Routledge.

Lobbestael, J., Vreeswijk, M.F. van & Arntz, A. (2007). Shedding light on schema modes: A clarification of the mode concept and its current research status. Netherlands Journal of Psychology, 63, 76–85.

Roediger, E. Stevens, B.A., & Brockman, R. (2018). Contextual Schema Therapy. An Integrative Approach to Personality Disorder, Emotional Dysregulation & Interpersonal Functioning. Oakland, CA: Context Press.

Young, J. E., Klosko, J. S., & Weishaar, M. E. (2003). Schema therapy: A practitioner's guide. Guilford Press.

Chapter 3: Case conceptualization and treatment

Christof Loose, Gerhard Zarbock, Peter Graaf and Ruth Holt

3.1 Introduction

The way in which we conduct mode work with children and adolescents in ST-CA is organised into five steps, elaborated on in chapter 12. These steps do not have to be completed in a linear fashion, and in fact may be repeated and elaborated on throughout therapy. However, they provide a broad framework for ST-CA, within which the therapist can tailor the treatment plan to the individual client.

Step 1: Identify the presenting modes
Step 2: Access the Vulnerable/Lonely/Abused Child
Step 3: Determine each mode's functionality (in dialogue)
Step 4: Strengthen adaptive modes and weaken dysfunctional modes
Step 5: Generalize therapeutic gains to everyday life

3.2 Key interventions

There are four main intervention strategies in ST-CA, comparable to adult Schema Therapy with some adaptations based on the developmental needs of children. These adaptations are spelled out in detail in the age-specific chapters of this book (chapters 4-8).

1. **Limited Reparenting Therapeutic relationship**

A key intervention in ST-CA is the climate created by a special kind of therapeutic relationship: Limited Reparenting. Young defines this in ST for adults as 'providing, within the appropriate boundaries of the therapy relationship, what patients needed but did not get from their parents as children' (p.177, Young *et al.*, 2003). In ST-CA we have an opportunity to not only to meet the child's needs within the therapy relationship, but also to impact the parenting of the child outside it. During assessment and treatment, the schema therapist should ask 'what kind of reparenting does this patient need?' This will guide the approach to the child and the therapeutic intervention with the parents, giving them support to begin more effectively meeting the needs of their child. Of course, some parents will not have the capacity for this shift, and this is further explored in chapter 13.

2. Cognitive Techniques

From preschool age, children can use cognitive interventions to learn how to recognize and label modes. With school-aged children, the therapist can help the young person to make connections between mode triggering and thoughts, emotions and behaviours. It is also important to use cognitive techniques to question modes and evaluate impact, so that alternative behavioural strategies and cognitions can be developed. As therapy progresses, cognitive strategies are also used to consolidate new learning from experiential techniques. All traditional approaches from cognitive therapy can be used in ST-CA, in age-appropriate ways.

3. Experiential Techniques

Experiential techniques are central to ST-CA as they assist clients in becoming aware of their emotional needs and give those needs appropriate expression. Chapters 9-11 explore many ways in which play and other experiential techniques can be useful. However, two of the most important experiential techniques are mode dialogues (chair work) and imagery exercises. Chair work allows the modes to 'speak' to one another, to be externalised, understood and modified in order to strengthen the healthy modes. Chair work is also very helpful in working with parents and others to build more adaptive responses. Imagery work allows therapists to harness children's amazing imaginary capacity when assessing and treating schemas, and strengthen healthy coping. Imagery re-scripting is an intensive method of treating traumatic experiences in early development. It provides space to experience and reframe difficult events that have contributed to maladaptive schemas. Using imagery, the therapist is able to meet the needs of the child, confront the abuser and change the way a distressing event has been evaluated, providing a corrective emotional experience. This is a powerful way to reduce schemas and dysfunctional modes.

4. Behavioural Interventions

Behavioural techniques are mainly found in the final phase of ST-CA and ST with adults, as they build on earlier cognitive and experiential work. This timing increases a client's capacity for behavioural pattern breaking. However, there is a role for introducing behavioural skills earlier in order to interrupt damaging behaviours (e.g. skills training), or when the formulation suggests a strong behavioural component, particularly with younger children (see Chapter 4). ST also provides a way to conceptualise issues with implementing behavioural interventions, understanding a parent's capacity to stay in Healthy Adult mode when using behavioural approaches. All behavioural techniques from CBT can be used, such as social skills training or behavioural activation, but there is also scope to focus on building corrective relationship patterns as the healthy modes are developed.

3.3 The relationship between schemas, needs and modes

Schemas can be defined as a consistent experiential pattern or belief, formed through repeated negative experiences related to unmet needs, and easily triggered by partial similarities of stimuli. A mode can be defined as an overarching 'predominant state that we are in at a given point in time' (Young *et al.*, 2003). This predominant state comprises different ingredients: the primary emotions of the activated schema are present, but may be partly overruled by secondary emotions associated with the mode (for example an Abandonment schema, characterized by anxiety or sadness, may be overruled by anger as an Overcompensating mode). A mode is further sculpted by steering the inner or outward-directed attention, as well as by bodily sensations, physiological activation patterns, and other behaviours designed to reduce inconsistency and aid emotional coping. One could define a mode as a momentary 'way of meeting the world' as an answer to an inner or outer challenge.

In general, Schema Therapy focuses on how maladaptive schemas and modes, rooted in past unmet emotional needs, are activated in the here and now. This question is central to understanding psychological disorders and symptoms. The key diagnostic questions in Schema Therapy are:

- Which basic need is being frustrated or not met, now or in the past?

- Which schema is being triggered?

- Which coping style is leading to what mode?

Table 3.1 depicts the connection between schemas, domains, unmet basic needs, and possible modes. The term 'domain' describes a group of schemas, which result from similar kinds of basic need frustration. Single schemas are a more precise differentiations of the respective domain.

Table 3.1 Schemas, domains, needs and modes (according to Grawe, 2017; Roediger *et al.*, 2018; Young *et al.*, 2003)

Schemas		Domains	Unmet needs	Possible modes
1	Abandonment/ Instability	Disconnection and rejection	Attachment	Vulnerable or enraged child
2	Mistrust/Abuse			
3	Emotional Deprivation			
4	Defectiveness/Shame			
5	Social Isolation/ Alienation			
6	Dependence/ Incompetence	Impaired autonomy and performance	Autonomy/ Self-efficacy	Vulnerable or enraged child
7	Vulnerability			
8	Enmeshment/ Undeveloped Self			
9	Failure			
10	Entitlement/ Grandiosity	Impaired limits	Identity/ Structure/ Limits	Undisciplined child
11	Insufficient Self-Control/Self-Discipline			
12	Subjugation	Other-directedness	Self-esteem acceptance Autonomy/ Self-determination	Surrender (behind demanding internal parents)
13	Self-Sacrifice			
14	Approval-Seeking/ Recognition-Seeking			
15	Negativity/Pessimism	Overvigilance and inhibition	Pleasure, spontaneity and play/Fun	Overcompensation/ Avoidance (behind punishing internal parents)
16	Emotional Inhibition			
17	Unrelenting Standards			
18	Punitiveness			

3.4 Primary and secondary emotions from a Schema Therapy perspective

In Schema Therapy, it is essential to uncover the primary emotions behind the secondary emotions that are present in coping modes. Secondary (or social) emotions include shame, guilt, pride, envy, admiration, gratitude and disdain. The primary (or basic) emotions are rage, sadness, anxiety, disgust, surprise, and happiness (Greenberg, 2006). These precognitive primary emotions are held within the Child modes. Table 3.2 shows the primary and secondary emotions.

Table 3.2 Primary and secondary emotions (based on Greenberg, 2006).	
Primary emotions (basic emotions)	**Secondary emotions (social emotions)**
■ Sadness	■ Shame
■ Anger	■ Guilt
■ Anxiety	■ Pride
■ Disgust	■ Jealousy; envy
■ Surprise	■ Admiration
■ Happiness	■ Gratitude
	■ Disdain

Clients can be helped to trace primary emotions by asking the therapeutic question: 'What feeling or emotion came first in this situation, even before guilt or the impulse to seek revenge?' Another way to differentiate between primary and secondary emotions is to ask: 'Was the client born with the secondary emotions?' The goal of Schema Therapy is to reach the unacknowledged emotions, to enable new ways of thinking and responding, and to find more healthy ways of coping and self-care.

3.5 Case Conceptualization and Psychoeducation

In Schema Therapy, case conceptualization and psychoeducation regarding schemas and modes play an important role. When working with children and adolescents, we encounter clients who are still going through the natural processes of emotional and cognitive development, so their capacity to understand theoretical models is limited. We have had good results visualizing the mode model with small figures positioned inside a bigger figure to represent the whole person (see the Inner Team,

Schulz von Thun, 1998). Additionally, we add red wedges onto the figure's skin to represent the client's schemas as 'wounds' (see Figure 3.1).

In ST-CA we conceptualize the schema mode model using Ellis's ABC model (or the SORCK model – see www.pavpub.com/resource-374CoCr). The activating event represents the trigger that opens the client's wound (the schema). The wound appears next to a small figure, representing the Vulnerable Child mode which is activated next. After this, other modes come into play, one after another, until a specific maladaptive coping mode comes to the fore, dictating the child's problematic behaviour. The Clever and Wise mode is there to soothe the Vulnerable Child and support other Child modes, but it requires assistance to find a need-oriented solution. The rule is: first Self-Compassion (towards the Vulnerable Child) then Self-Assertiveness (towards the Angry Child). The Parent (or Critic) mode must then be disempowered in order to help the Clever and Wise mode find and use a new adaptive behaviour.

Visualizing the processes taking place on the inner stage helps to shed light on the 'Mode Black Box', which allows young clients to understand better what is going on inside them and builds cooperation. This process will be explored in detail with practical demonstrations and examples in chapters 4-9; for more general explanations see chapter 12, or the online material (there is a relevant congress poster by Loose & Graaf, 2016, and a case study by Loose, 2018).

Figure 3.1: Pictorial Representation of Case Conceptualization. Adapted from Schulz von Thun (1999).

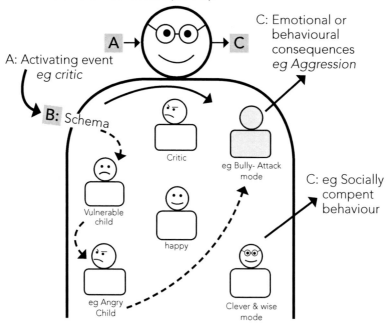

3.6 When to use Schema Therapy for children and adolescents

The indications and contraindications for ST-CA are, broadly speaking, the same as for adult Schema Therapy. Key issues in evaluating whether Schema Therapy is indicated or not are whether frustration of needs appears to be a factor, and whether a client would benefit from the emotion-focused techniques and intensive therapeutic relationship that are central parts of Schema Therapy.

In order to begin the assessment, we ask the parents about the child's biographical case history and temperament, and about successfully resolved or currently pending developmental tasks. For older children and adolescents, we ask the client themselves about their parents, symptoms and problem areas. We aim to get an idea of the relational styles of the client and relevant others. If possible, it is also helpful to include teachers or preschool educators in the process of evaluation.

With assessment complete, an initial hypothesis about predisposing, precipitating and perpetuating factors and problem areas may be formulated. If it becomes obvious that chronic frustration of basic needs can be shown, then ST-CA could be very helpful and is indicated. Occasionally, for disorders such as eating disorders, addictions and psychosis, some form of crisis intervention may be needed to stabilize the client before ST-CA treatment can begin.

Schema therapy may be especially helpful if a child or adolescent:

- is not motivated to engage with CBT methods or techniques
- does not complete therapeutic homework
- is unable to adapt or apply self-management strategies
- avoids emotions and cognition related to the problem behaviour
- has issues with self-control, or is attached to rigid behaviours and attitudes
- experiences problematic behaviour as ego-syntonic ('this is just how I am')
- is unable to define goals precisely, or has no faith that change is possible
- is overwhelmed by personality disorder traits
- has insufficient resources to work on problems effectively
- finds it difficult to establish therapeutic rapport.

Given that conditions such as lack of engagement and emotion avoidance occur often in therapy with children, a schema-oriented approach can be applied to a broad array of presentations with children and adolescents, including ADHD and OCD.

3.7 Schema coaching for parents and other caregivers

In ST-CA, and indeed any intervention with young people, it is generally helpful to think of and approach therapy as *systemic therapy* because one can understand children and adolescents best by considering the context of the environment and the groups that they live in. Lazarus's idea of transaction proposes that a behaviour emitted from person A elicits a response behaviour from person B, which then elicits a new and answering behaviour from person A. It makes sense to refer to this kind of mutual change, reinforcement, and escalation between individuals and groups as *transactional* rather than simply *interactional*, as the influences are multiple and complex. The concept of transaction also underlines the spiralling nature of these processes.

In addition to family relationship spirals, there may be specific family trauma, such as parental conflict, witnessing domestic violence, or the separation and divorce of parents, which may result in increased feelings of guilt and shame for the child. In this context, schema dispositions may be established and/or already-rooted schema dispositions further deepened.

In general, schema therapists can help parents to understand the development of maladaptive schemas using schema coaching or systemic approaches within a Schema Therapy framework. They can teach parents what successful coping and co-regulation for each developmental task looks like. Using a systemic perspective, therapists can also analyze how dysfunctional boundaries in the family system (for example family rules that are too rigid or too broad), as well as the parents' own dysfunctional behaviours, may contribute to the development of maladaptive schemas. They can also work with parents to increase protective factors, resources and positive schemas like self-efficacy, drawing on positive psychology. For detailed information, see Chapters 15-17.

3.8 Parent-specific and age-specific goals and strategies

In the following section we will look at how Schema Therapy addresses the five developmental phases for children and adolescents outlined in Erikson's developmental model. To recap, these are:

- Babies and toddlers from birth to age 3

- Pre-schoolers from age 4 to age 6

- Starting school to pre-puberty – age 6 to age 10

- Puberty from age 11 to age 16

- Late puberty and early adulthood from 17 to 23

For each phase we will give a brief overview of ST-CA areas of focus. Of course, the specific goals and strategies used in therapy will depend on the developmental stage of the individual young person. The phases will then be explored in greater depth in the five chapters that follow.

3.8.1 Babies and toddlers from birth to age 3

In this phase, Schema Therapy is primarily helpful in shedding light on the schema activations of parents. Schemas are triggered in the parent-child interaction when a parent's schema is activated. The seeds of schemas in a newborn baby can be observed in early parent-child interactions. The transaction between parent and child will fulfil, frustrate, or even dramatically harm the baby's basic needs, laying a foundation for the development of schemas over the course of childhood.

From birth to age 3, genetically based factors like temperament play an important role. At this early age, Schema Therapy provides an opportunity to look more closely at the interaction between temperamental factors, challenging pre- and perinatal conditions, and compensating or de-compensating developmental processes.

Dealing with babies or toddlers, parents can experience strong mode activations – for example, inner- or outer-directed Demanding or Punitive Parent modes are common. On the other hand, parents can themselves feel a sense of regression into their own Vulnerable Child, for instance if they feel overwhelmed. Angry and Enraged Child modes can also occur. Long or persistent crying can induce feelings of alienation in the parents, which can result in distance and a lack of mirroring such as a Detached Protector mode. Parents may also react with overcompensation and aggressive emotions and behaviour toward the child as well as toward the partner, with parents shouting at their baby or having heated quarrels with their partner.

3.8.2 Pre-schoolers from age 4 to age 6

With emotional and cognitive development, the acquisition of language, and more conscious embedding into family and preschool systems, the development of schema dispositions may begin during this developmental phase (or existing schemas may deepen if basic needs have not been met over the first three years of life). The influence of the parents and other significant caregivers is more explicit through education and modelling, for instance by teaching the child cultural norms in the areas of eating, cleanliness, and social behaviour.

Areas like fine motor, graphomotor, and sensorimotor development and achievement provide important avenues for building self-worth, self-efficacy, and self-understanding. However, these processes may also give rise to the child's first and/or further maladaptive experiences, which can foster the development of maladaptive schemas like Emotional Deprivation, Abandonment, Defectiveness/ Shame, Mistrust, and/or Social Isolation.

A helpful focus during this phase is on assisting parents and children to manage developmental tasks such as separating from parents to go to preschool, making friends and getting along with peers, and obeying school rules and regulations, in a context of meeting core emotional needs.

3.8.3 Starting school to pre-puberty – age 6 to age 10

This developmental phase is centred on dealing with social situations in different groups such as school, sports, and leisure activities. Challenges may also come from the academic setting where issues related to achievement, impairment of performance, motor and sensory shortcomings or disabilities may induce the development or further hardening of maladaptive schemas.

If a child has high intellectual potential, other schema risks are present: in situations where the school environment does not provide a challenging enough experience, a maladaptive learning and working attitude may be developed (e.g. underachievement), which could lead to schemas like Social Isolation, Subjugation, Self-sacrifice, Entitlement/Grandiosity or Impaired Self-Control/Self-Discipline.

Looking at the development and precursors of the Healthy Adult mode, competent modes like the Clever and Wise mode become more obvious at this age, enabling skills in frustration tolerance and delayed gratification as well as enhancing empathy. If these skills are developed, the child becomes more competent in emotional and social domains, and behaviour is managed by internalized rules and values.

3.8.4 Puberty from age 11 to age 16

Central developmental tasks in this phase are related to autonomy and identity.

Adolescents face changes in their body and the integration of sexual drives and gender role identity into their self-concept. In this phase, the relationship to one's own family of origin and the importance of the peer group is much more consciously evaluated and open to change. Separation from the family begins; if the family system is problematic, massive conflicts of values and norms may occur between family and peer groups. Enmeshed families can hinder the development of autonomy and misunderstand the importance of peer groups, or even prevent such normal development. Conversely, peer groups can become problematic as they can facilitate or even 'cause' dysfunctional coping modes.

In terms of identity, the young person formulates his or her own inclinations, values, competency judgments, and preferences. The schema Social Isolation can be established by negative peer group experiences. Sexual and physical abuse can lead to the development of Mistrust/Abuse or Subjugation schemas, as is true at any age. Coping reactions following such traumatizing events or frustrations may lead to Overcompensating modes like Bully and Attack, Surrender modes like Compliant Surrenderer or more Passive Overcompensating modes like Perfectionistic Overcontroller.

3.8.5 Late puberty and early adulthood from age 17 to age 23

The young person is now increasingly in adult roles (for example exploring intimate relationships and sexuality, dealing with alcohol and drugs, or building a career). These new challenges can be stressful and overwhelming and lead to emotional instability, partly because they are faced at the same time as the young person is continuing to pursue autonomy and separation from their parents.

Schema therapy provides helpful approaches to navigating the issues faced by adolescents and young adults. The concepts of treatment of borderline personality disorder are helpful as there is, to some extent, an overlap in the problem areas for this age group. With borderline clients, changes of emotional states (called mode-flipping) are frequent, as well as feelings of emptiness and an incoherent and unstable identity. These features are partly shared between borderline personality disorder and the developmental conflicts in adolescents and late adolescents.

The development of maladaptive schemas is usually complete by this point. In addition to the schema model, this age group can be helpfully understood using the mode model. In therapy, the coping modes can be significantly disruptive, as well as the Vulnerable and Enraged Child modes and the Punitive and Demanding Parent modes. These modes can help us to understand the heated dynamic of adolescents and young adults. Frequently in therapy, new modes can be formulated due to the internalization of peer group norms or the powerful manifestation of shame feelings.

Punitive and Demanding modes stemming from parental influences may be added to by modes stemming from dysfunctional peer relations, such as the Peer Tyrant or Peer Dictator. In this mode, the factual or at least perceived demands (norms and rules of conduct of the peer group) are internalized and directed tyrannically toward one's own person and the Child modes.

3.9 Treatment overview

In the following section, we will summarize the central features and phases in Schema Therapy, in order to provide a solid foundation to understand the chapters that follow. We have highlighted that schemas and modes are the basis of ST-CA. Once the schema-mode model has been formulated for the client, the following activities and interventions take place:

a. The therapist aims for therapy to impact significant others, systems or situations so that the client's previously unmet core emotional needs can be met more effectively in everyday life, both inside and outside the therapeutic environment.

b. Within therapy, the therapist will provide limited re-parenting and try to meet the basic needs of the client. The therapist will design therapy as a need-fulfilling interaction. This enhances motivation and is a first step toward alleviating symptoms, because self-worth and self-efficacy are enhanced, and new positive parent parts are internalized.

c. If fulfilment of basic needs is blocked by a maladaptive schema or mode activation, the therapist and client can work together to look for the hidden needs underlying the problem. When these are discovered, more adaptive possibilities for fulfilling them open up. The family system may need new boundaries or rules in order to help fulfil these needs.

d. If the presentation contains mainly disorder-specific behavioural vicious circles (as with obsessive compulsive disorders or school phobia, for example), then ST-CA will focus on this aspect in its early stages. Specific symptoms of such disorders may be understood as a coping mode or an intensified or developmentally inappropriate Child Mode.

3.10 Phases of treatment

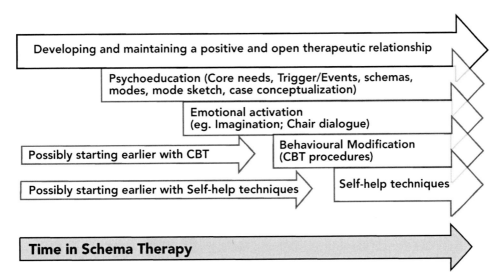

Figure 3.2 The phases of Schema Therapy over time

The first phase of treatment involves building a positive and open relationship, usually through focusing on the client's strengths, resources and achievements. This is followed (for clients of school age and older) by a phase of psychoeducation and case conceptualization, which provides the first opportunity for the client and family to understand what may up to now have been a perplexing and frustrating dynamic. The needs model is explained, the event/trigger identified, the coping mode clarified, and the belief as part of a schema identified; then the mode model is developed as a case conceptualization and presented in age-appropriate terms. The therapist is able to provide insight into frustrated needs, situational misconceptions, weighty emotions, and understandable coping approaches. Each facet of the problem can be identified and labelled, often for the very first time.

In the central phase of therapy, we aim to involve the client emotionally by using experiential techniques to address and challenge maladaptive schemas or modes. This often includes mode work (e.g. finger puppets, mode cards, chair work) and/ or imagery to understand and challenge in a developmentally appropriate way the roots of dysfunctional behavioural patterns. Often, we need to apply classical CBT procedures such as role play, exposure and problem solving to help the client and family put what they have learned in therapy sessions into practice in the real world. As is usual in CBT, new behaviours arising from the schema or mode formulation are practiced via homework assignments. In this phase, ST-CA resembles classical child and adolescent CBT; however, because the behavioural tasks arise from an understanding of schemas and modes, an emotional and experiential dimension is added to the behavioural and cognitive interventions.

In the final phase of therapy, the therapist implements self-help techniques to enable the client and their family to become independent of the therapist's sessions and interventions. In this phase, relapse prevention plays an important role – as well as general support in meeting core needs and strengthening and consolidating the client's competent modes.

3.11 Conclusion

Schema therapy integrates a developmental understanding, a focus on the relationship, mode analysis and emotion-focused interventions with traditional cognitive and behavioural interventions within an overarching systemic framework. Schema therapy aims to understand the learning experiences a client has had during their development. In doing this, we consider the different contexts of family, education, and other peer groups and subcultures. Schema therapy allows us to shed more light on the impact of both the inner and outer dynamics of development. Schema therapy also integrates the symptom-oriented analyses and interventions used in CBT, as these are considered very important in understanding and reducing problematic behaviour.

Schema therapy looks at disorders and symptoms from the perspective of inner conflicts, which have been insufficiently resolved. This complements the classical behavioural analysis of disorders and symptoms, which focuses on situational, personal and consequential variables. The perspective of 'inner conflicts', as well as the perspective of the environmental control of behaviour through trigger and reinforcer, can be integrated into an overarching schema- and mode guided behavioural therapy approach. Coping reactions or modes are triggered by (inner or outer) stimuli. Usually, such stimuli have the power to trigger maladaptive schemas, that can be interpreted as classically conditioned emotional reactions, followed by physiological responses, cognitions, and memories (schemas).

Schema therapy provides a new perspective, identifying problematic behaviour as part of an Overcompensating or Avoidant mode or as maintenance of age-inappropriate younger Undisciplined or Vulnerable Child mode. This provides a deep understanding of the complex emotional lives of our clients, and a richer comprehension of the presenting problem's developmental dynamic. These themes will be elaborated in detail, with worked examples, over the course of this book.

Literature

Grawe, K. (2017). *Neuropsychotherapy: How the neurosciences inform effective psychotherapy.* Routledge.

Greenberg, L. (2006). Emotion-focused therapy: A synopsis. *Journal of Contemporary Psychotherapy,* **36**(2), 87-93. doi:http://dx.doi.org/10.1007/s10879-006-9011-3

Loose, C. (2018). Schema therapeutic outpatient treatment of a 15-year-old boy with hypochondria against the background of a car accident caused paraplegia early in childhood. Amsterdam: ISST-Conference.

Loose, C. & Graaf, P. (2016). Pictorial Representation of Early Maladaptive Schemas and Modes - for Young and Old. Poster. Stockholm: 46th Annual EABCT Congress CBT.

Roediger, E. Stevens, B.A., & Brockman, R. (2018). Contextual Schema Therapy. An Integrative Approach to Personality Disorder, Emotional Dysregulation & Interpersonal Functioning. Oakland, CA: Context Press.

Schulz von Thun, F. (1998). Miteinanderreden 3 – Das innere Team und situationsgerechte Kommunikation. Hamburg: Rowohlt.

Young, J. E., Klosko, J. S., & Weishaar, M. E. (2003). *Schema therapy: A practitioner's guide.* Guilford Press.

Chapter 4: Schema Therapy from Infancy to Early Childhood

Katharina Armour, Sophie Kröger Gerhard Zarbock and Ruth A. Holt

Preliminary remark

The model that we introduce here focuses on regulatory disorders (excessive crying, sleeping and feeding disorders) in babies and young children. We use the label 'regulatory disorders' and refer you to changes in the definition of the disorders gathered under it. The term 'regulatory disorders' has been renamed 'Sleep, Eating and Crying Disorders' in the internationally recognised Diagnostic Classification of Mental Health and Developmental Disorders of Infancy and Early Childhood (DC:0-5) of the workgroup Zero To Three (ZTT-DC:0-5, 2016), and relates to clinical disorders in children.

The clinical focus is on the interaction between the infant and the main attachment figure or caregiver, usually the mother. The approach outlined in this chapter draws on behavioural therapy concepts from infant sleep dysregulation studies conducted by Mechthild Papousek at the Max Planck Institute for Psychiatry in Munich, from a Schema Therapy perspective. Psychodynamic approaches were also helpful in formulating our Schema Therapy approach. We are moving into new territory in the field of Schema Therapy with our parent–infant/young child therapy. Therefore, the concepts presented here are by no means complete, and will have to be worked out further and in more detail in the future. Further, empirical findings regarding the course and the efficacy of Schema Therapy interventions with infants and young children are needed to refine the approach and methods presented here.

4.1 Phase-specific developmental tasks, interactions, conflicts, and modes in young families from a Schema Therapy perspective

Case Example

Kim, a 39-year-old marketing manager, came for advice because her second child, a nine-month-old boy, had been waking up every 30 minutes for the preceding six months. He would only sleep when he was breastfed, which was also the only way to quiet him during the day. Kim was exhausted, and had begun to 'hate' her son. Kim told us during the assessment that with her first child she needed to supplement feeds with formula after four months as the child was not gaining weight. She felt like a bad mother because she was unable to feed her child herself. So with her second child, she had decided to breastfeed on demand in order to stimulate milk production and wanted to 'do everything right' this time. Kim's mother was quite critical of her, saying that the stress of working and caring for her child was the cause of the insufficient milk supply. Kim herself was unsure whether working had harmed her children.

The birth of a child is a big change for parents. There are mixed emotions during the pregnancy: there is joy about the new addition, but there can also be a fear of a loss of independence. Fears and worries related to parental responsibility also come into the mix: Can I provide for my child? Can I protect them? How will I cope with my new role? The change in the couple dynamic is also a challenge for many parents.

The reality of new parenthood also does not often match the idealised scenes that the parent imagined before the birth. Looking after the child, the tiring sleep–wake–feeding rhythm and periods of crying, and the frustration of the parent's core emotional needs (for instance, the loss of autonomy: 'I've got no time for me', 'What about what I need?') can result in parents feeling overwhelmed and permanently exhausted. This situation can unconsciously activate childhood experiences and feelings (schemas) associated with that time in the parent. As a result of this, the parent's childhood distress, feelings of abandonment or anger get mixed up with the perception of their own child's needs. When the parent's schemas are activated, the infant and their utterances or communication signals are then perceived through the lens of the schema activation.

4.1.1 Developmental tasks for parents and child

Parents have to adapt in many ways in the weeks after the birth of their child. These adaptations include the mother's physiological changes after labour and delivery, parents building confidence in their capabilities, a temporary loss of a professional identity, growing into the parental role and changing from a dyadic to a triadic relationship (for more information see Stern, 1995). In addition to the parental identity and relationship shift, there is also a need for parents to begin to find balance between the child's innate physical needs and emotional needs: bonding, autonomy, self-esteem and pleasure (spontaneity, fun and games). The child also undergoes huge changes in the first two years of life: mastering eating and digestion, regulating sleeping and waking cycles, regulating affective behaviour, focusing attention, balancing bonding and exploration needs and dependence and autonomy needs.

4.1.2 Coping and interaction

A child's ability to cope with developmental tasks and the challenges they bring can only be built with the co-regulatory help of the parents. However, child, parent and situational factors influence co-regulation. So as parents and children bring their own vulnerabilities, dispositions and limitations into this arena, the ongoing development of the child is impacted.

Not only are developmental tasks impacted by these factors; so is the quality of the relationship between parent and child. Factors such as the parent's personality factors, schemas and coping strategies, as well as current stressors, influence the quality of the relationship. The infant also impacts the parent–child dialogue through its constitutional factors that influence adaption and self-regulation (temperament, normal and 'maximal' levels of excitement, self-regulatory competence). If the child has a 'difficult' temperament they will get worked up quickly and intensely, and can be very difficult to calm down. When trying to train a 'difficult' child into regular rhythms of sleep, the parents will face challenges that can be distressing and schema or mode-triggering. Medical issues (such as a physical disability) and traumatic interventions (such as needing special nutrition) can make the process even more difficult.

In these early years, difficulties arise from mismatched parent–child interactions: the child's needs are not properly recognised or are misinterpreted, parents may not react sensitively enough and both child and parent can have distressing emotional reactions. The development of regulatory disorders can therefore be seen as a failure of the co-regulation of parents and infant when coping with developmental tasks. Regulatory disorders are then manifested in symptoms of extreme irritation, expressed through excessive crying, nutrition refusal and problems falling and staying asleep.

4.1.3 Where does the 'failure to communicate' come from? Schema Therapy approaches to explaining disorders of relating and communicating

Schema Therapy approaches suggest the following way of understanding relating and communicating issues. The baby expresses a need, which activates the parent's dysfunctional schema or modes (connected to the parent's unmet needs and childhood experiences), blocking 'healthy' parental responses to the child. As a result the child's cries and needs get mixed up internally with the parent's biographically-caused 'neurotic' problem activation. The intuitive parental competence that most parents have, according to Papousek (2008), becomes obscured, and parents interpret their child's signals according to their maladaptive schemas and react accordingly, often not very sensitively. Parents then feel overburdened, disoriented, overtaxed and desperate. For example, when her child has been crying for hours, a mother may think, 'It doesn't matter what I do, she's never happy.' Depending on the mode with which the mother reacts, she can become aggressive, for example, and shout at her child or even shake her (the mother's Angry Child or Bully/Attack coping mode). An apathetic reaction is another possibility (Detached Protector mode), followed by bouts of extreme overeating undertaken by the mother to distract herself (Detached Self-soother mode).

The mother may also mistake her child's signals as reactions to her, driven by her own schemas, such as *Social Isolation* ('My child is crying because she's lonely'). In this case the mother's Vulnerable Child mode is activated, which she copes with it by overstimulating her infant, exacerbating the child's crying. As the mother's schemas are activated they provide a framework for her understanding of the baby's behaviour. The mother's feelings and needs are imposed on the infant, masking the actual source of the baby's irritation. As a consequence of this, the mother has difficulty decoding her infant's signals correctly, and in a child-focused manner. Her Healthy Adult mode is 'off'. This is the reason why Schema Therapy focuses on disentangling the mother's and child's needs by helping the mother become conscious of the maladaptive schemas and modes that her child activates.

Schema Therapy focuses on balancing the needs of both mother and baby. The therapist always 'sees' the hurt or unfulfilled needs that are behind the mother's unhelpful schema or modes. The central therapeutic question is then 'What do you need?', which results in weakening the schema and diminishing the modes. This hypothesis, based on need orientation, has parallels with psychodynamic concepts such as the projective identification, or Fraiberg's 'ghost in the child's bedroom' (Barth, 2004; Fraiberg *et al*, 1975).

Below is a list of typical modes in parents that are activated by infants (other modes may also be relevant to individual case conceptualisation:

- Healthy Adult/Caring and Guidance mode
- Happy Parent (This mode should describe the harmony parents feel when they have successfully interacted with the small child, e.g. in cycles of joy (ca. 30,000 reciprocal joy reactions from the mother and baby in the first 6 months, Krause, 2006))
- Vulnerable Child (or Hurt or Isolated Child)
- Angry Child
- Punitive or Demanding Parent (directed inwards or outwards)
- Detached Protector (Coping mode)
- Detached Self-soother/-stimulator (Coping mode)
- Attacker mode (Bully and Attack coping mode)
- (Perfectionistic) Overcompensation (Coping mode)

Parent modes

Healthy adult/caring and guidance mode

Healthy Adult mode is characterised by foresight, frustration tolerance, empathy and the ability to defer needs. It is especially important for the care of infants that the caring role is devoted and capable of appropriate 'self-sacrifice'. The difference between appropriate self-sacrifice and a *Self-Sacrifice* schema is whether the parent is able to *choose* to delay their needs and then take up offers of help to meet those needs when appropriate. When a parent is acting from a *Self-Sacrifice* schema, they feel they have no choice and are unable to accept help even when it is available. In Healthy Adult mode they are able to accept help from others, such as the other parent, grandparents or even friends, providing time out and helping the main caregiver to be re-energized. This mode also reflects healthy attachment and caregiving capacity.

Happy Parent mode

We propose the Happy Parent mode in addition to Healthy Adult. This mode is especially apparent during positive interactions with the infant. The smile-confirmation-cycle is an example of the mutual affirmation between the caregiver and the infant. In this mode there are intense feeling of happiness, affection for the child, mutual gaze and connection with the infant.

Punitive or demanding parent mode

As experience shows, the parents' lack of sleep and other stress caused in the care of infants can result in an irritable atmosphere between the parents, which activates the Punitive or Demanding Parent mode. The internalisation of the demanding or punitive other, especially parental or authority figures, from the individual's childhood is often the origin of the Punitive/Demanding Parent mode. The *Punitiveness* schema, which forms the basis of the Punitive Parent mode, is an automatic assumption that one's own mistakes and those of others will and should be severely punished. This mode is characterised by harsh criticism, focusing on mistakes and punishment of omissions. A Demanding Parent mode is characterised by *Unrelenting Standards* schemas, perfectionism and a fixation on achievement.

If the Punitive mode is directed inward, then it expresses itself in self-accusation, self-doubt and rejection. If the Demanding mode is directed internally it results in inner restlessness, unrelentingly high expectations and searching for mistakes. Mothers who have doubts that they are 'a good mother' and believe that all other mothers 'are better than me' tend toward self-deprecation, can worry too much about their child and become self-sacrificing as well as depressed. In other words, they become their own demanding parent.

If the mode is directed outward, the infant's other carers are harshly criticised for supposed mistakes and clumsiness with the child and are put under high levels of pressure. This results in conflict between partners, exposing the child to arguments and tension in the environment.

Child modes

The infant's signals can also activate the parent's innate child modes.

Angry Child mode

When an individual's needs (for sleep, quiet, free time or solitude), are constantly frustrated, and they feel permanently stressed because of the pressures on the rest of the family as a result of caring for the infant, then the infant's crying can activate the parent's Angry or Enraged Child mode. The parent ideally is able to shift back into Healthy Adult mode and manage their Angry Child mode. However, if they have less resilience or resources, their Angry Child response can lead them to feelings of shame or guilt. In extreme cases, physical and emotional abuse of the infant can occur (such as in the Bully/Attack coping mode)

Hurt or Vulnerable Child mode

Being confronted with a baby's enormous neediness and its demand for protection can activate the mother or father's Vulnerable Child mode. Schemas such as *Emotional Deprivation* or *Abandonment* or *Social Isolation* can be triggered.

When these schemas are activated, the parent experiences feelings of lack of care or nurture, or re-experiences traumatising emotions from their own history. In that moment the baby functions as a representative of the parent's past: parents can then describe their children exactly as they, the parent, would have felt when they were young children (Barth, 2004).

Coping modes

The emotions that are connected to schema activation, such as fear, anger and shame, are very painful and usually bring forth coping modes in the parent.

Avoidance

Avoidance (fleeing from the activation of feelings of *Abandonment* and *Isolation*) may result in a mother caring for her older infant in age-inappropriate ways, such as breastfeeding until they fall asleep, or carrying them around to avoid separation so that she can meet her own needs for closeness and care. In order to support the child in his or her developmental task (falling asleep alone), it would be more appropriate to put him or her down to sleep. Another form of avoidance (resulting from a *Mistrust/Abuse* or a *Defectiveness* schema activation) is when the mother avoids eye contact with her child and carries out her caring duties mechanically and without interest. She spends no time playing with her child, hardly reacting, neither answering nor mirroring, which leaves the child under-stimulated. This raises the danger of an insecure attachment being formed. A consequence of an insecure bond with the primary caregiver is that the infant will reduce the amount of affective expression they use or (depending on temperament) develop an exaggerated liveliness in order to gain the attention of their carer.

Overcompensation

Overcompensation results when the parent's Vulnerable Child mode is activated ('I'm at someone else's mercy; I'm helpless and abandoned') and is then compensated for with Perfectionistic Over-Control. Overcompensation begins when anxiety increases, focused on something happening to the child (Sudden Infant Death Syndrome, for example). The anxiety leads the parent to keep very close watch over the child, despite a complete lack of medical indicators for this behaviour. Parents with a *Mistrust/Abuse* schema can overcompensate for their threat activation arising out of not understanding their child's behaviour. When they don't understand the signals their child is giving, they interpret them as threatening in some way. For example, the baby's crying can be perceived as hostile by the parents. They may then try to control their baby's need signals or dominate the relationship. They tend to overstimulate and ignore the child's attempts to self-regulate. If the child withdraws into itself as protection from the (parental) overstimulation, then the parent interprets this withdrawal as rejection.

Detached Protector mode

Detached Protector is another dysfunctional coping mode that can occur with postpartum depression and is expressed as a numb switching-off or disconnection, 'not feeling myself' or being unable to connect with the baby.

Bully/Attack mode

The activation of the Bully/Attack mode, which is also known as the Bully and Attack mode, is characterised by the parent's anger or even hatred of the child. The child can be seen as a 'greedy black hole'. The demands of a child are so challenging that they are seen as unbearable and unjustified. Such parents usually have violent fantasies regarding their infant, which in extreme cases may lead to actual abuse. Table 4.1 summarises behaviours that are apparent when the coping modes are activated.

Table 4.1: Parental behaviour by mode activation

Parent's mode activation	Observed behaviour in parents
Angry, Enraged Child initially, then Bully/Attack coping mode	Angry responses to the infant such as loud shouting or scolding; in extreme cases, physical abuse
Vulnerable or Hurt Child initially, then Avoidance coping mode	Breastfeeding or carrying while infant falls asleep; avoiding infant's eye contact; mechanical washing, diaper-changing, and dressing; little playful contact
Perfectionistic Overcompensation	Overanxious supervision of the infant with constant checking during the night (disturbing the infant's sleep)
Detached Protector	Numb, switched-off and inadequate reactions to the infant

Case example

The complexity of the interaction between the parent's needs and the child's needs becomes obvious in our case study: Kim felt like a failure, like she was a bad mother (schema: *Defectiveness/Shame* and *Punitiveness* inward). Her intuitive parental skills felt undermined after the birth of her second child, and so she started to consult various breastfeeding advisors and Internet forums (Perfectionistic Overcontroller mode as overcompensation). Her son's crying activated Kim's Vulnerable Child mode ('he feels so lonely when I'm not there'), and it became clear that Kim herself had an *Abandonment* schema. As a child she had a month-long stay in hospital because of a respiratory illness, without any close family members, as at the time it wasn't normal to let a parent stay with their child. Kim remembered how she used to watch her mother walking off to the parking lot, and how lonely and abandoned she felt. Her own childhood needs for closeness are now being played out in her inability to expect her son to bear the separation every evening. Kim is answering her own childhood needs through her behaviour with her son.

4.2 Schema Therapy approach to the role of the father

Once the child is born, the father is faced with considerable transitional tasks that can also induce certain modes. The needs frustration that he faces can trigger experiences of needs frustration in childhood or in the course of his life which can play out in the following way. With the birth of the infant, the father is faced with a new task; he has to lose a large part of his previous independence and freedom. This conflict occurs especially when the father imagines himself in the role of a modern father, where both partners are involved in a large part of the infant's care. The father's instinctive wish is to be a good father and supportive partner, yet he also faces an unfulfilled need for autonomy. Various modes can be activated here. The Vulnerable or Impulsive Child mode might be expressed as aggressive thoughts directed at the child, such as 'You've ruined my life'. This then induces guilty feelings (Punitive Parent mode: 'How can you think such a thing! You are a terrible father'). A typical overcompensation is evident, for example, when the father plays overstimulating games and activities with the child every evening and ignores the child's needs for sleep and quiet. This pattern can set the stage for sleep disorders or excessive crying. Reactions like these from the baby strengthen the father's feelings of insufficiency.

If the father has an *Emotional Deprivation* or *Abandonment* schema, which has previously been soothed by the female in the couple concentrating on caring for him, the transfer of affection to the infant can be destabilising for the man. A competition can be created between his needs and the baby's. The triangulation (by extending the dyadic relationship to a triadic relationship) results in ongoing distress. The husband can start falling into the Vulnerable Child mode more often, more intensely and for longer periods of time. This sets up the dynamic that is described by mothers as having 'two children' at home. Other possible responses may be increased quarrelling with the partner (Enraged Child mode activated through needs frustration). The father might start fantasising about leaving the family (Impulsive Child mode) and might even do that. Other strategies to manage the distress of the schema activation include escaping into work (Detached Protector avoidance mode), spending more time with friends (active Detached Self-soother or active avoidance) or eating and drinking more (passive Detached Self-soother). The scenes just described are worsened if the child has a more 'difficult' temperament.

Ideally, the parents are able, if the infant–parent interaction is sufficiently successful, to stay in Healthy Adult mode for the majority of the time. In this mode the parents display a measured self-sacrifice and devotion to the infant's care and there is a successful completion of the parenting role. The mode enjoyed when there is a balanced meeting of needs is the Happy Parent mode, where the children's happiness is central and positive relationship interactions are plentiful. In this mode, parents initiate positive bids for a relationship and the child answers such offers with smiles and contentment.

The couple's relationship and the infant's care can be made more manageable if the father and mother can learn to give space for each other to be in Vulnerable Child mode from time to time ('I've had enough, you do something'), provide comfort and support to one another and then equally participate in looking after the child, relieving the other partner.

4.3 Schema Therapy assessment, psychoeducation and therapy for regulatory disorders

Schema Therapy formulations and interventions are closely connected in the case of regulatory disorders. An individualised formulation focusing on the needs and wants of the parents and their infants is always the starting point. Parents who seek professional help for their infant are often desperate, greatly stressed and exhausted, so in addition to assessing and meeting the child's needs, an important initial goal is to provide options for relief for the parents.

Assessment, formulation and therapy begins by hearing the parents' description as well as observing the parent–child interactions in typical situations such as quieting, putting to sleep and playing (Papousek, 2008). The behaviour during the interaction can be observed during the first few sessions or can be video-based. During these observations, issues to be addressed are noted and raised throughout treatment.

4.3.1 Initial assessment

The initial assessment encompasses a thorough biopsychosocial history of every family member concerned.

Organic causes of the presenting problem need to be considered (Groß, 2016) during the assessment phase (for example neurological anomalies, perinatal brain damage or breathing difficulties caused by blocked airways). The parents are then interviewed separately and asked about difficulties related to crying, sleeping and eating disorders (these often co-occur), and the length and the extent is described. The infant's temperament-based issues and self-regulatory capabilities (sucking on fingers, for example) need to be assessed (Groß, 2016). For further information we refer you to the multi-axial Diagnostic Classification of Mental Health and Developmental Disorders of Infancy and Early Childhood (DC:0-5) from the early childhood policy non-profit Zero To Three, providing a multi-axial approach to diagnostics. Also helpful is the Research Diagnostic Criteria – Preschool Age (RDC-PA; Postert *et al*, 2009).

4.3.2 Exploration of parental issues

Once the child's presenting problem has been described via the parental interview and any medical investigations have been completed by medical personnel, the next step is to explore the parents' subjective perspective of the issues.

At this point it can be helpful to provide appropriate psychoeducation about the normal development of infants and their needs (as well as those of their parents).

4.3.3 Assessment of the parent–child interaction

Following interview-based information gathering, recording of the parent–child interaction and/or behavioural observation is carried out for all forms of regulatory disorders. In addition the parents are asked to keep behavioural, crying and sleeping diaries, feeding and nutrition protocols, and so on. These are explained to the parents in the first session and then worked on and evaluated in subsequent sessions (examples are available in the online materials: www.pavpub.com/resource-374CoCr).

While watching the video material or observing interactions, the appropriateness of the infant's behaviour when relating to the parents is assessed. It is important to evaluate how ready the child is to interact and what kind of attachment is apparent. At the same time, the parents' sensitivity and the appropriateness of their responses is also evaluated in connection to the child's behavioural pattern. Video recordings of normal routines, such as changing, feeding, dressing, playing, as well as separation and boundary enforcement situations, are watched with the mother. It is then possible – in the framework of eating disorder, for example – to observe how the mother and child deal with the transition from the breast to the bottle and later to eating at the table.

The mother or father is asked, while watching the video, to say out loud what was going through their head in the situation and what is going through their head at that time of watching. As this is being discussed, the therapist is developing empathetic understanding (verbalisation of supposed emotions, feelings, thoughts) and validating the parents (making clear, relieving, depathologising).

Following this, an interactional schema and mode analysis of the presenting problem is developed. Questions that are helpful in developing this formulation are:

- Which interactions with the infant activate/trigger strong emotions, in connection to which schema or mode in the parent?
- How is that schema activation coped with?
- What is outwardly visible?
- What reactions does the child's behaviour cause in the mother/father, or vice versa?

In addition, questionnaires (such as parents' schema and mode inventories) can be used to complete the formulation.

During this process parents are generally (in Healthy Adult mode) involved as experts in the analysis of themselves and their child. It is important to understand their feelings, interpretations and explanations of their child's behaviour. It is also important to explore their expectations of their child. Old wishes, expectations and experiences during the pregnancy are discussed, as well as parental emotional states before and after the birth. The therapist's initial hypothesis (therapeutic working hypothesis) then includes which maladaptive schemas and modes are activated by the baby's presence and behaviour, and which of the parents' core emotional needs (which were chronically unmet during their childhood) are contributing. Relevant childhood memories (for example a compendium of key experiences; Young *et al*, 2003) can be of special importance for the development of the relevant schemas and modes, as well traumatic life events such as parental separation, loss and abuse. A mother's possible eating disorders may also play a impacting role in her child's feeding disorders (Agras *et al*, 1999).

4.3.4 Observation procedures and instruments for assessment

In order to adequately understand the dimensions of the interaction between the mother/ father and the child, additional characteristics such as visible behaviours, verbal remarks, non-verbal aspects such as eye contact, body language, voice volume and so on (see Lebow, 2012), and both negative and positive affect can either be observed directly or from video material.

There are various observation procedures that can be used in structured and semi-structured situations (e.g. playing, feeding, tidying up) that differentiate between various modalities of expression during the observed interaction. The CARE index (Child-Adult-Relationship Experimental Index; Crittenden, 2005) is an example of an observation procedure in an unstructured situation that allows sensitivity to be recorded in a dyadic way. Seven behavioural aspects are looked at (facial expression, verbal/vocal expression, position and body contact, expressions of affect, pacing of turns, control and choice of activity) for the child as well as the caregiver. These aspects are listed under the dimensions 'sensitivity', 'control' and 'unresponsiveness' for adults and 'cooperative', 'over-adjusted', 'difficult' and 'passive' for the child. In addition to the possible evaluation of appropriate vs. inappropriate for the child and closed vs. open for the significant other, clues can be gained from the Schema Therapy assessment as to the schemas behind the 'suboptimal' or 'dysfunctional' behaviour.

Questionnaires that the patient can answer themselves or that others can answer about them, such as the Young Parenting Inventory (YPI; Young, 1994) or the short Young Schema Questionnaire (Young, 1998) are useful in gaining more information about the presenting problem. The Parenting Stress Index (PSI) by Abidin (1995) can also be used to find out more about parental stress factors.

The parents are also asked about their relationship, their experience of the transition to parenthood and any possible change in the quality of their relationship ('What has changed in your relationship since you became parents? What has worsened? What has improved?') This process allows for an analysis of dysfunctional relationship structures and the dynamic between the parents and the family as a whole.

4.3.5 Summary of the assessment process

The therapist should be able to form a working hypothesis that serves as the basis for a multifactorial disorder formulation within the first five sessions. As a guiding concept, the therapist will reflect on which of the parents' schemas and modes (from their own childhood experiences) have been activated by the infant's birth and how parenthood is impacting on the fulfilment of the parents' and partnership's core emotional needs. The therapist should also be able to understand, through direct observation and the schema and mode questionnaires, which maladaptive schemas and modes are activated by the child and why the positive modes (Happy Parent and Healthy Adult) are blocked, if that is the case. In order to be able to set realistic goals and plan the therapy appropriately, an assessment of the resources within the family is also made. This includes functional and helpful personality characteristics, amount and quality of social networks and fulfilment from work or career. Situations in which there are positive parent–child interactions are also identified and validated. From a Schema Therapy point of view, it is always important to explore how parents can fulfil their legitimate basic emotional needs (connection to their partner, autonomy, self-esteem, pleasure) at least partially and temporarily, despite the challenge that arises through caring for an infant.

Figure 4.1 shows the interaction between factors which play a role in the success of the parent–child triad and which can, under certain conditions, lead to regulatory disorders. The parents and the children bring certain issues into the interaction: for the parents, this could be underlying schemas that get triggered by the child's behaviour, which then affect the interactional behaviour and impact negatively on the child. An important element in this situation is how many psychological and physical stress factors are present in the parents, and also what resources are available. The child also brings individual factors like their temperament, level of excitement, and so on into the interaction. In addition, the parents and the child are faced with the challenges of adapting and completing developmental tasks (for the adult, the deferment of their own needs, etc and for the child eating, regulating behaviour and sleeping/waking states, etc).

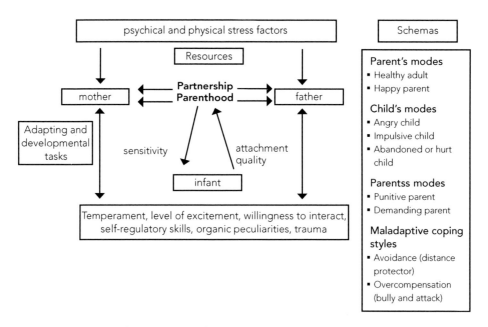

Figure 4.1: Important factors that influence the parent–child triad

4.3.6 Goals and therapy

In parent–infant and young child therapy, the relationship unit 'parent and child' is seen as the patient, rather than the infant alone. Below we outline various therapeutic approaches to this treatment unit.

Developmental guidance

Development guidance can be seen as a less obtrusive form of intervention: lots of parents benefit from pedagogical, psycho-educative interventions where their questions regarding their child's development (core emotional needs, sleep needs, fear of separation, the 'terrible twos', individual variability, etc.) are answered. From a Schema Therapy point of view, the parent's Healthy Adult mode is strengthened by the provision of this information. The therapist responds to specific, pending developmental tasks (self-regulation, self-calming, independent eating, 'guided' falling asleep, etc.), offers coaching for parents, and supports the parents to form realistic expectations of their child. If the parents have unrealistically high levels of expectations around control (Demanding Parent mode), then this should be discussed with them, and the impact on their child's core emotional needs pointed out (Groß, 2016). Psychoeducation helps parents know, for example, that their child's crying and sleeping isn't always under their control. As long as the parents' modes or schemas aren't greatly activated, then this level of intervention will suffice to bring about positive behavioural changes and more appropriate reactions as they connect with their child.

Communication guidance

Communication guidance makes sense when the parent falsely perceives the child or doesn't recognise the infant's signals and has little trust in their own capabilities. The therapist has the opportunity, during the session with the parents, to point out dysfunctional communication patterns and to talk about which schemas may be activated, and the therapist can help to separate these 'old' central life themes from the new life task of 'caring for your infant'. This approach can be complemented with video recordings of parent–child interactions if necessary. Parents can be supported in replacing dysfunctional communication patterns with functional ones and increasing their sensitivity so that they can recognise and respond to their child's signals effectively (for example, a modified mother–infant transaction programme: see Newnham *et al*, 2009). The parents are supported in accessing their Healthy Adult mode, which can help them to better understand their baby's changing needs for attachment, safety, self-efficacy, autonomy and discovery, and also assist them to react more appropriately to the actual needs of the child, promoting stronger self-regulation.

Schema Therapy guidance

Schema Therapy guidance can be helpful in all forms of regulatory disorders as either complementary or parallel to psycho-educative and behavioural therapy methods. If the therapeutic rapport is well developed this intervention will help parents feel that they are being understood and they are more able to talk about their ambivalence, disappointment, feelings of insufficiency, anger and other taboo subjects. At this point, the Schema therapist provides psychoeducation and normalises the parents' experience of the schema activation (using phrases like 'You experience your own childhood again when you have your own children'). The term 'schema' can be introduced using terms such as life themes and 'family rules' which can be used to refer to spoken and unspoken feelings, expectations and behaviour patterns inside the family of origin. The parents are then encouraged to fill out the schema questionnaires. The therapist can then usually form the first hypotheses about the background of the child's regulatory problems. The important schemas and modes are connected to the current problem and based on observations made during parent–child appointments. It is important at this stage to clarify which are the most prominent or dominating modes in operation.

4.4 Schema Therapy practice: therapeutic strategies, age-specific techniques

There are parents for whom psychoeducation and interaction-focused counselling alone will not be sufficient. Indicators of a need for Schema Therapy can be assessed by asking the following questions:

- Is the child still being perceived in a distorted manner, despite psychoeducation and communication guidance?

- Do the parents interpret the child's behaviour as malicious and hostile?

- Do the parents still act dismissively or inappropriately toward the child?

- Are vicious cycles still present?

- Are the couple's problems still a big stress factor affecting the parent–child relationship?

If concern is raised by these questions, the Schema Therapy goal then becomes focused on addressing interaction problems, parents' schemas, coping styles and critical modes with the parents.

Important goals in the mother's or the father's Schema Therapy include:

1. Recognising their own inner Vulnerable Child. Further steps concentrate on recognising, accepting and comforting innate child parts as they occur.

2. Dysfunctional Punitive and Demanding Parent modes (e.g. the Inner Punisher mode) need to be weakened and 'deprived of power'.

3. Avoidance and overcompensation modes need to be minimised in favour of more 'grown-up' Healthy Adult solutions to problems and conflicts.

4. Finally, the parents' Healthy Adult mode can grow through modelling, corrective experiences and catching up on developmental stages. The innate Happy Child mode can then be rediscovered and become a resource. Subsequently, pride, joy and identification with parenthood can be experienced and the Happy Parent mode can develop – maybe for the first time in their lives.

Schema Therapy approaches are underpinned by the assertion that unhelpful reactions activated by the infant can be changed by addressing the parents' own experiences from early childhood. The parents' perceptions of situations as an infant or small child are evoked in visualisation. Then, through Imagery Re-Scripting, the parent can experience having those unmet needs recognised, appreciated and validated. In imagery the child's wishes can then be not only named but also fulfilled by the therapist providing a corrective or symbolic satisfaction of the unmet need. If necessary, the adult patient's own parents can receive helpful advice from the therapist during the visualisation about how to treat the infant or how to improve the family situation. The parent's Vulnerable Child mode receives limited re-parenting from the therapist.

Following Imagery Re-Scripting, the therapist identifies core messages and key sentences that address the parent's schemas, and gives them to the patient on flash cards. Throughout therapy the therapist focuses on helping the adult identify their mode and schema activations, asking: 'Which mode or modes are active now?' As there is more moment-to-moment awareness of feelings, the therapist is able to connect these experiences to the parent's history. The distressing experiences and emotions, such as sadness or jealousy, can be expressed and connected to the causative situation, allowing the parent to see the origins of the distress. These experiences are then processed in therapy, finding symbolic and verbal need fulfilment. Parental schemas can be 'healed' or at least 'weakened' by dealing with the past and experiencing a re-staged need fulfilment. This frees up the parent to be able to bond in the here and now with their own, more realistically perceived baby.

The therapist can, in addition, use the age progression technique borrowed from hypnotherapy, asking the question: '*If Little Sally (the parent as child) had experienced this need being met and if your parents had been able to communicate this message in a way you could understand, what would have been different as a baby … as a toddler … as a school child, etc?'* Once the adult has experienced more nurturing care, the therapist can then direct the parent to visualise this more caring approach in the parent's interaction with their actual child. This Healthy Adult mode can be signalled and developed using phrases that connect the parent to their experience of being nurtured in the therapeutic relationship. There are many ways to help a parent connect with the nurturing Healthy Adult mode: using key phrases, self-calming techniques ('You can do it', 'Cuddle the baby – that you once were') and coping statements ('Strong parents – strong kids'); building self-regulation ('Pay attention to your own breath') and interactional regulation ('Breathe with the child,' 'Sing the baby your special song'). These ways of connecting to the Healthy Adult can be visualised and practised at home.

The therapist provides, through their validation and acceptance, a space in which 'all' feelings can be expressed, allocated to the appropriate mode and processed through appropriate interventions (e.g. visualising comforting the Vulnerable Child, depriving the Punitive Parent of power). The parents will then be better able to perceive their child (unaltered by their own schemas and modes) in a more attuned way, seeing more clearly the child's needs and emotional states.

The therapist can, as a sort of 'limited grandparenting' or 'limited co-parenting', then take the role of a helpful grandparent or co-parent who not only re-parents the adult patients themselves but also acts as a caring and guiding figure who can stand by the family's side in the current situation.

4.4.1 Disorder-specific Schema Therapy considerations

Sleep disorders

Parents that have been impacted by their children's sleeping disorders say that trying to get their child to sleep arouses strong feelings in them. These feelings can range from abandonment to powerlessness, helplessness, disappointment and aggression. Because the parent has had their own schemas activated by the distress of this situation, they often misinterpret the reasons why their child is not sleeping. Parents will then push themselves beyond their own limits in order to fulfil the child's supposed needs. For example, if the parents see their child as helpless, abandoned and lonely, this indicates that the problem isn't a self-regulation disorder of the child; it is a much more unconscious separation problem that lies primarily with the parent (Barth, 2004). The parent is often really dealing with his or her own schemas of *Social Isolation* or *Abandonment* or *Emotional Deprivation*. The child's crying activates their Vulnerable Child mode, which impairs the parent's capacity to respond adequately to the child's needs.

Parents presenting for therapy are often at the end of their tether because of lack of sleep, reporting that they sometimes react inappropriately aggressively (Angry Child mode) to their child and in extreme cases become physical (shouting or shaking: Bully and Attack mode). This quickly leads to feelings of guilt (Punitive Parent mode), which they then have to compensate for by indulging the child or through excessive soothing. From a learning theory point of view, the parents are intermittently reinforcing the child's behaviour and are not maintaining clear boundaries, which does not provide the security children need. This pattern then ensures that the child behaves in such a way that the parent's schemas are no longer triggered, and they don't have to deal with their own Vulnerable Child fears of separation. One way in which this can play out is that the parents, in misjudging their child's own needs (sleep), react with overstimulating interaction or breastfeeding. They thereby miss the chance to support their child in the important developmental step of learning to fall asleep alone. The child doesn't learn to associate its needs (sleep) with the corresponding appropriate answer to that need (being put to bed) because they are always being answered by an unhelpful answer (stimulation followed by parental distress).

Case example

Back to the therapy of Kim and her son: Kim was able to comfort 'little Kim' (Vulnerable Child mode) with the help of visualisations in which adult Kim (Healthy Adult mode) held and comforted herself as a little girl. At the same time, as a form of developmental guidance, Kim was able to learn what a secure bond is and what expectations were appropriate for her child, and understand how to scale down her reaction to something more appropriate for her child's developmental age. The Punitive Parent was reduced and Kim's identity as a working mother was legitimised. Assisting in this process was Kim's husband, who displayed a high level of Healthy Adult and Healthy Parent mode. He was able to provide emotional stability and nurture to Kim and told us he would take over the sleep transition. He altered the Tweddle method (Cummings *et al*, 2000) a bit and stayed sitting next to the bed so that his son could see and hear him. He spoke calmly, in a soft voice, to the child ('Daddy's here, I can't pick you up at the moment. You can fall asleep yourself. We can do it!') and managed, within a few days, to get the child to fall and stay asleep.

Excessive crying

Babies often cry in the first three months without apparent reason. Lots of parents get through this period quite well because they assume all young babies cry. If the duration and intensity of the crying phases do not decrease, the parents can lose control and feel helplessness and despair. They talk about taking their children for long drives at night, putting them on spinning washing machines or contorting their bodies, all in an attempt to calm their child down. The child's long bouts of crying can make the parent feel tense and aggressive. Typical modes that are triggered are the Angry or Enraged Child or, in extreme cases, the Bully and Attack mode in which the parents shake their child, which can be life-threatening. Sometimes, parents experience the Punitive Parent mode which can lead to feelings of insufficiency ('I will never be able to calm my child').

The goal in Schema Therapy, along with behavioural therapy and psychoeducation, is to help the parent to see that the dysfunctional modes are a response to extreme stress, to learn how to comfort the hidden Vulnerable Child mode and/or limit the Punitive Parent mode. It is often helpful to give parents phrases that they can use as a reminder in crying phases to calm themselves so that they stay in their Healthy Adult mode (e.g. 'I am here, I can hold you, but there's nothing else I can do for you at the moment'). It can be helpful for parents to have the knowledge that the crying can trigger their own Vulnerable Child mode ('I am just as abandoned' or 'you are feeling desperate just like I felt desperate') or Punitive Parent mode ('The crying is aimed at me; you (the baby) are accusing me', 'It will never stop', 'You're being ungrateful, trying to hurt me'). When the parent understands the Schema Therapy conceptualisation (focusing on central life themes and family background: see above), that also helps to anchor the parent in the here and now of the Healthy Adult mode.

Feeding disorders

It should be pointed out that the Schema Therapy treatment of feeding disorders only applies to those forms of feeding disorder which present no acute threat to life or where there is no imminent physical risk. Schema Therapy approaches to feeding disorders are only indicated when the issue is exacerbated by the interactions of the parent and child or the reactions of the parent to the child. When babies and young children don't eat and/or digest appropriately, this can release in the parents an existential fear for their child. Brief instances of food refusal by the child can be escalated, become rigid and be made more chronic through unhelpful, schema-driven responses to the food refusal. Parents can experience, for example, their child's food refusal as a rejection of their person, and then the Vulnerable Child or the Punitive Parent mode (aimed internally) is activated. The mother can then feel helpless in the Vulnerable Child mode, which can awaken strong experiences of feeling isolated and overwhelmed. If there is an unfulfilled need for autonomy, or if the parent emotionally re-experiences an old relationship conflict, she can, in the overcompensation mode (Perfectionistic Over-Control), get into a power struggle with the infant.

Furthermore, the mother can, in Punitive Parent mode, blame herself and obsessively brood upon what she might have done wrong during her pregnancy or the first few weeks after the birth. A Punitive Parent mode that is aimed internally like this can lead to depressive symptoms. If the Punitive or Demanding Parent is aimed externally (which is displayed by hard and unyielding rules around eating and table manners or statements such as 'you eat what's put in front of you' or 'children are starving elsewhere'), then the food-refusing infant is perceived as ungrateful, disobedient and 'bad'.

Parents who have these strong reactive responses to food refusal can then escalate into force feeding their child 'to get some nutrition into the child', increasing everybody's distress. The child's growing resistance to the force feeding is then part of the vicious cycle in which child and parent find themselves. In Schema Therapy, the biographical themes or the parents' schemas need to be identified and modified in the ways described above. The background issues that fuel the presenting problem can then be defused. The only thing then that needs to be resolved is the child's 'learned' dysregulation. This can usually be treated with the behaviour therapy techniques described below.

4.4.2 Classic Behaviour Therapy intervention techniques within the framework of Schema Therapy

Behaviour therapy interventions are thought of as supports for the modification of dysfunctional behaviours in parent–child interactions. They are based on the laws of classical ('associative learning') and operant ('learning through rewarding') conditioning, which apply to all life forms. Parents can find behaviour therapy methods overly regimented and negative because they are very structured, and the therapist can thereby be perceived as taking the role of the Punitive Parent and no longer as warm and accepting. Schema Therapy can sensitise for such relationship traps ('therapist as punisher'), providing a context of parental care which allows parents to feel supported rather than judged, increasing levels of acceptance and compliance with behavioural approaches. The therapist can recognise when the schemas or modes are activated and can provide feedback in a way that is more likely to be heard, by first acknowledging the underlying fears and distress (in the Vulnerable Child mode, for example):

'I know that Little Sally is really scared that she will never be able to cope with your baby and you feel criticised by your Demanding Parent voice; maybe I even sound like your Demanding Parent? But I want to stand with you, holding onto Little Sally, and help your Healthy Adult stick with the plan. We can do it!'

Coping styles, such as Detached Protector forms of avoidance, need to be taken into account in this context and empathically challenged with the parent.

'I know Detached Protector wants to shut you down because it's really hard, but your son wants to feel your love and care, even when we are doing things that are hard.'

Taking into account the emotional background and schema dynamic, the therapist and the parents can integrate the behaviour therapy interventions detailed below into the therapy.

Behaviour therapy treatments for regulatory disorders

Problems falling and staying asleep

If there are problems falling and staying asleep then a regular daily rhythm to clearly differentiate between day and night has to be created for the infant. Any forms of overstimulation (rough carrying, physical or exciting games in the evening, etc) have to be identified and reduced. Progressive extinction, or the Ferber method, can be used in connection with a clear bedtime ritual and has been proven successful for small children from six months on. In this method the parents stay until just before the baby falls asleep and come back if it cries, but they don't pick up or stroke the baby; instead they use verbal calming by saying things like 'Mummy and Daddy are here, you don't need to worry' (Mindell *et al*, 2006). The recommendation is that in the first two nights parents go to the child after five minutes, and then after ten minutes, and then after 15 minutes, and so on (Wolke, 2009), although there are variations in specific timings (Mindell *et al*, 2006).

Alternatively, the Tweddle method (Cummings *et al*, 2009) is very useful with very anxious or excited children and is said by some parents to be less distressing and easier to carry out. The time intervals are shorter with the Tweddle method and the child is calmed not only with the voice but also with calming stroking and gentle rolling from side to side in the child's bed. When using the Tweddle method, the recommendation for the increasing time intervals between the parental calming attempts is 2, 4, 6, 8, and 10 minutes for 6 to 12-month-old babies.

Excessive crying

It is also important in the case of excessive crying to structure the rhythms of sleep, feeding and play times, to avoid the overstimulation that is often the case with crying babies. Parents are informed that too much carrying and robust swaying as well as the offering of various different stimuli (such as rattles, for example) can be too much for their child. The baby has no chance to relax and reacts with increasing irritation (Cierpka, 2016).

Feeding disorders

One behaviour therapy technique for feeding disorders is to structure the daily routine and feeding and reduce distractions during feeding (Thiel-Bonney &

von Hofacker, 2016). The desired behaviour can be reinforced through selective attention giving and contingent rewarding or extinction (e.g. smile when the child swallows, look away when it spits the food out or refuses it). The problematic behaviour is defined and time out methods (e.g. mother leaves the room if food is refused) are used when that behaviour occurs. Behaviour can be modified also through desensitisation, for example to address avoidance of feared food (stepwise change of purée consistency from very fluid to more substantial) (Kerwin, 1999).

Learning by modelling behaviour can also be used to increase food curiosity. For instance, if the child doesn't display any explorative behaviour or has had a long break in feeding, the child can be led by the hand or the parent can model the approach behaviour. Another technique is to hold the spoon near the child's mouth even if the child closes its mouth and refuses to feed or starts to cry (Kerwin & Eicher, 2004). Furthermore, it is very important that aversive stimuli or unpleasant experiences through pressuring or forcing should be avoided at all costs, especially in the case of post-traumatic feeding disorders. By limiting the duration of the feeding to 10 to 15 minutes you can gradually increase food acceptance by reducing the frustrating experiences of failure.

The play picnic is another way of treating feeding problems and contains behaviour therapy elements such as desensitisation to stimuli that are initially aversive (Linscheid, 2006). The idea behind the concept involves an interdisciplinary group therapy for infants and small children with feeding disorders and their caregivers for whom we want to 'replace fear and nervousness with curiosity and playful discovery' (Strauss, 2011). This can also be done in individual therapy. The children can approach food at their own pace and through their own experimentation and can then reduce their fear of food in their own autonomous space. The goal for the mother or caregiver is, through observation, to become more relaxed and to develop trust in their child's autonomy and reduce negative associations they have with eating (Groß, 2016 and Linscheid, 2006).

4.4.3 Couple therapy and systemic issues in Schema Therapy

In the course of the therapy with parents, the individual life themes and the pair's common narratives are discussed in order to understand the origin and role of maladaptive schemas in the presenting problem. The therapist conceptualises how pregnancy and birth and the connected developmental tasks have changed the schema dynamic of each individual and also the schema dynamics of the couple and family. Systemic aspects such as boundaries and alliances inside the family play a role in this aspect of the formulation (the systemic observation of Schema Therapy is discussed in detail in Chapter 10).

The main goal, from a systemic point of view, is that the couple strengthens their dyad despite all the burdens of birth and infant care. The first step is an emotional 'detoxification' of the couple's relationship in which mode or schema clashes or escalating problems are explained and modified through chair dialogues. It is often essential at this point that the parents can clearly express their feelings of being overburdened, their Vulnerable Child mode, and also see the Vulnerable Child mode in the other, be able to reach out, understand and 'comfort' that part. Punitive Parent modes that throw accusations at the other person need to be deprived of power (Simeone-DiFrancesco *et al*, 2015).

One key sign of improvement is when the quieter partner overcomes their avoidant mode and is able to express their desperation and feelings of being overwhelmed (Vulnerable Child). As the quieter partner gains confidence that they will be heard they may then also articulate their disappointment and frustration (Angry Child), suggesting increased safety in the relationship for those feelings as well as an increased ability to vocalise their own needs.

The partner who is most talkative (and often the more openly aggressive partner) also needs to identify their role as an outwardly directed Punitive Parent mode and must learn how to weaken it in favour of a more Healthy Adult method of expressing needs. A further step toward meeting the need for freedom for the adult is then to see if the couple or single parent can get regular time away from the infant care each week or month so that they can do something for themselves or the partnership.

The issue of re-commencement of sex also plays a role at this time. This will require the couple to negotiate, especially if the breastfeeding mother's sexual desire is reduced. One approach in Schema Therapy, if there are significant barriers to resuming sexual intimacy, is to encourage conscious abstinence (decided by both partners in Healthy Adult mode) as a more helpful and constructive approach rather than a silent 'avoiding the topic' of sex (avoidance mode) or aggressive refusal or defensive behaviour (Angry Child mode).

The two main goals of the couples work are, first, to de-escalate the vicious cycles caused by schema and mode clashes, and second, search for possible compromises to help each person have their basic needs met, individually but also as a couple, in spite of the considerable developmental task of now having to look after an infant.

If the presenting problem is related to the fact that the family already has several children (who also have unmet needs) then these children and their reactions will be included in Family Schema Therapy. In this case the mode induction and escalation pattern needs to be mapped out for the problem situation. The goal of this analysis is primarily to recognise age-appropriate modes, which are to be found in the natural course of development, like the Angry or Impulsive Child. As these modes are identified, the parents are coached in strategies to stay in their Healthy Adult modes despite the child's provocation and provide appropriate responses to the children's problem behaviour. The parent's goal in this situation is to deal with the situation in such a way that their distressed offspring shifts into Contented Child mode by comforting the (real) Vulnerable Child and co-regulation of the Angry Child (see also Chapter 10).

Child Schema Therapy techniques, like mode work with hand puppets, can be used in parallel to classical psychoeducation interventions so that, for example, a jealous sibling can find more helpful ways of behaving with the small new arrival.

The focus of the Family Schema Therapy work is based on the family schema and mode transaction model that is part of the assessment process. Sessions with the whole family work toward a goal of creating a set of family rules and interrupting dysfunctional mode interaction cycles. These sessions can alternate with parent sessions, or individual child sessions, or older children-only sessions (see Chapter 11). For a more detailed look at Couple-Focused Schema Therapy see Simeone-DiFrancesco *et al*, (2015).

4.5 Outlook

Regulatory disorders in infancy and early childhood have been identified as a risk factor for the development of later behavioural disorders and poor school performance when development is delayed, if treated insufficiently, or if multiple stress factors are present (DeGangi, Porges, Sickel, & Greenspan, 1993; Porges, Doussard-Roosevelt, Portales, & Greenspan, 1996).

Schema Therapy can be helpful in infancy and in supporting the parents in the first few weeks and months after the birth of their child. Classic symptom-orientated approaches with regulatory disorders are complemented, but not usually replaced, by a Schema Therapy perspective and work on the parents' biographical past. The Schema Therapy approach allows parents and carers a nuanced way to understand problems, even complicated ones, in the parent–child and parent–parent dynamics and provides a direction for treatment. Schema Therapy with infants and small children and their parents is still in its early stages. Further development of the concepts and empirical evaluation of the approaches is planned.

References

Abidin RR (1995) *Parenting Stress Index: Professional Manual* (3rd ed.) Odessa, FL: Psychological Assessment Resources, Inc.

Agras S, Hammer L & McNicholas F (1999) A prospective study of the influence of eating-disordered mothers on their children. *International Journal of Eating Disorders* **25** (3) 253–262.

Barth R (2004) 'Gespenster im Schlafzimmer'. Psychodynamische Aspekte in der Behandlung von Schlafstörungen. In: M Papousek, M Schieche & H Wurmser (Eds) *Regulationsstörungen der frühen Kindheit. Frühe Risiken und Hilfen im Entwicklungskontext der Eltern-Kind-Beziehungen*. Bern: Hans Huber.

Chatoor I (2009) *Diagnosis and Treatment of Feeding Disorders in Infants, Toddlers and Young Children*. Washington DC: Zero to Three.

Crittenden P (2005) Der CARE-Index als Hilfsmittel für die Früherkennung, Intervention und Forschung. Frühförderung interdisziplinär **3** 99–106. (English commentary available at http://www.patcrittenden.com/include/docs/care_index.pdf)

Cummings R, Houghton K & Williams LA (2000) *Sleep Right, Sleep Tight. A Practical, Proven Guide to Solving Your Baby's Sleep Problem*. Milsons Point: Doubleday.

DeGangi GA, Porges SW, Sickel RZ & Greenspan SI (1993) Four-year follow-up of a sample of regulatory disordered infants. *Infant Mental Health Journal* **14** (4) 330–343.

Fraiberg S, Adelson E & Shapiro V (1975) Ghosts in the nursery: a psychoanalytic approach to the problems of impaired infant-mother relationships. *Journal of the American Academy of Child Psychiatry* **14** (3) 387–421.

Groß S (2016) Approaches to diagnosing regulatory disorders in infants. In *Regulatory Disorders in Infants* (pp17–33). Springer International Publishing.

Kerwin MLE (1999) Empirically supported treatments in pediatric psychology: Severe feeding problems. *Journal of Pediatric Psychology* **24** (3) 193–214.

Kerwin ME & Eicher PS (2004) Behavioral intervention and prevention of feeding difficulties in infants and toddlers. *Journal of Early and Intensive Behavior Intervention* **1** (2) 129.

Krause R (2006) Emotion, Gefühle, Affekte – Ihre Bedeutung für die seelische Regulierung. In: A Remmel, O Kernberg, W Volmoeller & B. Strauß (Eds) *Handbuch Körper und Persönlichkeit. Entwicklungspsychologie, Neurobiologie und Therapie von Persönlichkeitsstörungen* (pp22–47). Stuttgart: Schattauer.

Lebow JL (Ed) (2012) *Handbook of Clinical Family Therapy*. Chichester: Wiley.

Linscheid TR (2006) Behavioral treatments for pediatric feeding disorders. *Behavior Modification* **30** (1) 6–23.

Mindell JA, Kuhn B, Lewin DS, Meltzer LJ & Sadeh A (2006) Behavioral treatment of bedtime problems and night wakings in infants and young children. *Sleep* **29** (10) 1263–1276.

Newnham CA, Milgrom J & Skouteris H (2009) Effectiveness of a modified mother–infant transaction program on outcomes for preterm infants from 3 to 24 months of age. *Infant Behavior and Development* **32** (1) 17–26.

Papousek M (2008) Disorders of behavioural and emotional regulation: Clinical evidence for a new diagnostic concept. In: M Papousek, M Schieche & H Wurmser (Eds) *Disorders of Behavioral and Emotional Regulation in the First Years of Life* (pp53–84). Washington, DC: Zero to Three.

Porges SW, Doussard-Roosevelt JA, Portales AL & Greenspan SI (1996) Infant regulation of the vagal 'brake' predicts child behavior problems: a psychobiological model of social behavior. *Developmental Psychobiology* **29** (8) 697–712.

Postert C, Averbeck-Holocher M, Beyer T, Müller J & Furniss T (2009) Five systems of psychiatric classification for preschool children: do differences in validity, usefulness and reliability make for competitive or complimentary constellations? *Child Psychiatry and Human Development* **40** (1) 25–41. Available online at: doi:http://dx.doi.org/10.1007/s10578-008-0113-x

Simeone-DiFrancesco C, Roediger E & Stevens BA (2015) *Schema Therapy with Couples: A Practitioner's Guide to Healing Relationships*. Chichester: Wiley.

Stern DN (1995) *The Motherhood Constellation: A Unified View of Parent–Infant Psychotherapy*. New York: Basic Books.

Strauss MP (2011) Wieviel Gramm braucht eine Seele – Psychosomatische Behandlung von Fütter- und Gedeihstörungen im Säuglings- und Kleinkindalter. *Praxis der Kinderpsychologie und Kinderpsychiatrie* **60** (6) 430–451.

Thiel-Bonney C & von Hofacker N (2016) Feeding disorders in infants and young children. In: *Regulatory Disorders in Infants* (pp89–118). Springer International Publishing.

Wolke D (2009) *Regulationsstörungen. Lehrbuch der Verhaltenstherapie*. Heidelberg: Springer.

Young JE (1994) *Young Parenting Inventory*. New York: Cognitive Therapy Center of New York.

Young JE (1998) *Young Schema Questionnaire Short Form* (1st ed.) New York: Cognitive Therapy Center.

Young JE, Klosko JS & Weishaar ME (2003) *Schema Therapy: A Practitioner's Guide*. New York: Guilford Press.

Zero to Three (2016) *DC: 0–5™ Diagnostic Classification of Mental Health and Developmental Disorders of Infancy and Early Childhood*. Washington DC: Zero to Three.

Chapter 5: Schema Therapy for Pre-School Aged Children

Christof Loose, Peter Graaf, Katharina Armour & Ruth A. Holt

> **Case example**
>
> Chiara was starting at her second preschool following a family move. The shy four-year-old had not adjusted well to the first preschool, expressing lots of anxiety. However, Chiara was a different child at home. She helped her mother pack boxes and had been brave enough to ask her cranky neighbour for some packing tape. At home she showed no anxiety whatsoever. After the move, her anxiety increased. After lots of encouragement, she finally attended the new kindergarten. The teachers thought she had adjusted well, but soon Chiara developed head and stomach aches, experienced dizziness and refused to come downstairs from the bathroom in the mornings. Sometimes she would cry and cling to her mother, breaking her mother's heart. She couldn't force Chiara to go, could she? As a child, she herself had been anxious because her father often drank and then hit her mother. During her own kindergarten years, she used to worry about what was happening at home. But that was a long time ago. The situation was completely different with her daughter, Chiara. The parents got along well and there was harmony in the house. Chiara then said she wanted to sleep in her parents' bed. The parents became desperate and decided to consider therapy. What was wrong with their child?

5.1 Phase-specific developmental tasks, interactions, conflicts and modes from a Schema Therapy Perspective

As the case example suggests, kindergarten entry sometimes represents a major obstacle that requires considerable effort from children as well as parents. Themes from early parent–child interaction during infancy (e.g. the attachment and caregiving system) and the development of attachment (e.g. attachment styles) are built on by the developmental challenges and opportunities of the kindergarten environment. This new developmental stage requires adaptation in the areas of cognition, intelligence, emotion, language, self-concept, gender identity and moral and social relationships (see Lohaus & Vierhaus, 2009). Given all these developmental tasks and adaptations, it is not surprising that Chiara would rather stay at home with her mother: the strange environment of kindergarten can seem oppressive to some children and it can be difficult to manage all the developmental tasks. Nevertheless, developmental tasks are essential for ongoing healthy growth. These will be outlined in the following section.

5.1.1 Phase-specific developmental tasks and needs

Developmental tasks

In the first few years of life, children must master general developmental tasks (e.g. eating and motor development) that generally occur at expected times, although development can also fall outside the typical timeframe. Heinrichs and Lohaus (2011) view social communication and language skills as the most important tasks children need to master during the preschool and kindergarten years. These skills also assist with age-appropriate emotion regulation. The child experiences numerous socio-emotional challenges, especially from their peer group, that catalyse the emotion-regulation learning process. From a Schema Therapy perspective several additional tasks include the ability to integrate with a peer group, accept authority and understand social norms (socialisation). These new skills present difficult challenges alongside trying to satisfy personal and emotional needs.

Developmental deviations versus psychological disorders

- The most frequent problems in preschoolers reported by families in counselling services, child and adolescent psychotherapy and psychiatric clinics are developmental delay (e.g. motor, language or play skills), oppositional or aggressive behaviour, hyperactivity, shorter attention span during play, toileting problems and separation, touch, or social anxiety, including difficulties with social integration (Holland *et al*, 2017). These difficulties can be challenging for parents to address on their own, and parents frequently see no other option than seeking professional help. To avoid pathologising children during the preschool years, we recommend using terms such as 'developmental obstacles,' 'developmental delay' or 'developmental deviations' at the early stages of a problem.

Schema Therapy suggests that whether these issues develop into psychological disorders depends on how the core needs of the child are met. This brings us to the central question asked in Schema Therapy: What core needs does the child have during this life stage?

Needs behind symptoms

One way to focus on needs is to look beyond the symptoms by asking: How has the child learned to deal with needs frustration and what emotional support does the child need from their family?

A six-year-old child with enuresis has attachment needs in addition to need for the treatment of symptoms. The emotional attachment between parents and child and the parents' empathic support of the child in managing frustration is at least as important as the practical strategies employed. Even if the original problem (in this case, enuresis) has already resolved, the emotional support, or lack thereof, given by parents to their children can become a problem in itself. In Schema Therapy the focus is therefore always on the child's needs underlying the symptoms. In the case of enuresis, to continue the example, thorough psychological treatment targets the attachment needs beneath the obvious symptoms. When therapists plan and conduct their therapy too superficially, in the best case scenario, the symptoms will decrease. However, the underlying, un-emphasised needs could, if frustrated or unmet, contribute to the creation of schemas (e.g. *Abandonment / Instability* or *Emotional Deprivation* schemas). If unmet needs are not identified or if the child does not receive sufficient support from caregivers, unmet needs continue and can interfere in the resolution of new developmental tasks. When a similar experience is repeated (e.g. superficial treatment of later developing ADHD-like symptoms without sufficient attention to the child's core needs), schemas are reinforced and tend to become chronic, in the worst case leading to a psychological disorder (e.g. depression).

5.1.2 Psychological distress, conflict and trauma in schema development

Psychological distress, conflict and trauma result from core childhood needs being unmet or overly indulged in the past and present, according to Schema Therapy.

When Chiara (case example) knows on the one hand that she is old enough to handle kindergarten without her parents, but on the other hand feels little and helpless, she experiences a conflict that is not adequately resolved. Her needs for autonomy, mastery and pleasure are left unmet, while her needs for security and attachment are overly emphasised in an age-inappropriate manner. In Chiara's case, this imbalance in needs leads to avoidance, which in turn interferes with having age-appropriate, positive experiences. For Chiara, a precursor for the *Dependence / Incompetence* schema develops, which she attempts to address via a strategy of avoidance. This avoidance not only deprives Chiara of age-appropriate positive experiences (e.g. growing independence in social relationships); it also increases her general insecurity and feelings of incompetence. In a later case description we will explore what role her mother's schemas play in Chiara's avoidant behaviour.

Parental reactions to children's fears can also feed into the development of schemas. Parents can react in ways that traumatise a child for having age-appropriate responses. For example, the reaction of a parent to a fearful child can develop or increase that insecure attachment when the parental 'safe harbour' is questioned by the child's fearfulness. A parent may over-react in ways that can be traumatic (e.g. unpredictable and harsh discipline), when the symptom (fear) is suddenly 'attacked' with great intensity.

What factors impair meeting a child's needs and result in maladaptive schema development?

In general, there are four factors that play a role in developing maladaptive schemas by perpetuating frustration of needs: parental schemas, needs, parenting style and attachment style.

Parental schemas

The initial assessment needs to provide an understanding of the parents' experiences in their own childhood and any resulting schemas that may have been triggered by parenting (e.g. personal negative experiences and anxiety regarding kindergarten, which could be unconsciously projected onto the child). We will further discuss Chiara's family and their issues below.

Parental needs

Another important question is: What are the parents' needs in the system within which the child lives? This question is discussed in depth in Chapters 15–17 (parent-based techniques), to which we refer the reader.

Parenting style

Parenting styles are particularly important for the development or prevention of early maladaptive schemas. According to Baumrind (1971), four unique parenting styles can be differentiated on orthogonal dimensions of Responsivity (R) and Management (M) (see section 5.1): neglectful style (R-, M-), permissive style (R+, M-), authoritarian style (R-, M+) and authoritative style (R+, L+).

Table 5.1: Parenting styles according to Baumrind (1971) and possible maladaptive schemas that can develop

Permissive style	Authoritative style
■ abandonment/instability ■ emotional deprivation ■ entitlement and grandiosity ■ insufficient self-control/discipline	■ positive psychosocial adjustment ■ positive self-concept ■ fewer behavioural problems
Neglectful style	Authoritarian style
■ abandonment/instability ■ emotional deprivation ■ failure and avoidant coping ■ insufficient self-control/discipline	■ emotional deprivation ■ mistrust and abuse ■ defectiveness/shame ■ subjugation ■ punitiveness

The Authoritative parenting style results in positive psychosocial adjustment, better academic achievement, a positive self-concept and fewer behavioural problems (Lohaus & Vierhaus, 2009; McIntyre & Dusek, 1995; Milevsky *et al*, 2006). To our knowledge there has not been any empirical examination of how schema development or a schema tendency in the child and parenting styles correlate. The relevant Schema Therapy literature (e.g. Young *et al*, 2003; Arntz & Jacob, 2012) regarding parenting styles suggests that the Neglectful parenting style promotes schemas such as *Abandonment/Instability*, *Emotional Deprivation*, *Failure*, *Insufficient Self-Control*. The Permissive style leads to *Abandonment/Instability*, *Emotional Deprivation*, *Entitlement/Grandiosity* and *Insufficient Self-Control*. The Authoritarian style can cause *Emotional Deprivation*, *Mistrust/Abuse* and *Defectiveness/Shame*, as well as *Subjugation* and *Punitiveness*, and the Authoritative style – as illustrated above –functions as a protective factor and can serve to regulate needs.

Attachment styles

Last but not least, attachment style (secure, insecure-ambivalent, insecure-avoidant, disorganised) can greatly influence the development of maladaptive schemas (see Roediger *et al.*, 2018). From a Schema Therapy perspective, attachment styles are precursors to coping styles. For example, when a young child reacts in an ambivalent or distant manner to an insensitive mother, they are attempting to cope with the pain of deprivation via distancing. Over time these repeated experiences are the precursor of the *Emotional Deprivation* schema.

5.2 Schema Therapy assessment, psychoeducation and Therapy

In the assessment process either the DSM 5 or the ICD-10 can be used to clarify the nature of the disorder. DSM 5 features modifications to criteria for psychological disorders, and the revised ICD-10 more specifically differentiates types of these disorders in childhood and infancy.

5.2.1 Interviewing Preschoolers

There are important considerations when working with preschoolers in the assessment phase (Holland *et al*, 2017) that are also a core part of the relational style of Schema Therapists: early on during the assessment process it is important to focus on the child's opinion, ideas, thoughts, feelings, and so on (communicating 'you have my full attention!'). It is also helpful to alternate interview and play phases in working with preschoolers. Interview phases need to be tailored to the child's attention span or be paired with play. Longer periods of sitting still can result in restlessness that impacts on a child's ability to focus and can also impact their answers. Therefore, frequent opportunities for movement and activity are recommended. Sentences should be brief, clear and easy for a small child to understand.

Interview techniques

Open and closed interview questions are suitable interview techniques; however, the latter are not recommended for diagnostically important themes. The therapist should ask for more details in an open and casual manner whenever a question is diagnostically important ('and what happens next? … and then?'). Leading questions should generally be avoided even when dealing with therapeutically meaningful facts and observations. Questions regarding important themes may be rephrased in order to ensure that the child is properly understood.

5.2.2 Important diagnostic considerations

There are few standardised tests and instruments for diagnosis of schema-relevant indicators in preschool children. The important information is often gained by evaluation and clinical observation of the child as well as their environment (parents, grandparents, caregivers, etc). A few methods are, nevertheless, available that the clinician should be aware of.

Need considerations

In German-speaking countries, the External Assessment Sheets for Satisfaction of Core Psychological Needs (GBJK) from the SDS-KJ (Borg-Laufs, 2011) is available and normed for children aged four and up. It is important to note that only current and not past need satisfaction is recorded by this measure.

Attachment considerations

For pre-school aged children, Ainsworth's classification system for infants (Ainsworth *et al*, 1978) or Crittenden's (1992) approach are both useful tools for understanding attachment patterns. History taking can help to determine attachment of 5- to 8-year-olds (using concepts from the Adult Attachment interview; George *et al*,1984, 1985, 1996). A helpful tool to assess the parent's perspective on their attachment is also included in Zeanah *et al* (1995).

Attachment models that are already present are suggestive of specific schemas and coping styles (e.g. *Emotional Deprivation*, *Abandonment / Instability*, *Mistrust / Abuse*). From a Schema Therapy perspective, the insecure-avoidant attachment style (Type A) can be viewed as a precursor to an avoidant coping style (the child wants to avoid the painful feelings of abandonment). In the case of the insecure-ambivalent attachment style (Type C) the child vacillates between the emotion-avoiding coping mode of a Regressive Protector (clingy) and an Angry Protector mode. In the case of a disorganised attachment style (Type D) we can often see bizarre or changeable behavioural patterns, such as freezing, turning in circles, rocking and other stereotyped behaviours as a precursor of emotionally avoidant modes.

Evaluation of parent–child interaction

Suess and Roehl (1999, cited in Borg-Laufs, 2005) recommend attending to three significant markers in parents during conversations with families and younger children:

1. Sensitivity towards the child

2. Respect for independent activities of the child

3. Empathy of parents towards the child (rejection versus acceptance).

It is important to consider, however, that observation in an assessment context represents an unusual situation in which bias (e.g. social desirability) can be superimposed. Therefore, less structured, more open-ended situations, such as the waiting room or greetings and goodbyes, are more helpful for observation. Home visits are also meaningful in order to develop a realistic impression of daily life.

Attachment models of parents

Of diagnostic interest are also the more remote attachment models of parents, categorised as secure-autonomous (F), insecure-distant (Ds), insecure-entangled (E) and disorganised (U) in the Adult Attachment Interview AAI (originally George et al, 1984, 1985, 1996, explained in Hesse, 1999). Further information about the connection between parental attachment representations and child attachment style can be found in, for example, George et al, 1984, 1985, 1996.

Temperament

The fact that the temperament of the child plays a large role in the development of schemas and also has an important influence in the selection of schema coping style (surrender, avoidance, overcompensation) suggests that it is meaningful to assess the child's temperament. The exploration of early competencies and difficulties in self-regulation (self-soothing, screaming, sleep, feeding and attention span) are part and parcel of this evaluation, as is behavioural observation during the therapy session.

Questionnaires and inventories are also helpful in this regard. Zenter & Bates (2008) provide a helpful overview of measures. The Junior Temperament and Character Inventory JTCI (Luby et al, 1999) is a useful tool normed for 3–18 years, as is the Integrative Child Temperament Inventory (ICTI), for 2- to 8-year-olds (Zentner & Wang, 2013).

Assessment with play therapy

Play therapy approaches provide one form of especially useful behavioural observation in an assessment context. Two different methods are typically highlighted: directive play therapy, whereby the responsibility for leadership and interpretation is the therapist's, and non-directive play therapy, whereby the responsibility for play is left with the child. When using a directive approach, the focus is on diagnostic questions. There can be a focus (or direction) on certain emotions, thoughts, behaviour patterns or needs during play – a time-efficient approach. However, with this approach there is the risk that important and relevant aspects are missed. We therefore recommend a non-directive method for assessment and diagnosis and a directive method for the therapy, although both phases may overlap or be closely connected, depending on the presentation and the child's requirements.

When using play therapy to conduct assessment or therapy, the therapist needs to be alert to staying within the child's attention span; if the limit is reached (e.g. the child becomes tired or bored), the therapist then accepts this and closes that play intervention. Any outstanding questions (e.g. how does the father handle the argument?) should be skillfully integrated in an upcoming play session (directive) in order to then continue to anticipate the ongoing open development of the play (non-directive).

5.2.3 Psychoeducation

Psychoeducation regarding background factors and the process of therapy, which is typical in Schema Therapy, is kept very brief when working with this age group. Specific questions can absolutely be addressed in an age-appropriate manner; however, the therapist should avoid being pulled into explaining more than what was asked. The primary forum for question and answers is play. During play problems reveal themselves for which the best solutions are 'played out' and their suitability tested. Educative work with the child can also take place within this age group (see Chapters 11 and 12 for more specific instructions).

5.3 Schema Therapy in action: age-appropriate therapeutic interventions

Schema Therapy treatment of a preschooler consists of therapy for the child and parent dyad where the parent is the primary focus (see Chapters 15–17). This does not mean, however, that preschoolers may not also receive Schema Therapy. Play is available as the medium of choice to the therapist to build a positive and trusting relationship and is useful in the introduction and implementation of assessment and therapy.

In general, play during childhood is of central importance for the entire development of the child, as the child learns how to handle themself and their environment during play. Thus, play is a natural medium for self-representation (Axline, 1947). A child gathers important experience during play that they apply not only in the play space but also in the real world. Play allows children to communicate personal experiences and their impacts (needed for assessment) as well as solutions (therapy) at a symbolic and a concrete level. In therapy, thoughts, feelings, behaviour patterns and anticipated results or consequences can be tried out without negative real-life consequences (i.e. it is 'just' a game).

One of the key goals of therapeutic play is to provide emotional support for the child, assisting them to be the protagonist in the space. This also enables recognition of the needs of the child. In this way the child's needs are affirmed verbally and symbolically in a space that the therapist has created. In this space the therapist affirms the importance of the child's needs and provides enforcement of those needs being met. The therapist supports personal management of emotions, offers help in expressing and understanding others, and emphasises how emotions can influence others in a positive or negative way. Through the accompanying verbalisation of play, the child becomes more able to express themselves verbally, an important aspect of providing clear information regarding their needs to caregivers.

5.3.1 Creating a mode sketch with a preschooler

Some information has already been provided regarding modes. However, given the cognitive development of a preschooler with average intelligence, an elaborate mode model is not appropriate. Rather, the focus is on the unhelpful state (mode) or a helpful state (mode) needed for conflict resolution or tension reduction. These modes then become actors in the play. The child may name that actor himself or herself, or the name could be agreed between the therapist and the child.

From the age of three, all children with normal cognitive and emotional development are able to differentiate between fear, anger, grief and joy. Their cognitive development also allows them to use their imagination, even though they have difficulty differentiating between fantasy and reality (see Holland *et al*, 2017). What is important in this context is that they engage fully and experience the Schema Therapy-relevant child modes – the Vulnerable, Impulsive-Undisciplined, Angry and Happy Child modes (see Chapter 2, tables 2.7 to 2.12). The modes may be renamed or personalised: the Vulnerable Child mode, for example, may be called 'Sad Trudy' or the Impulsive or Undisciplined mode 'Wild Tom'. When personalised names are used it is important that the therapist remains aware of which mode takes over which function.

The therapist is free to bring the child's interests and strengths into the naming of the child's modes. For example, a girl who enjoys grocery shopping games could name modes as different 'customer types'. She then could encounter her modes as if dealing with a 'customer'. If possible, each mode should have a 'voice' that provides information about mode-typical thoughts, feelings, behaviour patterns and needs. The challenge is to find an appropriate compromise between directive and non-directive aspects of therapy: the sensitive therapist responds to the child's interests and ideas with patience and, at the same time, sets an appropriate 'stage' for the conflicting modes and appropriate resolutions.

5.3.2 Use of finger and hand puppets

We suggest working with hand and finger puppets for mode-driven and need-oriented play therapy, whereby each puppet must be created for a feeling-state also known as mode ('now 'Mischievous Frank' wants to join in, do you know him already?'). These finger or hand puppets can even play on a puppet stage using a hand puppet theatre. This acquisition is especially helpful when the finger or hand puppet play is video-recorded and viewed with the child as well as the parents. A first step is to develop brief video sequences, no longer than five minutes, which graphically demonstrate the conflicts occurring on the inner stage of the little child. This helps many parents to develop a new view of the problem behaviour of the child (often in the form of an 'a-ha moment') and thereby increase their patience and understanding when dealing with the presenting problem.

For the exact process and subtleties of implementation, sections 12.2 and 13.1 are recommended.

5.3.3 Mode-led, need-oriented play therapy

During mode-led, needs-oriented play therapy the goal is to assign wishes and needs to all actors of the play, which they can express during the play (see section 9.1). This method initially needs to be modelled. The therapist performs a play for the child showing how wishes are formulated and needs are articulated without shame or guilt or developing fears of failure. This encourages the child to designate needs to his own protagonist and model these needs on the example of the therapist, which not only provides insight into childlike feeling and thinking, but also increases a child's capacity to communicate their own needs (e.g. 'I am sad, Mum, I want a hug from you'). The goal of mode-based play is the development of a kind of 'chat room for needs' or 'wishing corner', 'wishing machine', 'dream weaver' etc integrated into the play (a space for the child to focus on needs).

5.3.4 Mode- and need-oriented play protocol

After each play session the therapist should assess and record which core needs (see 2.1) the child met independently, and which needs were less satisfied. Table 5.2 shows a worksheet that provides the therapist with an overview of need satisfaction during play.

In the 'Issue/Topic of the session' (2nd column) the subject of any conflict is outlined; in the 'Mode dynamic' (3rd column) the suspected conflicting modes are identified; and in the last five columns it can be noted what need was met and to what extent. Often there is an emphasis on one need to the neglect of other needs. The goal of the therapeutic work then becomes to support the strongly emphasised need (which the child felt was important) without disregarding other needs.

Mode and needs-focused record of play therapy

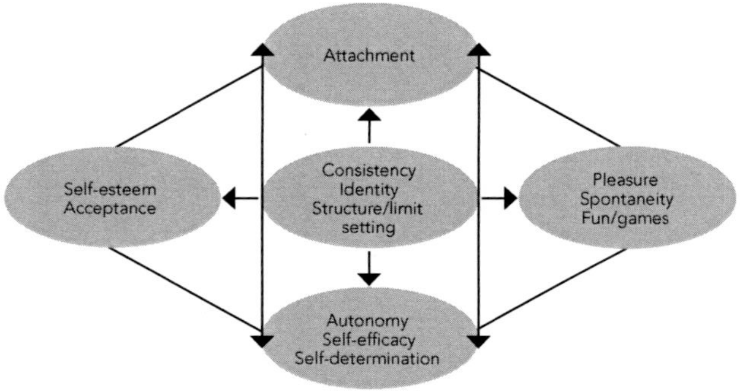

<u>Legend</u>:
- ++ fully met
- \+ met
- 0 not or rarely addressed
- \- unmet (minimized to support another need)
- -- fully unmet (minimized to support another need)

Date & time	Issue/Topic of the session (e.g. Child role plays an argument/conflict at school; he/she lost his/her control and became violent towards children and teachers)	Mode – Dynamic (eg. Lonely, hurt child vs. demanding mode)	Psychological core needs				
			Attachment	Autonomy Self-Efficiacy Self-Determination	Self-Esteem Acceptance	Pleasure Spontaneity Fun/Games	Consistancy Identity Structure/Limits

Figure 5.1: Mode and needs-focused record of play therapy (see online worksheets)

> ## Case example
>
> During play, Chiara repeatedly expressed anxiety regarding leaving her pet alone at home (e.g. when shopping). The dog also would not let Chiara go during play and begged her: 'Stay with me, Chiara! Then I can protect you and nothing will happen to you.' The dog was likely saying out loud what Chiara was experiencing in the kindergarten situation.

For this play scene the therapist recorded in his ledger: 'Mode dynamic: Wise and Clever Child mode versus Vulnerable Child mode'. For the needs, he noted (on the scale '++' = strongly satisfied to '- -' = strongly neglected) for Attachment: '++', Autonomy/self-efficacy/self-determination: '+', Self-esteem: '- -' , Spontaneity/play/fun: '- -' , Identity-structure/limit setting: '+'. When reviewing the worksheet (where other play scenes had been reported) it was apparent that Chiara obtained significant need satisfaction in the areas of attachment and autonomy/self-efficacy/self-determination (e.g. 'I'm staying with my mum and I decided this myself'). This generated, however, notable deficits in self-esteem needs as well as in spontaneity/play/fun needs (e.g. 'Over time I don't dare to do anything').

This combination results in a risk for maladaptive schema development in the long run, such as *Incompetence / Dependence*. The remaining need categories of identity/structure/limit setting would not have interfered with this schema because of the fear-based ego-syntonic belief – something like 'this is just what I'm like' or 'this is typical for Chiara, you can't do anything about her fear.' How these findings were managed in therapy is further described below.

5.4 Case example: Chiara case formulation and therapeutic process

In the family history it was noted that Chiara's mother herself had experienced an anxiety disorder as a child. In the background of distress in her own family (including addiction, among other problems), *Emotional Deprivation* and *Abandonment / Instability* schemas had developed that were now sparked in Chiara's mother by her daughter's age-appropriate development of independence. The mother unconsciously transmitted her own fears in moments of separation (e.g. via gestures, facial expressions, tone) and tended to project overemphasized needs regarding emotional care (which were insufficiently met during her own childhood). Chiara's mother's own *Abandonment / Instability* schema may also have been retriggered after the move (Lonely, Vulnerable Child mode), a state that made her more needy and unconsciously longing for Chiara's company ('In Chiara's presence I don't feel as alone and foreign!'). Chiara felt the unspoken, subliminal need and melancholic state of her mother and therefore stayed with her ('I'm not leaving you alone!'). Several causal mechanisms were likely involved here (child and mother having a similar temperament, mother's mode model, tendencies towards parentification).

Chiara has already showed precursors of one schema, namely *Incompetence / Dependence*, which she partially dealt with via overcompensation (e.g. asking for packing tape from cranky neighbours). However, for the most part Chiara attempted to avoid the schema via defiance, exhibiting anxiety or somatising.

Because of her own history, Chiara's mother was particularly sensitive to Chiara's insecurities and fears. The combination of the mother's insecure over-involved attachment representation (alliance with her own mother against a drinking father) and her own deeply ingrained *Abandonment / Instability* schema led to overcompensating behaviour. The mother overcompensated in the form of overprotection, which in turn promoted Chiara's avoidant behaviour and separation anxiety and the formation of the *Dependence / Incompetence* schema. Thus, a vicious cycle had started which was formed by Chiara's *Dependence / Incompetence* schema ('I am so little and weak') and her mother's *Emotional Deprivation* and *Instability / Abandonment* schemas ('I [mother] feel alone and abandoned at home'). When both mother and child submit to their schemas or act on them, Chiara stays home and her mother is not alone – a relief in the short term, but in the long term this cycle creates increasingly chronic schemas. We call this situation schema collusion (colludere (lat). ~ play), that is, the schemas are 'playing' with each other and are enhanced in their impact.

On the ICTI (Zentner and Wang, 2013), the parents rated Chiara's temperament on the factor of *Self-Consciousness* as high and on *Activity* as low. This combination often results in children choosing a more passive coping strategy (surrender, avoidance). This was also the case with Chiara: she was, when she gathered all her energy and courage, capable of brave behaviour (e.g. at home), but typically she chose the less costly route of avoidance (e.g. in public).

During mode work with puppets, tensions dominated between the socially and emotionally Demanding Mode ('you have to...') and the insecure, anxious, Vulnerable Child mode ('I am still so small'). This conflict was complicated by her mother's ambivalence about having to let Chiara go (and thereby create space for personal experiences in kindergarten) and the fear that she would be unable to protect Chiara in a crisis situation (e.g. conflict in kindergarten). Chiara sensed her mother's ambivalence (e.g. the half-hearted encouragement to go to kindergarten) and learned that mother actually did best when she stayed at home with her, even when she demanded again and again that Chiara should go to kindergarten ('She always just says it like that!').

Via schema-focused parental work (schema diagnosis, education, imagery and chair work) with Chiara's mother and father (who became involved as a resource), as well as mode-focused play therapy with Chiara in which new ways to handle anxiety were found (e.g. phone mother when Chiara wished to do so, increasing time periods in which Chiara remained in kindergarten without mother), progress was made. Eventually both Chiara and her parents resolved Chiara's separation anxiety and her mother's abandonment fears. In addition, system and subsystem limits were worked through (grandparent, couple and parent areas), dysfunctional role assignments within the family were detected (parentification, Chiara as partner substitute for mother) and core needs of family members were addressed (e.g. hobbies for both mother and father). Following these interventions, exposure treatment with Chiara, initially in play, then imagined ('pretend…'), and eventually in vivo (using shaping), was uncomplicated and expeditious. A summary of the therapeutic techniques with parents can be found in Chapters 15–17.

5.5 Summary of Schema Therapy with preschoolers

Schema Therapy with preschoolers is based in large part on Schema Therapy focused on parents (see Chapters 15–17), and to a lesser extent on mode-focused, need-oriented play therapy with the child. The assessment phase is based on the general recommendations from 'Guidelines for diagnosis and therapy of psychological disorders' (DGKJP, 2007), with special attention to needs, attachment styles and representations, and parenting styles, as well as the temperament of the child, which significantly influences the coping style (surrender, avoidance, overcompensation) when schemas are triggered. The therapy with the child occurs in part in a non-directive and in part in a directive play therapy.

One key medium for mode work is finger and hand puppets. This provides a voice for diverse needs in a playful manner and thereby enhances awareness. For education and reflection, video recordings of finger and hand puppet role plays is helpful in order to clearly represent for the child and parents the thoughts, feelings and needs of the inner world of the child. As this awareness grows, a deeper understanding of the presenting problem is developed. Because the child's and parents' emotional needs are more effectively being met through Schema Therapy approaches, classical behavioural techniques such as graded exposure to anxiety provoking situations are met with greater acceptance and application.

References

Ainsworth MDS, Blehar MC, Waters E & Wall S (1978) *Patterns of Attachment: Psychological Study of the Strange Situation*. Hillsdale, NJ: Erlbaum.

Arntz A & Jacob G (2012) *Schema Therapy in Practice: An Introductory Guide to the Schema Mode Approach*. Chichester: Wiley-Blackwell.

Axline V (1947) *Play Therapy*. Cambridge, MA: Houghton Mifflin.

Baumrind D (1971) Current patterns of parental authority. *Developmental Psychology Monograph* Part 2. **4** 1–103.

Borg-Laufs M (2005) Bindungsorientierte Verhaltenstherapie – eine Erweiterung der Perspektive. In: J Junglas (Ed) *Geschlechtergerechte Psychotherapie und Psychiatrie* (pp127–136). Bonn: DPV.

Borg-Laufs M (2011) *Störungsübergreifendes Diagnostik-System für die Kinder- und Jugendlichenpsychotherapie (SDS-KJ): Manual für die Therapieplanung* (2. Aufl.). Tübingen: Dgvt-Verlag.

Cassidy J & Marvin RS, with the MacArthur Working Group on Attachment (1992) *A system for classifying individual differences in the attachment-behavior of 2½ to 4½ year old children*. Unpublished coding manual, University of Virginia.

Crittenden PM (1992) Quality of attachment in the preschool years. *Development and Psychopathology* **4** (2) 209–241.

DGKJP: Deutsche Gesellschaft für Kinder- und Jugendpsychiatrie und Psychotherapie et al. (2007) *Leitlinien zur Diagnostik und Therapie von psychischen Störungen im Säuglings-, Kindes- und Jugendalter* (3. Aufl.). Köln: Deutscher Ärzte-Verlag.

George C, Kaplan N & Main M (1984, 1985, 1996) *Adult attachment interview protocol*. Unpublished manuscript, University of California at Berkeley.

Heinrichs N & Lohaus A (2011) *Klinische Entwicklungspsychologie kompakt. Klinische Störungen im Kindes und Jugendalter*. Weinheim: Beltz.

Hesse H (1999) The adult attachment interview: historical and current perspectives. In: J Cassidy & PR Shaver (Eds) *Handbook of Attachment,* pp395–433 New York: Guilford Press.

Holland, ML, Malmberg J & Gimpel Peacock G (2017) *Emotional and Behavioral Problems of Young Children: Effective Interventions in the Preschool and Kindergarten Years* (2nd ed.). New York: Guilford Press.

Lohaus A & Vierhaus M (2009) Parenting styles and health-related behaviour in childhood and adolescence: Results of a longitudinal study. *Journal of Early Adolescence* **29** 449–475.

Luby JL, Svrakic DM, McCallum K, Przybeck TR & Cloninger CR (1999) The Junior Temperament and Character Inventory: preliminary validation of a child self-report measure. *Psychological Reports* **84** (3_suppl) 1127–1138.

McIntyre JG & Dusek JB (1995) Perceived parental rearing practices and styles of coping. *Journal of Youth and Adolescence* **24** 499–509.

Milevsky A, Schlechter M, Netter S & Keehn D (2006) Maternal and paternal parenting styles in adolescents: associations with self-esteem, depression and life-satisfaction. *Journal of Child and Family Studies* **16** (1) 39–47.

Roediger, E. Stevens, B.A., & Brockman, R. (2018). Contextual Schema Therapy. An Integrative Approach to Personality Disorder, Emotional Dysregulation & Interpersonal Functioning. Oakland, CA: Context Press.

Suess GJ & Roehl J (1999) Die integrative Funktion der Bindungstheorie in Beratung und Therapie. In: GJ Suess & KW Pfeiffer (Eds) *Frühe Hilfen. Die Anwendung von Bindungs- und Kleinkindforschung in Erziehung, Beratung und Therapie*. Gießen: Psychosozial-Verlag.

Young JE, Klosko JS & Weishaar ME (2003) *Schema Therapy: A Practitioner's Guide*. New York: Guilford Press.

Zeanah CH, Benoit D & Barton M (1995) *Working model of the child interview*. Unpublished manuscript, Brown University, RI.

Zentner M & Bates JE (2008) Child temperament: an integrative review of concepts, research programs, and measures. *International Journal of Developmental Science* **2** (1–2) 7–37.

Zentner M & Wang F (2013) *ICTI. Integrative Child Temperament Inventory*. Oxford: Hogrefe Ltd.

Chapter 6: Schema Therapy for Primary School Children

Peter Graaf, Christof Loose and Ruth A. Holt

Case example

Kevin, 9 years old, has refused to attend school for the past five months. He has had no contact with his peers during this time. He has some long-term fears, such as of being treated by a doctor (e.g. being weighed), of strangers and of separation. At home he shows oppositional behaviour for even routine requests (e.g. homework, bedtime). He often says 'no' or shouts loudly, and demands something in return when his parents ask or order him to do something. He provokes and insults his mother (calling her names such as 'stupid cow'). He had problems concentrating in his lessons at school, but no notable achievement deficit. In therapy, Kevin appears so withdrawn and uncooperative that the therapist treating him suggests inpatient treatment. Kevin also refuses to participate in the admission assessment and hides himself in the new apartment at the parent–child clinic. As he was so challenging, the interviewer could not find the reason for school refusal during the initial evaluation.

6.1 Phase-specific developmental tasks, interactions, conflicts and modes from a Schema Therapy Perspective

Erik Erikson formulated a model of phase-specific conflicts, first developed in the 1950s and then published in the 1960s (Erikson, 1968). The main conflict in the 4th stage (from 6 years to puberty) of his stage model was between 'industry and inferiority'. While this has not been empirically proven, it does describe this developmental period very succinctly. The child's need to do something useful and good is called 'industry', or competence, by Erikson. Children no longer want to just pretend to do something; the child wishes to fully participate in the adult world. Children in this phase are therefore more susceptible to feelings of inadequacy or inferiority, which build up when the child has too few opportunities to prove their abilities in the world of the grown-ups. Feelings of failure develop when the child is challenged beyond their competence and experiences ongoing failure.

6.1.1 Developmental tasks and potential crises

Havighurst (1972) labels the developmental tasks of the school aged child as follows: social cooperation, self-confidence (meaning diligence and efficiency), learning cultural techniques (reading, writing, calculating), playing and working in groups.

We have developed these development tasks from a clinical perspective with more detail, supplementing Havighurst's approach with new findings.

New challenges

School children face challenges from their cognitive, physical, and psycho-social developmental processes, as well as from the requirements of the school system. As children move beyond early school years expectations of conformity increase, and children are expected to become more organised and manage social interactions. For example, they are expected to pack a school bag, follow directions and complete homework. Children of this age are increasingly expected to be able to act independently. They are also required to work on tasks with persistence and follow rules without constant encouragement or external incentive. They need to manage their time and the tasks they are expected to achieve. They are also expected to curb their impulses and to focus their attention and be able to sit and listen for longer periods of time. So school provides both opportunities and challenges to a child having their needs met.

Increased expectations provide opportunity for needs related to gaining autonomy and self-worth. However, school also challenges children to postpone other needs. For example, the child's need for movement and fun is challenged when they are required to attend to a cognitively orientated lesson with very little activity, or the standardised syllabus might challenge their need for autonomy and self-determination. The fulfilment of the need for recognition is also more carefully dosed than previously, with less frequent praise as the child ages. Often the need for bonding in the first few school years is met by the comparatively close relationship with the school teacher playing the parental role (a 'motherly teacher'), which may change as teachers expect more autonomy from their students as they progress through school.

Children from the ages of 7 or 8 are also faced with the challenge of performance, reproducing what they are learning. Most children respond with optimism and expectation that they will be able to master these new challenges. The abilities to read, write and calculate are milestones on the road to independence and prestige; however, for those who are struggling in these areas, these challenges also present frequent opportunities to 'fail' and internalise maladaptive beliefs.

Group belonging

The school-age child needs to position him or herself within the social setting of his or her peers. They need to fit in to different groups in class, recess and free time. The child may be forced to the edge or feel themselves an outsider in these settings. These social situations present opportunities for a child to develop an understanding of self and a narrative related to these situations. Even though these social settings may appear to be simple to an adult, they of course have great significance to a child. A situation that appears harmless to an adult can present to a child as a great challenge with serious effects. If there have been social problems in the nursery or kindergarten, then the school situation may activate the memories, feelings and experiences of being different and the practised coping methods become more entrenched.

Fears

Children's fears change according to their development (Carr, 2005). Age-specific fears in preschool children are fears related to fantasy figures (monsters), natural occurrences (thunder and lightning), separation, animals and being alone at night. In school children, you are more likely to find fears of failure, negative evaluation, injury, illness and loss such as death, or catastrophe (or highly publicised events such as kidnapping or war). The amount of fear varies according to biological factors (temperament) and environmental factors. Other important factors are media consumption (e.g. seeing news reports), the passing on of dysfunctional belief systems over generations, and also the modelling of an anxious parent's behaviour. Interpretation of threat is very strongly influenced by the evaluation of the nearest person to whom the child closely relates (Murray *et al*, 2009). These challenges are often met by growing competence and skills in normal development.

6.1.2 Psychological distress, conflict and trauma in schema development

Self-image

Personality development during school age is often an unfolding of the child's self-image in relation to the world around them. From a Schema Therapy perspective the child at this age is developing a growing association (instead of disassociation) between the different modes and a reinforcement of the integrative sense of self. The forerunner of the Healthy Adult mode is created at this point, which consists of appropriate frustration tolerance, the ability to defer gratification and increased empathy and the Clever and Wise mode. As these skills become more developed the child is able to regulate emotion, manage social situations and develop pro-social behaviour.

Children up to the age of 5 see themselves as having individual characteristics that are discrete and not integrated (Oerter, 2008), but over the next few years these characteristics are incorporated together into a more cohesive whole. From the age of 9 to 12, the ability to coordinate self-representation grows. Certain achievements are categorised and thought of as personality traits ('I am musical' instead of 'I like to sing'). Children can also see themselves as simultaneously containing conflicting characteristics. For example, they may describe themselves as brave or afraid (with strangers) and sad or happy (with friends). Feedback from the child's social environment concerning their position in the group or their performance leads to a more realistic and complex self-image that is also relatively stable (Marsh *et al*, 1998; Measelles *et al*, 1998) – e.g. with help from the Berkeley Puppet Interview (BPI).

Studies focusing on 8 and 9-year-olds show a rise in the correlation between school performance and self-image. In addition, studies have repeatedly confirmed the effects of the teaching methods (and not only the performance) on children's self-esteem. The teaching methods are also variable in their impact. For example, there appears to be a weaker connection between self-image and school grades in teaching methods where feedback is based on effort rather than social norms (Jerusalem, 1984). However, engagement and achievement at school are also impacted by whether a child has a sense of having some influence over their performance at school (locus of control). All of these elements impact on a child's developing sense of self, and either a virtuous or a vicious circle is formed (Skinner, 1998).

In summary, to paraphrase the words of Oerter (2008), you can say: where preschoolers judge their own performance as mostly free of external factors, primary schoolchildren increasingly measure their performance not only against their own effort but also against external markers of achievement, such as the grades they receive.

Image of others/evaluation of others

One key aspect of a child's psycho-social development is their developing appraisal of others. At this age a child can evaluate others' behaviour and use that evaluation to assist in regulating their emotions more independently of their caregiver. If they are able to make positive attributions they may be less distressed by interactions (saying to themselves 'the other person just wants to help me'). However, in a negative example, if a *Mistrust* schema is developing, the child will interpret other's behaviour as intended to harm. At this age children are capable of assuming the intentions of those who frustrate them. They can distinguish between malicious and reckless behaviour (Dodge, 2006). In later school years, children are also capable of more complex insight. They are able to consider the motive of the one causing annoyance and can assume pro-social intentions even if the behaviour is personally annoying. This allows for a new ability to manipulate others and excuse or apologize behaviour, but can also assist with emotional regulation as a child learns to tolerate some frustration if the person has good intentions (Olthof *et al*, 1989).

Insight has both positive and negative implications. Insight into others allows children to empathise with others and help them. It also allows children to provoke others more effectively and to offend them more precisely. At the same time, children are more able to modulate their emotional behaviour (Southam-Gerow & Kendall, 2002).

'*Children are increasingly able to control their facial expression of their own volition [and] the repertoire of emotional expressions that they are able to put on their faces on command increases constantly*' (von Salisch, 2008, p201, with reference to Lewis *et al*, 1987).

However, this capability encourages the development of dysfunctional coping styles (e.g. 'playing tricks' or manipulating for own advantage). If manipulation or cheating becomes a permanent 'habit', a maladaptive coping mode is formed (Conning mode). Similarly, the capability to distract from unpleasant or uncomfortable feelings can also have an unhelpful outcome if used as emotional avoidance. Emotional avoidance coping styles like the Detached Self-Soother/ Protector modes may develop. The capability to perceive and ignore emotionally triggering stimuli improves at this age. If there are problems with friendships, children are increasingly able to take their minds off those problems. However, children with externalised behaviours are noticeably less able to direct attention in helpful ways. They have problems using distancing strategies to deal with problems with friends (Southam-Gerow & Kendall, 2002).

6.1.3 Effects of limited capability and group dynamics on schema formation

Negative external factors and difficulty negotiating normative developmental tasks can impact on a child's individual needs being met, resulting in maladaptive schemas developing. The following illustrates the most common new or reactivated schemas that solidify at this age.

Learning difficulties can frustrate the central needs of autonomy and self-worth. The *Failure* schema can therefore easily be caused at primary school age. The child may have undiagnosed learning problems, or may have other difficulties resulting in poor grades. However, without awareness of those complications they may attribute failure to their own 'stupidity'. Our clinical experience has shown that for many children testing reveals learning difficulties caused by dysfunction in phonological awareness, memory function (connected to auditory processing) or a visuospatial problem (compare Schröder, 2010). However, because these presentations are not obviously classical dyscalculia or dyslexia, they frequently go unnoticed during routine school evaluations such as special needs assessments. The child's poor learning can be accompanied by feelings of shame and failure in the case of pronounced developmental disorders. Even if these issues are identified, there are not always sufficient resources to adequately address them and recover progress.

The development and consolidation of the *Failure* and *Defectiveness / Shame* schemas is highly likely in intellectually disabled children who, after one or two school years, notice that their schoolmates are increasingly moving academically in another 'world'. This may then be coupled with a *Social Isolation* schema when invitations to schoolmates' birthdays and play dates become rare because intellectual interests are becoming growingly disparate.

At this age an *Unrelenting Standards* schema is usually formed through conscious or unconscious parental expectations and modelling. This schema can also be entrenched by social or cultural values (e.g. 'you're nothing without a good career'). In our view, the new possibility to compare (if only illusory) scholarly performance in different countries has increased competition with the other imaginary competitors on the world market. There is also a movement toward testing from a younger age, with published rankings adding to the sense of school as a competition. A rarer problem is schema development in the intellectually gifted: schemas such as *Entitlement / Grandiosity* and *Insufficient Self-Control / Self-Discipline* can develop as a result of being under-challenged in the standard school system. If an especially bright child can achieve adequately with no effort, those schemas can be developed.

Children with limited self-control (e.g. those with ADHD) often develop an *Insufficient Self-Control / Self-Discipline* schema as a result of these symptoms. They also have opposing pressures: external pressure to sit still and internal pressure urging them to move, resulting in *Defectiveness / Shame, Insufficient*

Self-Control and even *Subjugation* schemas because rules are perceived as an aversive demand for submission. These children experience everyday school life as a constant imposition of boring routine demands whose sense or sensory qualities do not meet their higher needs for stimulation. These children can then feel suppressed by authority figures and react according to their 'temperament', more impulsively and with a higher degree of overcompensation, rebelling against rules in general. Sanctions that are then applied are seen as punitive and aimed against them, reinforcing the schemas listed above.

Peer groups

Repeated negative experiences with children (e.g. being used, put down, threatened or hurt) can cause the *Mistrust* schema to occur at primary school age, or can reactivate it if it had already developed in the family of origin. Many parents who experienced their school years as traumatising because of bad experiences with schoolmates can be re-triggered when their children are this age. Dark memories come back to life when their own children speak of similar experiences.

In our school days, peers become more important and contribute greatly to our self-image. Belonging to peer and social groups (preferably ones which are highly regarded) is very important for self-esteem. The connection to their peers is vital to the formation of a child's social identity (Tajfel, 1981). School-age children identify themselves increasingly with their own groups, and are especially sensitive to being ostracised, put down or bullied. Bullying or mobbing can therefore be the cause of a *Mistrust/Abuse* schema.

Children often use immature methods of demarcation to keep their social territory safe (which might not be easily observable by adults) and maintain their position in the group. Violence is one method that children use to maintain their position. Children's violence can be a way of defining their spaces and those of their friends against those who try to invade these territories or cross invisible borderlines (Dodge, 2006). Underlying this behaviour is a need to connect; therefore, some forms of violence can be understood as immature ways of trying to meet the need to show belonging.

Bullying can also be seen through the lens of maintaining group position. It should therefore be seen not only as an individual issue (focused on identifying the 'perpetrator') but also as a group phenomenon. Perpetrators can only reach their position of strength through focusing on the weaker, the person without 'defenders'. The perpetrator's role can be sanctioned by the 'victims' and 'reinforcers', 'assistants' and 'outsiders' (as discussed in the participant-role approach by Salmivalli *et al*, 1996). Cautious children are sometimes 'used' so that the perpetrator gets a better position in the group. Mobbing then occurs as an exaggeration of age-typical competition, ultimately to increase one's own value within the group. Therefore, bullying needs to be understood as a complex group process, where individuals can take on sometimes contradictory roles.

'Victims' of verbal and physical abuse who have been pre-conditioned by their familial history are especially prone to the development of schemas. Offenders are often also victims, and vice versa. Victims have (in contrast to a large percentage of perpetrators) lower self-esteem (*Shame* and *Defectiveness* schemas) and feel that others do not accept them, and ostracise them (*Social Isolation* schema). Victims also contribute to the concealment of the act (Avoidance coping strategy). Therefore, they seldom speak to parents or educators because they are afraid of the perpetrator. They are afraid of not being taken seriously and of facing accusations. Victims are often held responsible for their own experience of violence. They get blamed: 'If you'd behaved differently, then you wouldn't have become a victim.'

There are a range of typical coping styles for the above-mentioned schemas, including overcompensation, which can lead to different disorders. Victims can respond to their experience in the following ways:

- **Surrendering**. The silent endurer is less noticeable and often has symptoms of depression; their experience of failure, ostracism or violence is borne or endured without resistance.

- **Overcompensation**. The most common forms of overcompensation are particularly harmful for those in the victim's surroundings, e.g. externalising or social behaviour disorders in the form of disturbing school lessons; rebelling against rules; acting out or attention-grabbing, aggressive behaviour; belittling others; mobbing and forming gangs.

- **Avoidance**. Often expressed in avoidance of demands or social withdrawal culminating in school absenteeism, but also emotional avoidance through daydreaming, somatisation (headache or stomachache) and excessive media consumption.

6.1.4 Effects of a lack of external resources

Family resources play a big role in coping with normative developmental tasks. Many school aged children, for example, need practical direction and help in doing their homework. As well as this instrumental support, emotional support is also required, such as teaching children how to deal with emotions (e.g. providing comfort when sad) and modelling frustration tolerance. A lack of social support in the family is seen as a risk factor for poor academic achievement and low intelligence (Heinrichs & Lohaus, 2011) and through this for the development of schemas such as *Shame/Defectiveness* and *Failure*. The synthesis of many risk conditions – anxiety, mental health, mother's level of education and detrimental minority status – is, according to studies (Sameroff *et al*, 1993), the cause of between 33 and 50% of IQ variation in the 4–13 age group.

6.2 Schema Therapy assessment, psychoeducation and therapy

For the general diagnosis of mental health problems we refer you to the DSM-5 or the ICD-10 and to Carr (2015). From a systemic standpoint, a multi-informant approach to assessment is preferable. For example, information from staff at the childcare facility, teachers from the school, attachment figures from clubs or extracurricular activities and, if appropriate – and as long as the child agrees – important 'peers' of the same age or older are helpful in the assessment process, hypothesis formulation and later intervention.

We also think it is necessary, from a Schema Therapy viewpoint, to carry out a thorough cognitive and psycho-social assessment so that you can exclude any specific learning or functional disorders or developmental delay and formulate therapeutic or pedagogical interventions.

Diagnosis, psychoeducation and therapy often interlock in practice. A thorough diagnostic assessment (e.g. memory), making connections between bodily functions and emotional distress (e.g. with enuresis/encopresis) and identifying schemas and modes can have a therapeutic effect. As the patient (and their parents) are freed of blame they are also given a new way to perceive the issue and a more helpful self-image can begin to develop. The assessment begins the process of 'self-consciousness' – a process of getting to know all parts of the self, even the unloved parts (Roediger, 2009). Indeed, the 'experience of not having to hide anymore, of even being accepted as you are' can free 'many patients from years of playing hide and seek' with others and themselves (ibid., p. 183).

The goal of the Schema Therapy assessment is the completion of a case conceptualisation that will help the parents and the child (as far as there is sufficient differentiation) to understand their presenting problem and to define appropriate goals. When establishing goals, it is important to verify whether the goals are 'healthy' or whether they are serving a maladaptive schema. Goals such as 'becoming the best in the class' or 'belonging to the cool kids' group', for example, need to be questioned, because they obviously serve dysfunctional coping and reinforce the maladaptive schema. Further useful diagnostic questions are:

- Which needs are currently not being met?

- Which needs were unmet in the past?

- Which schemas hinder the meeting of needs?

- What are the typical triggers for schemas?

- What influence do schemas have on the child's view of their surroundings?

- Which coping styles have been useful up to now? Which have not?

- Which modes (emotional states and beliefs) are blocking?

Parents and children ideally agree on a coherent explanatory model and an agreement on objectives (Zandt & Barrett, 2017; Walter & Döpfner, 2009). For primary school children, this needs to be simplified according to their developmental level, and ideally as pictorially as possible.

6.2.1 Contextual assessment

We identify as many different layers of the child's problem as possible: these layers consist of temperament, needs, attachment and relationship with the parents (parenting style), the cognitive and social competence of the child, their main interests and their resources/strengths. Naturally of importance are what schemas and modes are occurring, along with a clear understanding of typical thoughts, emotions, body responses and behavioural tendencies, as well as the choice and use of coping styles. Also the family, social, scholastic and cultural backgrounds of the patient and their attachment figures is very important, as well as the conflicts and expectations of the surrounding system (e.g. in school). For systemic approaches to assessment we refer you to Chapters 15–17, and for the diagnosis of needs and temperament, Chapter 5.

6.2.2 Important diagnostic considerations

As assessment progresses, schema-specific formulations inform the questions asked of parents and other attachment figures ('Does your child have any particular sensitivities to anything? Is there anything they cannot stand?'). Also helpful are the questions regarding parents' feelings about performance from Walter and Döpfner (2009, L21/1), in which relevant parental evaluations and attributions can be explored. Assessment of parental schemas and their part of the problem is covered in the section dealing with parental work (Chapters 15–17).

A schema questionnaire for schoolchildren has been developed for ages 8-14, the Schema Questionnaire for Children (DISC). See www.pavpub.com/resource-374CoCr. Observations of the child's behaviour at play, in therapy and with the parents (optimally under natural 'conditions', e.g. when visiting the home) often yields hypotheses about relevant schemas and (met and unmet) basic needs for the Schema Therapist.

Using a chart (prepared by the therapist) with situation boxes, thought bubbles and 'gut' feelings is helpful when questioning the child as to their (often schema based) thoughts in certain situations. Situation-specific sentence completion tasks also fit in here (Walter & Döpfner, 2009, L02).

Projective techniques often offer a source of information when forming hypotheses. Good examples are the island fantasy ('If a wizard could magically transport you to an island, who or what would you take with you?'), the sentence completion test, the CAT (Bellak & Bellak, 1955), the kinetic family drawing (Burns & Kaufman, 1970) and the 'family as animals'. It also makes sense to have structured pictorial material with speech and thought bubbles in which the child can enter thoughts, feelings, beliefs and how they imagine their parents will act in socially or emotionally ambiguous situations. It's very useful to have a collection of pictures with coloured representations of typical feelings (such as Bear cards, from Saint Luke's Innovative Resources).

- *Free drawing* ('draw your family', '... how you want to be', '... a favourite place', '... a nice dream') can also give the therapist a good insight into the child's needs – just like the well-known miracle or fairy question ('Imagine you have three wishes. What would you wish for?').

- *Mode drawings* (for more information see Chapter 12) are also useful for the diagnosis of important emotional states in children.

- The exploration of modes using *finger puppets* is described in Chapter 12, as well as working with story completion.

- The *story completion procedure* for 5–8 year olds (Bretherton & Oppenheim, 2003).

- The MacArthur Story Stem Battery is helpful, as it can test the quality of the attachment but also, indirectly, help form hypotheses about modes and schemas.

Role play in the form of an interview is useful in assessing lively, restless children. The therapist plays a reporter who is asking the child about their life. Another interesting role play is a fictional dialogue with one of the parents, in which the child plays their own father or mother and is interviewed. For instance, the therapist may ask: 'Imagine you are your mother or father and I'm about to interview you. We'll talk about you. Who would you like to be – father or mother?' From that point on, the therapist addresses the child by the chosen parent's name. 'Mr N., what are you proud of when you think of Stefan?

What are you concerned about with Stefan? Which advice would you give to your child? What should Stefan do with his life so that you are happy? What did Stefan give you for your last birthday? When did you last hug Stefan? How did Stefan hurt or anger you? How did you disappoint Stefan? What does it mean for you that Stefan is growing up?'

Case example

Let's come back to 9-year-old Kevin, who is avoiding school and peers. Various projective procedures were used during the assessment, e.g. sentence completion test, the family as animals and the island question ('Who or what would you take with you to a desert island?'). This process activated feelings of isolation and deficiency. Kevin expressed that he sometimes thinks he is 'stupid' (for example, while doing his homework). He also described violent thoughts and revenge fantasies as a solution to his conflicts when other children annoy him. Cognitive testing showed an average intelligence according to the K-ABC and phonological and memory problems when reproducing pseudo-words (Mottier test) and sequences of numbers. There was no indication of anxiety or stress symptoms when required to perform.

During the behaviour and interaction observation, Kevin was dominating and accusatory toward his mother (although this usually occurred in private rather than public). In the first sessions, his mother appeared to be too cautious and patient with Kevin, and unnecessarily justified her behaviour. She vacillated between making pleas for cooperation and getting angry with him. Kevin behaved provocatively and jealously when his mother turned to other children. He could also trigger strong emotions in his mother, who once cried helplessly over his absolute refusal to participate. It was also noticed that Kevin's mother would stand protectively in front of Kevin, in a posture that suggested hostility or mistrust, and in so doing was modelling impulsive and gruff ways of dealing with others. Kevin closed himself off to repeated attempts (from his mother and other attachment figures) to get him to clarify his feelings and wishes in connection with participating in group and school situations. In group situations with children and adults (if he dared to take part), his reactions were quick, angry and over the top, but also clumsy. If another child stood in his way, Kevin would threaten them – 'Move your foot or I'll hit it!' – or make snide comments about other children. During a school observation, he was restless and irritable, with little discipline or willingness to work in the classroom. When presented with a new type of homework, he showed reluctance and fear of challenging tasks, even with a task that he could easily have completed; however, he had no anxiety about making mistakes.

Part of the assessment included a thorough survey of the parent's schemas and modes over the course of a few sessions.

Case formulation

The result of the assessment was the creation of a case formulation with the following hypotheses about causative and maintaining aspects of Kevin's symptoms, taking underlying schemas and coping styles into account.

1. **Defectiveness/Shame schema** in connection with
   - his gross motor (also partially phonological) difficulties
   - subtle familial messages (father's and grandfather's perfectionism and high standards concerning their son's/grandson's performance)
   - mother's norms of perfectly correct behaviour.

2. **Entitlement schema.** His mother's soft, pampering manner at home resulted in feelings of being small and insecure elsewhere. This attitude, along with being an only child, complicated the development of age-appropriate social competence when asserting oneself with peers. As a protective defence when an attempt to establish contact was made, Kevin responded with retreat or gave a curt response.

3. **Mistrust/Abuse schema:** Various encounters with aggressive or annoying schoolmates had hurt Kevin and were part of his reason for avoiding school.

4. **Avoidance of schema-triggering situations** led to a typical vicious circle of avoidance. The initial denial of insecurity and fear also served to avoid unpleasant feelings.

5. **Reinforcing factors in the family interaction:** Kevin's mother is reluctant to push him to face certain frustrations, because she is afraid of 'breaking' the already stretched relationship. Because she experienced violence and harsh punishment in her own childhood, she has avoided using physical means of limit-setting. Behind her caution and permissiveness of Kevin's contrariness are biographically conditioned schemas (*Emotional Deprivation* and *Subjugation* under her own dominant foster mother, resulting in *Shame/Defectiveness*). She has over-identified with Kevin, and felt it was harsh to expect too much from him. She formed, thereby, a subliminal coalition against the father, who was very rational and emotionally distanced. As a result Kevin and his mother were aloof with his father (role polarisation: strict distanced father and 'good' soft mother). The mother also identified herself with Kevin's fear (she recognises the 'twinge' in the stomach when flustered).

6. **Fear of separation (*Abandonment* schema):** Between the ages of 3 and 6, Kevin didn't outwardly show any worries, despite his parents' conflict. He was emotionally shaken by his parents' temporary separation and believed he needed to stand by his disappointed and sad mother, even when his father looked after him. Presumably Kevin also hoped to take the part of a strong male (the ersatz partner role) at his mother's side. His mother's planned re-entry into the workforce re-triggered Kevin's fear of separation (walking to and from school alone, coming home and having to spend a short time there alone).

7. **Temperamental factors:** Kevin appears to have a genetic predisposition to anxiety. He had been observed from early age to be irritable and to have difficulties controlling his emotions. He has always found it challenging to be faced with change, even in moving to positive activities, and had difficulty adapting to change.

For issues related to education, please see section 9.3 of this book.

6.3 Schema Therapy in action: age-appropriate therapeutic interventions

The general therapeutic strategy for schoolchildren (not focused on a specific disorder) will be briefly mentioned. Many of the interventions named are known from other therapeutic contexts or schools. They will, however, be embedded into the Schema Therapy conceptualisation in the appropriate place. This helps therapists to have a road map of how to proceed.

Element 1: Meeting of core needs

Limited re-parenting during therapy as a way to meet needs
The Schema Therapist's tone is attuned to the unmet core need and schemas. For example, with a timid, more submissive child, the therapist's approach is focused on improving their autonomy and confidence; with an unruly or undisciplined child, the focus is on guidance toward more self-discipline (need for structure and orientation). For example, if a child has a *Defectiveness / Shame* schema it is important to build up their self-esteem in therapy interactions. In each interaction with the child the therapist's goal is to meet the child's core emotional needs and boost the child's ability to be open to that process.

Encouraging connection with people who are ready and capable of meeting needs
The child is (after prior agreement between the therapist and the parents) encouraged or guided toward building relationships with people who are safe and nurturing and also able to manage the child's needs for autonomy and fun. This increases the level of modelling available to children and also builds more positive experiences of getting needs met.

Modifying interactions with people who haven't supported needs fulfilment up to now

The child is shown how they can communicate so that the parents understand their issue and take it seriously. The child can then be given permission during therapy to ask the parents for support when feeling helpless, instead of stubbornly withdrawing. In this way the therapist supports both the parents and the child to communicate and interact in ways that are more effective, to learn a new 'dance'.

Addressing the child's environment

The therapist also guides attachment figures in new ways to meet core needs. It may be necessary for the family to formulate new 'rules' in order to adequately meet a child's needs, or there may need to be changes in the daily and weekly schedules (e.g. creating a time pie chart that allocates activities and time to meeting identified unmet needs). The therapist may also advise educators to help them understand and meet previously unmet core needs at school. It may be necessary, with some schoolchildren, to change schools if there is no possibility to modify that environment.

Element 2: Correction of schemas

Recognising the schemas (and modes)

As therapy progresses the child is encouraged to recognise and name their 'sore spots' and typical emotional states, so that it is possible to address them. If possible, the child is assisted to also recognise the cause of their schemas and the functionality of the modes (For elements of mode work see section 10.2; for chairwork see section 12.3).

Checking the validity of schemas

To begin this work the therapist needs to help the child work out the cause of their schema (e.g. *Failure*) and explain the disappointments/challenges that they have faced. If necessary, the therapist can identify dysfunctional evaluations and false attributions and contrast those with the evidence – for example, discussing the results of psychological tests and contrasting those with the *Failure* schema: 'You aren't stupid, that's been proven!' It helps lots of children with low self-esteem when they can see their strengths and weaknesses in front of them on their test profile and have these explained to them. The test manual and its norms are used as a counter-argument to self-criticism. Mapping a child's competencies and strengths can enable the child to expand their self-image if things like social or artistic abilities (making friends, singing), creativity (good ideas for games) or physical strength are listed there as well.

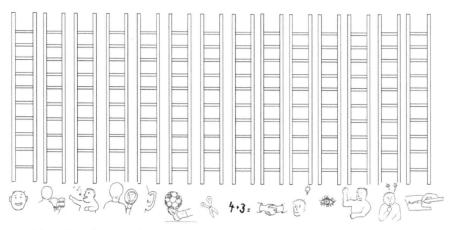

Figure 6.1 Ladder of strengths and weeknesses

The reader will find a 'ladder' for assessing strengths and weaknesses in the online material (www.pavpub.com/resource-374CoCr), which the child can fill out first on their own. They can also take it home with them and get feedback from safe others. Improvised 'tests' involving self-evident bodily functions (hearing, sense of smell, taste, sight, test of strength) can bring about positive revaluation, if these include believable feedback from others (parents/peers/educators).

Dealing with chronic limitations (e.g. asthma) or physical limitations (e.g. hip dysplasia) is very difficult for children at school age to accept because, understandably, they can feel inferior and disadvantaged. They need not only the above-mentioned reminder of their strengths, but also a clear definition of their limitations (for example, in the case of learning difficulties: 'You just need a bit longer to learn and sometimes, someone who can explain things to you at your pace. But that doesn't change the fact that you can ... (name a strength), which others are nowhere near as good at'). The therapist needs to help the child answer each serious and appropriate worry with a consolation, helping the child to place their limitations in a broader context. The therapist may also need to intervene with the family to assist them in managing and talking about the disability in a more helpful way. Children may also require spiritual help to deal with issues of shame, fear or isolation prompted by exposure to religious material that has been misunderstood, or by abstract thoughts of death and dying. Group games and activities are another important way to improve self-esteem through positive feedback and increased awareness of qualities that may have been unrecognised (Plummer, 2008).

Sometimes, situations have to be created or sought in which the child can perform equally or even better than others (sports club, music, scouts). These interventions help address *Social Isolation* and *Defectiveness* schemas, by providing children with experiences of connection and mastery. Strengthening the child's social network can also be schema-correcting (in the case of *Defectiveness* or *Social Isolation*, for example).

Drawings (Shore, 2007) can be used to develop latent resources. One technique is to ask the child to represent their relationships using inner, middle and outer circles. The people in their lives are drawn in as circles, with more important people drawn as larger circles. The child is represented as a square in the centre, and they reflect closeness to the people by placing people in closer or more distant circles. As the therapist reflects with the child on the important people in their lives, suggestions may be made about ways to bring important people closer to the child, or there may be reflection on why the child feels isolated even with people in the inner ring.

Psychoeducation can also provide challenges to dysfunctional thoughts and self-evaluations, such as helping a child to see that their feelings and behaviour are normal. Hearing how many other children suffer with enuresis or ADHD, for example, can normalise a child's experience, or they may be encouraged to hear how common mistakes and failures are in the course of a school career. The child may then more easily distance him or herself from an *Unrelenting Standards* schema. Of course, when dealing with this schema, parents will also need coaching on changes that they need to make in order to provide a more supportive environment for their child. Children (especially those with *Unrelenting Standards* or *Insufficient Self-Control* schema) also benefit from clarification and reinforcement of reasonable parental expectations: 'your parents really want you to be happy and healthy, not just doing well at school' or 'Mum and Dad would like to have their belongings respected and not destroyed'. In this way the therapist can help children increase their awareness of parents' good intentions, rather than the child continuing to read their parents' behaviour through the lens of the schema.

Imaginary or play-based re-scripting

The goal of re-scripting work is to provide a corrective emotional experience by revisiting key schema defining moments and over-writing these negative experiences with new experiences of connection, mastery and safety. Imagery re-scripting is conducted with adolescents and adults by revisiting a significant memory connected to a schema and delivering a corrective experience in imagery. The therapist meets the needs of the child in imagery by bringing in a safe person who can provide what the child needs (Arntz & Jacob, 2012, p. 160). When working with school aged children (just as with younger children), re-scripting occurs more effectively through games and play (see Chapter 11). This process fits well with the urge children often have to re-enact difficult experiences. Many children have the need to re-enact undigested experiences and, through that play, process the experience. In therapy the child can take on different roles, such as the role of director of the film, and gain a sense of control over the scene (see sections 5.3 or 11.1 for the importance of games). Very often children do not acknowledge or even recognise the real experiences behind the enacted scene. As play progresses the therapist supports the creative change of similar play situations. This process allows negative feelings (of guilt, shame or threat) to be replaced by positive feelings (safety, attachment, joy). The alternative play situations help the child to develop solutions to future similar situations.

A key goal in this aspect of therapy is the de-coupling of ingrained negative emotions from trigger situations. In order to help a child to practice different responses in relation to trigger situations the therapist brings realistic elements from the child's everyday life into the new play sequences, so that the child can vividly see the difference between then and there and here and now. The new responses are further supported by structured cognitive interventions such as reframing from the therapist ('He used to think no one loved him, now he knows how to get love'). This emotional processing via decoupling is used less with children over 12, with whom imagery (section 13.3) and cognitive interventions such as the memo or flash card (see section 14.2; compare Arntz & Jacob, 2012) are more appropriate.

Element 3: Developing healthy coping responses

In this phase of therapy the therapist is focused on ways of reducing surrender, avoidance and overcompensation coping responses and strengthening appropriate communication of feelings and needs.

Behavioural pattern breaking is an important part of changing schema-driven coping responses. Once the child understands the effect of avoidance cycles they are guided to approach difficult situations. They may be encouraged to, for example, take the risk of making a mistake – but now with the new knowledge of how realistic the fear is, and skills in assessing their own and others' responses (for example, being able to make more accurate assessments of their parents' opinions, or schoolmates' likely thoughts). Classic behavioural therapy techniques are used here (role play, planning of graded exposure, homework, observation protocol, etc). The child often also needs practical help and practice in using assertiveness techniques.

The child with a *Failure* schema needs tangible help in various areas where performance is required (class work, reduction of poor behaviour, reducing knowledge gaps, building self-discipline and suitable learning strategies). Parental support needs to be negotiated, agreed upon and tested in the therapeutic session so that any schema-activating behaviour that the parents show is addressed. When appropriate (for example, if there are some knowledge deficits), professional help can be introduced in the form of a private tutor, or another appropriate resource. Cooperation between the therapist, the parents and the educators is important in facilitating this. A five-minute phone call alone is very helpful in the intensive phase of the therapy. For example, on Friday afternoons, the teacher can provide information to the parents so that they can make a timely intervention. Special appointments can be made to give feedback (e.g. reinforcement schedule) and progress monitoring so that all the child's attachment figures are in the loop and up to date.

Behavioural changes will then start to shift a child's position in the class and can impact on schoolmates. These educational and social successes need to be monitored (compare Walter & Döpfner, 2009) as there can be resistance to acknowledging success when a child has a schema such as *Failure*, which seeks to maintain a narrative of underachievement and selectively remember experiences, which can undermine progress in therapy. Impediments such as unhelpful relabelling of adaptive coping by peers (e.g. accusing the child of becoming an 'overachiever') need to be caught and strategies provided for the child. As the child becomes more confident they can be helped to understand and accept that not everyone will be supportive of their progress – some may even be jealous.

When persistent avoidant patterns are present, the child needs determined guidance from their attachment figure and the therapist to help the child approach the feared situation. This approach is needed in the case example, where fear has led to school refusal. While cognitive strategies can be helpful, there are some children who only overcome their fear when they are placed into the situation that they perceive as terrible (using the principle of classic exposure therapy). Intensive parental work needs to occur in this situation so that the parents can learn a more confident approach to overcoming threshold situations (see case example, below).

Case example

We decided together with the parents on a behavioural interruption of the avoidance cycle, once Kevin's mother had done sufficient work to improve her capacity to stay in Healthy Parent mode. Kevin was given skills to, in increasing intervals, attend school and therapy. When he had sufficient skills he would be helped and if necessary, forced to attend school. Indeed, his mother had to propel him in the direction of the school entrance and classroom and prevent him from running away by blocking his way. She resisted Kevin's blazing anger after some encouraging support. It was very important for her that she alone carried this out, and that no one else physically blocked Kevin (partly out of fear of him being treated too roughly). After this determined attitude from his mother, Kevin gradually overcame his own resistance until he eventually took part in almost all group activities and attended school and therapy appointments himself (also without his mother accompanying him). However, he fell back into school refusal over time. Kevin also continued to swear at his mother quite often and behaved disrespectfully when she wanted him to do tasks such as homework.

Element 4: Mode work

This aspect of therapy has specific goals related to each mode. The dissociated modes are integrated; the Caring Parent, Inner Helper and Clever and Wise modes are strengthened; problematic coping styles are overcome; the Punitive Parent mode is disempowered; and the Angry/Impulsive/Undisciplined Child modes are channelled and guided.

Mode work in Schema Therapy offers more potential for change than the classic forms of CBT. There are a number of ways in which Schema Therapy is particularly useful when working with children. Schema Therapy provides ways of addressing children's resistance in therapy, particularly avoidance of vulnerability. Schema Therapy also provides a way to conceptualise unhelpful behaviours, and suggests a way to help a child meet the emotional needs driving those behaviours (see methodology outlined in Chapters 9–17). Mode work can be done with drawing, finger puppets and stories, as these techniques are intuitive with children.

Case example

During mode work with finger puppets, Kevin increasingly revealed problematic parts of himself (for example, the Angry Red Kevin and the Mean Red Kevin). There was also an Unhappy Kevin who increasingly moved into the focus of the therapy sessions (Figure 6.1).

Kevin found it very difficult to talk about Unhappy Kevin. He denied that this was still the case (Detached Protector mode). He repeatedly resisted coming to the sessions (Avoidant Protector mode), and his mother often had to push him into the room, where he sometimes relented and let a dialogue take place with his drawings and therapy puppets. Eventually, Kevin had more and more fun in the sessions and could gradually admit to the existence of an insecure part of himself. With a view to the imminent school visit we decided which parts would play the main role in that visit and which sides he could increasingly trust to help him cope more adaptively.

In the course of the therapy sessions (partially as a result of his mother's presence), Kevin came more readily and showed, through the finger puppets, that he used the red puppets as protection. As the therapy progressed Kevin gradually showed less need of them as defence and put them aside in favour of the Vulnerable, previously hidden part. Kevin began to realise that he had felt poorly treated by aggressive schoolmates and wanted to run from them. As a result of a mode dialogue with 'the Hider' (name of flight/avoidance mode), role plays were developed in which Kevin practiced reacting differently when having contact with other children. He played out aggressive, defensive, mean and friendly responses.

After six weeks of inpatient treatment, Kevin revealed to his mother a new thought and positive experience: he had learned that playing with children is fun. He increasingly shared his experiences with her in the daily exchange meetings we had suggested, where they could talk about the experiences of the day. He began to talk with her about how things had gone in group and therapy situations. At the end of his inpatient stay he left his new 'friends' with sadness and expressed that he wanted to see his fellow patients again.

Outcome of therapy

One year after the end of therapy, Kevin has been continually attending school. The first day at school was one of the hardest, for Kevin and also for his mother. As a result of interventions with Kevin's parents they were able to be supportive but also directive, encouraging him to get through the door and into the classroom.

6.4 Conclusion

Child-centric work is more important in primary school children than in preschool, where the parents are the focus. The needs of the child and family member are at the heart of the assessment and therapy and more attention is paid to the developing of schemas and coping styles. Play therapy approaches are complemented with psychoeducation (often done with drawings) and practising elements. Finger and hand puppets have been proven as a medium for mode work. This approach allows each mode to voice different needs, thoughts, emotional states, body feelings, action tendencies and beliefs and increase the child's awareness of modes, making them more accessible. The finger puppets make visible – as representatives for the modes – the conflicts on the child's inner stage and give a deeper understanding of the dynamics beneath the presenting problem. Once there is awareness and insight into the modes that are triggered, classic behavioural therapy interventions such as graded exposure to fears, for example, are more readily accepted and put into effect.

As therapy progresses, changes and mode interventions need to be generalised to the child's everyday life. With all schema and mode interventions, the therapist needs to take into account systemic issues in the family and also the school context. Therapy can be seriously undermined if these broader issues are not recognised and addressed. For example, if a child is always having to face mobbing or ostracising, the therapist needs to provide practical strategies that might be very different from the ones that are needed at home. The therapist can also call for interventions at the school level (for example, through school counsellors or psychologists, or similar, as in Redlich, 2002). Group therapy measures in the form of social competence training are also helpful to concurrently assist children with deficiencies or problems with assertiveness.

References

Arntz A & Jacob G (2012) *Schema Therapy in Practice*. Chichester: Wiley-Blackwell.

Bellak L & Bellak SS (1955) *The Children's Apperception Test. C.A.T.* Göttingen: Hogrefe.

Bretherton I & Oppenheim D (2003) The MacArthur Story Stem Battery: development, administration, reliability, validity, and reflections about meaning. *Revealing the inner worlds of young children: The MacArthur Story Stem Battery and parent-child narratives*, 55-80.

Burns RC & Kaufman S (1970) Kinetic family drawings (KFD): An introduction to understanding children through kinetic drawings. New York: Brunner/Mazel.

Carr A (2015) *The Handbook of Child and Adolescent Clinical Psychology: A contextual approach*. London: Routledge.

Dodge KA (2006) Translational science in action: hostile attributional style and the development of aggressive behavior problems. *Development and Psychopathology* **18** (3) 791–814. Retrieved from https://search.proquest.com/docview/201695609?accountid=178506

Erikson EH (1968) *Identity: Youth and Crisis*. New York: Norton.

Havighurst RJ (1972) *Developmental Tasks and Education* (3rd ed). London: Longman Group.

Heinrichs N & Lohaus A (2011) *Klinische Entwicklungspsychologie kompakt*. Weinheim: Beltz.

Jerusalem M (1984) Reference group, learning environment and self-evaluations: A dynamic multi-level analysis with latent variables. *Advances in Psychology* **21** 61–73.

Lewis M, Sullivan M & Vasen A (1987) Making faces: age and emotion differences in posing of emotional expressions. *Developmental Psychology* **23** 690–697.

Marsh HW, Craven R & Debus R (1998) Structure, stability and development of young children's self-concepts: a multicohort-multioccasion study. *Child Development* **69** 1030–1053.

Measelle JR, Ablow JC, Cowan PA & Cowan CP (1998) Assessing young children's views of their academic, social and emotional lives: an evaluation of the self-perception scale of the Berkeley Puppet Interview. *Child Development* **69** 1556–1576.

Murray L, Creswell C & Cooper PJ (2009) The development of anxiety disorders in childhood: an integrative review. *Psychological Medicine* **39** (9) 1413–1423.

Nicholls JG (1984) Achievements motivation: conceptions of ability, subjective experience, task choice, and performance. *Psychological Review* **91** 328–348.

Olthof T, Ferguson T & Luiten A (1989) Personal responsibility antecedents of anger and blame reactions in children. *Child Development* **60** 1328–1336.

Oerter R (2008) Kindheit. In: R Oerter & L Montada (Eds) *Entwicklungspsychologie* (6. Aufl.) Weinheim: Beltz.

Plummer D (2008) *Social Skills Games for Children*. London: Jessica Kingsley Publishers.

Redlich A (2002) Die kooperative Methode im Unterricht. In: HP Nolting (Ed) *Störung in der Schulklasse. Ein Leitfaden zur Vorbeugung und Konfliktlösung*. Weinheim: Beltz.

Roediger E (2009) Praxis der Schematherapie. Stuttgart: Schattauer.

Salmivalli C, Lagerspetz K, Björkqvist K, Österman K & Kaukiainen A (1996) Bullying as a group process: participant roles and their relations to social status within the group. *Aggressive Behavior* **22** (1) 10–15.

Sameroff AJ, Seifer R, Baldwin A & Baldwin C (1993) Stability of intelligence from preschool to adolescence: influence of social and family risk factors. *Child Development* **64** 80–97.

Schröder A (2010) *Evaluation eines Therapieprogramms für Kinder mit entwicklungsbedingten räumlich-konstruktiven Störungen*. Dissertation zur Erlangung der Würde des Doktors der Philosophie am Fachbereich Psychologie der Universität Hamburg.

Shore A (2007) *The Practitioner's Guide to Child Art Therapy: Fostering Creativity and Relational Growth*. New York: Routledge.

Skinner EA (1996) A guide to constructs of control. *Journal of Personality and Social Psychology* **71** 549–570.

Southam-Gerow MA & Kendall PC (2002) Emotion regulation and understanding: Implications for child psychopathology and therapy. *Clinical Psychology Review* **22** (2) 189–222.

Tajfel H (1981) *Social Identity and Intergroup Relations*. London: Cambridge University Press.

von Salisch M (2008) Emotionale Entwicklung. In: B Herpertz-Dahlmann, F Resch, M Schulte-Markwort & A Warnke (Eds), *Entwicklungspsychiatrie, Biopsychologie – Grundlagen und die Entwicklung psychischer Störungen* (2. Aufl.) (pp96–108) Stuttgart: Schattauer.

Walter D & Döpfner M (2009) *Leistungsprobleme im Jugendalter, SELBST-Therapieprogramm für Jugendliche mit Selbstwert-, Leistungs- und Beziehungsstörungen*. Göttingen: Hogrefe.

Yee MD & Brown R (1992) Self-evaluations and intergroup attitudes in children aged three to nine. *Child Development* **63** 619–29.

Zandt F & Barrett S (2017) *Creative Ways to Help Children Manage BIG Feelings: A Therapist's Guide to Working with Preschool and Primary Children*. London: Jessica Kingsley Publishers.

Chapter 7:
Schema Therapy with Adolescents

Christof Loose, Peter Graaf and Ruth A. Holt

Case example

Lea-Marie is 15 years old and in 9th grade. She lives with her mother and 12-year-old half sister in a small two-bedroom apartment. Her parents separated when she was two years old and her mother has been unlucky with new partners; no relationship has lasted longer than six months. During those early years Lea-Marie's mother had five unsuccessful relationships and was in emotional turmoil. Lea-Marie frequently assumed the supportive role with her mother, consoling her and providing emotional support. As she did not like some of her mother's new partners, Lea-Marie did what she could to stir up conflict. However, when the relationship broke up Lea-Marie would feel guilty, especially when her mother complained about feeling lonely. When Lea-Marie was 10 years old, her mother promised to distance herself from men once and for all. She dedicated herself solely to looking after her two daughters and working as a part-time administrator in a mail order company, run by one of her mother's friends. Later, both her mother and her boss frequently got involved in Lea-Marie's personal life, discussing her romantic relationships. While this bothered her, she did not raise the issue with them.

Lea-Marie reached all developmental milestones during toddlerhood and primary school age with ease. She had a quiet nature, and was inhibited and hesitant. However, she could also present as a strong-willed, persevering and resolute child. Her athletic ability was a source of pride. Due to her slim figure, she had always been the fastest and most flexible of all the children in her gymnastics and ballet classes. Then she entered puberty. Her first period caught her by surprise one night, her breasts grew within a few weeks and she developed more feminine curves that changed her whole body shape. She also gained weight and was no longer number one in her gymnastics class. Boys looking at her made her feel even more self-conscious, and so she began to withdraw, initially from her peer group, then from activities organised by the gymnastics club, and finally also from her family. At school and when doing homework, she found it difficult to concentrate. She also developed sleeping problems, nightmares, headaches and stomach aches which made her increasingly irritable and discontented. Her grades deteriorated, and when she received five warning letters indicating she was in danger of failing subjects, it was obvious that Lea-Marie needed help and support.

7.1 Phase-specific developmental tasks, interactions, conflicts and modes from a Schema Therapy perspective

Puberty (derived from the Latin word *pubertas*, meaning sexual maturity) refers to a time during adolescence characterised by a series of physiological developments to reach sexual maturity and enable further development into a fully grown adult body capable of sexual reproduction. The time between childhood and full sexual maturation is also called adolescence (ages 14–17 years). Early adolescence refers to 10 to 13-year-olds. Middle adolescence covers ages 14 through to 17, while late adolescence occurs between ages 18 and 22 (see Table 7.1 from Steinberg, 2005).

Table 7.1: Adolescence and age limits

Description	Age
Early adolescence	10–13 years
Middle adolescence	14–17 years
Late adolescence	18–22 years

Unless otherwise stated, we will focus on middle adolescence, which is also synonymous with the terms 'youth', 'teenager' and 'adolescent'.

7.1.1 Developmental milestones and themes

Adolescence is a phase during development characterised by many opportunities and possibilities, yet also possible risks and excessive demands.

'The transition from childhood to adulthood means stepping into an unknown world that is much less structured and offers much more freedom compared to what the adolescent has experienced thus far. The dramatic changes in body shape, along with experiences of new bodily sensations, produces confusion, particularly since the environment also responds to these changes'

(Oerter & Dreher, 2008, p317, own translation)

According to Dreher and Dreher (2002, as cited in Oerter & Dreher, 2008, p279), the central developmental goals during adolescence are:

- Developing new and more mature relationships with male and female peers
- Starting a close companionship with a girlfriend or boyfriend
- Taking on a male or female role in society
- Developing a clear self-image (getting to know oneself and knowing how one is seen by others)
- Being accepting of bodily changes and appearance
- Detaching or becoming independent from parents
- Preparing for romantic relationships (and developing an idea of such)
- Developing career aspirations
- Adopting values to guide behaviour
- Developing a view of the future, planning one's life, and working toward goals.

Common issues

According to Carr (2015) and also Döpfner and colleagues (2000), the most common problems in this age group stem from trying to accept one's self-image, establishing relationships with male and female peers, initiating intimate relationships, detaching from one's parents, examining career goals, developing a value system and learning to act in a socially responsible manner. In light of these difficult tasks and processes, it is not surprising that compared to other stages in development, adolescence is a particularly labile and sensitive phase.

7.1.2 Phase-specific developmental tasks, interactions, conflicts and modes from a Schema Therapy perspective

From the age of approximately 10 or 11, parents are increasingly replaced as confidants by same-sex peers (von Salisch, 2001). This yields a certain risk (e.g. antisocial peers exerting a negative influence), yet it is unavoidable given the developmental task of separating from one's parents.

Where attachment figures of the same age exert a negative influence, drug and alcohol abuse and/or risky, antisocial or delinquent behaviours may be facilitated (e.g. Gardner & Steinberg, 2005; Lundborg, 2006). As such, adolescents who are easily manipulated can be incited to act illegally.

Parent–child relationship

During this stage in development, conflicts between adolescents and their parents tend to become more frequent and revolve around themes such as dress, music and hairstyle. With older adolescents, discussions about political standpoints and curfews are also common. It has been shown that children who have a positive relationship with parents and whose parents possess good parenting skills are less likely to give in to peer pressure (Farrell & White, 1998). However, along with the adolescent's developmental tasks, attachment figures also have to master parental developmental tasks (Carr, 2015). The parents need to be able to facilitate an adolescent's requests for autonomy, understanding the developmental need for more detachment. Adolescents with parents unable to make this transition may develop schemas such as *Enmeshment* or *Dependence / Incompetence*, while adolescents with parents who are psychologically or physically ill may go on to develop schemas such as *Self-Sacrifice* and *Social Isolation* as a result of a blocking of their need for independence.

Successful adaptation of parent–child interactions

According to Fend's research (1998), the ability to successfully adapt parent–child interactions depends on the following factors:

- Maintaining moments of shared joy and keeping conflict free areas

- Being fair and just by negotiating rules rather than arbitrarily implementing rules

- Engaging in educational activities together in early adolescence

- Adopting a less punitive, more democratic parenting style

- Avoiding over-involvement

- Continuing supportive measures

- Creating steps toward independence

- Building a more realistic image of their own child, where parental images of their child and reality are largely aligned.

Capacity for emotional regulation

Adolescence is known as a phase of intense emotional experiences and mood swings. However, research shows adolescent emotions to be less fluctuating than previously thought (Mullis *et al*, 1992). Studies indicate a significant decrease in positive emotions among students between the fifth and ninth grades (Larson & Lampman-Petraitis, 1989). Increases in depressive feelings, low mood and self-consciousness are associated with dissatisfaction with one's own body image, particularly in girls. At this age, romantic relationships are the main source of stress and emotional distress (Larson *et al*, 1999) while hormonal and physiological changes during puberty appear to only have an indirect effect – or at least a smaller influence than expected. These effects are mediated by individual experiences and reflection (Oerter & Dreher, 2008, p314).

Goals in the development of self-identity

Gestsdottir and Lerner (2008) regard emotional regulation and integrating emotional experiences to be important tasks in the development of a person's self-identity. Developing a self-identity aims to achieve the following key goals, as outlined by Rosenblum and Lewis (2003):

- Regulating strong emotions
- Modifying rapidly changing emotions, including the ability to self-soothe
- Recognising others' emotions without being overwhelmed by them
- Being able to distinguish between experiencing emotions and expressing them
- Distinguishing between emotions and facts ('I feel it's true, but my perception of the situation may be wrong' rather than 'I feel it's true, therefore it must be true')
- Separating present emotional experiences from self-identity, which can remain intact despite changes in mood
- Handling social relationships in moments of heightened arousal
- Using symbolic thinking to process negative emotions
- Utilising cognitive functions to understand emotions.

In addition, many adolescents have difficulty finding a good balance between being compassionate to others and distancing themselves from others when the relationship is unhelpful. Those lacking the ability to self-regulate their moods tend to perceive empathy as threatening and avoid it altogether, which may deeply disrupt interpersonal relationships (Eisenberg, 2000). The ability to regulate one's emotions is therefore an essential prerequisite for the adequate development of empathy.

Adolescents often strive toward emotional control: in particular, being 'cool' is often a socially desirable state. 'Cool behavior is when someone does not show any emotions, even in situations that evoke strong emotions' (Oerter & Dreher, 2008, p316, own translation). Schema therapists therefore always look at the function served by being 'cool' and how frequently it is displayed. This apparent lack of affect could be an indication of the Detached Protector mode, which requires specialised 'treatment' (see Chapter 9), but it may also be an age-appropriate expression of confidence.

Friendships with peers represent an important and indispensable support system which helps overcome emotional turmoil as the individual experiences biological, cognitive and social changes that mark the transition into adolescence (von Salisch, 2001). Adolescents draw on their peers' opinions in learning how to control one's emotions 'properly': 'Which emotions are normal and how should I exhibit them?' is a common direct or indirect theme among youths. In this way, peers that are considered trustworthy can exert a positive or negative influence on one another (e.g. learning through modelling), as mentioned earlier. Given the importance of friendships generally, the ability to self-regulate emotions may be the greatest challenge adolescents face.

Another key challenge during adolescence is the ability to manage autonomy needs versus belonging needs within peer groups. In order to maintain their support system and put themselves in a good position to face future challenges (e.g. work, relationships, etc), individuals need to learn social skills which will allow them to manage their own interests and those of their peers. If this process fails, maladaptive strategies, e.g. avoidance, subjugation and overcompensation, can develop and form a vicious cycle leading to dysfunctional behaviours, such as withdrawal.

Withdrawing or discontinuing relationships with one's peer group risks widening the gap between social competence and the developmental challenges during adolescence, thus increasing social and emotional insecurity. Frequently, adolescents then escape into a virtual world through excessive computer use, which may satisfy emotional needs in the short term. However, in the long term this leads to deficient social and emotional skills, and a lack of preparedness for the challenges that lie ahead in adulthood (see Chapter 8).

7.1.3 Cognitive development and emotional comprehension

Cognitive development

Oerter & Dreher (2008) connects the major cognitive changes during adolescence to neurophysiological factors in brain development, among others. These factors are shaped by individual experiences. During adolescence there is an increased ablity to engage in more complex thinking, such as developing alternatives, abstract reasoning and perspective taking, as well as more advanced information processing, attention and memory.

Metacognition

'Metacognition develops during adolescence. It is the ability to think about one's thoughts and feelings. This greatly extends the ability to (re-)evaluate emotional situations and experience them differently. Adolescents are now able to systematically reflect on their judgements of antecedents and their subjective feelings in response to these. They can also compare their feelings to previous episodes or the reactions of others in similar situations. This enables individuals to identify their own triggers for sadness, anger or anxiety in a particular situation.'

(von Salisch, 2008, pp204–205)

Emotional comprehension

Cognitive developments during adolescence also enable more sophisticated emotional comprehension which relies less on conventional descriptions used within peer groups. Following the shift from spending time with one's parents to spending more time with peers, the adolescent starts to develop more independence from their peer group during the next phase in development. During this process, maladaptive strategies for social judgement and emotional regulation can develop (e.g. loss of sense of self-worth or dysfunctional rumination) which need to be targeted and modified in therapy.

While the newly developed metacognitive abilities and new ways of seeing the world can lead to dysfunctional thoughts and emotions, they also enable the questioning of assumptions, which is invaluable for therapy. The therapist can intervene on a metacognitive level. If, for example, a dysfunctional thought is present, the therapist can direct attention toward the needs of the Vulnerable Child mode. As the adolescent reflects on their own needs they are able to build the observer self, the beginings of Healthy Adult mode.

When working with adolescents who are able to review their previous choices of maladaptive coping modes, it is important that the therapist assist them to see this with compassion. These modes developed as adaptive solutions for problems that they had insufficient skills to cope with. Adolescents tend to self blame and put themselves down ('How could I?'). The therapist needs to be a strong advocate for the child's use of what was a necessary survival strategy (thereby instilling self-worth).

An important aspect of Schema Therapy is the differentiation between old and current coping strategies. The goal is to explore the coping modes and reflect on them in such a way that the adolescent becomes less identified with the mode. If this aspect of Schema Therapy is not accomplished, significant resistance during the change phase may result. Therefore, the shift from an ego-syntonic stance (e.g. 'This is how I am') to an ego-dystonic perception of a coping mode (e.g. 'That was the way it was up until now; however, today I can develop new strategies') is of critical importance.

Needs underlying adolescent behaviours

In Schema Therapy, children's experiences and behaviours are thought to be influenced to a large extent by the drive to meet core emotional needs. The five basic emotional needs are of particular importance in this context. During adolescence, autonomy, self-worth and questions around one's own identity become more and more central. As long as attachment needs are satisfied, therapists can identify needs that are characteristic during adolescence, e.g. autonomy, and explore these in greater depth together with the adolescent.

However, it is not unusual for attachment needs to remain unmet during early childhood (e.g. *Emotional Deprivation* schema), so insecure attachment bonds and relationship patterns may exist in addition to stereotypical adolescent needs, which makes therapeutic work more difficult. Therefore, to be safe, the therapist should assume that, even in an adolescent striving for autonomy, there may still be more basic needs that have not been met and which openly contradict the desire for autonomy. This conflict between needs becomes more complicated when adolescents look and present like adults (including the development of primary and secondary sexual characteristics) while at the same time showing the attachment needs of a child ('Go away, but hold me tight').

The case study at the beginning of this chapter describes the discrepancy between physical and psychological development: Lea-Marie does not yet want to deal with her sexual attributes. In her eyes, everything was going well and, if she could have it her way, things would have stayed as they were. However, the onset of puberty meant she had to face new roles in li fe (coming to terms with her gender role). At the time, this was too overwhelming for her. Consequently, she began to withdraw, partly due to her determination to refuse help and partly to avoid having to face her physiological changes. Lea-Marie's case will be discussed later in this chapter, but first we will look at key concepts of Schema Therapy with adolescents.

7.2 Schema Therapy assessment, psychoeducation and therapy

For general diagnosic principles with psychological disorders we refer the reader to Carr (2015); for German speakers, we highlight the *Guidelines for diagnosis and therapy of psychological disorders in infancy, childhood and adolescence*, issued by the German Society for Child and Adolescent Psychiatry, Psychosomatics, and Psychotherapy (DGKJP, 2007). Carr (2015) provides helpful descriptions and information on standards around guidelines, diagnostic processes, materials and tips for diagnostic interviews. The *diagnostic interview for psychological disorders in childhood and adolescence* (Schneider *et al*, 2009) also offers a structured interview format with room for exploring issues and is therefore another critical tool for evidence-based and careful diagnosis.

7.2.1 Important diagnostic considerations

Assessment of unmet needs

According to Grawe (2017, p176), there are 'many clues suggesting that a severe and enduring failure to meet basic needs is, ultimately, the most important cause in the development of mental disorders, as well as an important factor in the continued maintenance of such conditions'. We therefore cannot forego investigating past and current satisfaction of needs. To start with, the Assessment Questionnaires for the satisfaction of basic psychological needs (GBJK) from the SDS-KJ (Borg-Laufs, 2011, not available in English, although concepts are discussed in Borg-Laufs, 2013) are recommended, particularly the parent and self-report forms for children and adolescents (norms exist for ages 11–18 years). However, these questionnaires only assess current, not past, satisfaction of needs. In order to thoroughly assess the extent to which core emotional needs have been met, the clinician can use games, conversations and other interactions. During these interactions the therapist also needs to observe transference, tone and their own instinct.

For example, at each session, the clinician or therapist can record on a form (see below) the mode dynamic that is present in session (e.g. Vulnerable Child mode vs. Bully/Attack mode) and to what extent needs, such as attachment, autonomy, self-worth, spontaneity/fun and striving for consistency (or structure), were met or unmet. Using pluses, zeros and minuses to register the extent to which these needs are met or unmet gives an overview of the dynamic of modes developed over a few sessions (see Zarbock & Zens, 2011, p45; Roediger, 2011, p130). Figure 7.1 shows a worksheet which can be used as a template (mode and needs-focused record of conversation).

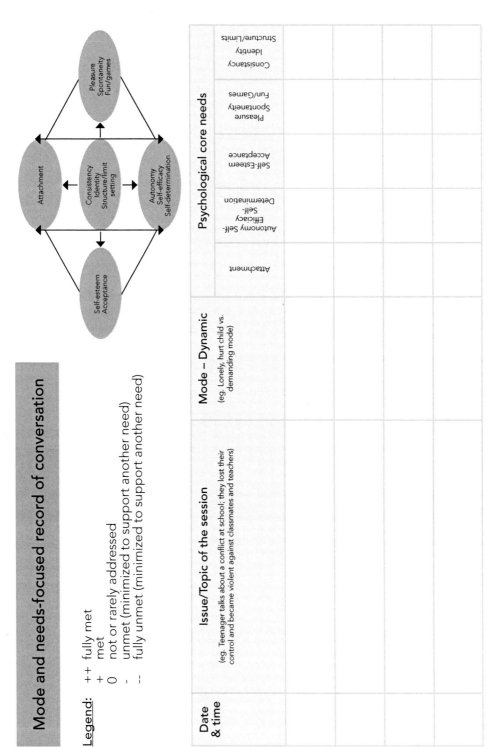

Figure 7.1: Mode and needs-focused record of conversation (see online worksheets)

Assessment of attachment style

When assessing attachment styles, the clinician should consider how attachment is expressed with peers and other important figures. During adolescence, an attachment gap has been reported (Shumaker *et al*, 2009). This refers to the lack of stability of attachment behaviours between early childhood and adolescence. The lack of stability of attachment behaviours may be due to the great developmental challenges and changes in adolescence, such as a move toward independence from parents and a reorientation toward social networks and partnerships.

More recent research into attachments (see Brisch, 2012) describes children and adolescents developing a number of attachments and forming a hierarchy of attachments with different people. The term 'attachment hierarchy' describes the concept of primary and secondary attachment figures and challenges Bowlby's attachment concept of monotropy, which suggested that there can only be one bond with one person at a time. According to Brisch, the attachment figure that will be at the top of the hierarchy depends on how much time the person devotes to the child and whether this is quality time; the level of the adult's emotional engagement; and whether the person is regularly available. Different attachment patterns can emerge with different persons, e.g. secure attachment to father (type B) and an insecure-ambivalent attachment to mother (type C). As a result of the attachment gap in adolescence, individuals are able to compensate to some degree, e.g. where primary attachment figures have not been able to form a secure (type B) or adequate attachment to the child (see Markiewicz *et al*, 2006), or possibly an insecure attachment pattern has emerged (types A, C or D). However, despite the attachment gap and the resulting opportunities, it is clear that insecurely attached children have already experienced disadvantages during childhood, at least in relation to sociability, popularity and social skills (Vondra *et al*, 2001).

According to Seiffge-Krenke (2005), attachments in adolescence display the following characteristics:

- **Securely attached adolescents:** When securely attached, adolescents are able to manage conflict with their parents. They can build on the foundation of a positive relationship and can solve problems effectively. There is a balance between their needs for attachment and independence (e.g. desire to explore).

- **Insecurely attached adolescents** often display little autonomy. At the same time, there is often little attachment to their parents; they tend to demonstratively display their independence. These adolescents commonly have a tendency to idealise their parents and have difficulties identifying negative affect in themselves and others.

■ **Insecurely-ambivalently attached adolescents** tend to display greater yet ineffective attempts to engage their parents, where the attachment system is activated disproportionally compared to the desire to explore.

The Adult Attachment Interview (AAI; originally developed by George *et al*, 1984, 1985, 1996) can be used to capture attachment patterns during adolescence.

Temperament

An adolescent's temperament plays an important role in the development of schemas and also influences the selection of schema coping strategies (surrender, avoidance and overcompensation). It is therefore necessary to develop an understanding of the adolescent's temperament. Exploring early abilities or inabilities to self-regulate (self-soothing, crying, sleeping, feeding and attentiveness) and behaviours and experiences at preschool, primary and secondary school, as well as behavioural observations during therapy sessions, also contribute to a better understanding (Shiner & Caspi, 2003). Additionally, questionnaires and inventories can be used, such as the Junior Temperament and Character Inventory (JTCI – Luby *et al*, 1999) which is currently used for 9 to 13-year-olds or the revised Early Adolescent Temperament Questionnaire for 9 to 15-year-olds (Ellis & Rothbart, 2001).

Ability to regulate emotions

In order to gain insight into adaptive and maladaptive coping strategies to manage feelings such as sadness, anxiety and anger, the Difficulties in Emotion Regulation Scale (DERS – Gratz & Roemer, 2004) is useful. Adaptive strategies such as problem-focused behaviours, diffusion, lifting mood, accepting, forgetting, re-evaluating and cognitive problem-solving need to be investigated. In addition, the presence and development of maladaptive strategies (giving up, aggressive behaviours, withdrawal, loss of self-worth and rumination) are evaluated. Other strategies, such as emotional control and asking for social support, are also important for a comprehensive analysis of the ability to regulate emotions. This analysis enables us to better identify strategies conceptualised in Schema Therapy, such as surrender, avoidance and overcompensation.

Assessment of coping modes

Extroverted people with a high degree of assertiveness tend to overcompensate. Introverted people with social insecurities, on the other hand, lean more toward avoidance. Surrender, which is reminiscent of the concept of learned helplessness (Seligman, 1974) and can lead to depression, is a reflection of having no ability to deal with the schema other than to 'obey' or submit to it. Clinicians can also consult Tables 2.5 to 2.8 (see Chapter 2) to look up typical adolescent behaviours and the relationship to preferred coping mechanisms. In the same row, characteristic behaviours for other coping styles (columns 4–6) and cognitions (column 3), as well as characteristic parental behaviours (column 2), can be compared to a teenager's presentation. Using the table provides the clinician with clues as to which maladaptive schema may be at work (column 1).

7.2.2 Psychoeducation

Detailed psychoeducation plays an important role in Schema Therapy, particularly when working with adolescents. Adolescents possess the neural structures that enable metacognition. This capacity should not only be recognised but be used as a strength in therapy. Due to the increasing need for autonomy, self-efficacy and self-determination, the therapist should address the adolescent as a responsible and capable person. In some cases, more in-depth psychoeducation is warranted, particularly if autonomy needs have not been met over time (expressed as a *Dependence / Incompetence* schema).

Prior to commencing assessment and therapy, the client (the term 'patient' should be avoided in the presence of the adolescent) should be informed of their rights and the regulations of the profession, e.g. confidentiality. Not all adolescents are interested in the details, but nearly all appreciate the opportunity to receive more detailed information. Therapists can also provide information around lodging complaints with regulatory bodies, law enforcement and child services, reducing adolescents' anxiety that they are helpless. The websites of such organisations usually provide helpful Q&A sections. For adolescents who are mistrustful (a possible *Mistrust / Abuse* schema), this process promotes trust and can be extended until the adolescent has fulfilled his or her need for information and autonomy. If the process takes a long time, this in itself provides valuable diagnostic information about the way basic psychological needs are met. On the worksheet depicted on p134 (see Figure 7.1), two pluses could be noted for autonomy. Of course, this approach is consistent with good practice. Openness and informed consent (e.g. explanation of imaginative procedures and chair technique) are an important prerequisite for Schema Therapy interventions.

7.3 Schema Therapy in action: age-appropriate therapeutic relationships and therapeutic interventions

The nature of the therapeutic relationship is of critical importance, but is made more complex when you are working with both the adolescent and their parent. As outlined previously, a patient's needs largely provide the structure for Schema Therapy. In adolescence these are focused around autonomy and self-determination. Since adolescents are not yet of legal age, they are also not yet autonomous, which means that they have to obey more rules in more areas of their lives than if they were an adult with their own income and accommodation.

These factors also make parenting an adolescent child complex because of the risks during this developmental phase, as outlined in section 7.1. Parents often turn to their child and adolescent psychologist to seek guidance as how to implement rules and appropriate consequences. However, this kind of alignment with the parents runs the risk of straining the therapeutic relationship with the adolescent. Providing insights into effective, quick and targeted interventions to help the parents discipline the child should be considered and weighed up carefully, as adolescents may then perceive the therapist in the role of a Demanding or Punitive Parent. Therapy with adolescents requires a careful balance of providing space and allowing them to step into it while also encourgaing a healthy relationship with parents (Geerdink *et al*, 2012). A therapist should never try to be the 'better parent', or seek to put themselves in this role by winning the client's affections as a result of denigrating the parent. Aligning with the client in this way can result in adolescent patients feeling guilty on behalf of their parents.

Managing the internalised Parent mode and the external, actual parent is one of the complexities of working with this age group. The Punitive Parent mode can have a negative impact on progress in therapy. Viewing the 'punitive voice' as an internal force, i.e. coming from within the adolescent, rather than just an external force, i.e. coming from their parents, can help reduce this negative impact (ibid., p. 120). This facilitates differentiating between the Inner Parent mode and the actual parents.

On the other hand, adolescents with less assertive parents often have a greater desire for structure and boundaries, even though they are commonly unable to articulate this. In these cases, a good relationship built on trust is required between parents and therapists because educating them on boundaries and structures too early on in therapy can have negative consequences for the therapeutic relationship with the adolescent. Therefore, in order not to jeopardise the fragile relationship with the pubescent child, parents need to be patient while the therapist needs to remain calm. The adolescent has to come to understand for themselves that their parents' lack of assertiveness or inconsistency in setting and following through with negative consequences is not helpful. This realisation results in a common desire for change which helps to establish new goals for more structure and effective discipline. Socratic questioning (e.g. Sudak, 2006) and working with schema modes are useful techniques to help in this process. This enables the adolescent to accept that their Spoilt or Selfish Child mode was given too much freedom by their parents but in actual fact still needs direction.

Other needs (attachment, self-worth, enjoyment and consistency) are easier to communicate because the therapist can side with the adolescent while working to satisfy these needs, in line with the concept of re-parenting.

Back to our case study: using the broad band measure for diagnosing disorders in children and adolescents (Child Behaviour Checklist – Achenbach & Edelbrock, 1991, or SDS-KJ – Borg-Laufs, 2011) as well as information derived from interviews, behavioural observation, questionnaires, psychometric tests and other assessment tools, the following insights and results were established.

Presenting problems

Lea-Marie presented for treatment because her grades at school were deteriorating and she had received five warning letters indicating she was in danger of failing subjects. To rule out intellectual difficulties, we conducted an intelligence test (WAIS-IV) in which Lea-Marie achieved a full-scale IQ score of 112. In the 'd2 test of attention' she also obtained a good average score (109) (or the Test of Everyday Attention for Children (TEA-Ch), by Manly, Robertson, Anderson, & Nimmo-Smith, 1994 could be used). During testing, she appeared motivated, focused and not prone to stress or performance anxiety. Therefore, intellectual difficulties or avoidant coping style deficits were ruled out.

Background information

Lea-Marie's impaired socio-emotional development within her family was the main cause of her problems: when she was two years old, her parents separated and her father disappeared from her life completely (*Abandonment / Instability* schema developed). Her mother's responses remained brief and unhelpful, even years later, whenever Lea-Marie asked her about her father. Lea-Marie paid little attention to her mother's boyfriends, presumably so that she would not be hurt again if they decided to leave (Avoidant coping strategy). Her introverted, withdrawn personality (NEO-FFI: high on introversion and inhibition) may be due to genetic factors, yet – from a Schema Therapy perspective – it may also be interpreted as an avoidant attachment style as an attempt to deal with an *Emotional Deprivation* schema.

Even though it was unclear where Lea-Marie's reserved nature came from (temperament or schema), the consequences were the same: her mother was too busy with her own life and romantic relationships for Lea-Marie to approach her with her needs. Lea-Marie often wished her mother was more present, not only for herself but also for the care of her younger half sister (*Emotional Deprivation* schema). Instead, she was often emotionally unavailable, lost and sad, which prompted Lea-Marie to assume a consoling role (parentification, producing a *Self-*

Sacrifice schema). If she did not follow the rules, something all children fail to do every now and then, Lea-Marie felt guilty (internalised Demanding, Criticising Critic mode) because, with an unstable mother and a little sister who needed her, she felt she had undermined the family bond. Even just looking at her mother brought up thoughts such as 'I must not do anything that may worry Mom' and 'I have to make sure there is peace at home'.

Her own emotional needs (e.g. for attachment and enjoyment) were second to her mother's and her sister's (*Self-Sacrifice* schema). She was often responsible for her little sister (Compliant Surrenderer mode) which resulted in role conflict: 'I feel as though sometimes I am a mother for my sister, then a counsellor for my mother, and then I am a child again who has to do what I am told.' Due to years of going through this emotional rollercoaster, Lea-Marie developed an *Abandonment/Instability* schema as well as an *Emotional Deprivation* schema. Coping strategies such as Surrender and Avoidance protected her from unrealistic expectations and painful disappointments. She had observed her mother using these strategies (modelling), e.g. when her grandmother and her mother's friend, who was also her boss, got involved in parenting questions.

With the onset of puberty, Lea-Marie's appearance and identity changed: she went from being a number one athlete to an adolescent with female curves – at least, as perceived by others. There may be a number of conflicts here: the process of sexual maturation presents Lea-Marie with the next developmental challenge (toward autonomy) for which she does not yet feel emotionally prepared (because her child-like need for attachment has never been adequately met). Potential friendships with boys were probably viewed negatively (through the lens of the *Abandonment/Instability* schema) and associated with subjugation, as a result of watching her mother. The symptoms Lea-Marie developed, such as sleep problems, nightmares, headaches and stomach pains, could be interpreted as compromise formation in depth psychology, or as dysfunctional (Avoidant) coping mode in Schema Therapy. Lea-Marie's avoidant coping resulted in her mother caring for her and enabled her to withdraw from club activities (although this resulted in weight gain). She also avoided spending time with her girl friends, who always talked about gender-specific topics. Eventually she also withdrew from her mother, to whom she felt she was too close. In addition to the aforementioned symptoms, she then developed difficulties concentrating and paying attention, as well as dysphoria, which became evident when her grades at school declined and prompted her to seek psychological help.

Therapy
It took a few sessions for Lea-Marie to assess the therapist's honesty, genuineness and trustworthiness: she did not open up when discussing emotional topics, denied or played down problems and claimed to have everything under control

(Detached Protector). She attributed her deteriorating school grades to teachers who did not like her.

Mode model

Lea-Marie's defensiveness was reduced by the introduction of the mode model. The therapist sat at the table with her next to an empty chair and said: 'You see, Lea-Marie, I understand where you are coming from and, if I were you, I would be just as defensive as you (eye contact). I know that I am still a stranger to you and that I have no right to impose myself on you or make you do something. In this regard, I am very like you.' Lea-Marie looked skeptical while the therapist continued: 'However, there is also a different side to me. And this side says (therapist changed chairs): "My god, what a stubborn child this is; I have had enough; what else can I do? This makes me angry!" (therapist returned to the first chair) Lea-Marie, what can we say to this side?' He pointed to the empty chair, on which he had just sat. Lea-Marie frowned and, critically, looked at the therapist.

Talking to the empty chair, the therapist then said: 'You have not understood anything. Don't you realise that Lea-Marie does not trust you yet? Who do you think you are? You have no idea what is going on here!' At first, Lea-Marie was confused, but she eventually accepted the therapist's offer, and told the empty chair what she thought. Because she was still holding back, the therapist swapped chairs again: 'Yes, I know I have no idea. That's why I asked her to tell her story. Do you think I have all the time in the world? Girl, hurry up, the hour is nearly up and the next person will be waiting outside.' After swapping chairs again, the therapist was pleased to see Lea-Marie exploding and using swear words, telling off the impatient, Demanding therapist mode.

That dialogue allows key issues to be explored: the therapist could voice his dissatisfaction (i.e. his lack of patience) but Lea-Marie could also open up emotionally and voice her negative emotions. In this way, a common enemy was defined: the therapist's impatient side. The therapist demonstrates acknowledging this (not entirely unfounded) side and weakness and also demonstrates apologising for this. The last step encourages collaboration. Both the 'patient and kind' therapist and Lea-Marie could search for a solution for how to deal with the impatient therapist, which amuses Lea-Marie ('What a weird guy!') but also gets her attention ('Funny guy, I wonder what else he will do?'). Finally, she opens up more to enable a therapeutic relationship with the patient and kind therapist.

Presenting the therapist's different modes (Patient and Demanding mode) is the first step toward introducing the idea of modes: 'Lea-Marie, you have just seen that different sides can be active in me. Do you know which sides you have?' After a while, Lea-Marie reported nine different emotional and motivational states (e.g. the

'Angry Girl', the 'Jealous Girl', etc). We referred to these as modes henceforth (Angry Child mode, Jealous Child mode, etc.). Following some prompting by the therapist, she could also identify with the 'Self-Protection' (Detached Protector) mode. This mode has an important defensive function, yet may also end up derailing therapy. Lea-Marie could recall situations in her life where she had used this mode. The therapist helped Lea-Marie to become more aware of this mode, linked to her desire to withdraw, which helped her explain to her attachment figures that she needed space and was changing into her Detached Protector mode.

Therapist and client spoke about psychological needs and slowly approached the topics that were important to Lea-Marie. Possibly in order to test whether the therapist was really trustworthy, she initially requested to work on her learning difficulties (with the goal of developing a better attitude toward learning and working). Understanding psychological needs enabled Lea-Marie to anticipate the effects a better attitude to learning would have on these needs.

Other goals, such as weight loss, were also discussed from the perspective of needs and how to satisfy these. Lea-Marie described a Vulnerable, Angry, Rebellious and Happy Child mode on one side, and Demanding and Critical modes on the other. She recognised very quickly the conflict that existed between the Child modes and the Demanding Critic mode. So-called quick fixes (e.g. denial of one side in order to reduce tension) were identified as beneficial in the short term but problematic in the long term. She could now learn how to apply to herself the Caring and Guidance mode (with other words Clever and Wise mode) that she had not experienced, and therefore not developed early on in life due to her emotionally labile mother (and needy sister). Therapist and client imagined the adolescent Lea-Marie (in the Clever and Wise mode) looking after the little, happy Lea-Marie (in the Happy Child mode), and supporting her, having fun, playing and enjoying life.

After some time in therapy, Lea-Marie began attempts to become more independent from her mother (whom she felt was too close for comfort), and it was clear that more autonomy and self-determination needs were starting to surface. By talking to her mother, the therapist was able to ensure that Lea-Marie was granted more freedom to engage in hobbies (reading, chatting, dancing).

Within the family, each individual's need for space and other desires were discussed. Clear rules around who was responsible for which household chores resulted in less arguments and dependence. These early successes encouraged Lea-Marie to talk to the therapist about her relationship with her mother and sister. She explained that she often felt let down by her mother (*Abandonment/Instability* schema) and that she was 'fed up with all the men and could not stand having to pretend to be happy when these men came around to visit' (*Emotional Deprivation* schema triggering a Detached Protector mode).

Using the three-chair technique (see Chapter 12), her Demanding Critic mode ('You have to look after your sister now! Don't be so selfish!') and her Vulnerable Child mode ('I want to be comforted, act like a child, have fun and do silly things') were placed on two chairs facing one another. Lea-Marie swapped between the two chairs and verbalised thoughts, feelings, expectations, and desires. After seven swaps she was exhausted (she had run out of things to say and the discussion had become quite heated), so she sat down on the third chair, between the other two ('nurturing chair'; Clever and Wise mode). She paused and caught her breath. Then she looked to her left, where the first chair was (Demanding Critic mode), and to the right, where the second chair was (Vulnerable Child mode). Meanwhile, the therapist encouraged her to feel the tension between the two sides. Tears rolled down her cheeks and a look of helplessness crept into her eyes. After 45 seconds, Lea-Marie indicated that she had felt enough.

Following the therapist's request, she turned to the Vulnerable Child mode (second chair) and asked what it needed. She then sat down on the second chair and expressed what she – in the Vulnerable Child mode – wanted the nurturing side (Clever and Wise mode) to do and the kind of support she was looking for. After a few clarifying questions and swapping chairs, she sat on the nurturing chair and turned to the Demanding Critic chair: 'Now, you Demanding Critic, I ask you to leave the little Lea-Marie alone with your constant demands. Lea-Marie needs support and encouragement, so give her a break! She does not always want to do things for you. Am I making this clear?' Swapping chairs, she said: 'We only want the best for her – don't be so rude. Without us, Lea-Marie would not have done so well at school.' She swapped chairs again: 'Little Lea-Marie does not care about school. I will look after her from now on and make sure that you are not always asking her to do things she cannot do and does not want to do.' After three swaps and a seemingly unsuccessful discussion, the therapist instructed Lea-Marie in the nurturing role (Caring Parent mode) to disempower the Demanding/Criticising mode by taking the chair and turning it around. Therapist: 'Lea-Marie, how does that feel (with the turned chair)?' She looked to her left to the chair and to her right to the Vulnerable Lea-Marie and said, 'I still feel trapped'. Therapist: 'Now take the chair and put it down the way you like it in your Nuturing mode or your Clever and Wise mode.' (Pause) Therapist: 'You can put it in the far corner of the room or even take it out of the room.' (Pause) Lea-Marie took the Demanding Critic chair outside the room, into the hallway, and came back smiling. She then spoke to the Vulnerable Child's chair with tender and loving care: 'I will look after you from now on.'

Even though this sounds like a fairy tale, it is completely accurate to the therapy session. It is the procedure for implementing a mode dialogue – a technique that adolescents will only engage in once a relationship of trust has been established.

Talking to an empty chair is not something adolescents are used to doing. Because Lea-Marie had developed trust, she could openly investigate her schemas and coping modes with the therapist. Further advice around how to develop good rapport can be found in section 10.1 (Building relationships).

Imagery

Imagery rescripting (described in Chapter 13) enabled Lea-Marie to express her feelings and needs toward her mother (who was not present at that time) for the first time, with the help of a Inner Helper ('Peter Pan') who provided the required support during this process. Lea-Marie experienced emotional outbursts of anger and sadness during the three imagery rescripting exercises. She perceived these heated, emotional moments to be particularly helpful in terms of opening her eyes to the hurt she experienced and clearly identifying her own needs (self-awareness). As her self-awareness increased during therapy, she realised how much she had neglected her own needs in the past. Once she was able to understand her emotions and had practised adaptive and healthy coping strategies in difficult situations (e.g. arguing with her mother, pressure to perform at school, boys teasing her about her breasts), she could engage in behavioural therapy aimed at developing her social skills, assertiveness and boundary-setting capabilities. These skills were practised in role plays, which were videotaped to enable the therapist to provide feedback, before implementing them in the real world.

Parent sessions

Initially the sessions wih Lea-Marie's mother were aimed at educating her about developmental milestones, e.g. adolescent's need for independence from parents. Lea-Marie's mother was able to identify that she had not completed this process and at times still acted like a little dependent child (Vulernable Child mode) around her own mother. The book *Reinventing Your Life* (Young & Klosko, 1993) helped her understand her own schemas, and she started undergoing psychotherapy herself, to help her work through her own childhood.

7.4 Conclusion

The processes of meeting needs for autonomy and self-determination are central to Schema Therapy with adolescents. A good rapport is critical in order to effect change in the adolescent. One of the most difficult tasks during therapy is developing a nurturing role toward the adolescent in a way that doesn't result in the parents' need to nurture being undermined. If required, working with the parents can even be outsourced (e.g. parent counselling, separate therapy). Mode work, involving understanding different modes – their respective feelings, thoughts, physical sensations, and behavioural patterns – are identified. This process provides the patient with insight and explains the reason for the existence of each mode. The mode model enables therapist and adolescent to investigate intrapsychic tensions and develop an understanding of why the adolescent is behaving in a certain way, thus allowing the client to let go of their egosyntonic view regarding the problem behaviour. Where there is good rapport ('I trust you') and the person has let go of their egosyntonic view ('I want to get rid of the problem'), the stage is set for the key phase of therapeutic work.

The therapeutic relationship then becomes the basis for focusing on unmet needs, dysfunctional modes and maladaptive schemas. In addition to understanding why symptoms have started (based on biography) and how problems are maintained, experiential interventions such as the chair technique/mode dialogues and imagery rescripting are helpful to deal with past hurt, deprivations, traumas and chronic need frustrations. Once past needs have been met (e.g. through imagery rescripting), traditional behavioural interventions gain more traction and can be successfully implemented.

Finally, it is important to note that adolescents need a mix of freedom to decide and specific ideas and clear instructions (Geerdink *et al*, 2012). The therapist should also be aware that for adolescents, there are some developmentally normal factors that can complicate therapy. Adolescents can have acute feelings of shame in front of peers ('You have a psychotherapist?'), can lack reliability in engaging with therapy ('I can't talk about that today/don't ask me to go there today') and have varying levels of motivation to engage in therapy ('I can do this on my own, I didn't ask to come to therapy'). Therefore, if the adolescent does not honour commitments, the therapist needs to be mindful not to present as a Demanding Parent ('I am disappointed, you promised to come'). The therapist's 'door' should always be open, even if the clinician does not feel appreciated or accepted. This unconditional positive regard is recognised by adolescents and can enable them to come back at a later stage.

References

Achenbach TM & Edelbrock C (1991) Child behavior checklist. *Burlington (Vt)* 7.

Borg-Laufs M (2011) *Störungsübergreifendes Diagnostik-System für die Kinder- und Jugendlichenpsychotherapie (SDS-KJ): Manual für die Therapieplanung* (2. Aufl.) Tübingen: Dgvt-Verlag.

Borg-Laufs M (2013) Basic Psychological Needs in Childhood and Adolescence. *Journal of Education and Research* **3** 41–51.

Brisch KH (2012) *Treating Attachment Disorders: From Theory to Therapy*. New York: Guilford Press.

Carr, A. (2015) *The Handbook of Child and Adolescent Clinical Psychology: A Contextual Approach*. London: Routledge.

DGKJP Deutsche Gesellschaft für Kinder- und Jugendpsychiatrie und Psychotherapie *et al* (2007) *Leitlinien zur Diagnostik und Therapie von psychischen Störungen im Säuglings-, Kindes- und Jugendalter* (3. Aufl.) Köln: Deutscher Ärzte-Verlag.

Döpfner M, Lehmkuhl G, Heubrock D & Petermann F (2000) *Ratgeber Psychische Auffälligkeiten bei Kindern und Jugendlichen*. Göttingen: Hogrefe.

Dreher E & Dreher M (2002) Familienstatus und Ablösung. In: B Rollett & H Wernek (Eds) *Klinische Entwicklungspsychologie der Familie*, pp137–157. Göttingen: Hogrefe.

Eisenberg N (2000) Emotion, regulation, and moral development. *Annual Review of Psychology* **51** 665–697.

Farrell AD & White KS (1998) Peer influences and drug use among urban adolescents: family structure and parent-adolescent relationship as protective factors. *Journal of Consulting and Clinical Psychology* **66** 248–258.

Fend H (1998) *Eltern und Freunde. Soziale Entwicklung im Jugendalter*. Bern: Huber.

Gardner M & Steinberg L (2005) Peer influence on risk taking, risk performance, and risky decision making in adolescence and childhood: an experimental study. *Developmental Psychology* **41** 625–635.

Geerdink M, Jongman E & Scholing A (2012) Schema therapy in adolescents. *The Wiley-Blackwell Handbook of Schema Therapy: Theory, Research, and Practice*, pp391–396. Chichester: Wiley-Blackwell.

George C, Kaplan N & Main M (1984, 1985, 1996) *Adult attachment interview protocol*. Unpublished manuscript, University of California at Berkeley.

Gestsdottir S & Lerner RM (2008) Positive development in adolescence: The development and role of intentional self-regulation. *Human Development* **51** (3) 202–224.

Gratz KL & Roemer L (2004) Multidimensional assessment of emotion regulation and dysregulation: development, factor structure, and initial validation of the difficulties in emotion regulation scale. *Journal of Psychopathology & Behavioral Assessment* **26** (1) 41–54.

Grawe K (2017) *Neuropsychotherapy: How the Neurosciences Inform Effective Psychotherapy*. London: Routledge.

Larson R & Lampman-Petraitis C (1989) Daily emotional states reported by children and adolescents. *Child Development* **60** 1250–1260.

Larson RW, Clore GL & Wood GA (1999) The emotions of romantic relationships: do they wreak havoc on adolescents? In: W Furman, BB Brown & C Feiring (Eds) *The Development of Romantic Relationships in Adolescence*, pp19–49. Cambridge: Cambridge University Press.

Luby JL, Svrakic DM, McCallum K, Przybeck TR & Cloninger CR (1999) The Junior Temperament and Character Inventory: preliminary validation of a child self-report measure. *Psychological Reports* **84** (3_suppl), 1127–1138.

Lundborg P (2006) Having the wrong friends? Peer effects in adolescent substance use. *Journal of Health Economics* **25** 214–233.

Manly T, Robertson IH, Anderson V & Nimmo-Smith I (1994) *The Test of Everyday Attention (TEA-CH)*. Bury St. Edmunds: Thames Valley Test Company.

Markiewicz D, Lawford H, Doyle AB & Haggart N (2006) Developmental differences in adolescents' and young adults' use of mothers, fathers, best friends, and romantic partners to fulfill attachment needs. *Journal of Youth and Adolescence* **35** (1) 121–134.

Mullis AK, Mullid RL & Normandin D (1992) Cross-sectional and longitudinal comparisons of adolescent self-esteem. *Adolescence* **27** (105) 51–61.

Oerter R & Dreher E (2008) Jugendalter. In: R Oerter and L Montada *Entwicklungspsychologie* (6. Aufl.) Weinheim: Beltz.

Roediger E (2011) *Praxis der Schematherapie. Lehrbuch zu Grundlagen, Modell und Anwendung* (2. Aufl.) Stuttgart: Schattauer.

Rosenblum GD & Lewis M (2003) Emotional development in adolescence. In: GR Adams and MD Berzonski (Eds) *Blackwell Handbook of Adolescence,* pp259–269. Malden MA: Blackwell Publishing.

Salisch M v (2008) Emotionale Entwicklung. In: B Herpertz-Dahlmann, F Resch, M Schulte-Markwort and A Warnke (Eds) *Entwicklungspsychiatrie* (2. Aufl.) Stuttgart: Schattauer.

Schneider S, Unnewehr S & Margraf J (2009) *Kinder-DIPS. Diagnostisches Interview bei psychischen Störungen im Kindes- und Jugendalter* (2. Aufl.) Heidelberg: Springer.

Schroeder CS & Smith-Boydston, JM (2017) *Assessment and Treatment of Childhood Problems: A Clinician's Guide* (3rd ed.). New York: Guilford Press.

Seiffge-Krenke I & Beyers W (2005) Coping trajectories from adolescence to young adulthood: links to attachment state of mind. *Journal of Research on Adolescence* **15** (4) 561–582.

Seligman ME (1974) *Depression and Learned Helplessness*. Chichester: Wiley.

Shiner R & Caspi A (2003) Personality differences in childhood and adolescence: measurement, development, and consequences. *Journal of Child Psychology and Psychiatry* **44** (1) 2–32.

Shumaker DM, Deutsch RM & Brenninkmeyer L (2009) How do I connect? Attachment issues in adolescence. *Journal of Child Custody* **6** (1–2) 91–112.

Steinberg L (2005) *Adolescence*. New York: McGraw-Hill.

Sudak DM (2006) *Cognitive Behavioral Therapy for Clinicians*. Philadelphia: Lippincott Williams & Wilkins.

von Salisch M (2001) Children's emotional development: challenges in their relationships to parents, peers, and friends. *International Journal of Behavioral Development* **25** (4) 310–319.

Vondra JI, Shaw DS, Swearingen L, Cohen M & Owens EB (2001) Attachment stability and emotional and behavioral regulation from infancy to preschool age. *Development and Psychopathology* **13** 13–33.

Young JE & Klosko J (1993) *Reinventing Your Life*. New York: Dutton Books.

Zarbock G & Zens C (2011) Bedürfnis- und Emotionsdynamik – Handlungsleitende Konzepte für die Schematherapiepraxis. In: E Roediger and G Jacob (Eds), *Fortschritte der Schematherapie*. Göttingen: Hogrefe.

Chapter 8: Schema Therapy with Young Adults (17–23 Years)

Christine Zens and Silka Hagena

Case example

Mona was 17 and a half years of age, an only child and in her final two years of school. Her doctor and mother referred her for therapy after inpatient cognitive behavioural therapy was discontinued because of her failure to comply. She had suffered for a year from anorexia nervosa, restrictive type (limited food intake and obsession with calories and body weight). At the start of treatment, she weighed 43 kilos, was 1.68m tall and had a body mass index of 15 and disordered body image. She was also experiencing depressive symptoms (particularly low mood, loss of interest, social isolation, lack of motivation and, at times, suicidal thoughts, from which she detached herself). As well as these symptoms, she had a distorted self-image and mood swings. Further investigations into the case history indicated a tendency to engage in impulsive and self-destructive behaviours (drinking alcohol, cannabis consumption, self-harm in the form of scratching herself and superficial wounding); she also reported being fearful of losing those close to her. This was especially evident in her relationship with her boyfriend, who was quite contemptuous and often ignored her needs. Mona stated that 'sex meant nothing' to her; she just 'tolerated it for his sake', to keep him from leaving her. While earlier in high school she had performed well academically, her results had been slipping for some time now. She had long-term friends who were supportive. However, she was engaging less and less in activities with her friends and becoming more withdrawn.

Her mother worked in insurance and her father worked for the government taxation department. Her parents were divorced. She told us that she was her 'mother's pet' and her early years (kindergarten and initial school years) were relatively problem free. She recalled many happy memories of this time with her mother. Her relationship with her father had always been difficult. He suffered from periodic bouts of deep depression during which he became unresponsive to those around him. Because of the burden of her father's mental health issues, at 10 years of age Mona began to help her mother more and more. Mona's mother became increasingly reliant on this support, especially when the fighting between Mona's parents became more intense. Mona reported that she often felt alone and helpless during these times. When she was 13 her parents separated and her contact with her father ceased for the most part. Shortly afterwards her mother found a new partner. This partner treated Mona in a lecherous and degrading manner. After a few sessions in therapy Mona was able to talk about how, when she was 15 years old, he had regularly sexually abused her when he was under the influence of alcohol. She was very ashamed of this. Her mother blocked all of Mona's attempts to tell her ('you're exaggerating, your interpretation is wrong … we need him, think about that'). At 16 Mona finally left home and ran away to live with her father. Her father took her in but ignored her, not talking to her or looking after her in any way. During this time she began to focus on her food intake and started to lose weight. She still felt 'much too fat' and ugly. Her only support was her 20-year-old boyfriend (who was living at home, had left school early and was unemployed), whom she had met at 16. Although it was not easy to live with him, she could not imagine a life without him. He didn't like her girlfriends and tried to keep her away from them. Over time Mona began to see her friends as being less important. Mona's mother had separated from her partner in the meantime and Mona therefore moved back to live with her. She still felt misunderstood in that relationship. She and her mother were unable to talk to one another and there was a lot of conflict because of her eating issues.

Mona had no idea what she wanted to do after school. She had very few interests and she chose subjects she felt able to do without much effort. She chose biology as a major because it gave her information about the human body. When asked about current affairs and opinions about the world Mona appeared to lack awareness, and had no real views on those subjects.

From a young age, Mona had displayed an emotionally unstable temperament. According to her mother, she had been very sensitive to any negative environmental stimuli all of her life. In spite of this, up until she was 11 she appeared to be able to manage developmental tasks relatively well. However, when the conflict at home between her parents became more intense, her mother noticed Mona had become more distressed.

8.1 Phase-specific developmental tasks, interactions, conflict and modes from a Schema Therapy perspective

In this chapter, we are concerned with the late adolescent period of life, up to and including early adulthood (Carr, 2015). This stage roughly corresponds to the ages 17–23, referred to here as the 'young adult phase'. The age range of late adolescent/young adult overlaps with the adolescent period. Adolescence is the stage of life between late childhood and adulthood. The exact definition or description of the 'age' is dependent on cultural, social, gender-specific and economic factors (wealth, for example). Adolescence encompasses not only physical maturity but also, more importantly, the mental and psychological development toward independence and responsibility as an adult.

8.1.1 Phase-specific developmental tasks and themes for young adults

In developmental psychology there are numerous descriptions and concepts related to the development of a person's sense of self. In order to simplify, we will focus on those concepts that are more relevant to Schema Therapy for young adults. Erik Erikson's (1968) model of the stages of psycho-social development and crises is a helpful model, as is the development tasks model of Robert Havighurst (1972), complemented by the description of developmental tasks in youths from Carr (2015).

In his stage model, Erikson describes the development of identity as a result of the interplay between the child's needs and desires as an individual and the constantly changing demands of the social environment. Erikson's developmental theory gives the child's relationships and interactions with their personal (and objective) environment a very important role. There is an obvious connection between Erikson's tasks and a child's basic needs from a Schema Therapy perspective. We will focus in this chapter about therapy for young adults on Young and colleagues' (Young *et al*, 2003) formulation of a child's basic needs of safety and attachment, autonomy, self-esteem, play and spontaneity, as well as limit-setting, guidance and monitoring. We will also draw on the work of Grawe (2017) concerning the need for consistency.

For both male and female young adults there is a tendency to devote more and more time to questions about the self. These issue of how a young person relates to their body continues and there is especially a fixation with attractiveness.

There is also an emphasis on the acquisition of independence from parents, as well as the restructuring of relationships to peers, which reaches its peak in middle puberty, with questions such as: Who am I? What are my values, attitudes, perspectives on life? What will my future look like?

Ideally, a realistic self-image will have developed and individual weaknesses and strengths become acknowledged. Identity formation is, however, not yet finished. According to Erikson and Havighurst, this does not occur until the young adolescent can answer questions about career, partner choice, family and political and moral standpoints and has attained sufficient social and intellectual competence to follow these aspirations.

Havighurst asserts that each developmental task appears to be particularly suited to stages where the individual is able to master the appropriate learning process – the teachable moment. He differentiates between task areas which are time-limited and tasks which can be mastered over more flexible amounts of time. These tasks may be difficult to complete because there is a state of tension between the individual's needs and the society's demands. Also, the developmental tasks of the adolescent and those of the young adult are closely interconnected (Carr, 2015). According to the above mentioned developmental theories, the following topics are of central importance to the age group of young adults which we are looking at in this chapter: identity; family; the meaning of family and detachment from family (development of autonomy); love and partnership; choice of career and development of perspectives; creation of stable social relationships; and financial independence.

Questions about one's identity are a lifelong pursuit. However, in young adulthood there are manifold physiological, cognitive and social changes that impact on the development of a stable identity. Therefore the question 'who am I?' is of special importance in the young adult age group. Erikson frames this issue as the developmental crisis regarding 'identity versus role confusion'. A sense of self is established by connecting past and present experiences with anticipations of the future. It is important that a young adult has the ability to accurately evaluate their capabilities in order to imagine realistic possibilities for the future 'self'. Therefore, a young adult needs to understand his or her own abilities, strengths and weaknesses. A critical analysis of social conditions and expectations also occurs during this stage of life. This then informs personal values and morals which are part of identity formation. During this intense conflict with the above themes, a person's ability to take responsibility is formed. Active integration into society also takes place, carrying with it experiences such as loyalty, faithfulness, commitment, well-being and self-esteem.

According to Erickson, further developmental crises are focused on the ability to form intimate relationships versus alienation. If successfully negotiated, an ability to form intimate relationships with another human without losing one's own sense of identity is achieved. If this is not successful then feelings of loneliness, isolation, subjugation or confusion in terms of intrinsic worth, wishes, expectations and viewpoints can occur.

In summary it appears that, from the theories mentioned and our clinical experience, the following themes are especially relevant for this age group:

1. Emotional and economic individuation from parental home (autonomy)

2. Entering a sustainable partnership

3. Creation of stable social networks

4. Consolidation of values, norms and social attitudes

5. Ability to take responsibility for own decisions

6. Development of realistic career and personal goals

7. Attainment of necessary social, practical and emotional competencies e.g. development of healthy frustration tolerance as well as dealing with difficult or strong emotions

The individual's own experiences of attachment and thereby their ability to bond are of great importance in resolving these developmental tasks and phases, all of which have one thing in common: the development of autonomy and a striving for independence and self-responsibility. The quality of attachment is (partly) decisive for the prognosis of how easy and problem-free separation from the parental home and transition into an independent, responsible life will be.

These developmental tasks also bring demands on parents and significant others. For example, parents must encourage increasing autonomy in the young person and promote the process of detachment. However, the parent's personal background impacts on their ability to cope with these demands. The parent's schemas and modes can be activated by the stress of these changes. Therefore, the background and schemas of significant others needs to be taken into consideration when conducting treatment.

8.1.2 Phase-specific developmental tasks, interactions, conflicts and modes from a Schema Therapy perspective

Young adults find themselves in a special field of developmental pressures, as they have to cope with the tasks of a youth as well as those of being a young adult. In contrast to the stage of mid-adolescence, the need for autonomy continually increases, and the young adult progressively takes on the role of the adult and the corresponding responsibilities. At the same time, dependency on the family often still exists, and this needs to be taken into consideration. This area of conflict can lead to excessive demands being placed on the young adult as well as on the significant others. These competing demands need to be assessed in setting realistic therapeutic goals, balancing the desire for autonomy with the limitations on that autonomy.

From a Schema Therapy perspective, the young person's ability to achieve developmental milestones is significantly impacted by their history of having core emotional needs met or frustrated. A young person whose basic needs have been sufficiently fulfilled will have much more capacity to achieve developmental tasks described in both the short and long term. However, when there has been a history of emotional needs frustration this sets the stage for lower levels of capacity to cope with frustration of basic needs by significant others. Outbursts and high irritability with others in peer groups can be seen as normal developmental deviations and should not be judged too harshly (Offer *et al*, 1981). So individual crises should therefore not be hastily judged, as they are often part of the 'normal course of development'.

Frustration of emotional needs can result in difficulty in achieving separation from parents and developing adult autonomy. For example, attachment and autonomy needs can be frustrated by the experience of not having an emotionally reliable attachment figure (for example through variable attention, frequent changes in caregivers, isolation, emotional coldness, neglect or rejection) or through controlling or overprotective parenting (e.g. overcautious and fearful parents or an authoritarian, controlling parental style). If these needs have been chronically frustrated the psychological ground is prepared for the development of eating disorders, fears, compulsions or depression. Romantic relationships are also impacted by a history of ongoing frustration of attachment needs. Impaired attachment often forms schemas, such as *Emotional Deprivation, Abandonment* or *Mistrust/Abuse*, which are at play in triggering attraction to others who will perpetuate the maladaptive schema. When this occurs a young adult forms relationships with others who are not capable of providing commitment, trust and dependability (e.g. being drawn to relationships with a married person, etc), and they then experience more *Emotional Deprivation, Abandonment* or *Mistrust/Abuse*-reinforcing experiences.

Case example

Frustration of core emotional needs

With Mona, accumulated frustration of basic needs in areas of attachment, guidance, limit-setting, control and self-esteem has occurred. First, Mona experienced attachment trauma and was burdened by responsibilities in excess of her ability to manage because of the father's illness and the unstable marital relationship that resulted. Mona ended up taking responsibility for her mother, who was not able to meet Mona's needs, which resulted in parentification. Mona also suffered from a lack of attention, protection and affection because of her parents' separation and her father's severance of all contact, as well as the humiliation and abuse experienced at the hands of her mother's new partner, and finally her mother's dismissive reactions (negating Mona's feelings and her perception of her needs) and lack of protection from the abuse. These experiences came during a time when Mona was busy with developmental tasks such as adopting gender-specific roles, accepting her body and separating from the parental home. Given that Mona's capacity was being overwhelmed, she then developed a fear of loss and self-esteem deficits, leading to the onset of anorexia nervosa and inappropriate coping strategies like self-harming. In addition, Mona's attraction to another emotionally depriving and dismissive partner ('schema chemistry'; Young *et al*, 2003) perpetuated the degradation and emotional neglect.

Formation of values and norms

During the development and establishment of values, rules and political attitudes the satisfaction or frustration of the basic needs for guidance, direction, limit-setting and control can play a vital role. A young person can seek support in a functional family in order to clarify their value system, finding role models in the family. However, when there is an absence of guidance and limit-setting there is no input regarding the formation of pro-social norms. Moral views are not imparted, or they may be delivered in an arbitrary or whimsical fashion or subject to the pleasure principle. Predispositions for delinquency or drug abuse can be formed within this environment, especially through strong suggestibility and impressionability, even with weak influences. The development of difficulties in controlling impulses and low levels of self-discipline then results in social deficits and disorders, e.g. depression.

At the beginning of therapy Mona had no clear idea of her own norms and values. As a result, it was difficult for her to reflect on the appropriateness of a partner, deciding with whom one should be allowed to meet. It became clear that all her energy was directed in two areas: stabilising her self-esteem through striving to be thin and avoiding abandonment by fixating on her partner.

Mona's parents were not able to provide reliable guidance and protection. As a result there was not sufficient emotional safety to progress to the more advanced developmental task of evolving viewpoints, social and political values and norms, personal interests and hobbies. Since the age of 10, Mona had been managing existentially basic issues such as insecurity and loss and had developed a very limited repertoire of solutions, consisting of stabilising self-esteem and devotion.

Young adults with frustrated core emotional needs in the areas of self-worth and the development of autonomy frequently exhibit patterns of helplessness and experiences of dependency. The fear of making one's own decisions and of taking responsibility for them can contribute to the emergence of disorders and impaired ability to develop a sense of self or set appropriate life goals.

If the needs for spontaneity, play and the attainment of pleasure were frustrated in development, e.g. because of an unemotional and achievement-oriented parental home, interpersonal inhibition can often emerge. Social competences, such as developing relationships and teamwork skills, cannot be sufficiently formed. In that case, young adults can tend to do things like avoid social contact and isolate themselves, or hide in pseudo-realities (video games etc.), or seek refuge in achievements (sport, hobbies, school). Emotional awareness and expressiveness is also restricted. Mona learnt, for example, to behave in a careful and controlled manner and to deny her own needs. This led to considerable problems in managing developmental tasks in the area of friendship and intimacy, which in turn contributed to the occurrence of a variety of disorders and interactional problems.

8.2 Schema Therapy assessment, psychoeducation and therapy

In this age group, almost all standard clinical disorders can be present. Particularly common are depression, obsessive-compulsive disorder and eating disorders. The development of personality disorders can also be found, or at least indicated, in this age group (Newton-Howes et al, 2015).

Schema Therapy for young adults differs from the approaches discussed previously in this book because it resembles, in many respects, the approach applied to adults. The diagnostic and therapeutic concepts are essentially the same as those used in Schema Therapy with adults, because the intellectual and verbal skills at this stage of life are already fully developed. There are, however, some limitations in emotional development at this age, and therefore the therapeutic relationship needs to provide support in perceiving and expressing emotions.

8.2.1 Indications, contraindications and diagnosis

As with patients of all ages, the following indications for Schema Therapy are required.

First, information is collected about the patient's main symptoms and problem areas, as well as about the patient's interaction with others. The case history is compiled. In addition, the clinician evaluates the patient's temperament and which developmental tasks have been successfully resolved or are pending, as this could provide clues to which basic needs have been met. Finally, as is the case with all psychotherapies, diagnostic features are part of the assessment stage, e.g. assessment of intelligence and possible performance impairment (like dyslexia), as well as the patient's personal and social resources. A list of diagnostic test methods used in developmental psychopathology can be found in Carr (2015). The diagnostic guidelines for diagnosis of and therapy for psychiatric disorders in adolescents should be observed (German Association for Child and Youth Psychiatry and Psychotherapy, 2007). The current interviews, questionnaires and inventories (e.g. SCID-II; First *et al*, 1997) for adults can be deployed with increasing age.

A phase of self-observation of the problematic behaviour (symptoms and interaction styles) makes sense at this point. In Schema Therapy we pay special attention to feelings and needs. Self-observation for adolescents offers even more than in adult therapy. In addition to identifying the problem behaviour and naming it, self-observation offers a chance to increase motivation for change and compliance. As the young adult observes and records the 'problem', an awareness of the impact of this results. Often motivation is an issue when treating young adults. As Geerdink *et al* (2012) suggest, the motivation to change is often less than one would find with adults, because adolescents have not suffered for as long and are prone to experience quick attitude changes. A short introductory period of problem observation and description is advisable, without the need to reduce the problem behaviour as quickly as possible. This offers you, the clinician, a chance to meet a short-term goal with the patient, building up the desire for change and providing time for the therapeutic relationship to develop.

In addition to the patient's report, and depending on the age and needs of the patient, the primary significant others (parents, partner, friends or teachers etc) should be consulted as a form of third party collaboration. Here you need to make sure you respect the patient's needs. This means that any external collaboration should be discussed and agreed with the patient in advance, as well as the form these conversations should take (whether in the patient's presence or not) and what topics should be discussed.

Case example
Case (medical) history provided by a third party

At an early stage a conversation was planned with Mona's mother, which was primarily used as a third party case history. Both parties expressed the wish that the mother be consulted alone after the therapist and Mona had prioritised a list of possible topics. It was important that the therapist remained impartial in the conversation, while reassuring Mona that all points and concerns would be addressed in therapy. Future conversations would occur with Mona present, as per her wish.

Mona's mother told us how difficult her relationship with Mona had become. She was very worried about her eating disorder, had informed herself about the effects and constantly tried to get Mona to eat. This led to accusations and fights with Mona, which she later regretted. She did not understand why Mona had become so closed off and why she couldn't get through to her anymore.

In the conversation, Mona's mother appeared to be totally overwhelmed. She began to cry and displayed a lot of helplessness. She reported that she was considering getting help herself because she was not able to deal with the problem any longer and didn't want to make the problem worse. Mona's mother was also very keen to help her because she believed that she failed to understand Mona's animosity toward the previous partner.

After the third party corroboration is completed, the first hypotheses, based on the patient's biography, current concerns, and the presenting and maintaining factors of the presenting problem, can be formulated. If there are indicators that basic needs have not been met and if the problems have a biographical component, then Schema Therapy should be considered. In addition, if there has been stagnation in the therapeutic process, or if the case is chronic or a personality disorder is present, Schema Therapy is also indicated.

In many parts of the world there are reports of Schema Therapy being used successfully with adolescents and young adults, although systematic evaluation of outcomes has not occurred on a large scale. This is because youths from the age of 17, and some even at 16, are frequently treated as outpatients in adult clinical settings. In these settings many of the adult symptoms and indicators are also used to assess young adults, particularly traits associated with personality disorders (e.g. borderline personality disorder) and chronic axis 1 disorder symptoms, e.g. anxiety, obsessive-compulsive disorders and eating disorders (Zens & Jacob, 2012). Further applications of Schema Therapy have been developed for non-acute addictive disorders (Kersten, 2012) and as a gentle approach to trauma work. In addition, Schema Therapy has been successfully developed for group therapy (Farrell & Shaw, 2012). In The Netherlands there are positive progress reports of the use of Schema Therapy for young adults in forensic settings (Geerdink *et al*, 2012).

Contraindications to this treatment are, just as in the treatment of adults, when a focus is needed on managing physical safety in acute disorders (e.g. life-threatening weight in the case of anorexia nervosa or acute suicidality), which should be treated with appropriate crisis-focused therapy techniques and medical intervention. For patients with psychotic symptoms, severe substance abuse problems, significant cognitive impairment or distinct early developmental disorders, Schema Therapy is not recommended, although there are increasingly positive reports anecdotally from Schema Therapists working with these conditions.

The most important consideration is whether the patient will benefit from the main components of Schema Therapy, particularly the emotion-focused approaches and the intensive therapeutic relationship. A key contraindication is if there is still contact with a perpetrator which a young person cannot escape from without institutional help, especially if they are not yet of age. In this case safety conditions must be created so that a reduction of defensive, symptomatic patterns of behaviour is possible.

The treatment of young adults using Schema Therapy puts the mode approach at the forefront because it is intuitive and easy to administer, and provides a young person with a good understanding of their underlying problem. This concept is fully described by Arntz and Jacob (2012), focusing on the 18 modes, reflecting states that are triggered by schema activation. In order to ascertain further relevant modes, the SMI (Lobbestael *et al*, 2010) can be used.

It is also helpful to gain an overview of the relevant schemas, utilising the Young Schema Questionnaire. This can suggest a possible 'emotional tone' of a particular mode and help to provide a suitable approach for therapy, particularly limited re-parenting. According to our experience, young adults are often able to complete the Schema Therapy questionnaires on their own (YSQ). Nevertheless, the therapist should offer help, especially if problems with understanding or motivation are expected. Before administering questionnaires it is helpful to assess the extent to which a young person's coping modes may interfere with their ability to effectively self-report on schemas. For example, for patients who tend toward overcompensation, the Young Compensation Inventory (YCI – Young, 1995) may be more helpful. Similarly, if there are strong avoidance modes, the Young-Rygh Avoidance Inventory (YRAI – Young, 1994b) may be more instructive. Also, in order to assess the parents' behaviour, the Young Parenting Inventory

(YPI – Young, 1994a) may provide additional information. These approaches should be decided from case to case. Completing all inventories can be too taxing and demotivating. Moreover, loyalty conflicts can often emerge when filling in the YPI, especially when there is enmeshment with parents.

Table 8.1: Overview of modes (compare Arntz & Jacob, 2012)

Functional Healthy modes

Clever-Wise mode (or Healthy Young Adult for this age)
Caring Parent mode (internalised care-giving mode)
Good Protector mode
Happy Child mode

Dysfunctional Child modes

Vulnerable (lonely, abandoned, abused) Child mode
Angry, Enraged, Impulsive, Spoiled or Undisciplined Child mode

Dysfunctional Parent and Peer modes

Demanding Parent/peer mode (parents or peers who expect high achievement or are emotionally demanding).
Punitive Parent/peer mode (parents or peers who harshly criticise or abuse the child)

Dysfunctional Coping mode

Surrender	Compliant Surrenderer mode
	Currying Favour mode
Avoidance	Detached Protector mode
	Dissociated Protector mode
	Angry Protector mode
	Detached Self-Soother mode
	Regressive Protector mode
	Complaining Protector mode
	Hyperactive Protector mode
	Avoidant Protector mode
Overcompensation	Defiant-Oppositional mode
	Dominator mode
	Perfectionistic Controller mode
	Excessive Controller mode
	Self-Aggrandizer mode
	Dramatist mode
	Intimidator mode
	Bully and Attack mode
	Conning mode
	Predator mode

Typical schemas with 17–23-year-old patients

Psychotherapy questionnaires and case descriptions of patients between the ages of 17 and 23 who took part in group Schema Therapy in an inpatients clinic between 2011 and 2012 were analysed. These patients had various diagnoses, e.g. depression, eating disorders, social phobia, compulsive disorders and comorbid personality disorders. The results showed that the most common schemas, independent of disorder, were: *Abandonment, Defectiveness/Shame, Failure, Emotional Inhibition, Entitlement/Grandiosity* and *Insufficient Self-Discipline*.

- **Abandonment/Instability:** This schema can be expressed as fears that cover the spectrum from the age-appropriate need/desire to separate from the parental home to the fear of being alone or being left alone. 'I have to go but don't know where I'll end up!' is how a 20-year-old succinctly describes this conflict. Often a young person with this schema has the impression that you cannot rely on anyone or anything, and a pronounced fear of loss and rejection.

- **Defectiveness/Shame:** The typical adolescent question 'How do others perceive me and what do they think of my weaknesses?' and the sharpened self-monitoring of potential deficiencies are exaggerated with this schema. Problems in the family are attributed to oneself, especially in high-conflict families. This also occurs because the natural desire to have a 'Good Parent introject' has no accepting and compassionate parent to model from and emotional detachment is not yet complete. Perceptions that one needs to meet high ideals of perfection (such as appearance and success, fuelled by popular media) can also encourage the development of this schema (as well as the next).

- **Failure:** At this age, choice and long-term prospects are central to identity. This is, for young adults, related to the question of whether they have sufficient skills and capacities to cope with these tasks, which can lead to enormous fear and pressure.

- **Emotional Inhibition:** Late adolescents can often experience strong pressure to behave 'correctly' (first within the family, but also with the peer group). The fear of embarrassing oneself, appearing weak or being the centre of attention can lead to explicit avoidance of emotional expression. When this schema is activated the young person strives, for example, to appear untouchable in order to prevent others seeing insecurity. However, the more the young person avoids 'being him or

- **Entitlement/Grandiosity:** Frustrated basic needs for guidance and boundaries are commonly at the centre here. 'Being normal' or being a 'team player' are seen as unattractive for those with this schema because they often have a narrative of being better than others and deserving better. This schema can also be an over-compensatory counterweight to *Defectiveness/Shame*.

- **Insufficient Self-Discipline:** This schema results in young adults having low frustration tolerance as well as a tendency to give up quickly when experiencing distressing feelings, often countering those feelings with problematic or impulsive behaviour.

One limitation of these results is that the generalisability is restricted by the relatively small numbers of predominantly female patients that made up our sample.

8.2.2 Psychoeducation

Excursus

Educating the patient about Schema Therapy is especially important with more complex disorders, so that the patient can make a connection between symptoms, schemas and modes. Following this comes a more detailed Schema Therapy psychoeducation. It is not always necessary to go through the schema questionnaire fully with the patient. This really depends on the patient's current level of motivation, their intelligence, the extent of the disorder, the number of presenting schemas and the patient's stage of development. However, it often makes sense to explain and discuss the main schemas that are apparent from the assessment process, along with the core emotional needs frustration model. This creates a deeper understanding of the disorder and how it occurred, and a shared nomenclature, which can then foster motivation and trust in the therapeutic relationship. In doing so the therapist often also receives further biographical information.

At this point the first pieces of information about the mode model are shared, i.e. what a mode is and how it relates to schemas. During this process it should be pointed out which modes could be involved – for example, child modes or coping modes. If the SMI has been completed then those results can be incorporated into the framework of the individual case conceptualisation.

Furthermore, the late adolescent can also be given general information concerning the course of therapy, the importance of their cooperation and their rights. Patients' questions should be answered extensively in order to create an atmosphere of trust and to encourage the greatest possible sense of autonomy in the relationship.

8.3 Schema Therapy in action: age-appropriate therapeutic relationships and therapeutic interventions

As already mentioned, Schema Therapy with young adults is focused on the mode model as this can be appreciated independent of intellectual and cognitive abilities. In doing so the approach is similar in most respects to the Schema Therapy treatment of adults, as described by Arntz and Jacob (2012).

Building on the assessment process, the focus of early sessions is on the formation of a stable therapeutic relationship and increasing motivation. The therapist creates an individual case conceptualisation, resulting in a Schema Therapy treatment plan, which is collaboratively shared with the patient. This allows the patient to gain an intellectual and emotional understanding of their presenting problem/s and helps them to distance themselves better from those symptoms as a result. It is easier for young adults to name and allocate the root of problematic thoughts, feelings, body sensations and behavioural patterns because of the temporal proximity of the schema origins. Young adults quickly learn to recognise when schemas or modes are activated in situations and how to observe their thoughts, feelings and behaviours. Gaining such understanding at this early stage of the young person's development allows the patient to learn how to care for themselves and how to take a self-monitoring perspective, and thereby to focus on building corrective experiences early.

There is a special opportunity presented by Schema Therapy with young adults. This age group has greater flexibility and openness, which allows for a much larger change potential. At the same time, schemas and modes haven't become as rigid through ongoing reinforcement in everyday experiences. There are also more opportunities to change environmental factors, such as living conditions, than is possible with older patients. Often there is a good chance of a career (re-) orientation and a capacity to shape long-term relationship dynamics. However, there is also a challenge that comes with this age group: emotional distress often fluctuates, which can complicate the therapeutic treatment.

8.3.1 Case conceptualisation and treatment plan

The first step after diagnosis and psychoeducation is the creation of an individual mode based on case conceptualisation in which the thoughts, feelings, body sensations and behaviours that are disorder-relevant are assigned to the various modes (according to Arntz & Jacob, 2012; also dependent on age and stage of development: section 2.3). Even if there are generic mode models (overview in Loebbestael *et al*, 2007) for personality traits or disorders, the mode model should be formulated individually. In our experience modes are less fixed and rigid in this age group than in older people. During this process, both the dysfunctional parts (e.g. dysfunctional Parent or Peer modes, or maladaptive coping modes) and the functional modes (e.g. Happy Child, Healthy Young Adult) are identified.

For clarity, no more than five to seven modes should be named at the beginning of treatment. Further distinctions and variations can be made in the course of treatment. When identifying modes it's often best to begin with a concrete situation to identify which modes were triggered, and then make generalisations about typical mode dynamics in the young person's presentation. We also recommend beginning with the Vulnerable Child mode and then the Parent and Peer modes, which then give a basis for a good understanding of the coping modes. Theoretically it is possible to begin with any mode but the therapist's approach needs to be clear and based on the treatment formulation. The process of understanding modes and intervening is always done in collaboration with the patient. It is often helpful to provide some visuals on, for example, a whiteboard. Nowadays, there are also many supplementary and additional materials available (see Jacob *et al*, 2015 and also sections 9.3 and 12.1).

Figure 8.1 depicts a mode model that is useful for all common disorders and can be used to portray an individual case conceptualisation.

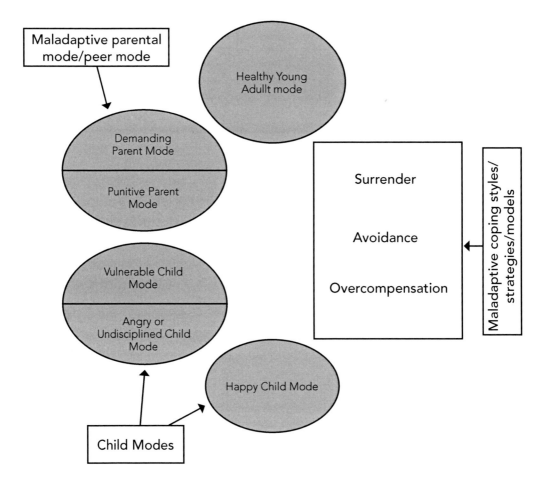

Figure 8.1: The general mode model

Mode dialogues

To assist with conceptualising the case, mode dialogues can be used to both understand and explore each mode. This is a helpful way to identify problem behaviour as a coping mode. By interviewing the 'coping mode' the corresponding chair can be attributed with feelings, thoughts and responsibility for behaviour. The patient and therapist can recognise which thoughts, feelings and needs are tolerated, kept at bay or avoided by the coping mode. These thoughts, feelings and needs are then assigned to the other chairs, e.g. fear or sadness as the Vulnerable Child and shame or underlying feelings of pressure as Punitive or Demanding Parent or Peer modes. Inner conflicts are externalised and the patient can, together with the therapist, attain a more healthy perspective. Mode dialogues (see mode work with chairs in section 12.3.9) are often very helpful for this age group. In our experience, it usually does not require much convincing for a young person to engage in chair work, because the playful components of experiential interventions connect to a young person's sense of fun.

Another way to deepen understanding is using diagnostic imagery. Here the patient is encouraged to connect a currently distressing situation to a childhood memory. This helps the patient gain an emotional understanding of their schemas and modes. Of course, it is important to be aware that young adults sometimes have difficulties with these kinds of experiential exercises, especially at the beginning of treatment, as they can feel watched and thereby embarrassed. The therapist can provide options such as not facing the patient or give the option of the patient keeping their eyes open or focusing their attention on a point in the room (see 13.2 for further information).

If there is resistance to the use of experiential techniques then pressure should not be put on the patient, as this could endanger further therapeutic work and the therapeutic relationship.

Case conceptualisation

Diagnostically speaking, anorexia nervosa has been present for approximately a year, along with body image disorder and a moderate level of depression with a background of emotional instability. Mona reports a lack of self-worth, mood fluctuations and deep 'emotional holes' (sadness, helplessness, guilt, anger) and fear of loss in relation to her partner, as well as an inability to establish healthy boundaries. Mona also misuses alcohol and cannabis and occasionally engages in superficial self-harming. As a result of the sexual assault by her mother's ex-partner, Mona feels dirty, disgusting and worthless. She does not experience flashbacks. Mona also reports high levels of self-loathing. Mona explains that the restrictive eating patterns allow her to prove to herself and others that she is able to deal with something and can endure difficulty easily. She is disappointed with her parents, and particularly her mother, but at the same time longs for their attention and love. She also feels guilty because of the heartache she brings her mother, who has always 'had such a difficult life'. Mona's goal is to help her mother. In the assessment, her mother reports not being able to get through to her daughter anymore, not being able to understand Mona's problems or their causes and feeling totally helpless. She says that although she would like to tell Mona how she feels, it would not change anything.

The results of the YSQ showed that the main schemas were: *Mistrust/Abuse; Abandonment/Instability; Defectiveness/Shame; Emotional Deprivation; Subjugation; Self-Sacrifice;* and *Unrelenting Standards/Hyper-Criticalness* and *Punitiveness*. Because of Mona's initial lack of ability to deal with pressure and her low level of motivation, further questionnaires were not carried out.

Mona's distorted self-image, feelings of worthlessness, 'emotional holes' (sadness, powerlessness, guilt) and fears of abandonment are conceptualised as the Vulnerable, Abused Child mode. Based on her reports, anger is attributed to the Angry Child mode. Self-degradation and self-loathing are ascribed to the Punitive mode, while the feelings of having to take responsibility (and the resulting *Self-Sacrifice* schema) can be seen as a consequence of the Demanding Parent mode. She regularly subjugates herself to her partner ('bearing' sexual intimacy), suggestive of the Compliant Surrenderer mode. The substance abuse and self-harm are identified as avoidant modes (Detached Self-Soother mode). In addition, she tends toward overcompensation in the form of restricting her eating (Perfectionistic Controller). Her willingness to undergo therapy and to continue to open up is conceptualised as Healthy Young Adult mode.

During case formulation with this age group, it can be more meaningful for the patient to use their own names for the modes. As long as they are conceptually suitable, these names can be used throughout treatment. After the collaborative formulation of the mode model, the primary origins of each mode, the sustaining factors and the influence of triggering events and situations are determined.

Young adults can generally adopt this model very well. They often find it easy to identify with the beliefs and emotions connected to modes and, due to the temporal proximity to the experiences which have contributed to schema creation, find the formulation fits their experience in a very validating way. Therefore, Schema Therapy approaches help the patient to feel understood. It also provides opportunity to collaboratively develop ideas about what needs to happen in order to improve their symptoms, what they require in a given mode and what skills are needed to develop more Healthy Young Adult mode.

Conducting the treatment plan discussion

T = *Therapist*; **P** = *Patient (Mona)*

T: Let's have a look at the model again. There is the 'Inner Offender' (Punitive Parent mode), the one who does and says mean things and is full of hate. We know from people who have experienced sexual abuse and other distressing things that they often blame themselves and hate themselves for it, even though another person was responsible for the abuse.

P: (softly) Yes … it was exactly like that with Frank *(the ex-partner of the mother)*.

T: How do you feel when this inner voice speaks to you?

P: Really horrible. Helpless, small, weak, disgusting, at everyone's mercy … all that… (swallows).

T: And here we see the Little Mona on the whiteboard (Vulnerable, Abused Child mode) who often feels sad, helpless and powerless, but also dirty, worthless and disgusting. It is no wonder she feels like that when she hears this voice so often.

P: No … not really.

T: Together we have looked at how Little Mona tried to protect herself. She ran to her backyard (Avoidant mode), put up with things she didn't like (Surrender mode) or 'controlled' whatever she could (Overcompensation). And that was a good thing because otherwise she would not have got through all of those horrible situations. But we want to strengthen this part of you – the Healthy and Confident Mona (Healthy Young Adult mode). What do the other modes need, so that this part can get bigger? What must happen to them? Do you have an idea? What does 'Little Mona' really need?

P: (hesitating) Ah well … she needs lots of reassurance, that she will not be left alone. And perhaps less pressure? So that she can do what she would like to do.

T: Exactly. In order for Little Mona to be less frightened she needs reassurance. And the voice that demands so much, the 'Pressure Voice' (Demanding Parent mode), must become quieter?

P: Yes. And I would also like not to have to feel so terribly dirty all the time.

T: That means somehow the voice, the 'Offender' (Punitive mode) must disappear.

P: Yes, that would be great (disbelieving).

T: And for us to bring this about we must find 'Little Mona' and protect her. And provide assistance to the 'grown-up and Confident Mona' so that she can protect Little Mona herself eventually. And to combat and change this inner voice together we must get past the coping modes which are standing here on the right-hand side. They are blocking the way to 'Little Mona' and preventing us from protecting and helping her to feel better. Does that make sense to you?

P: Yes.

8.3.2 The therapeutic relationship

Establishing the therapeutic relationship with young adult patients is quite different to working with adults using Schema Therapy. Since the process of development is not yet complete, the Inner Parent modes have not yet been fully formed (Geerdink *et al*, 2012). As a result the therapist will usually fulfil the function of guidance and norm provider.

The acquisition of necessary skills to enable autonomy, the development of an identity, attachment and intimacy are of central importance for this age group. Therefore, as work progresses, the therapist needs to be able to adapt to assist with these developmental tasks.

In addition, as already described for this age group, there are complex stresses associated with increased autonomy within a family environment, which can reduce motivation and hinder compliance with therapy. This is often made worse by the person's immature frontal cortex, which reduces impulse control (Spitzer, 1999) and results in emotionally driven behaviour.

The quality of the therapeutic relationship – how safe and accepted the younger patient feels – is central to the success of the therapy. As safety grows, so does the ability to work collaboratively with patients. The connection between therapeutic rapport and progress is even more central in this demographic compared to working with adults, as the developmental stages are not yet complete and may be impaired by a lack of therapist attunement.

The key element of the therapeutic relationship is to meet the need of 'partial parental care' or 'limited re-parenting'. It is therefore useful to pick a form of address that helps to create an atmosphere that accentuates the position of an important significant other and the special aspects of care and support for the young adult.

We agree with Geerdink *et al* (2012) that it is helpful and positive in therapy with this age group to use self-disclosure, if used for a therapeutic purpose within the formulation and treatment plan. Obviously, sharing the therapist's own experiences related to different circumstances that do not fit the patient's world is of little help and should be avoided.

Limit-setting and empathic confrontation

In Schema Therapy, one of the therapist's roles is to model suitable adult behaviours and reactions. Therefore, basic needs which have been neglected are discussed and fulfilled in therapy ('limited re-parenting'). The limited parenting role of the therapist – which is common to working with adults in therapy –

comprises not only providing an attachment figure and a sense of security, but also providing guidance and 'limit-setting' in the case of unsuitable behaviour. However, care needs to be taken, considering the developmental stage these patients are at. Sometimes empathic confrontation is necessary; however, it is important to make sure that those moments always encompass a caring approach. All of this demands a high degree of empathy.

The Vulnerable Child mode should be cared for within the therapeutic relationship, not only in the therapeutic interaction but in the framework of all interventions. Each intervention should be understood in terms of how it meets a core emotional need/s. The Angry Child mode needs validation, addressing the distress and basic needs which lie behind it. The Angry Child mode, like the Impulsive Child mode, must also be confronted about the negative behavioural impact, and healthy boundaries set. Dysfunctional coping styles are recognised for their initially protective role. However, it should be clearly stated that getting in touch with the Vulnerable Child mode is essential to treatment and that the part played by dysfunctional coping modes needs to be reduced. It may be that a patient behaves in a very damaging or obstructive way in therapy when in their coping mode. In such a case therapists can carefully, but clearly, empathically limit this mode.

There is a fine line in the therapist's stance between nurture and support, on the one hand, and setting boundaries and giving consequences, on the other. On the one hand, support, encouragement and care is foundational to emotional safety in therapy. Yet on the other hand, boundaries and guidance, as well as highlighting and carrying out consequences if rules are broken, are also necessary to encourage emotional maturity. One must always consider the developmental aspects, i.e. that young adults often behave impulsively, which can mean breaking rules and agreements. By emphasising understanding and care, the patient can be empathically confronted and at the same time made aware of the need to take on age-appropriate adult responsibility – e.g. 'It's really important that I understand what you are feeling and needing, but when you are shouting, that gets in the way of me being able to hear you' or 'I know Impulsive James only wants to come to sessions when he feels like it, but Little James needs to have this time with me'. In this way the Healthy Young Adult mode is continually addressed and fostered and is able to get its needs met more effectively.

The empathic framework provided by limited re-parenting also addresses one of the challenges of empathic confrontation and limit-setting: the therapist being lumped together with parents, teachers and carers as those who 'hamper' the young person's independence. However, an empathic framework and a reminder that more Healthy Young Adult behaviour will lead to emotional needs being met provides motivation for accepting limits and reframing challenge as support for deeper needs: 'I'm not going to tell you what to do, but I also want to make sure Little Angela doesn't keep missing out on what she needs because that impulsive part of you keeps creating drama, so she still doesn't get heard. What does your wise side think about this?'

Another challenge in working with this age cohort is that the therapist can end up as a rival to other parents or attachment figures. The therapist is advised to keep sufficient distance in the areas where caregivers are able to meet the young adult's needs, so as to not provoke a loyalty conflict. Also, when conceptualising and working on the Parent modes, a thoughtful use of therapeutic terminology is needed. If the young person's Parent modes have their origin in the current caregivers, it is important to find a way to deal with those introjects without creating an unhealthy alignment with the therapist against the caregiver. Even so, it is very important in the setting of the therapeutic relationship to protect the young adult from their inner dysfunctional 'Parent or Peer modes' and to limit or disempower these. One way to do this is to identify the unhelpful aspects of the caregiver's relational style and challenge that behaviour, while acknowledging the healthy aspects of the relationship. Helping the patient to 'take the good and leave the bad' in their relationships with their parents/caregivers can alleviate the problem of the therapist becoming a 'rival parent'.

An additional challenge for this age group is that parents and others who are perpetrators may have ongoing contact with the young person. They may be in the same house, or the young adult may be dependent on them (financially, practically, etc). Therefore, care needs to be taken with terminology when doing mode work. It is also important that the therapist be mindful of how much therapeutic progress is possible if there is ongoing damage occurring. Working with the parents is of central importance to provide the young person with a more healthy and safe environment.

Case example

'Limited re-parenting' visualisation

Mona talked in the therapy session about something that had happened at school that had upset her greatly. A substitute teacher had told her off in a very harsh manner. This caused her to completely switch off inwardly and stop listening. She subsequently burst into tears. She had been very upset since that time and had played truant. During the following visualisation (using an affect bridge), she recalled an experience at 14 years old where her mother's ex-partner had shouted at and insulted her. She felt very afraid, powerless and unprotected. At her request, the therapist entered the scene, stood beside 'Little Mona' protectively and threatened to call the police and social services. As a result, Mona felt relieved and safe. The therapist asked if there was anything that 'Little Mona' needed. Mona asked that the therapist tell her mother, which the therapist then did in imagery. The therapist took 'Little Mona' to her mother in the kitchen, where 'Little Mona' told her mother everything. The therapist confirmed 'Little Mona's' report and told the mother about how her partner had been treating 'Little Mona', demanding that she takes immediate measures to protect her daughter. Then she took 'Little Mona' into the garden and reassured and comforted her.

8.3.3 Age-specific Schema Therapy techniques with young adults

Starting with the case conceptualisation, which provides a shared understanding of the presenting problem and a rationale for treatment, the patient begins the process of externalising the problem. They develop an intellectual and emotional understanding of their issues which provides perspective. They increasingly learn to recognise and name these modes in their everyday life. These early therapeutic steps already strengthen the Healthy Young Adult mode. Throughout therapy the Healthy Young Adult mode is a focus; the development of functional behaviours and the language used are overt in fostering and promoting this mode.

The dysfunctional coping strategies are usually targeted first. The therapist and the patient discuss the advantages and disadvantages of these strategies in order to understand their role and then reduce their activation both in and out of session. Working with the patient to reduce maladaptive coping modes in everyday life needs careful consideration given that there may be negative environmental factors, such as critical peers or bullying in the workplace. Therefore the clinician needs to evaluate how much Healthy Young Adult mode the patient has, and whether that mode has sufficient resources to manage these situations. As the coping modes are reduced, the Healthy modes need to grow to meet needs more adaptively.

As there is progress in noticing and bypassing unhelpful coping modes in session, the patient is able to focus on the Vulnerable Child mode. The therapist is then able to activate this mode and use limited re-parenting and experiential techniques to provide a corrective experience within the therapeutic relationship. In order to limit or combat the often increasingly Punitive or Demanding/Guilt Inducing Parent or Peer modes and to further validate and meet the needs of the Vulnerable Child mode, intensive 'limited re-parenting' from the therapist is necessary in this phase. Because of the unfinished development of this age group, this therapy phase is particularly delicate. It is possible to create a corrective experience more quickly here than in older adults if there is a strong therapeutic relationship and authentic, attuned re-parenting. At the same time, invalidating therapeutic interventions, e.g. if the therapist is unclear or behaves dismissively, can be equally formative and can strengthen maladaptive schemas.

Mode-led goals

In summary, the following goals summarise Schema Therapy work with young adults:

- Dysfunctional coping strategies are empathically confronted, their advantages and disadvantages are discussed and their role in the present is assessed and replaced by Healthy Young Adult coping in therapy and everyday situations.

- The Vulnerable/Lonely/Abused Child modes are identified and their feelings and needs validated, supported and comforted. Therapy provides corrective experiences for these modes.

- Angry Child modes are given space to vent their anger. The underlying basic needs are validated and suitable expressions of anger are fostered in the patient.

- Impulsive Child modes are identified and the mode's feelings and needs are assessed as to their suitability and, if necessary, limited.

- Dysfunctional Parent or Peer modes are identified; their role is explained as well as limited and maybe partly combated (Punitive Parent modes are banished rather than partly combated).

- Functional modes (Happy Child mode and Healthy Young Adult mode) are strengthened and built up.

As already mentioned, Schema Therapy for young adults largely resembles adult therapy. Cognitive, emotion-focused and behavioural intervention strategies are thereby flexibly brought together into an overarching framework (Zens & Jacob, 2012). Schema Therapy provides a model to conceptualise and formulate with the patient, which then produces a treatment plan. This approach applies for the whole course of treatment as well as for the individual therapy sessions). Schema Therapy strategies are used within a therapeutic relationship that provides containment in which a patient can model and internalise healthy adult behaviour and experience corrective emotional experiences.

Cognitive techniques

Cognitive interventions are used to help the patient learn how to recognise and label modes. Particularly at the start of therapy, the therapist helps the patient make connections between mode triggering and thoughts, emotions and behaviours. Questions are asked about whether the mode is appropriate to the situation so that alternative behavioural strategies and cognitions can then be developed. As therapy progresses, cognitive strategies are used to consolidate new learning from experiential techniques. Generally speaking, all traditional approaches from cognitive therapy can be used. An important cognitive approach in the treatment of young adults is psychoeducation about the normal rights and needs of children, which can provide validation and relief for the Child modes. Thematically appropriate children's books can also be brought in as a support. In Schema Therapy schema diaries are used for self-observation and schema-memos or flashcards are developed as self-help instructions for triggering situations.

Inappropriate demands, guilt-inducing behaviour and punitiveness coming from the dysfunctional Parent or Peer modes and can be labelled as such and challenged cognitively with the goal of clearly limiting or combating their influence. Psychoeducation about appropriate behaviour of parents and peers is also an important cognitive intervention. Maladaptive coping modes are also explored cognitively, providing links to the modes and their survival benefit in the patient's history. Exploring the pros and cons of the coping modes is also helpful in developing motivation for change. Strengthening the understanding of what a Healthy Young Adult mode is and introducing more healthy thoughts assists in the goal of building the Healthy Young Adult mode and reducing the coping modes in the present.

Case example
Cognitive assessment of the 'control mode'

During one session Mona reported an increase in her restrictive eating habits. Together with the therapist, this behaviour was identified as an overcompensation mode. They collected the arguments that supported this strategy and wrote them on the whiteboard. From this exercise it became clear that Mona feels more protected when she displays this behaviour because she can control something within herself and she also has a certain amount of control over her environment. The therapist identified that the Control mode offers protection, which it had done for years, and asked Mona if there are any ways in which the mode does not protect her. She then asked about various areas of Mona's life that were being impacted by the Control mode, and from this a pros and cons list for the coping strategy was generated.

Experiential interventions

These techniques form one of the central parts of Schema Therapy. The young adult is assisted in becoming aware of their emotional needs and give them appropriate expression. Often sadness and helplessness as well as anger are all emotions that may have previously been disavowed. Two of the most important experiential techniques are mode dialogue (chair work) and imagery exercises (Arntz & Weertmann, 1999; see also section 13.2). Role playing can also help to activate emotions. It is important when using experiential techniques that the patient's affect is aroused, resulting in Vulnerable/Angry/Abused Child modes. These Child modes need to be activated to achieve therapeutic effect. These techniques are helpful when negative emotions arise, which can happen when triggered by the patient's outside world as well as during therapy itself. When these experiential techniques are used positive and healing experiences can then occur. However, if the patient is not willing to engage in emotion-focused techniques like chair work, they can be substituted with dolls, symbols or other items. Whichever technique is used, the clinician will need to ensure that a sufficiently intensive emotional activation occurs so that a therapeutic effect is realised.

The focus when working with the Vulnerable Child modes (including Lonely/Abused Child modes) is meeting needs. Initially, Angry Child modes should be allowed to vent anger in order to correct early experiences, when often anger was repressed. Dysfunctional coping modes should be addressed often through mode dialogue, so that the patient can clearly feel their different parts. Dysfunctional Parent modes need to be weakened or banished using imagery and chair work. At this stage of development the young adult patient often finds it difficult to distinguish between the externalised and internalised parent voices, which means that the patient can end up feeling responsible for protecting an actual parent, even though the focus needs to be on the parental introject. Being open about the confusion and challenges of identifying Parent modes assists with this process.

Case example
Chair work to limit the demanding mode

Mona recounted a fight she had with her mother, where her mother tried to talk to Mona but Mona refused. Mona described feeling helpless in that situation, but mainly she felt 'wrong'. The therapist suggested a chair dialogue, which Mona agreed to after initial hesitancy. The feelings of helplessness and guilt were put on 'Little Mona's' chair and the demand 'talk to me' on the 'Demanding voice' chair (Demanding Parent mode). In between, a chair was put a bit closer to 'Little Mona' for the Healthy Young Adult Mona. At the start, Mona sat on the 'Demanding voice' chair and repeated its phrases. Next, in 'Little Mona's' chair, she talked about how she felt, experiencing fear, shame and feelings of guilt that suddenly arose. It became apparent that this experience was connected to earlier experiences when Mona felt responsible for the well-being of her mother. On the Healthy Young Adult chair Mona practised, initially with the help of the therapist, countering demands and putting in place some boundaries. She also comforted Little Mona and assured her that she is doing the right thing and that she is too little to be responsible.

This mode dialogue gave Mona better understanding and a lot of relief. In the subsequent sessions she herself said that she would like, with the therapist's help, to have a conversation with her mother in order to tell her about what had happened at that time. At the therapist's suggestion, this was prepared in a role play beforehand. Mona cried a lot in the process but described feeling as if a huge weight had been lifted off her shoulders.

Behavioural interventions

Behavioural techniques are mainly found in the final phase of Schema Therapy to build up and train the Healthy Young Adult mode. However, there is a role for earlier behavioural skills to interrupt damaging behaviours (e.g. skills training). Early in therapy many of the changes have been made on an emotional and cognitive level. When behavioural pattern breaking is being focused on, all CBT techniques can be used, such as social skills training or behavioural activation.

Child modes need to have needs met, by engaging in healthy relationship patterns as the Healthy Young Adult mode is built up and corrective experiences become more regular. As this occurs, coping styles become more and more superfluous. Patients learn to be less demanding of themselves and to refuse to punish themselves (reducing Demanding Parent and eliminating Punitive Parent mode).

Case example
Development of healthy eating habits

With increasing understanding of her modes and greater ability to meet needs in healthy ways, Mona expressed the desire to normalise her eating habits. However, she shared that, even though she wanted to change her restrictive eating, she felt she would not be able to free herself from her habit. Having said that, the thought of putting on a few more kilos no longer terrified her. Mona worked with a nutritionist and was quickly able to build up trust, and a nutrition plan was worked out. This was regularly discussed and revised. Emerging feelings and difficulties were regular themes in therapy. Mona succeeded in normalising her eating habits within a few months. At the same time, she was happy with her increase in weight and, observing herself on video, could rate her body in a clearer and more realistic manner (more Healthy Young Adult).

Parent work

The question of whether to involve the parents in therapy has first to be clarified by looking at the role they play in the patient's life and how ready and able they are to engage in the patient's therapy in a responsible, dependable and self-aware manner. If they are able to do that, then most young adults will happily agree to sessions with the parents when needed, or even to the therapist advising and explaining things to them alone (with the patient's awareness and consent).

As already described in the assessment process, the patient's needs should certainly be respected where additional conversations with parents or significant others are concerned. It is helpful to discuss beforehand if such conversations are helpful and if they should occur in the presence of the patient or with the significant others alone. The topics to be discussed must be well prepared in advance. Although the therapist can suggest particular topics, the decision always needs to rest with the patient. Also, it is beneficial while the sessions are running to have a signal that the patient can give to the therapist, e.g. non-verbally, that a topic should no longer be discussed if they are becoming uncomfortable.

During regular joint sessions with the parents we suggest using Schema Therapy terms and interventions. The whole family system can discuss the issues using the mode model. As many parents feel very helpless and can often feel guilty about their child's illness, it can be useful in joint sessions not only to illustrate the patient's problem behaviour with reference to the mode model, but also to show the parents' actions and reactions in mode terms (for further examples of education with illustrations see section 16.2). Parents can frequently identify themselves astonishingly well in mode terms and reframe their own behaviour toward the patient using mode language. These reflections can be very useful for the young adult because they aid understanding without needing to deny their own needs. It is not helpful to focus on the Parent modes in the joint sessions, as that topic involves too many vested interests to be easily managed therapeutically. If it is indicated, given the formulation and the parent's capacity, discussions of the patient's Parent modes can happen (following discussion with the patient) in additional individual sessions with the parents, or if there are significant issues then therapy for the patient's parent should occur separately.

Case example
Conversation with the mother

Mona wanted a joint session with her mother after she became aware of how impactful her feelings of responsibility and guilt were. She wanted to confront her mother with the abuse and the humiliation she had experienced at the hands of her mother's ex-partner. She also wanted to confront her mother over not believing her about the abuse. She wanted to have this conversation in therapy so that she could access the help and support from the therapist if needed. The confrontation was prepared for in role play. In the subsequent joint session, Mona spoke about her experiences and showed how hurt and angry she felt about the fact that her mother did not believe her. Her mother appeared very affected by it. She assured Mona that she now believed her and apologised for her behaviour, trying to comfort her, which proved successful after Mona's initial scepticism. At the end of the session the therapist advised them both to do something positive together. Mona said she would like to go and eat some ice cream with her mother and then go shopping. Following this conversation, mother and daughter became much closer. Further conversations appeared unnecessary and were not desired by Mona.

End of treatment

Because the therapeutic relationship with this age group can be a powerful corrective relational experience, there needs to be a careful tapering off of therapeutic contact. This topic must be addressed openly in order to reduce fear and avoid leaving the patient feeling abandoned. Sessions should be held less frequently and with wider intervals between conversations, telephone calls or contact via email, although the young adult should have the opportunity to contact the therapist if new problems arise.

In the closure phase, so-called transitional objects, i.e. symbols or unique items associated with the therapist or schema-memos concerning the end of therapy, are particularly helpful. A further option would be to record especially important and comforting things said by the therapist as MP3s/on the patient's phone for them to take home. Further help can include suitable self-help literature, e.g. Jacob *et al* (2015) or Young *et al* (1993).

8.4 Conclusion

The aim of treating young adults using Schema Therapy, similarly to treating adults, is to develop behavioural and cognitive strategies to disrupt schema and mode-dependent automatic reactions. In the process, biographical patterns regarding unmet emotional needs and the resulting schemas and modes are illustrated and the rigid connection of primary and secondary emotional networks is dissolved and/or relaxed. Besides the cognitive and behavioural elements of Schema Therapy, the experiential techniques and the therapeutic relationship itself play a major role. Limited re-parenting, limit-setting and empathic confrontation of the Demanding and Punitive modes and problem behaviours resulting from maladaptive coping modes are important elements in treatment. As a result, young adult patients are able to have corrective relationship experiences and satisfy basic needs relating to attachment and security, guidance, protection and control.

Even more than in therapy with adults, a therapeutic goal is to guide the young person through the developmental tasks which have not been completely resolved. One needs to be aware that the therapeutic relationship operates within a very sensitive developmental phase. The intellectual competencies are almost completely formed in young adults; however, the emotional development is not yet concluded, suggesting that the therapeutic relationship needs to support healthy development of emotional perception and expression. Here Schema Therapy provides avenues for the expression of emotions and mode activations, which can be more helpfully processed in therapy. Both positive and negative relationship experiences need to be managed with this awareness, in order to build a Healthy Young Adult mode competent to manage emotional needs.

Schema Therapy with this age group also differs from work with adults regarding when to provide corrective experiences. Young adults normally become aware of the causes of the problem earlier than adults and don't have a long sequence of various contributing and consolidating life events. Because of this, frustration of core emotional needs is countered at an earlier stage in therapy, allowing for schema healing sooner. The schema coping processes are addressed earlier and progress can be quicker, a suggestion confirmed through clinical experience.

In Germany, Schema Therapy is increasingly used with this age group, on an individual basis in outpatient clinics as well as in inpatient settings with individuals and groups. There are also many positive reports from the Netherlands, particularly from forensic settings (Geerdink *et al*, 2012). Due to the peculiarities of treating this age group, further research on Schema Therapy for young adults is desirable.

References

Arntz A & Jacob G (2012) *Schema Therapy in Practice*. Chichester: Wiley-Blackwell.

Arntz A & Weertmann A (1999) Treatment of childhood memories: theory and practice. *Behaviour Research and Therapy* **37** 715–740.

Carr A (2015) *The Handbook of Child and Adolescent Clinical Psychology: A Contextual Approach*. London: Routledge.

Erikson EH (1968) *Identity: Youth and Crisis*. New York: Norton.

Farrell JM & Shaw IA (2012) *Group Schema Therapy for Borderline Personality Disorder: A Step-by-Step Treatment Manual with Patient Workbook*. Chichester: Wiley.

First MB, Gibbon M, Spitzer RL & Benjamin LS (1997) *User's Guide for the Structured Clinical Interview for DSM-IV Axis II Personality Disorders: SCID-II*. American Psychiatric Pub.

Geerdink MT, Jongman EJ & Scholing A (2012) Schema Therapy in adolescents. In: M van Vreeswijk, J Broersen & M Nadort (Eds) *The Wiley-Blackwood Handbook of Schema Therapy. Theory, Research, and Practice*. Chichester: Wiley-Blackwell.

Grawe K (2017) *Neuropsychotherapy: How the Neurosciences Inform Effective Psychotherapy*. London: Routledge.

Havighurst R (1972) *Development Tasks and Education*. New York: David McKay.

Jacob G, Genderen H & Seebauer L (2015) *Breaking Negative Thinking Patterns*. Chichester: Wiley.

Kersten T (2012) Schema Therapy for personality disorders and addiction. In: M van Vreeswijk, J Broersen and M Nadort (Eds) *The Wiley-Blackwell Handbook of Schema Therapy: Theory, Research, and Practice*. Chichester: Wiley.

Lobbestael J et al (2010) The reliability and validity of the short Schema Mode Inventory (SMI). *Behavioral and Cognitive Psychotherapy* **38** 437–458.

Newton-Howes G, Clark LA & Chanen A (2015) Personality disorder across the life course. *The Lancet* **385** (9969) 727–734.

Offer D, Ostrov E & Howard K (1981) The mental health professional's concept of the normal adolescent. *Archives of General Psychiatry* **38** 149–152.

Spitzer M (1999) *The Mind Within the Net: Models of Learning, Thinking, and Acting*. New York: MIT Press.

Young JE (1994a) *Young Parenting Inventory*. New York: Schema Therapy Institute.

Young JE (1994b) *Young-Rygh Avoidance Inventory*. New York: Cognitive Therapy Center of New York.

Young JE (1995) *Young Compensation Inventory*. New York: Cognitive Therapy Center of New York.

Young JE & Klosko JS (1993) *Reinventing Your Life*. New York: Plume Books.

Young JE, Klosko JS & Weishaar ME (2003) *Schema Therapy: A Practitioner's Guide*. New York: Guilford Press.

Young JE, Klosko JS & Weishaar M (2005) *Schematherapie*. Paderborn: Junfermann.

Zens C & Jacob G (2012) Schematherapie bei Persönlichkeitsstörungen. In: HH Stavemann (Ed) *KVT Update*, pp159–178. Weinheim: Beltz.

Chapter 9: Basic Principles of Schema Therapy

Christof Loose, Peter Graaf & Ruth A. Holt

9.1 Therapeutic relationship as an essential feature in Schema Therapy

In each form of therapy, relationship building plays an important role. For example, in CBT, which is focused on symptom-related treatment, a working alliance between therapist and patient is needed. However, Schema Therapy elevates the therapeutic relationship to the position of a main agent of change. Young and colleagues (2003, p177) suggest that the 'schema therapist views the therapy relationship as a vital component of schema assessment and change'. Compared with traditional CBT the Schema Therapist seeks to develop a deeper relationship that is designed to meet emotional needs for a limited time and purpose: Limited Re-Parenting. In Schema Therapy the therapist seeks to provide an emotional, experiential and regulating space in order to access the Vulnerable/Lonely/Abused Child. The therapeutic relationship required for Schema Therapy therefore makes more intense relationship building necessary.

9.1.1 Relationship building with the patient

Since children do not have a fully developed understanding of their own personality, clinical symptoms such as anxiety, depression, conduct disorder, ADHD, and so on are perceived as part of their sense of self. For example, a therapist could say to a child with ADHD: 'I want to help you with your attention deficit problems, impulsivity, and restlessness, but apart from that I think you're great and you can stay the way you are.' However, that child can hear: 'I want to change you', because he experiences these behaviour patterns as a part of himself (Ego-Syntonic). Thus, the child can view the offer of treatment as a kind of ruse: although my therapist says he wants to help me to reduce *problem xy*, he pushes himself – without being asked – into other areas of my life (e.g. family, social, emotional, cognitive aspects). Even if this is not a conscious thought, there can be a diffuse, implicit feeling of being disregarded and encroached upon, frustrating the child's needs for autonomy and self-determination. Formulating goals (such as the reduction of ADHD symptoms) – no matter how well intentioned – can therefore be unconsciously interpreted as an attack on the innermost part of the child. This can, often unconsciously, lead to a cautious attitude, a lack of compliance and even termination of treatment. Such behaviour could be expressed as a failure to complete therapeutic homework, persistent lateness or cancelling of appointments or silent behaviour in therapy.

An additional problem in child and adolescent psychotherapy is the fact that it is normally the adult caregivers that see a need for therapy in the child, resulting in only external motivation (see Chapter 8.1). Therapy may already have been threatened as a form of punishment, especially with externalising behaviours (as well as some internalising issues): 'If you cannot behave yourself, we're going to a therapist!' If this is the case, the already charged image of child psychotherapy ('Only crazy people have to go there') is additionally damaged because therapy has been declared as a negative consequence for failure. The core psychological needs of the child for autonomy, self-determination and avoiding discomfort are violated here, and the need to seek consistency results in a child beginning to integrate an unhelpful sense of self ('Am I crazy? What makes me crazy/wrong?'). The more important need for connection with parents can also be undermined, as the child concludes that he is now supposed to work on his problems with a stranger. Self-doubting thoughts like 'my parents can't stand me anymore' or 'I'm too hard for my parents to cope with' may act as an assault on the child's concept of self-efficacy and family integrity.

Repairing these impressions and creating safety are important foci when building the therapy relationship. The therapy room has to be a 'safe place' and the therapist a warm, caring parental presence, so that the underlying causes, and not just the symptoms, can be comfortably worked on in safety. This requires the child to have a high degree of trust, especially when there are attachment injuries, insecure attachments in place or trauma. Roediger (2009) speaks of the therapeutic environment in Schema Therapy as providing a 'laboratory of subsequent maturation', i.e. the therapist seeks to meet the core emotional needs of the child against the background of frustrated needs (the concept of limited re-parenting).

Limited re-parenting

During assessment and treatment the Schema Therapist should repeatedly ask themselves what kind of re-parenting this client requires. Given the child generally still has daily contact with parents, the therapist can also use these 'resources'. A significant goal in therapy is therefore that the parents are given support to begin to more effectively meet the needs of the child. The therapist must be aware that unmet needs from the past can only be partially satisfied. If the parent or caregiver is not able to learn to do that (for whatever reason), it is the therapist's job to do this using 'limited re-parenting'. It is, however, important to ensure that professional boundaries are maintained in the relationship between the therapist and the client. If the mother or father has withheld physical affection, it is not appropriate for the therapist to provide direct physical affection in the context of limited re-parenting. Instead, the therapist can reflect how precious and lovely the child is through verbal and non-verbal communication rather than physical affection, or use puppets and dolls to act out physical affection such as hugging, as appropriate.

Therapist requirements

Young and colleagues (2003) suggest that a Schema Therapist needs high levels of empathy, warmth, acceptance and authenticity, creating an emotional connection and building rapport with the client. We would like to add patience to that list. Particularly when working with children whose caregivers may be demanding, a therapist may be tempted to aim for quick behaviour change. However, the therapist needs to be mindful of the child's environment and incorporate the high level of pressure (Demanding Critic mode) coming from the parent into the formulation. The therapist should also recognise the limits of their therapeutic abilities, though, and be aware that insufficient trust between therapist and client can reduce the effectiveness of all interventions and undermine the therapeutic process. When 'strategies' are rushed, even well-proven approaches (e.g. positive reinforcement) can fail, fuelling negative expectations in the family (e.g. 'we already know about sticker charts, they don't work'). A trusting and supportive relationship with the child, once established, opens the door to all other Schema Therapy interventions.

Strengths-based work

Particularly with children and adolescents, strengths-based approaches, highlighting achievements or already achieved skills, have been found to be beneficial (Tedeschi & Kilmer, 2005). Beginning therapy with this approach combats some of the mistrust previously discussed and begins an alternate narrative. The strengths-based approach says to therapists: 'Immerse yourself in the wonderful world of your client! Let yourself be inspired by what the child is already able to do and what they have already learned.' Therefore, once the assessment is completed, the therapist moves away from focusing on problems. Ideally, the therapist focuses on the young person's achievements and capabilities for long enough that the child begins to ask: 'When do we start with the actual therapy?' The therapist can explore this as an invitation to speak about more difficult things, at least briefly. This would be the ideal foundation for work on the issues that have been presented and a good time to introduce the mode formulation. Highlighting strengths and capabilities also sets a foundation for identifying and building the child's Clever and Wise mode.

9.1.2 Relationship building with parents and caregivers

Building rapport with the parents plays an equally important role. The amount of time spent with the parents and the tone of the relationship needs to be adjusted depending on the age of the child. The younger the client, the more parental work is required. The qualities needed in the therapeutic relationship with the child discussed previously also apply to the parents, especially the primary caregiver of the child (usually the mother). The parent needs a similarly high level of comfort with the therapist. Parents need to perceive the therapy room as a 'safe place' and the therapist as a trustworthy person with whom they can be sufficiently open and address shame-inducing or taboo subjects. Parents also want to have their psychological needs met. Without empathy, warmth, acceptance and authenticity, a sufficient basis of trust cannot be established. In the introductory phase it may be useful to offer a weekly appointment to the parents as well as the children. As a rule, parents need support and acceptance to let go of feelings of guilt and repair their self-worth so that past mistakes can be acknowledged and parenting skills can be addressed. Often the parent's maladaptive schemas need to be addressed in order for the parent to have capacity to relate differently to their child. More detailed information about working with parents (i.e. parent-related techniques and procedures) follows in Chapter 17.

It is important with adolescent clients to proceed carefully with parental work. The therapist needs to involve the adolescent in determining the extent of parent involvement as conflict often exists between the parent and the child. Parents can tend to see the therapist as an extension of their interests (e.g. to get tips on how to get compliance with family rules). In these situations it may be useful to outsource the handling of these issues (e.g. limit-setting) to a more appropriate resource, such as a parenting course, in order to not burden the therapist–client relationship. However, later in therapy, it may be useful to integrate the Schema Therapy work with adolescents into one formulation of goals for both parents and child, such as combating the *Defectiveness/Shame* schema. The formulation guides the level and timing of the parent's involvement. So, for example, when separation difficulties are part of the presenting problem, the timing of parent involvement is guided by the client's interests, rather than the parent's preferences.

9.2 Empathic confrontation

Once a warm and nurturing relationship is established between the therapist and the child (based on the qualities discussed in section 9.1), the therapist will also need to confront the child with the impact of their maladaptive modes and schemas. Young and colleagues (2003) call this an 'empathic reality check'. Empathic confrontation is not so much a technique but rather a therapeutic attitude. The therapist tries to empathise with the unmet needs present in the child and doses the quality and quantity of the confrontation prudently, where an optimal balance is desirable. Here, 'optimal' is defined highly individually, depending on the day and the situation. For this purpose, the therapist must observe the client very sensitively and assess in every moment when the scale of empathic confrontation gets out of balance. An over-emphasised weight on the side of empathy to the detriment of the reality check can result in the child trivialising the impact of their actions or maladaptive modes. However, understanding and empathising alone will only bring the client short-term relief. On the contrary, a too harsh or too quick confrontation of the problematic behaviour and its consequences may trigger considerable self-worth issues and feelings of shock, unless authentic emotional warmth is radiated by the therapist and accepted by the client. An imbalance in empathy and confrontation can cause a strain on the therapeutic relationship, which can lead to resistance to the therapeutic process. The following two case studies illustrate how to proceed when children are resistant to therapy or relationship building and show no motivation.

Case example Annika

Annika, an 8-year-old girl, was in third grade at a primary school. She stood out because of her tendency to be disrespectful, disobey rules and disturb the class, and also because she was highly distractible. She refused to co-operate or discuss any problem behaviours in the first five sessions. She had the impression that her teachers and classmates were being unfair and that she was the class scapegoat. Before beginning empathic confrontation, the therapist took a supportive position toward the Vulnerable and Angry Child modes (e.g. 'It is horrible when so many people complain about you, I would be sad and angry as well'). When the therapist heard reports of what had happened, they empathised with Annika's descriptions and experiences. From this subjectively coloured plateau, the therapist explored what Annika's actual problem was: 'What do they blame you for? Ah, so I understand, they think that you...'. By accessing the perception, thoughts and feelings of others from Annika's description, the therapist was able to summarise and reflect the differing perspectives in Annika's narrative back to Annika. Thus, the two perspectives were defined and could now be further investigated in terms of background and causes. The analogy of being a detective was used to explore this history; Nancy Drew and the Pines twins from Gravity Falls were used as models for finding hints and clues about where these two perspectives originated. After reviewing the occupational therapy report from the school and her grandparents' accounts, Annika was gradually able to understand a little of the teacher's and students' perceptions. Then she was able to tackle, together with the therapist, her share of the problems in the class. As Annika was able to trust her therapist more, the therapist was able to gently confront Annika about her own part in the problems.

Case example Fynn

Fynn, an 11-year-old boy, experienced typical ADHD-related problems. As with Annika, the therapist used a high level of empathy to build rapport and understand Fynn's point of view. However, Fynn remained unable to see other's perspectives and stubbornly fixated on his position. He stressed repeatedly that he felt unfairly treated. His parents found it difficult to take an alternate perspective, too. They would often excuse his behaviour and say 'he seems so believable, this can't be made up'. Fynn had refused therapy previously, and was angry during the first five sessions, which he saw as a great 'injustice'. Given Fynn's rigidity and the low level of rapport, empathic confrontation, as in Annika's case, was not possible with Fynn at this stage. The therapist then applied the principles of empathic confrontation with Fynn's parents: 'It has become clear to me how difficult these accounts of the situation are for you. You probably no longer know who or what to believe, right?' After some confirmation of ambivalent feelings by the parents, the therapist suggested, 'Let's say the teachers' descriptions of the disturbing class behaviour are not made up, and we assume at the same time that your son is telling the truth from his point of view – which may be a bit distorted, okay, but from his point of view still true. It's very hard to know what's true, but perhaps we could have a different goal, a goal that Fynn be respected and liked at school. If this were the case then perhaps, instead of focusing on finding the truth, it could be our goal to encourage Fynn to make different choices when he feels a sense of injustice? Choices that don't get him into trouble?' By experiencing empathy, Fynn's parents felt understood and taken care of, regardless of what had actually happened before and of the circumstances which may have motivated Fynn's behaviour.

As a result of this new perspective, the parents were able to expect Fynn to co-operate in therapy for the first time without the need to accuse their son of being a liar. The parents were then assisted in empathically confronting Fynn about participating in therapy and working toward respecting other's perspectives. At the request and direction of the therapist, they conveyed emotional warmth and appreciation toward Fynn and his subjective view, but also the firm expectation that he respects the perspectives of others (in this case, the teachers). They also let Fynn know that they expected a willingness to participate in the therapy. Fynn had great difficulty accepting this at first and accused his parents of 'betraying' him. The parents confirmed their loving support (empathic attitude), but also calmly and empathically expressed the concern that the current problems could endanger his future schooling. That was definitely not what they wanted for their beloved Fynn. They consulted with the therapist and then also told Fynn that their concern was so great that they would agree to a possible hospital admission if he could not engage with the therapist. After some tears had been shed, a clear and unambiguous framework was created that made it clear to Fynn that the co-operation was actually necessary and desired by the parents. It was the parents' warm, clear and resolute message to Fynn that made it possible for him to come to terms with the therapeutic context, to engage with it and to allow empathic confrontation.

With another child who has difficulty accepting other points of view and is completely closed to new ideas, a dialogue might look like this: 'When I listen to you, I can see how much the situation worries/upsets/annoys you, and that you do not agree with any other alternatives or ideas. Is that true?' ... 'My problem is that now, as a therapist, I would really like to suggest a different perspective on the situation, but I get the impression that you would not like that at all. Is that true?' ... 'I also understand that part of my job is to propose new ideas and perspectives from time to time and to discuss them with you. If you're so determined to control what is said and what ideas are allowed to be expressed, I start to feel very small and very uncomfortable. Do you know situations in which you are not allowed to say anything, but really want to? How does it feel?' With such a patient, a willingness to listen and accept different points of views needs to be created first. The therapist has a sympathetic understanding of how challenging this task is, and yet also a gentle, loving, patient and above all persistent approach toward the client. We are borrowing here from the concept of parental presence (Omer & Lebowitz, 2016; Omer *et al*, 2013), which is similarly focused on being patient, appreciative and persevering. In practice, the therapist displays an ongoing willingness to engage in relationship building and strengths-based work, while gently and repetitively reiterating the desire to provide a different perspective on the problem behaviour.

If a child behaves aggressively toward the therapist, we suggest naming the problem behaviour: 'I have to state very clearly that I will not accept you yelling at me and insulting me. I expect that you control yourself, even if you are very angry. We will later think about how you can vent your anger, but I do not want you to continue to hurt others, and at the moment you are hurting me' ... 'If I let that happen, I would be a bad therapist, because I want you to learn to express your anger, but without harming yourself or risking your friendships' ... 'I really want to help you have great relationships but if this keeps happening people won't want to stay and one day you are going to be alone out there, you're such a nice and thoughtful boy ... you do not deserve that. I will not allow you to keep going like this. This also applies to me!' Here, the limited re-parenting role is about setting necessary limits to behaviour. The therapist should be very careful to not use fear or physical intimidation to draw appropriate boundaries; instead, the motivation for change is focused on needs for connection and the future of the child who needs to learn how to deal with intense feelings. Therapists should also be careful to not escalate the situation by shouting or abruptly ending therapy ('This child is not capable of engaging with treatment'). This is only possible, though, with an underlying foundation of goodwill, empathy, skill and a lot of determination. At a minimum, the principle of parental or therapeutic presence also applies: as long as the child comes to therapy (regardless of the emotional state), there is a chance to connect with the child.

Basic rule: authenticity

It is important that the therapist acts authentically in the exploration of the child's viewpoint. The therapist adopts the position of learner, rather than expert, when exploring the world of the child, without acting in an exaggerated, stupid or naïve way. The therapist asks the child to teach them something from the child's own world. Initially the objective is to make the child aware that the therapist is an advocate for his basic needs, and that the therapist is not there to enforce a change in the child's behaviour. If the therapist is relatively sure that they have the child's confidence and are seen as an expert able to help with the problem, they should gradually begin discussing the impact of their behaviour and alternate approaches. This confrontation must always take place in the context that the child's viewpoint is never wrong. The child's view should, however, be supplemented by others' views. In this interactive dialogue – perhaps even over several hours of therapy – a motivation and willingness is gradually built within the child, comparing their viewpoint with that of others.

Building awareness and motivation for change is probably the most difficult step in the, often extrinsically motivated, therapy with children and adolescents. If the therapist notices that the child is disengaging, the confrontational aspect is probably too strong and the therapist should increase the focus on empathy for the child's perspective. The relationship with the child is the beginning and end of therapy: if the relationship between therapist and child is substantially impaired then therapy has little chance of success, even Schema Therapy interventions.

9.3 Psychoeducation

When working with schoolchildren and young people, Schema Therapy provides a particularly helpful way to explain and overcome distress and entrenched behavioural patterns. To effectively educate clients about the mode model, various materials can be used, depending on age.

9.3.1 Materials

- Hand or finger puppets or animals, representing internal states and their underlying needs (allowing the child to play different characters)

- Dolls

- Malleable objects that stand for the modes (e.g. play dough, clay, balloons, threading characters, etc)

- Painted figures or paper dolls (people, animals)

- Stories from picture books, films or children's television series, reflecting the child's experience

- Photos or images from known prevention programmes or literature dealing with mode-specific topics

- Games that involve ascribing feeling state to characters

- Feeling cards that can be modified to shape different facial expressions (e.g. by completing with tears, wrinkles on the forehead and eyebrows raised in anger or fear)

9.3.2 Psychoeducation at different age levels

Preschool children

Psychoeducation with preschool children is more likely incidental during play rather than structured and cognitive in focus. Psychoeducation and therapy are not separate processes at this age. They are fluid and intertwined and need to occur naturally during sessions. The child is not cognitively able to understand the concept of schemas. However, they can differentiate emotional states and triggers and can practice noticing emotions, expressing them and testing solutions in play. The therapist can encourage the child to explore underlying core emotional needs connected with the mode states while also practising alternative coping strategies.

Primary school children

Primary school children are able to understand the concept of the connection between activating events, beliefs and consequences, as outlined in Ellis' ABC model (Gonzales *et al*, 2004), depicted in Table 9.1. By using practical examples from the child's experience, children can begin to understand the connection between schemas and responses. This awareness should be practised and deepened with ongoing examples. Here the child's beliefs come into play as they reveal schemas more explicitly. With the help of examples (e.g. classes are cancelled due to the teacher's illness) the therapist can make it clear that the teacher being sick (Activating event) does not cause the respective feelings (Consequences), but what the person thinks about the events (Beliefs). An example is provided and explained in a child-friendly way (Table 9.1).

Table 9.1 ABC model according to Ellis (1957)

A: Activating event	B: Belief	C: Consequence
Everyone laughs at me	I am dumb	I feel ashamed
	Everyone makes mistakes	I am OK and I keep working

Once the basic idea is understood the therapist can introduce different scenarios where the child is then asked what different people would probably think and feel. Do all the other children in the class think and feel the same, for example? And what might the teacher think and feel?

The core concepts of Schema Therapy (basic needs, schemas and modes) can be easily visualised with child-friendly material. One way to do this demonstrated by Schulz von Thun (1998) who suggests an 'inner team', drawing the modes as characters in the belly of the client. The schemas are symbolically painted as wounds in the body. In Chapter 10 we have provided illustrations and a number of formulation options to show different ways of providing psychoeducation. The examples in that chapter focus on children aged from 6 to 12, to illustrate how to simplify complex connections with that age group. Adjustment of language for adolescents is also helpful and will be familiar to most readers.

Secondary school children

With children over 10 years old, the inner house (Chapter 13) is a helpful image linking core memories to relevant schemas and modes. This age group also responds well to imagery exercises (13.2), paintings and drawings (12.1) and finger and hand puppet work (12.2). It can also be helpful to externalise schemas in the form of objects that stand symbolically as hurdles for the client to jump over or get stuck on. Another way to deliver psychoeducation is to use biology as an example, where schemas are like 'genes' that are expressed or 'switched on' by situations (an example is available in the online material , www.pavpub.com/resource-374CoCr).

Basic steps of psychoeducation with children

1. The child is shown a picture/a scene from a story. In one picture the child 'Frank' experiences something nice; in another, something unpleasant. Examples of the latter: Frank's parents are arguing (Fig. 9.1); Frank falls and a group of boys are laughing about it (Fig.9.2).

Figure 9.1: Representation of parent conflict and thoughts connected to a child's anxiety

Figure 9.2: Representation of a memory of falling down and being laughed at

2. The child is asked about Frank's possible thoughts and feelings: 'What do you think? What does Frank think or feel? Why does he feel this way?' Using the ABC model, the therapist conveys age-appropriate information about how emotions are associated with situations.

3. The therapist and the child now note appropriate words and symbols for those events. Children can draw an appropriate expression on the face of the child (sad, anxious, ashamed). Or they can assign certain feeling cards to the scene. Speech bubbles or thought clouds can illustrate possible interpretations: 'My parents are splitting up'; 'I am probably the reason for it'.

4. The therapist then asks what the needs and coping strategies might be. 'And what happens next? How does he feel then? What does he really want?'

5. The therapist asks the child to recall a similar scene from his or her own experience: 'How would you feel? Have you experienced anything similar before?'

6. The therapist offers different ways of viewing the situation: they ask the child if another child would have the same thoughts and feelings, or maybe even completely different ones. The therapist could also talk about another child and insert them into the sketch and imply a positive schema: 'I know a boy who had completely different thoughts. His name was Francis, and he thought, "When my parents argue, it is stupid, but they always stay together, I know that".' Or: 'The kids can laugh, this does look funny. It can happen to anyone.'

7. The therapist explains the formation of a schema: 'If Frank experiences this often, then the experiences take root deeply or in a younger version: 'Then the feelings and thoughts can get stuck there.' Here, different terms or metaphors are suitable: 'Like a wound, it hurts all the time, like a movie that's stuck'; 'Frank will not forget this quickly'. The therapist-selected metaphor for the child can also stand for a visual symbol in the work with school children, such as drawing a wound in the stomach, or a film reel/movie in the child's head. The therapist explains the activation of a schema or mode: 'And when the child has become much bigger, the thoughts and feelings are still there.' The therapist can then visualise this in different ways – by drawing the same child again, only a few years older, with a smaller 'inner child' in his stomach (Fig. 9.3):

    Look, little Frank is still there. What do you think, what does big Frank now think and feel when his parents fight again / children laugh at him or his behaviour once again? Well ... then little Frank feels unhappy inside again and thinks ... the old wound aches / the old film starts again. This runs automatically, because he has learned it like that.

Figure 9.3: Representation of little Frank in big Frank, who goes through the same fear as when he was little

8. The therapist explains the change of perception on the basis of the schema:

    'If Frank still has the old stories inside, then he sees the world through those stories. He pays attention to certain things much more closely. Why is that [include child]? Correct, because he is afraid that the stories from before might happen, that argument could lead to separation or those children could laugh at him when he falls or something embarrassing happens to him.'

Figure 9.4: When small mishaps happen, the fear from the past comes up again – when little Frank was laughed at because he fell down

9. *'Then Frank is on the lookout for any children who might laugh. And if they do, what is he going to think then [include child]? They are embarrassing him all over again.'*

10. The therapist then discusses the possible consequences of a schema including the formation of Coping modes based on Frank's schemas, describing the avoiding, surrendering or overcompensation modes. The child is asked what they think Frank will do when he feels embarrassed, etc. The child can then come up with their own ideas of Coping modes.

11. The therapist discusses ideas with the child about how Frank could choose healthy Coping modes that allow him to meet his core emotional needs, and begin to heal the wound or turn down the volume and brightness of the movie.

9.3.4 Using metaphors with schemas and modes

Another aid to understanding schemas or modes is metaphors such as glasses that alter visual perception. A dialogue might look like this: 'If you've ever experienced something like Frank has, then you have probably developed and begun wearing some special glasses – maybe you didn't even know you were wearing them?' The therapist explains: 'These glasses can completely change the way you remember situations or objects, so things appear bigger or more important than they would have been without the glasses. They are just like a magnifying glass – small things become quite large. It's similar to the curved mirrors in a funhouse, at carnivals that make you look really fat or really thin. Have you ever seen them? With the glasses that come from our difficult experiences, the world looks a bit different. They change the way we perceive things. These glasses cause misunderstandings, because one person sees one thing and another person sees the same thing totally differently.'

The special glasses are described as a protective mechanism to notice the slightest signs (hypervigiliance) that could indicate a similar painful experience.

The therapist then describes the client's pattern (e.g. *Social Isolation* schema) and its coping strategy (e.g. Bully/Attack mode). This pattern must be identified over and over with the child, otherwise it will be forgotten. In order to help the child become more aware, objects such as stones, stars, balls, and so on, which symbolise the problematic schema and mode activation, are helpful.

Important therapist attitude toward maladaptive modes

The therapist, while identifying that unhelpful modes are maladaptive, should also model appreciation for their services, because they represent an intelligent solution at the time of creation to reduce intra-psychic tension and conflicts in the short term. Therapist appreciation of the 'protective' function of the modes also encourages the child to develop a more compassionate stance toward their younger, vulnerable self (Vulnerable Child mode).

Psychoeducation about the 'detached protector' mode

When working with children, and often also with parents, it is important to be aware of the impact of the 'Detached Protector' mode (or Dissociated Protector mode) and other Avoidance modes. Roediger (2011, p114) identified how this mode expresses itself in children. When the child uses the Detached Protector mode they:

- come to school with no motivation

- regularly lose or leave homework at home, or don't complete homework

- trivialise their situation ('everything is fine')

- constantly talk about unimportant things that have nothing to do with the problem behaviour

- feign confusion or play dumb when asked about thoughts and feelings ('I don't know')

- behave very rationally, emotionally cool or precociously

- do not say anything, or behave in a taciturn or sarcastic manner

- appear bored (or the therapist may feel bored when the child is talking)

- just want to play, not talk (Detached Self-Soother mode)

- are charming, open, easily distracted, absent-minded (Hyperactive Protector mode)

- blame parents, teachers, classmates, etc. for their own misbehaviour (Angry Protector mode)

- refuse to talk, appear grumpy or moody (Angry/Oppositional Protector mode)

- and many other avoidant behaviours.

These hindering modes should be addressed with the child. Chair dialogues can help to demonstrate the idea of an avoidant Coping mode (see Chapter 12.3). Another approach is to use visualisations that illustrate the function of the Surrendering, Overcompensating or Avoiding modes, presented below.

Initially, the therapist can engage a child in a quiz on the subject of protection.

Why do people wear clothes? Why do they wear – at least in winter – several sets of clothes over each other, like a T-shirt, shirt, sweater and jacket? And why is a T-shirt enough in summer?

Let's have a look at this book about knights: Why do the knights wear armour? And why do motorcyclists wear leather suits and helmets? Why is there a law about having to wear helmets?

Let's have a look at how traffic works: what are pedestrian crossings for? Why is there a speed limit for vehicles? What is a seat belt for, what do turn signals do, why are so many traffic lights built, what are bike paths for?

Now let's take a look at school: Why are there class rules, e.g. the rule of raising your hand? Why do you have a classroom instead of having class outside on the lawn? Why are there names on your exercise books?

And now let's look at the world out there, in the shops: Why do adults address each other as Mr or Ms? And at what point do they get on a first-name basis? Why can it be uncomfortable when people stand too close to each other? Why do two people who like each other usually exchange glances before they start a conversation?

The answers to the questions above relate to the need that every human being has for protection. Appropriate protective actions should be justified as intelligent and helpful solutions in everyday life. Everyone needs some form of protection! When this message is understood, more adaptive approaches to protection can be discussed with the child. The aim is to develop staged protection arrangements: there are more than the two options of protection or no protection. For example, several picture frames can be placed or pushed in front, which are activated depending on the need for protection of the child (Fig. 9.5).

Figure 9.5: Picture frames are covered with different materials: the first frame is empty, the second has got a mosquito net, the third a rough net, and the last is covered with plastic wrap. The second and third frames partially protect against the fan air; the fourth, however, completely protects.

The picture frames shown are only examples and too complex for therapists to recreate. However, they might encourage the reader to develop their own ideas about how they can explain this concept to the child, and how degrees of protection can be illustrated. The goal is to shift from the all-or-nothing thinking and demonstrate different degrees of protection. Other options are to put on a construction worker or hockey helmet, sunglasses or headphones, or to pull down an imaginary blind when a conversation or a situation becomes threatening or unpleasant. To stay in touch, the slats of the blinds can be adjusted to the right level of sight, so that the child feels safe.

There are also many examples in nature of how creatures protect themselves. All living creatures on earth (plants, animals, humans), and especially the young and small, including children, develop special protective mechanisms to stay out of harm's way. The goal is not to demonise protective mechanisms (and therefore devalue the Detached Protector mode), but rather to help the child find appropriate forms of protection. One way of demonstrating appropriate levels of protection for the child is by using differently coloured mosquito nets (see Figure 9.6).

Figure 9.6: Dark mosquito net (left) for more protection and brighter (right) for a lower need for protection

The child sits on the chair, which is placed behind the mosquito net and looks through the net. Depending on the situation, the child may feel more comfortable in the dark net (e.g. when parents argue and insult each other), but mostly children feel more comfortable in the lighter net, because this gives them a clearer outside view. If they feel safe, they can also open the net and look out as if from a window, or come completely out of the net. Again, the therapist works with the child to ensure they are able to transfer this understanding into everyday life. What does appropriate protection look like in daily life, such as when the child is being bullied? 'Which net would you want when…? Are there times when you could peek out from the net? Or even when you would feel safe enough to leave the net for a while?' In this context, the therapist reminds the child that everyone has the same basic needs (using psychoeducation) and these needs (for safety and protection, for example) should not be violated. It is important that Detached Protector mode is seen as helpful in offering protection to the Vulnerable Child mode, although the level of protection offered by Detached Protector mode is not appropriate for everyday use and is not helpful in therapy. The aim is to explore alternative options such as developing the Caring Parent or Good Protector modes that might provide appropriate levels of protection in situations when Detached Protector mode is offering too much, too little, or unsuitable protection.

References

Ellis A (1957) Rational psychotherapy and individual psychology. *Journal of Individual Psychology* **13** 38–44.

Gonzalez JE, Nelson JR, Gutkin TB, Saunders A, et al. (2004) Rational emotive therapy with children and adolescents: a meta-analysis. *Journal of Emotional and Behavioral Disorders* **12** (4) 222–235. Retrieved from https://search.proquest.com/docview/214924708?accountid=178506

Omer H & Lebowitz ER (2016) Nonviolent resistance: helping caregivers reduce problematic behaviors in children and adolescents. *Journal of Marital and Family Therapy* **42** (4) 688–700.

Omer H, Steinmetz SG, Carthy T & von Schlippe A (2013) The anchoring function: parental authority and the parent–child bond. *Family Process* **52** (2) 193. Retrieved from https://search.proquest.com/docview/1424667979?accountid=178506

Roediger E (2009) *Praxis der Schematherapie. Grundlagen, Anwendung*, Perspektiven. Stuttgart: Schattauer.

Roediger E (2011) *Praxis der Schematherapie: Lehrbuch zu Grundlagen, Modell und Anwendung* (2. Aufl.) Stuttgart: Schattauer.

Schulz von Thun F (1998) *Miteinander reden 3 – Das innere Team und situationsgerechte Kommunikation*. Hamburg: Rowohlt.

Tedeschi RG & Kilmer RP (2005) Assessing strengths, resilience and growth to guide clinical interventions. *Professional Psychology: Research and Practice* **36** (3) 230–237. Retrieved from https://search.proquest.com/docview/224865236?accountid=178506

Young JE, Klosko JS & Weishaar ME (2003) *Schema Therapy: A Practitioner's Guide*. New York: Guilford Press.

Chapter 10: Starting Schema Therapy

Peter Graaf, Christof Loose and Ruth A. Holt

10.1 Preliminary remarks on increasing motivation for treatment in children and adolescents

While working with children is rewarding, there are barriers to engaging in treatment, which the clinician needs to address. Often children arrive for therapy thinking that their parents or teachers want to change something about them. Naturally, this causes the child to resist changing anything! Many children also find it difficult to delay their need for fun and gratification in order to focus on more 'serious' tasks, and don't like dealing with unpleasant topics (even less than adults do). They may try to avoid painful feelings for as long as possible. However, for children in distress, painful feelings are frequently triggered and often overwhelm the child. Given the child's suspicion that therapy is a possibly threatening environment, children often initially present in Detached Protector mode, not Clever and Wise mode. The Detached Protector mode will then make it difficult to access the Vulnerable Child mode, the 'place of therapy' (Berbalk, 2010, personal communication) where the work needs to be done. In contrast to adult clients, who are more able to accept – with appropriate psychoeducation – that dealing with negative emotions is part of the therapy process, children do not have the same perspective-taking capacities and therefore motivation. Children need to feel safe enough to be vulnerable, and require assistance to see the benefit of facing difficult emotions in order to effectively engage in therapy. Therefore therapists need to be aware and ready to work hard to build rapport and motivation for therapy.

Another element that therapists need to consider when working with children is the strong loyalty they have toward their parents. As the therapist begins to develop trust with the client and understand the family dynamics, they need to be sensitive to a child's perception that they must align with the therapist in opposition to the family. A child who feels that they are being asked to make this choice will sense that the family's unity and security is threatened, or that the family will come to harm in some way (for example, be devalued or criticised or accused of neglect). The child will then almost always align with their family against the therapist, undermining the therapy.

In order to address these aspects of working with children and adolescents in therapy and provide a medium that is familiar, there is a long tradition of play therapy methods which allow the child to use playful self-expression in the therapy situation. Play therapy allows a young client to express emotional conflicts, family distress and traumatic experiences in a modality that they are comfortable with. Play approaches also facilitate the observation of a child's main coping styles. The techniques used in Schema Therapy form an innovative bridge between classic play therapy approaches and cognitive behavioural therapy. Children respond very well to these techniques, enhanced by the exercises and supplementary material discussed in the other chapters. This approach also provides parents and children a structure for therapy, which orients them during the therapeutic process. Schema Therapy builds a solution-oriented bridge between the child and family's presenting problems and the changes needed in everyday life. It provides a practical approach to change without fixating on the symptoms that are presenting.

10.2 Mode work: basic elements and materials

Working chiefly with modes is the focus in children's Schema Therapy. The mode model closely resembles a child's play and experience, and is therefore more intuitive to present to a child than a schema-focused approach. For example, many children, without therapeutic intervention, choose imaginary friends or helpers when faced with losing a caregiver or when needing protection. Therefore, most of the techniques described in this book focus on the child's modes. When working with the parents there is often a more complex schema and mode activation focus. The basic tenet of Schema Therapy for children and adolescents is that therapeutic progress comes about as a result of re-orienting dysfunctional mode patterns. We assume that children and parents are quite capable of short-term behaviour modification. However, changes at the 'deeper' mode level are – in our opinion – more effective and sustainable, as they encapsulate a more complex mechanism of body reactions, thoughts, feelings, and behaviour producing longer lasting results.

Children and parents become aware of their modes in therapy. Once they have an understanding of the modes, they are able to test, inside and outside of therapy, the 'utility' of adaptive modes as an alternative way of coping with difficult situations. Patients are assisted to not surrender to a dysfunctional mode – in other words, to not dive as deeply into negative emotional states, and to improve self-regulation, working towards emotional maturity. Young articulated this approach for patients with borderline personality disorder: 'Bring the modes together, don't get so deeply into the mode' (Young, ISST-Congress 2010, Berlin).

Basic elements of mode work

Below is an overview of mode work for children and adolescents. This approach was inspired by the work of Berbalk (2009) and his 14 steps for mode work with dolls. Our list is intended as a guide for therapists and gives an overarching plan for using different media. Within each of the five steps for mode work there are more detailed sub-steps. It is not necessary to work through every small step in one session. Each sub-step is described in detail and references the individual chapters describing the various 'media' (e.g. working with pictures/drawings, chairs, finger puppets, stories, etc). In practice, the elements are not necessarily processed in a fixed order. Often the order is more circular, with 'steps backwards', going over the same steps in greater detail and with more understanding. For example, the second step may also need to be covered after the third step.

1. Identify the presenting modes

2. Access the Vulnerable/Lonely/Abused Child mode

3. Determine each mode's functionality (in dialogue)

4. Strengthen adaptive modes and weaken dysfunctional modes

5. Generalize therapeutic gains to everyday life

Caring parent mode

We assume, as Berbalk (2009) does, that each child has internalized both a Caring Parent mode and a negative (Demanding/Punitive) Parent or Critic mode. Both negative and positive aspects of caregivers have been internalised as modes in the child. One of the goals then is to help the child activate the Caring Parent mode more frequently. The Caring Parent mode doesn't quite correspond to the Healthy Adult mode for children, although Young readily attributes parenting tasks to Healthy Adult mode in adult clients (Young et al, 2003). For children, a separate Caring Parent mode better suits the attachment model. As children's early attachment experiences become a 'working model' (Bowlby, 1951), the mother–child relationship represents a resource for coping with unfulfilled needs. By therapeutically providing a positive source of comfort that is a 'parent' we are hoping to build a more secure internal attachment.

Another reason for using a Caring Parent mode rather than a Healthy Adult mode is that children are naturally drawn to 'protector figures' and heroes, who do not necessarily equate to an 'adult' in their imagination. Children often see this helper as coming 'from outside' to help the child in a way that is more external than the Clever and Wise mode.

1. Identify the presenting modes

- Capture and name important presenting modes (e.g. by assigning each to a finger puppet).

  It is important to include the following modes: Vulnerable Child mode, Happy Child mode and Clever/Wise mode.

- Activate typical experiences and behaviours when in each mode (each finger puppet talks and plays and thus gives the mode a living form).

- Express the emotions, body sensations, behavioural tendencies and cognitions of each mode.

- Interview each mode – the therapist engages in a mode dialogue with each mode.

2. Access the Vulnerable/Lonely/Abused Child mode

- Connect (with the child's permission) with the Vulnerable/Lonely/Abused Child.

- Explore needs (*What does little Felix need?*).

- Console, validate, offer protection from external of internal Demanding, Criticising or Punishing modes.

3. Determine each mode's functionality (in dialogue)

- Explore the mode's origin and intention (e.g. what is the history of the mode, what survival need did it meet?). What are the needs behind the modes?

- Establish connections between the modes and the current problem: How do the modes influence me? How are they connected with my problems?

- Identify the thoughts, feelings, situations and people that trigger each mode.

- Understand how the modes are related to each other. What effects do the other modes have on the Vulnerable Child mode? Typical mode flips can be charted.

- Discuss advantages (strengths) and disadvantages (difficulties) of the modes.

- Evaluate how functional or dysfunctional each mode is (i.e. assessing the results of the behaviour in each mode). Discuss the short-term and long-term impact of the coping modes, affirming their previous protective role, but increasing awareness of their unhelpful impact on current life.

4. Strengthen adaptive modes and weaken dysfunctional modes

- Discuss and try out alternative mode constellations or mode flips.

- Explore the impact of a different emphasis or a reconciliation between the modes.

- Strengthen the communication between adaptive modes and develop dialogues between Caring Parent/Clever and Wise mode and the dysfunctional modes that block those adaptive modes.

- Acknowledge that dysfunctional modes are a temporary solution. Develop techniques for distancing and increasing emotional and behavioural control. Integrate the positive facets of unhelpful modes into Clever and Wise mode.

- Encourage the Clever and Wise mode to assert itself in age-appropriate and reasonable ways. The Clever and Wise mode can now begin to take over the control of all other modes and assist in appropriate self-regulation.

- Strengthen the internalised Caring Parent mode and activate an internal Good Protector mode. The helping modes are introduced as loving and protective supports standing by the Vulnerable Child's side ('rescuing the Vulnerable Child').

- Help the Angry Child to appropriately and constructively express feelings and needs instead of destructive impulses

- Depower the Inner Critic and Punitive modes (analogous to Punitive/Demanding Parent modes). The therapist confronts the mode and banishes the mode or limits the mode.

- Increase the ability to observe and show compassion to self: 'If something like this was done to your friend, what would you think?'

- Guide the Undisciplined Child towards accepting self-control.

5. Generalise therapeutic gains to everyday life

- Mode monitoring: this process allows the child to become more aware of modes in order to be able to move to a more helpful response. In the therapy situation, awareness can be built by conducting experiments and structured role-plays with video feedback, possibly also with exaggerated body postures. Using worksheets for out-of-session tasks helps to detect functional and dysfunctional modes, noticing typical signs and cues for each mode.

- Plan and implement concrete steps (behavioural pattern breaking) for Clever and Wise modes in everyday life: talk through examples and role-plays: how do we bring Clever and Wise mode in to manage this situation?

- Discuss which modes should be used in which situations.

- Develop skills in everyday communication (practise dialogues between the Clever and Wise modes or Good Protector mode with real people in imagination or using structured role-play).

- Consider the impact of therapeutic gains on the system or family: How could they be affected? How can they adapt to a different kind of interaction? Are there any secondary gains?

- Install reminders in everyday life: flash cards or visual aids (e.g. cards or objects to carry around as prompts) to support the activation of healthy modes.

- Assign homework tasks to practise consciously changing modes and break unhelpful behavioural patterns.

Readers will find a notepad for the therapist with all the elements on a page of A4 at www.pavpub.com/resource-374CoCr (Basic Elements of Working with Modes).

Additional issues

Disempowerment vs. Fighting: Dealing with dysfunctional parent modes in children
Working with dysfunctional Parent modes is one of the key differences between Schema Therapy for adult populations and Schema Therapy with children, adolescents and their families. Jeffrey Young and colleagues (2003) speak of banishing the dysfunctional Parent modes, which are often introjects of demanding, harsh or abusive real-life parents. However, the child in therapy is still dependent on their actual parents, is loyal to those parents and is developmentally not able to differentiate the helpful aspects of a parent from the unhelpful aspects. Therefore, care must be taken not to undermine a child's loyalty to their parents and to appreciate the helpful aspects of the parent–child bond. Thus in Schema Therapy for children and adolescents the therapist should refrain from using the terms Demanding and Punitive Parent mode, but rather create separate labels such as Inner Critic mode or Punisher mode. The therapist should also speak about the parents with respect as individuals and express positive intentions toward them.

A helpful way to reframe the messages from these modes is to talk about the 'helpfulness' of the messages. The Punitive or Critic mode has provided unhelpful solutions to problems (e.g. anxiety). The content of these messages needs to be rejected, without rejecting the parents themselves. These issues need to be addressed in parallel with the parents, who are encouraged to identify their own schemas and mode triggers, which have prompted these unhelpful messages. It is also important to strengthen the child's internal Caring Parent mode by encouraging, coaching and highlighting the positive, caring, fun parts of the parents – the aspects of the parents that are able to meet the child's needs. This helps to create 'islands of good memories' (Peichl, 2007).

As the child's awareness of unhelpful messages grows, the therapist provides the parents with a parallel process of reshaping their parenting style. The therapist helps the parent connect to their healthy part (the adult's Healthy Adult or, in upbrining issues, the Caring and Guidance mode) and assists the child to notice these moments. The therapist can then strengthen memories of the times when the parent met the child's needs, and the child felt happy, safe, secure, protected and carefree. As a child experiences more of these moments they internalise these aspects of their parents, which eventually will contribute to the child or adolescent patient's own Healthy Adult mode in adulthood.

Destructive coping modes

In order to successfully work with the destructive coping modes, the therapist first needs to understand why the child needs, or needed, that level of 'protection'. The level of protection can range from an irritable Angry Protector mode to a violent and sadistic Destroyer mode. The very destructive offender modes (Bully and Attack mode, Destroyer mode, etc) are formulated as extreme forms of self-protection. The presence of these extreme protector modes is much more common in teenagers; in children, these behaviours are more likely to be introjects of abusers. In ego-state therapy (Watkins & Watkins, 1997) with traumatised patients, offender introjects formed in the child (we would view it as a special form of Parent mode in a traumatized child) had a positive function at the point in time when the trauma occurred. The therapist should recognise this. The content of the offender introjects needs to be clearly rejected. Adaptations need to be made so that the therapist's dialogue with the offender part is appropriate for young people as well.

CBT and Schema Therapy approaches

There are also similarities between CBT approaches and Schema Therapy in connecting cognitions or behaviours with biographical events (e.g. Zarbock, 2011). CBT tends to address thoughts, feelings, body sensations and behaviour as separate components. However, modes encapsulate a complex interplay of emotion, cognition, body sensation and memory as an 'inner state', triggered by external or internal events. In addition to environmental triggers, experiencing one part of the mode can also trigger the whole mode. For example, the body sensation of having stomach pain can automatically activate the feeling of fear, the thought 'I can't do this' and avoidance behaviours as part of a complete mode package. While traditional CBT may successively touch upon thoughts, feelings, body sensation and behaviours, mode work more deeply captures the experience of all four facets at once, thus promoting a deeper characterological change rather than a superficial, symptom-level change.

In CBT, children often have difficulty in accessing and challenging their cognitions, which decreases motivation. Further, viewing each of the above components (thoughts, feelings, body sensations and behaviour) as separate yet linked requires psychoeducation and assumes a certain level of verbal and cognitive development. Therefore it is often easier for therapists – at least at the start of therapy, and with younger children – to address the mode rather than taking out single components and changing them in isolation. Schema Therapy modes also have the advantage of needing only one label, simplifying the language for the child. Further, the mode label becomes part of a shared therapeutic language that has been developed in collaboration with the child. In this way the therapist expands their vocabulary to fit with how the child sees the world, rather than expecting the child's vocabulary to expand to fit with how the therapist sees the world.

Therapeutic materials

The therapeutic materials used in a session are chosen based upon the patient's interests, needs and developmental level. We supplement common play therapy materials with a variety of puppets, dolls and figurines to represent modes and real people (therapists, parents and peers). We also use whiteboards, paper and pens and worksheets when developmentally appropriate (from age 11 onwards). The worksheets include elements of traditional CBT within a Schema Therapy framework. They can be used as homework and are available in the online materials (see also worksheets for adults by Farrell *et al*, 2014 and Jacob *et al*, 2014). Worksheets provide avenues for cognitive work, and also a way of capturing new ideas resulting from experiential work. The written materials complement the experiential techniques and provide a visual structure or pictorial record as well as a way of recording progress. For example, we often use different methods and interventions to address the same idea, combining experiential work with a written worksheet, or even taking photos of experiential activities for the client to keep. Keepsakes (e.g. worksheets, photos or transitional objects) linked to experiential mode work are a helpful reminder when dealing with maladaptive schemas and modes. These documents can be used as a memory aid when dealing with maladaptive schemas and modes even years after therapy.

References

Berbalk H (2009) *Behandlungskonzept mit der MAP.* Unveröffentlichtes Manuskript.

Bowlby J (1951*) Maternal Care and Mental Health* (Vol. 2). Geneva: World Health Organization.

Farrell JM, Reiss N & Shaw IA (2014) *The Schema Therapy Clinician's Guide: A Complete Resource for Building and Delivering Individual, Group and Integrated Schema Mode Treatment Progra*ms. Chichester: Wiley.

Jacob G, Van Genderen H & Seebauer L (2014) *Breaking Negative Thinking Patterns: A Schema Therapy Self-help and Support Book.* Chichester: Wiley.

Peichl J (2007) *Innere Kinder, Tter, Helfer & Co, Ego-State-Therapie des traumatisierten Selbst.* Stuttgart: Klett-Cotta.

Watkins JG & Watkins HH (1997) *Ego States: Theory and Therapy.* New York: WW Norton.

Young JE, Klosko JS & Weishaar ME (2003) *Schema Therapy: A Practitioner's Guide.* New York: Guilford Press.

Zarbock G (2011) Praxisbuch Verhaltenstherapie. *Grundlagen und Anwendungen biografisch-systemischer Verhaltenstherapie* (3. Aufl.) Lengerich: Pabst.

Chapter 11:
Play and Story-Based Schema Therapy

Peter Graaf, Christof Loose and Ruth A. Holt

11.1 Schema Therapy using play therapy

Play is the most frequent and most intensely expressive medium of childhood, far beyond the infancy, toddler and preschool years. At the age of one and a half, children begin playing in intensely symbolic ways. Therefore, it makes sense to use this medium in therapy over a wide age range. Although behavioural therapists play with their clients in therapy, they use it for relationship building and later as reinforcement (first the therapy work, then we can play a game), or access other theories to shape the game's plot (e.g. person-centred). Play therapy can be non-directive (Axline, 1947), analytical (Freud, 1928; Klein, 1932) or client-centred (Landreth, 2012). In this section we will explain the basics of mode-guided play therapy in Schema Therapy.

Games and play are used to support the expression and fulfilment of a child's basic needs (see 2.1) in two main ways. First, we encourage the child to express feelings such as anger or sadness in symbolic and pretend play. Free play is an imaginative space for a young child's growing awareness of needs and represents an abundance of opportunities for the child to express their inner world in a familiar medium. Second, for children up to primary school age, animal figures or dolls (or similar) can be used to stage typical family events, relationship dynamics and roles that can occur in families, such as scapegoat, golden child or replacement partner (see 15.2.3). Play allows the child to narrate schema- or mode-triggering experiences in the present or in their history, without them being aware of the connection initially. Free play also allows opportunities for unconscious identification with inner parts that can then be built on.

Axline (1947) notes that in the framework of traditional non-directive play therapy, many children will use play to reproduce unprocessed experiences.

According to our observations, children also often present their previous coping modes, as if the story always had to run according to the same pattern. While playing, the child may process experiences that occurred in a pre-linguistic time or that they have no language for. As the director of play, the child has some control over unprocessed experiences. They may seek distance through the observer position, but also want to reenact what was suffered 'back then'. The child may get in touch with various previously dissociated feeling states. Thus, one can interpret the child's play as an integration and self-healing attempt. Therein lies the creative potential of dramatic play as a platform upon which stories can be reinvented and re-scripted, much like the Schema Therapy technique of 'Imagery Re-scripting' with adult clients (described by Arntz & Jacob, 2012). Similar to directors, screenwriters or other artists, the child externalises aspects of their internal world through various figures and takes over protagonists' roles to display different modes. This process often does not seem creative or free, but rather problem-fixated, repeatedly focusing on tragedies that are meant to produce pain and sadness (in the best case, communal mourning) in the audience (including the therapist); it does not offer a solution or a constructive horizon. Without intervention, therapists can become participants in endless repeating loops that can strengthen dysfunctional schemas or coping modes.

In Schema Therapy, play is used for creative mode changes and the modification of dysfunctional coping patterns. Different techniques in Schema Therapy are used to provide limited re-parenting with play. In this model the therapist does not take the role of passive spectator to destructive actions or unmet needs in the child's drama. Although the therapist will witness an event, they ultimately direct events according to Schema Therapy principles. The therapy space is the place where the core needs of the child appear and are met representatively, where primary emotions may be expressed and validated by the therapist. Play is a space for experimenting with different modes, a place for the integration of dissociated parts. Through trial and error, play motivates the creative development of ideas.

These ideas can then move beyond play and offer a model for ways to be in the real world. Schema-relevant situations can be investigated in play rather than be avoided. When the child plays out compensating coping patterns, the therapist can provide alternatives. When the child discusses Vulnerable Child parts, the therapist gives (as in classic imagery work with adults) limited re-parenting, and provides protection and care. The therapist's Healthy Adult provides the words for the previously unspeakable. Therapists should actively seek access to the Abandoned/Vulnerable/Lonely Child in the play scene and then soothe in the role of a character. They can take the Angry Child seriously in play and guide towards appropriate anger expression, but also limit excessive impulses (e.g. by protecting play materials or other dolls). Therefore the child can experience corrective emotional moments in the game that contribute to the weakening of maladaptive schemas or modes. Threatening, harassing or distressing figures are disempowered and limited in their movement (as an alternative to killing, dismembering and burning). For example, an evil dragon can be locked up in a sack, a monster can be made immobile with heavy leg irons and a ghost can be laughed at or have his own fear ascribed to him ('Help, there are people and they are laughing at me'). Vulnerable animals can be introduced as surrogates, to raise intuitive caretaking impulses, which are then internalised as self-compassion and build Good Parent modes ('as I take care of this bunny, I need that as well').

Therapeutic play also has emotion-regulating functions. With over-regulated and inhibited children the therapist can begin initiating lively scenes (such as a knight battle or even a game of catch) in a free play situation. The therapist can support the expression of child's feelings, for example: 'Doesn't it feel good to move? It's just a game, we can be silly in games, in here puppets sometimes actually fight.' With under-regulated children who react by externalising with an excess of open aggression, the therapist can provide opportunities for the child to learn to follow the rules, for example: 'Let's play a game where you get to disagree with me but you only get points for speaking softly/starting with "I don't like"', and so on.

11.1.1 Basic elements of mode-oriented play therapy

The basic elements of mode work (see section 10.2) are also useful as a rough guide in play therapy. Cognitive and behavioural interventions, however, are less important in giving direction to play approaches.

1 Identify the presenting modes

The identification of modes is done automatically as a child takes a figure and talks to it or acts through it. Typically, emotional arousal does not usually need to be activated, as children actively participate in games and can 'flip' between different modes easily. The therapist names the characters and interviews the child or the figure itself about their characteristics and thoughts. Initially many children prefer one-sided performance. For example, dominant military figures or coping modes are represented in play, while mature or caring parts are under-represented.

2 Access the Vulnerable/Lonely/Abused Child

Vulnerable Child modes usually occur in the victim role. Thus, the therapeutic task is to integrate and elaborate on the hidden parts or to directly address neglected Child modes. However, it is often unclear whether the child is displaying their own or another person's parts, or simply an expression of confusion. For example, a gorilla might represent an aspect of the angry father;

a turtle may be the closed, inward-looking sibling; and a giant bird may illustrate the unpredictable in the child's environment. Not every threatening figure is attributable to a specific person; often they act as a symbol for a world that is naturally hard to understand and is unpredictable from a child's perspective. Many play actions can also be an expression of a passion to experiment or have mastery. The delight many young boys find in roughhousing is not automatically an indication of pathological coping modes. As such, while the Vulnerable Child mode is often seen in the victim role, caution must be taken when exploring the origin or symbolism of the character in the perpetrator role.

3 Determine each mode's functionality (in dialogue)

The therapeutic interpretation of a child's character selection is often only possible after observing many 'cycles' of acted scenes, and by exploring their functionality. As a player (e.g. being given a role within the play by the child) or commentator, the therapist can ask appropriate questions during the play: 'Who are you, where do you come from? What powers do you have? What are you fighting for? Who do you want to protect? How happens next in the story?' The therapist can also describe or ask about the advantages and disadvantages or strengths and difficulties of certain characters or animals. Care needs to be taken in how the therapist comments on the play. The connection to the child's current problems is not necessarily revealed in play therapy. With preschoolers or younger children, who are not really able to deal with interpretations or explanations, these remarks are not helpful. Remarks such as 'You act like a gorilla sometimes' can elicit shame or anxiety and cause a retreat. Instead of linking the gorilla directly to the child, the therapist can highlight the gorilla's positives and offer ways of understanding the gorilla: 'Maybe he is just trying to make sure that no one laughs at him.'

4 Strengthen adaptive modes and weaken dysfunctional modes

The therapist takes care of the Vulnerable Child mode. This may be by providing safe places and activating other protective and nurturing characters. The therapist stands for justice and security, confronting any devaluing, humiliating or punitive or cruel characters. Working from the mode formulation, the therapist asks questions if the child does not develop an adaptive solution in play. Education concerning children's needs occurs via casual comments (for example, 'every animal has a right to food, no one should starve, that's not fair'). The therapist can introduce new characters themselves, such as an alternative Caring Parent mode that can instruct and limit the Angry Child mode in a non-punitive way.

5 Generalise therapeutic gains to everyday life

Given the cognitive limitations of young children transferring the experiences from play into the child's everyday reality is gradual and gentle, rather than through directly behavioural homework. Unconscious processes cannot be revealed completely; instead, they must be broached in a more measured fashion, with cautious references to concrete realities. For example, 'Just like the Bunny here, everyone wants to be looked after sometimes – you too? Does Mummy know about that? The turtle has a thick shell. Do you also need that? The dog can bark really loudly when it is scared ... What can you do when you are scared?' The play-based mode work described in this chapter is mainly suitable for children in preschool age or earlier, who are able to stage their own experiences using their own ideas, with the therapist participating. In the work with stories (in the next section), the therapist plays a more active role to involve the quieter or conflict-avoidant child.

11.2 Schema Therapy using stories

When working with stem stories, typical beginnings of family scenes are presented to a child of about 4 to 10 years, and are continued by the child using figures and objects. This approach, from Narrative Therapy, arises from the idea that people have a habit of becoming the stories they tell. With repetition the stories turn into realities, which can then keep the storyteller trapped within the 'walls' of the story, even though they themselves helped create it (Efran *et al*, 1990). From a narrative perspective, the goal is to question old, shaping and restrictive stories and co-create new stories (Stern, 1985). Schema Therapy story work is similarly focused on helping children become aware of their stories (particularly schema stories) and create different narratives.

Stem stories have been used in the context of attachment research in order to examine the play behaviour of children with different attachment patterns. The story completion task developed by Bretherton and colleagues (1990) investigates the reaction pattern of 5- to 8-year-old children to five classic conflict situations. In one such example, the child's doll spills juice. The child then plays out what happens next. These story beginnings were developed for diagnostic purposes (and for research) and should not be used outside a test environment. However, in the literature there are lots of similar ideas (Bretherton *et al*, 1990) that can be used therapeutically. Some of these are listed in the online materials at www.pavpub.com/resource-374CoCr (e.g. the hot soup stem story: although the mother has forbidden it, the child pours the hot soup from the pot and in doing so scalds their hand).

When using stem stories, the therapist sets up this type of scene, or an invented one similar to the family reality, as the starting point of their work with the child. The story plays out, led by the child, scaffolded by the therapist who comments on the events and asks questions, by taking a puppet's role or by giving tasks to the child. As different 'endings' are played out, the clinician asks how the child feels and what the child is thinking. The therapist also asks the central question in Schema Therapy:

what does the child need (or desire) now? These questions draw the child's attention to their core needs and they are encouraged to express these. If the child has no answer or is unsure, possible wishes/needs are put into words by the therapist. The child is thereby given a model of what can be felt and said. The therapist also takes the role of the child and plays out different modes (e.g. Lonely Child, Clever and Wise mode). In this way the clinician reflects the more hidden modes of the child and expresses them vividly, in order to support healthy coping. The therapist can also demonstrate or induce adaptive mode shifts. For example, if the child goes into a kind of combating mode to compensate for an injury, the therapist can acknowledge the hurt and model asking for support, or play out the consequences of an overcompensation mode and its impact on the Vulnerable Child mode. Typical components of mode work with stories follow.

1 and 2. Identify the presenting modes and access the Vulnerable/ Lonely/Abused Child mode

Initially, the child identifies the roles. The child takes individual characters, identifies spontaneously and thus expresses characteristic emotions, thoughts, body feelings and behaviour patterns. The therapist can then collaborate and give modes names ('Now that is a kind mum ... she is looking after you now and comforting' or 'This is a really grumbly (or Punitive) mum'). The therapist also identifies the subliminal or hidden Child modes ('I can see he is Sad Felix'). The therapist seeks to contact the Vulnerable, Lonely or Abused Child either indirectly through the child ('How's Felix now?') or through omniscient speech 'from above' ('Oh, he doesn't feel good, he's alone, what could he need now?'). The therapist can bring in care and comfort through suggestions to the child. If the child does not respond, the therapist can employ helper figures (e.g. neighbours or grandparents in the play story) who then turn to the child to offer care or support.

3. Determine each mode's functionality (in dialogue)

The functionality of each mode is not uncovered in this work in the same way as the other techniques (finger puppets, chair work, etc). However, the therapist can partially address the triggers of some modes ('If Dad scolds, Felix is quite silent'). It's also possible to ask about the pros and cons ('then Felix thinks that father will stop scolding ... does this work out?'). Dialogues between the modes are possible, such as siblings talking about how they respond to the scolding dad in the story. In Clever and Wise mode, the girl could address the boy in Combat mode ('You should not kick Dad, then he becomes angrier', 'It's better if we talk to him in another way').

4. Strengthen adaptive modes and weaken dysfunctional modes

The child initiates the transformation process alone, but is often prompted by the therapist's questions ('What can Sad Felix do now? Is he able to go to his dad like a clever guy and make a suggestion?'). The therapist recognises destructive Coping modes ('Of course he would love to stick his tongue out at Dad, or run away and lock himself in a room. But with this dad, Felix can also try something else out'). The therapist disempowers Punitive Parent parts by dealing with them in the role of a neighbour or caring adult friend, explaining the consequences of their actions and the children's basic needs ('Children can make mistakes, they are not trying to be difficult; they do not deserve to be hit for that. Children should have a chance to apologize and get things back on track'). Destructive modes should also be limited. If, for example, a boy always uses violence as a Coping mode, then the therapist can set appropriate boundaries in Caring Parent mode and, for example, demand respect from the child, together with other helpers (neighbours or trusted adults).

5. Generalise therapeutic gains to everyday life

With young children, we expect subsequent behaviour change based on processing difficult events in play, because the child will internalise the nurturing and adaptive experiences produced in the story. However, transfer from play-based stories into everyday life can be challenging, as the imaginative world doesn't directly parallel everyday life. It is important that the stories are creative, imaginative, magical and fun, thus engaging the child and leaving them wanting more. If the stories are too close to real life, modes can be triggered creating a barrier to engagement and leading instead to avoidance. In order to facilitate translating ideas tried out in story form, the therapist may gently introduce cross-references by afterwards reflecting on the play scene with the child, and thus building the Clever and Wise mode: 'What do you think? Can you do what Felix tried out there? And what will Dad probably do then? What should he do then? How could Dad know what he should do? Should I ask him if he wants to try it?'

Video recordings give the child and therapist the opportunity to think and reflect on the experience as well as deepen the processing. Video scenes can be stopped at any time to verbalise feelings or to consider needs or alternative solutions. They are also suitable for parent work. However, not all scenes generated in the child's therapy are suitable for showing parents, who may feel too confronted and get defensive. A selection can be shown that assist the parents to understand their child and meet their needs more effectively, without being too confronting or unhelpfully misunderstood.

11.2.1 Variations

Stories from the child's history provide the opportunity to address experiences that have not been processed. In this situation the therapist does not wait for the 'child's material' to come up as in client-centred play therapy, but brings those events up in a cautious, unobtrusive way. In this way the child can reconstruct or restage a part of their own story or explore what they and other participants may have felt. The therapist tells or plays episodes from the child's history, introducing the exercise as an anonymous story, beginning with 'many children have experienced…'. However, when working with school aged children, the therapist needs to be more transparent, disclosing the similarities and acknowledging that there is overlap with the child's own experience.

Case example

Four-year-old Jed is playing with his mother. She is fully engaged in playing with him, and has plenty of time to do so. The child can shape the scene. Then the therapist presents a schema triggering scene ('Then Jed had to go to kindergarten, because it's kindergarten day … How must he have felt? Maybe he was very angry and sad'). The therapist asks Jed what little Jed would have wished for and how he might have behaved. The therapist offers Coping modes which he suspects in the child, such as 'Then Jed gets angry with his mum; he yells at her and won't do what she wants him to do. And when Mum gets to the kindergarten, he tries to control what she does. And then he becomes the boss of Mum. When he's the boss he feels strong and not sad anymore. What happens next?'

11.2.2 Use of familiar stories and literature

Films, fairy tales or fictional characters (from literature, computer or video games) can be used as a vehicle to identify modes and situations that trigger modes within the child or adolescent. The child becomes the narrator and 'expert' for the therapist, who asks the child about the story of the hero, his fate and his injuries and the thoughts, emotions, behaviours and coping styles that the hero experiences. For example, Harry Potter fights evil with his 'protection' (the love of his mother). Cognitively, these illustrations help the patient see, from the hero's example, how they can overcome trauma and deprivation. 'What would Harry say now, if he was scared?' Storytelling and/or imagery work allows a child to travel back in time with the character at their side, or relive events through the eyes of the character, and rescript events using the character's strengths, in order to build a Clever and Wise mode.

References

Arntz A & Jacob G (2012) *Schema Therapy in Practice: An Introductory Guide to the Schema Mode Approach*. Chichester: Wiley.

Axline V (1947) *Play Therapy*. Cambridge, MA: Houghton Mifflin.

Bretherton I, Ridgeway D & Cassidy J (1990) Assessing internal working models of the attachment relationship: An attachment story completion task for 3-year-olds. In MT Greenberg, D Ciccetti & EM Cummings (Eds) *Attachment in the Preschool Years* (pp273–310). Chicago: University of Chicago Press.

Efran JS, Lukens MD & Lukens RJ (1990) *Language, Structure, and Change*. New York: Norton.

Freud A (1928) *Introduction to the Technique of Child Analysis*, trans. LP Clark: New York: Nervous and Mental Disease Publishing.

Klein M (1932) Psychoanalysis of Children. London: Hogarth Press.

Landreth GL (2012) *Play Therapy: The Art of the Relationship*. London: Routledge.

Stern DN (1985) *The Interpersonal World of the Infant: A View from Psychoanalysis And Developmental Psychology*. London: Karnac Books.

Chapter 12: Schema Therapy Using Drawings, Puppets and Chair Work

Peter Graaf, Christof Loose and Ruth A. Holt

12.1 Schema Therapy with drawings and other creative materials

Most children find it easier to talk about their own feelings or behaviours using drawings, rather than being asked a direct question. Even the therapist's simplest questions ('What are you feeling?') can easily hinder communication and trigger an avoidant Coping mode. Direct questioning can also stifle the child's need for activity and creativity. Looking at a picture together can deepen experiencing and make it easier for the therapist to get in touch with the Vulnerable Child. Drawing can also help overcome embarrassing moments and confused feelings. The child can actively participate and shape the content. Drawing also enables an observer self to be developed – an ability to look at themselves from a higher perspective and thus self-evaluate (developing their meta-cognitive skills). This process allows a perspective-taking that assists with introspective ability, developing self-confidence in the truest sense of the word.

12.1.1 Therapeutic traditions in work with images

Gestalt therapy

In child therapy, there is a long tradition of the use of free or guided painting – for example, in gestalt therapy (Oaklander, 1988). Here children are usually asked, after some guided imagery, to paint a dream, a favourite place or a beautiful world. The gestalt therapist avoids interpretations but stimulates the child to identify with parts of their image, such as a plant or animal: 'What part would you like to be (e.g. a dog)? Pretend to be a dog. How are you feeling? Imagine that you are in this part of the picture, speaking as if you are in it, what do you look like, what is your job? What do you do?' Or: 'What is he thinking at the moment? What will happen to him?' These and similar questions can also be used for mode work. A figure spontaneously painted by the child may represent an externalised part of the child, which the child can speak for. In this way, dialogues between parts of the image are encouraged, e.g. 'Can you speak as a dog to the man. What might the dog want to say to him?' or 'Imagine that you are the sun in the picture. Speak as the sun to the small point there!' The child may also be asked to play a part from the picture. In Schema Therapy terms, this intervention encourages the child to identify with a particular mode. The client can contact the Vulnerable Child mode, as the therapist asks, 'How is the mouse in the picture feeling? Do you want to talk to it? Do you sometimes feel like the mouse in the picture?' For example, Oaklander asked a 9-year-old client to lie down on a pillow as if he were a 'baby Jesus' that he had previously painted. Then, as the child played this role, she brought him gifts and talked about the wonderful baby (ibid. p17) – a limited re-parenting approach. Oaklander asked the child about the child's needs and feelings, which the picture expressed as a whole: 'Can you tell me a sentence that I can write on the picture (which expresses your feelings). Give your picture a title, such as "Me" or "My worries".' She also tried to connect the image to the child's experiences, for example, by asking questions such as: 'Do you sometimes feel like that as well? Does that fit with your life? Which parts of this picture are like what are you doing here (with me or with others)?'

Pictures generally provide projective material allowing the detection of hidden or unconscious burdens and desires, such as in projective investigation approaches like 'Enchanted Family/Family as Animals' (Biermann *et al*, 1975). Pictures are also used as an entry or starting point for a therapeutic conversation (e.g. images connected with anxiety or desire may indicate the child's ignored, unmet needs).

Pictures for building strengths

Pictures can encourage imaginative spaces that invite attempts to solve conflicts and distress ('Draw a beautiful dream', 'Draw the ghosts that scare you'. This image and thus the ghosts are then stored in a box at night and only let out again in the morning 'to let off steam during the day' – 'Draw how you want to be in the future'). When working with traumatised children, timelines of a child's life are used as a road map in order to reframe bad experiences as successfully survived events. In Schema Therapy work, images are used as anchors for change as the child draws problematic modes and adaptive modes. In following sessions, the child can use the images to help with transferring from one mode to the other. In addition to the free painting of pictures, art therapists offer children various other creative materials (such as clay). The child can then experience themselves as a creative artist and have fun, experiencing themselves as effective and feeling valued by therapists and parents.

12.1.2 Schema Therapy with drawings

The mode model allows depiction of difficult emotional processes in age appropriate ways. As children create drawings of each mode they are able to explore and understand each mode and create a visual representation of how their modes interact. The child can also remember this mode picture (including its messages) more easily and visualise it in the mind's eye when needed. Goals for change with each mode can also be visually represented and can provide a prompt on a conscious level that can help children to notice their own modes or communicate about them with caregivers.

Drawings can also assist with psychoeducation of schema concepts for children of school age (see Figure 12.1).

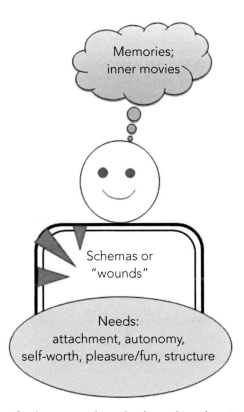

Figure 12.1: Education of schemas and modes based on drawings

Introducing mode work with drawing

As seen in Figure 12.1, the upper body of a person is drawn in front of the child. The thickness of the skin symbolises the current robustness. Depending on the physical and psychological strength of the child, the person can be drawn as thin or thick-skinned. Possible emotional injuries can be demonstrated with notches. The following is an example of how to describe these concepts to a child or young person while the therapist is drawing (see formulation aids for parents):

'Here I am drawing a man with a head and body. Over here, I'll paint the man's skin. The skin can vary in thickness depending on how well he is doing, for example, whether he has eaten or slept enough [for this child there are currently no physical limitations; however, the thickness of the skin can relate to physical or mental health]. Here is the story of his experiences [on the left of the figure] and here are the memories [in a thought bubble]. The small triangles are a symbol of the "sore spots" that almost everyone [normalisation] gets in the course of life because not everything goes well, for example, when someone was very mean to you. There are different types of wounds, such as those that occur when a person lets you down, or when you are excluded, or when your parents go through a hard time and you can't tell if they still love you. Or if you are beaten or threatened. If such an experience is very bad or happens again, the sore spots can become deeper. After a while they then form a type of scar that easily rips open or hurts when you experience something like that again. Then you can be very sensitive to that type of wound, because you expect that something like this will happen again. That's why most people also have kind of invisible special glasses that they use to look at other people, to recognise signs of danger. With the glasses you will feel that someone is angry. It may be that a person is not horrible or doesn't mean to hurt you, and yet it feels that way and does hurt somehow. Up here [reference to the thought bubble] are also the memories. In the head they are stored like movies in a library [or a cabinet in the brain]. So if someone comes across this wound, an "old movie" replays. It feels like earlier, even though you know it may not be happening now.'

The child could then begin to explore their own experiences with the therapist asking about whether they know their 'sore spots' or have examples of reacting sensitively, or which old films play in their head. Here the therapist can also provide psychoeducation about the challenge of managing trauma reactivation:

'Sometimes you just react and don't even notice that this has to do with an old wound. Other people might not know what's going on and wonder why you reacted like that. Some kids deal with this by avoiding people and not looking at their faces so that they don't have the wound re-opened. They say "I don't care". Some kids prefer to put on "rose-coloured glasses", so that everyone doesn't look so scary. This doesn't work for long, though, because other things might trigger the old movie to start running, even if you have tried to stop it. The movies are still up in

there and can make life difficult at times. That is why many people prefer not to be reminded of the old movies or think about them. In fact you might want to forget them, but can't. You can't get rid of them easily. However, in therapy we can change the strength and power of the movies. We could try that here, if you have an old movie you have always wanted to get rid of. We can watch old pictures together – and if you have them, even movies – you can get them out of your "inner library" here in our therapy session. And together we can change the message and the content, to help you feel better.'

A therapeutic step may be to paint/draw the scene (of a traumatic memory or image) that comes to the child's mind spontaneously or after further questions. When drawing the image, the child can access old scenes, not as the victim of the experience but as the creator of the image, and as a viewer who can talk about the image and change the image. This process helps the child to build up distance from the image and then re-evaluate those experiences emotionally with the support of the therapist.

Basic steps for mode work with drawings

For primary school aged children, drawing provides a great tool for identifying and beginning to challenge maladaptive modes (Chapter 10.2). The steps that follow are flexible, and do not have to be completed in full. However, is it important that the therapist makes sure that the modes are understood at an emotional level, not just a cognitive level. Otherwise the mode work will only have a superficial effect. When introducing mode work the therapist is simultaneously educating the patient and also exploring the way in which the child's modes are experienced and interact with each other. The main people in a child's life can be drawn along with the therapist, and the child can be shown as the outline of a human figure.

'This figure represents your mother, I am on this sheet, and here we can draw your body and head. Here is space now where we can draw the feelings that are inside of us. For example, here's a happy feeling, when you have a warm feeling in your tummy. That's why I drew a smiley face in my stomach here, where you can see how content I am. Do you feel that sometimes? Do you want (or should I) draw a happy mode on you?'

(See mode drawing of a child on p219).

1. Identify the presenting modes

'So this is happy Frank. When do you start feeling like him? What do you do then?' (The therapist encourages the child to illustrate and enhances the expression of the child). 'So happy Frank feels great. But, you don't always feel like that, do you? There are other moods, where you might feel completely different.'

Even though 'mood' can be used and is easily understood, it is important that the therapist be aware of technical distinctions. The term 'mood' as a synonym for mode is not technically accurate. By modes we mean latent (not necessarily currently expressed) states that are also associated with thoughts, memories and bodily sensations. In the common language of the child, these states are most likely associated with 'mood'. One can also use the term 'feeling', but this term is also not as accurate. If the child is able to understand and use the term 'mode', that is more accurate and helpful.

The therapist offers time to draw other faces and bodies and encourages the child to assign colours, symbols and characteristics to those modes and, if possible, also to give them names and list them. Different sizes can exemplify their dominance. Gradually problematic parts of the child appear and get a place in the belly. Now the child is invited to identify with a character and imagine that they are exactly this part. 'What would Evil Frank think or say right now – can you talk for him?' Typical sentences can be brought in as speech bubbles. The longer the child remains on a figure (for example, when colouring), the deeper the experience can go.

2. Access the Vulnerable/Lonely/Abused Child mode

In the next step, the therapist addresses separate internal modes. 'So this is Clever Frank, who can think through what is wise and unwise. When do you behave like that? And that is Sad Little Frank. When does Sad Frank come out? What makes him so sad? What would he need? Has he always been there? When did he show up? Can Clever Frank feel when Sad Frank is missing something important? When he gets the chance to speak, can Clever Frank remind Sad Frank of what a child needs, what would that be?'

3. Determine each mode's functionality (in dialogue)

The therapist addresses coping modes as a team with different characters. These modes are explored with the child to discover their strengths and weaknesses and the survival benefit that they have provided in the past. These modes can also be drawn within the family relationship: 'Which of your modes do your parents know? What do they do when … comes up?' This can lead to a conversation between the modes or between the modes and the family members, a variation on chair work or mode dialogue. This approach is useful in understanding the typical messages sent and received between the other modes and family members. The therapist asks the child how the characters relate to each other and what they might say to each other. Using this technique the child can begin to understand their internal 'dialogues' and become more aware of the need for more effective solutions (e.g. perhaps two modes always argue and don't ever get any resolution). At this point, you could change to using chair work, or the 'inner house' (see also Chapter 13.1).

4. Strengthen adaptive modes and weaken dysfunctional modes

Once the modes are drawn, the child is able to decide what they would like to do. 'When you see this picture, do you want things to stay as they are or should anything be changed? Do you have any ideas about how it should be? Who should be bigger, who should play a smaller role? Which mode would your parents most like? What would happen if, for example, Sad Frank were allowed to have a voice? How could the others respond when the "critic" or "complainer" (Complaining Frank) appears? Do you want to draw a picture of how you would like it to be?'

5. Generalise therapeutic gains to everyday life

The therapist's questions have so far been focused on the imaginary representation. In this step, the focus turns to practical actions. 'Let's see if we can make some of your solutions a "reality"?' It makes sense to be as concrete as possible in order to increase adaptive modes. One way to do that is to use speech bubbles that the child pastes onto the modes (starting with Post-It notes or reusable stickers). The caregiver needs to be added, as in a comic strip, providing support and encouragement or limits when necessary. Once the therapist and the child have formulated the changes they would like to make, the child can take important speech bubbles with them to help with testing or trying out the ideas discussed as homework.

The last step is including the system (parents/siblings/teachers/peers) into the child's strategies. The child is asked how parents or others could respond differently to the child, going over past situations to ensure that the Vulnerable Child's needs are not neglected.

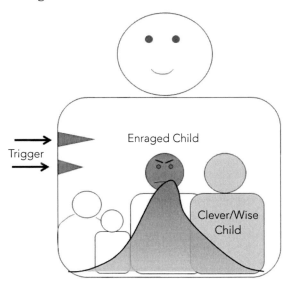

Figure 12.2: Mode picture with wave of excitement for triggers

It is also helpful to depict the way that different emotions relate to modes for children. Figure 12.2 demonstrates to the child how their own excitement can also contribute to the mode flip. Physical tension can be drawn as a wave of excitement. Many children relate to the metaphor of the volcano to represent increasing anger, which is best placed in Angry Child mode. Modes can disappear or be overrun when other modes take over, for example when arguing with others. The picture above shows the Clever/Wise mode remaining firm even when Enraged Child wants to take over. The solid colouring shows how the Clever/Wise mode can stay in control and remain calm.

The triggers of painful feelings can also be symbolised with arrows that hit the sore spots. The image graphically reminds the child of previous injuries, which increase triggering, as well as current options for getting protection or support. The best way to get the Vulnerable Child's needs met can be discussed in therapy and planned using the diagram, with its rich symbolism (see 9.3.1).

Case example
Figure 12.3 represents the different modes of a 12-year-old boy.

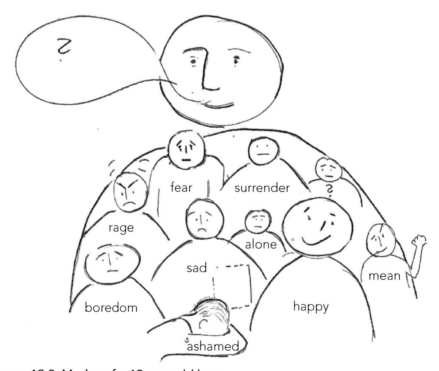

Figure 12.3: Modes of a 12-year-old boy

Figure 12.3 was developed working with a 12-year-old boy. When drawing each child's experience, the therapist needs to stay attuned to the child's way of seeing the world. For example, Figure 12.3 shows the division between the inner parts 'ashamed' and 'anxious', which are different facets of the Vulnerable Child mode. Even though we subsume those different emotions within the Vulnerable Child mode, the patient experiences fear and shame as different states.

In the first two sessions, the Vulnerable Child parts were not yet visible, but were hidden under the Camouflage mode (see Figure 12.4).

Figure 12.4: Mode image of the 12-year-old boy with camouflage

When the Vulnerable Child parts were understood, the therapist attached the Camouflage mode with self-adhesive paper which can then be swung open to show the hidden parts beneath.

Variations to mode work with images

Modes as playing cards

Semi-finished pictures on index cards or A6 size cardstock (or slightly larger, see www.pavpub.com/resource-374CoCr) for colouring are also suitable to represent individual modes. The child can change the outline of the figures to reflect their perception of the mode and can use them flexibly like playing cards. The cards can be spread on a table or put in the child's pocket or in a container as a collection. The child can also take them home and place them in a visible spot as a reminder to notice the modes and remind them of the changes they are making. The game cards principle reminds children of the popular Yu-Gi-Oh! or Star Wars cards that depict different characters with unique characteristics in battle against one other. This analogy can be extended so that each mode has a list of strengths and weaknesses (e.g. the modes can be labelled with symbols). Depending on the level of development, the cards can show complex relationships and contain, for example, the short-term consequences of certain behaviour patterns. One of the issues that can result from using playing cards is that the visual representation of the modes on a single picture can give the impression that the mode is fixed and unchangeable. Using different sized mode cards could offset this disadvantage, so that the changes in the internal dynamic can be illustrated by changing the size or the lineup. An alternative is to draw two images (a current mode image and a goal image).

Body images

Body images on large posters provide an even bigger space for mode maps. After tracing life-size body outlines, colouring with thick pencils begins. The space in the various regions of the body can be used for free colouring or as a space for laying out separately created maps or images. The head is a good place for Clever Frank. The child is offered a selection of visual cues so that he or she can choose one that is meaningful to them. The therapist can also provide all kinds of stickers or images (e.g. a small piece of jewellery, a pair of glasses, a 'bright bulb' for Clever Frank) as symbols or metaphors for strengths and weaknesses. The child can then select appropriate trinkets or symbols from a treasure chest and assign them to each mode (e.g. stickers for a crest, certificates, possibly weapons with warning signs as an indication of their dangerousness). The selected attributes can then be used as a 'trademark' or memory anchor for everyday use, and also as a nice souvenir of the therapy. The collage of modes can be rearranged again and again in the course of therapy, and thus represent a certain dynamic or change. At the end of the hour, the composition is hung on the wall and photographed, and the photo is given to the child as a reminder.

Images within a mode story

The concept of a timeline or lifeline is taken from integrative therapy and work with traumatised children (one example is described by Jordan, 2004). This technique allows the therapist to understand the history of modes and provide perspective to a child/young adult. Previous life stages are outlined or labelled on a poster, with 'milestones' drawn in. Another way to depict a timeline is to use a collage with old photographs or pictures from magazines (young people may prefer images from the internet). These can be flags, houses or any symbols that the child connects with important (positive and negative) experiences. The origins of certain modes can be included in this drawing. For example, when working with a boy with separation anxiety, the therapist can say: 'This was a wonderful time. The whole family was together. You could see lots of Happy Felix. Should we draw him in here? I think this Cheerful Felix is still inside you, but you don't see him as often now. This may have to do with that time (pointing to a difficult experience on the timeline). When your parents had that big argument, Very Sad Felix probably appeared. He was quite unhappy when they wanted to break up. Almost all children feel bad about that. Do you also want to draw Sad Felix in here? Is that Felix, who was so sad and felt so alone, still there? Does he appear again? When another big argument happens, does he worry that his parents will break up again? How old does he feel when that sadness comes up, maybe 4 or 5? But there is also a Clever and Wise Felix. He has become bigger and smarter. He also belongs to the image. What would he think/say?' More mature perspectives and resources can be ascribed to this part (marked or attached to the timeline, using speech bubbles so they can be summarized). Schema triggers can also be drawn as a 'sore spot' to clarify why someone reacts so sensitively to certain events.

Mode dialogues with drawings

A dialogue with modes can also be inspired by drawings. On an image with pre-drawn chairs (available at www.pavpub.com/resource-374CoCr), the child draws themselves and another person. This technique is drawn from a psychodynamic imagery approach (Wöller *et al*, 2012). If the child draws the other person as a friend, the therapist then asks what the friend should tell the child: 'What could your friend say that he likes about you? What do you want your best friend to say to you?' The messages are put in speech bubbles. Another safe person in the child's life can also be drawn sitting on a chair (favourite aunt, grandfather, etc.) and their words put in speech bubbles. The safe person can also be an imaginary friend. In Schema Therapy we call this figure a 'Caring Parent mode' or 'Good Protector'. The child is encouraged to draw the Caring Parent/Guardian mode and describe its attributes, keeping one image or combining all the images into a new image. The image can be copied and shrunk down to pocket size.

The chair drawings can be used to carry out dialogues with other modes. For example, the Enraged and the Clever and Wise mode can talk about how they help or hinder the child and come up with agreements about their roles. As each mode is drawn the child becomes more aware of the mode's feelings, memories and thoughts, and key phrases for each mode are identified. The healthy modes are then able to provide positive instructions or encouragements that the child can begin to internalize. As they carry around the pocket-sized image they can be prompted to access that part of themselves.

As a reminder: We conceptualise the 'Good Parent' mode as an internalisation of the helpful, safe and nurturing aspects of parents, teachers and other older caregivers. Such 'good parents' are protective and supportive of the child. In mode work they can be represented positively by drawing Inner Helpers or Heroes (which can be personified as a knight or other heroic figure), or the characteristics can enhance the Inner Friend or Adviser. Caring attributes can be derived from both parents and the child's peer group. The therapist assists the child to see these good Protector modes as constructive opposites of dysfunctional Coping modes. For example, the therapist asks the child what the Helper would do in certain situations, such as when someone steals the child's seat on the bus. What would the Helper say? What voice and posture would they use? The child needs to have a rich experience and understanding of the mode in order for it to be an effective model. One way to provide a more detailed understanding of the Inner Helper mode is to use different colours, symbols and speech bubbles. Finger puppets are another option and have the added benefit of being tactile. In play therapy, large animals or similar strong figures can play the role of the Inner Helper.

Mode work with masks

Another extension of the imagery technique is mode work with masks or dress ups. Costumes help children or teenagers identify with 'roles' (modes) and at times they can completely enter into the role, equipping themselves with swords and glasses and headgear. Mode work then follows the same steps as other media (see 10.2). However, the mask metaphor suggests the real person is hidden underneath the mask or costume. Therefore masks are most useful to represent Coping modes or negative Parent/Critic modes, while other modes can be presented unmasked, with props representing other attributes or resources (for instance a small toy, such as a bouncy ball, for Happy Child). The dramatic element of this kind of mode work can be extended to creating a film or theatre project, individually or in group therapy. As the young person develops the script they begin to understand the detail of their modes. Each mode can be played by a different person. The drama can take place in the natural world of the young adult (e.g. social scene, family vacation, etc.) or in a virtual world. In each role, different needs can be articulated and satisfied. This approach provides great insights into the child's needs (What is important for the child to say or hear?) and a road map for therapy (What does the child have to hear or know now?).

12.2 Schema Therapy with puppets (finger or hand puppets) and other figures

Work with puppets enables the therapist to access the Child modes in a playful manner. Childlike curiosity and natural playfulness are encouraged and allowed expression. Unlike the more distant work with images, touching and acting with real figures induces a spontaneous identification processes. This then facilitates emotional involvement. Quick associations with play material help reduce conscious control of critical or inhibitory thoughts. Finger puppets can be found on the internet for as little as $2 a piece, and there are a large number of types available with expressive characteristics. From our experience, children and adults connect readily with the figures and are able to find appropriate representations of modes out of a selection of about 20 to 40 figures. Teenagers, especially males, may think that this material is inappropriate or embarrassing and feel they are being treated like a child. In contrast, adults readily adapt to finger puppets for therapy and self-awareness. Heinrich Berbalk (2009) used this technique for the first time in workshops as 'mode work with puppets' as a Schema Therapy technique (documented in a diploma thesis by Rosenbusch, 2010). However, standard finger puppets only display a restricted spectrum of modes. Many popular doll brands only feature friendly and cheerful types of dolls; we have often reshaped such dolls, so that sad or serious faces are also available. For dialogues between therapist and Child modes, a therapist doll should be provided as well. This provides an additional opportunity for play dialogue when Child modes do not communicate with each other, or when communication directly with the therapist is difficult.

Figure 12.5: Therapist doll (self-made)

Figure 12.6: Dolls to represent mother and father

'Adult dolls' can also be added to represent the father or mother or other important adults, who can be a different size and shape to the finger puppets. For those people full-size puppets are suitable.

12.2.1 Elements of work mode with finger puppets

Below the ideal process of mode work is shown, following the steps listed earlier in the book (see section 10.2). In practice, the steps tend to be less sequential and do not have to be followed in full or in order. However, it is important that vivid emotional identification with modes is achieved. If this step is ignored or not achieved, the mode work will have limited effect. In order to adequately prepare a child for mode work, the assessment phase needs to explore the child's favourite and frequent modes and the therapist must effectively educate the child about each mode's functions (e.g. with drawings). This assessment element can also be done directly with finger puppets. If possible, the therapist presents the collection to the child in a well-ordered box. The child can choose (see below for restrictions) which of the provided puppets suit them best.

1. Identify the presenting modes

Allocating modes to puppets begins with the following introduction: 'Today I would like to present my collection of finger puppets to you. In this box are many different types of figures – they represent people with different feelings or moods. Some are the same as what you sometimes feel. Have a close look at them. Maybe you can find some that fit you. You can also touch them and play with them.' Whether the child chooses some spontaneously or after a longer time, additional questions can be asked, such as 'What do you like about this one?' The child is encouraged to describe the figures using all of their senses. 'How is the figure similar to you? What could we name him or her?' The naming can be influenced by the child, but should also be directed to ensure that the titles of the figures are close to the meaning of each mode.

Some children like to use several figures to depict certain modes. Boys, for example, tend to choose many knights at once, while girls often choose an array of princesses. The therapist may ask them to decide on just one of the figures in order for the therapist to keep track and not get confused. (However, the author [P.G.] has tolerated whole groups of fighters if the boy was really insistent on it, which would suggest that the child needs a strong power base.) Experience has shown that patients choose several different dolls for the Clever and Wise Child or the Healthy Adult modes (Rosenbusch, 2010). These often depict different aspects such as helping, friendship, nurturing or bravery. The Vulnerable Child mode can have different facets, such as the Lonely and Fearful child, which are important aspects to identify. Many patients also tend to mix modes in one doll (e.g. Clever/Wise Child and Detached Protector or Angry Child and Bully/Attack mode). Here, the therapist should encourage differentiation, with questions such as: 'I think there are two different parts to this, the Angry side and the Attacker, who really wants to harm others. Although they often act together, they are actually different. Let's choose an extra doll, so we don't get confused.'

When collecting puppets, aim to have at least five: at least one obvious Coping mode (e.g. Bully and Attack mode, Self-Soother mode), a Vulnerable Child mode (e.g. sad, lonely child), the Wise Child mode ('Clever', 'Smart' or 'Sensible'). A Punitive/Demanding Critic mode (Punisher Frank) and, if possible, a Caring Parent mode should also be added.

Another way to introduce the mode concept is to start with prototypes for each of the four mode types; child modes, coping modes, parent modes and healthy modes are set up to illustrate the various possibilities. The therapist then puts this puppet on their hand (or finger) and provides them with certain names and characteristics. Example with the Angry Child mode:

'Look, this is angry Will. He's really upset. He is annoyed that someone has overlooked or pushed him. Then he has loud tantrums. Sometimes he gets so upset that he slams doors or uses swear words. I've also been upset when someone has said something nasty to me, or when I was not allowed to join in a game. Do you sometimes feel like that as well? Does the figure fit you as well? Otherwise you can choose another one. What could we call this [preferably keep the child's name]?'

With shy or inhibited children, they may be more comfortable with attributing emotional states to other real persons ('Is your brother also like that sometimes? What do you do then?'). Another way to introduce puppets is to turn finding the puppet into a game: the child has the task of searching for the hidden dolls in the therapy room. Once he or she has found one, they can hold the doll up with both hands against his or her stomach and speak for the doll using 'I' statements ('Just feel what she feels ... and say how she feels, and what she often does, what she thinks').

2. Access the Vulnerable/Lonely/Abused Child mode

In the next step, the therapist may need to start a dialogue with the Angry Child mode using the therapist doll (it is often easier to interview the externalising modes first). They say, for example:

'I'm fetching the little man / the little woman now [name of therapist]. They would like to get to know Angry Felix in more detail. Can they talk to him? Hello, good morning, I'm little Mr. Graaf. Who are you? Do you belong to Frank? Are you a part of him? You look pretty upset. What's wrong? [The goal of the exploration is to activate the typical experience of the mode]. Tell me when and where you've been upset, what happened there? What are you thinking then, what are you feeling then?' The therapist focuses on a real scene and encourages the child to stay in this mode with the doll in their hand for a while in order to deepen the emotions. The therapist may also explore where the Vulnerable Child mode is by asking: 'What about Little Felix, where is he when you are yelling? Can I ask him what that's like for him?'

Vulnerable Child mode then is able to get special support and care. The therapist doll can validate the feelings verbally, but can also express limited re-parenting in actions (by petting, holding, protecting the Vulnerable Child puppet).

3. Determine each mode's functionality (in dialogue)

Problematic modes should not get too much space, but need to be appreciated for their survival function ('How long have you been with Felix? Have you always been here? Why does Felix need you? Do you have an important task?'). The consequences (advantages and disadvantages) for each of the dolls can also be discussed.

The protective function and techniques of dysfunctional modes are explored (e.g. Detached Protector as a temporary stopgap to deal with distress without sufficient support). Once the role is understood, an alternative that meets the same need is suggested – for example, a special protector is sought. This alternate way to meet the need can be a finger puppet as a model for protection, or tools that offer symbolic protection, such as a small wall, a shield, a helmet or glasses. These will be translated into action in the later step ('Generalise therapeutic gains to everyday life', opposite), and practised in real life.

4. Strengthen adaptive modes and weaken dysfunctional modes

This step involves a dialogue between the modes. The therapist asks (directly or as a therapist doll) what the individual dolls say in current situations faced by the child, what solutions come to their minds ('How do they try to help each other? What would Wise Felix say to Sad Felix?'). The Clever and Wise mode (Clever or Brave Felix) is addressed, and also – if available – caring modes: 'Which of you can comfort Sad Felix? Who can do or say something nice to him? What does Clever Felix think about the solution?' The therapist encourages the Vulnerable Child to express needs ('What do you want/need now?'). If the child detaches from the dialogue and discusses the action more 'from above', the Clever Child is asked about the Vulnerable Child ('What does Sad Felix need now?').

The Angry Child or Aggressive Coping modes must be managed or limited. It may be necessary, for example, to stop attacks on other dolls or the therapist doll through strong words or practical intervention ('It's my job to look out for everyone, as big Mr. Graaf, to make sure that no one gets hurt or broken. This is not OK. It's fine to say what makes you angry, but it's not fine to hurt anyone.')

One way to address the way that the dolls relate is to ask about 'friendships' between the dolls. As an introduction, the child can rank the dolls by popularity. 'Who is friends with whom among the dolls? Is anybody left out? How can the outsiders be included in a circle? Who from the others can help Sad Frank, what words can comfort him?

5. Generalise therapeutic gains to everyday life

One way to link the puppet work to everyday life is to have a dialogue between a puppet and a real person in the child's system. This is a kind of mode experiment to help prepare the child to bring their new awareness into everyday life. A great introductory question for example is: 'Hey Felix, does your mom even know how sad Sad Felix is, when he is so scared? What would happen if she knew that? What should she do or say? Should we play that out? Are you playing Sad Felix? How should I play Mom?' This can also be done in role play, in which the child uses different modes or only a single mode. The Vulnerable and/or the Clever Child mode speaks to the mother or the father, with the backing of the therapist. The patient practises expressing their needs in an authentic and appropriate way, either in their own words or modelled after the therapist's words ('May I try something?'). Afterwards the therapist and child evaluate the dialogue: 'How was it? Did it help you? Do you want to try that "in reality"? Have you ever tried it "in reality"? How did that work? What would happen if you were to do it in a different way? Do you want to try that? How would it be if your mom came to Sad Felix and comforted him?' This connects the experiential work to everyday life applications. During the planning of action steps, systemic 'control' is absolutely necessary. The therapist needs to be aware of what risks are involved if the child articulates their needs differently from before. Is it helpful to be braver, or simply more direct? The child should be offered help if they hesitate or have doubts ('Would it help if I talk to your mom "in reality"?'). The child can be made aware of parents' (or others') possible reactions and it is also helpful if the therapist discusses ideas for coping, e.g. via a Protective mode.

Games can be created to help the child identify different effects of the individual modes and weigh up the pros and cons. For strengthening and memorising, cards with a photo of a mode puppet and cards with matching speech bubbles can be matched together. Working effectively with modes can now also be given as a homework assignment (Let's see how many times Sad Felix speaks up this week. What does Clever Felix say if Dad wants him to clean up? Can we catch Angry Felix before he explodes and get stickers for each time he uses words rather than fists?). If the child has limited self-awareness about everyday mode activations, self-observation homework should be provided. In the vein of 'detective work', the child can 'search for clues' when certain modes appear. Making a large chart for the child to use at home is also helpful. A large A3 size sheet, with photos of finger puppets or one photo of the relevant finger puppets attached, helps the child to remember the experiential work done in session.

Figure 12.7: Finger puppets with speech bubbles with key phrases for the individual modes

The child can write diary-like keywords or draw little pictures to help them remember mode triggers. Support from parents is required to assist the child to notice the mode triggering and have accurate self-observation. Of course, the parents need to be capable of maintaining a sufficiently neutral and benevolent, friendly and interested attitude, without a punitive focus on errors and without seeming to 'gang up' on the child. One way to make an attractive visual presentation and memory aid for doll work is to insert photos of all the characters in a Power Point slide. Towards the end of a therapy session the child and therapist can name the dolls and attach appropriate speech on the screen together. The child can take this printed photo home.

Involvement of parents

In order to see ongoing change in family functioning, early involvement of key members of the system is especially important. The child needs to be consulted about how the therapist talks to parents about the session and how to prepare for the child's new approaches. Therapists can work with parents to shape their responses, so that negative reactions to healthy behaviour can be minimised and inadequate responses can be supplemented. Often parents gain a new and more compassionate understanding of the child as a result of this therapeutic work.

As therapy progresses, finger puppets should be available each session. They can be used spontaneously by the therapist or child. The issues of the child (or of the parents) can be discussed using the finger puppets and more mode work can be 'built in'. When the child talks about difficult experiences from everyday life, the therapist can take the dolls and ask if a certain mode played a prominent role. If the parents report a difficult situation (e.g. by telephone or before the session), the therapist can address this by himself and say: 'I have heard a story from home. Your mom said you had an argument. Should we find out together which of the people were playing inside you? Which of your modes were particularly active in this situation and who was more in the background? I, for example, would be sad [educative approach] in this situation. What was upsetting Sad Felix? What would he have needed to feel better? Which people could help to make it better? Most children want to be with someone who is nice to them. Is it the same for you? Could someone else talk so that your parents take it seriously or could someone help to get through that tricky situation better?'

The finger puppets provide a tolerable way of confronting unhelpful behaviour. The child is not attacked or questioned, but understood from all angles; even the hidden modes that are involved are discovered.

If the child does not raise a specific topic at the beginning of a session, the therapist can ask about the past few days and inquire about moments or situations where a mode may be activated. They may ask retrospectively ('Yesterday while watching TV, which part was with you there?') or explore in a more general way ('When your daddy comes/when you're at school, which of your modes show up then? How do you behave? How do you behave while with your friends/your mum/your dad? What problems may be caused by that mode? What if that mode takes a break for once and lets somebody else take the lead?')

Extending finger puppet work to the family system can involve discussing parents' modes. The child chooses dolls from the collection that display the parents' modes. The child can then show (possibly with the therapist's help) which modes occur together or which of the child's modes activate which parent mode. This can demonstrate how mother and child both send out their 'Warriors' or other destructive mode escalations. The therapist and child can then search for a healthier mode process, if possible, together with the parents. This makes it clear that both parents and child need a more deliberate use of healthy modes, in order to break the vicious cycle.

The presentation of the child's doll selection to the parents must be very carefully handled, especially when particularly ugly or unfriendly dolls have been chosen (which may offend or unsettle the parents). If that is too risky given the relationship dynamics, the parents can create a puppet arrangement similar to the child's.

Variants of the mode work with dolls

There are different ways to symbolise the mode model with children. For example, large hand puppets can be presented as a 'container' or a whole person, with the finger puppets inside them. To represent a whole child with inner diversity, the child can put all finger puppets on their ten fingers and hold them up. The child is then photographed with their own head as 'leader' of the modes. There are many ways to represent the Detached Protector: a cloth hiding a doll mask, building blocks as a wall or small boxes with lids are suitable. Patients often take the initiative and build a wall by themselves with the provided material (Detached Protector mode) in order to deny the therapist access to Vulnerable Child mode. (The author P.G. has experienced two cases where the guardian of this barrier has not been willing or able to step aside, in spite of long negotiations and the prospect of getting needs met more effectively.)

Large hand puppets can complement the play with finger puppets. They are suitable not only to represent parents or other adults, but also as a 'body' for the finger puppets. The big doll represents the whole person, the smaller ones the parts. The interaction between the dolls can also be put on a stage like a puppet show (through a specially built frame). It is also very helpful to film the play, which often encourages children to plan the play and to direct it towards a more healthy resolution. The video recordings are watched with the child, then possibly also with the parents, if the child allows. With very boisterous children, using a script helps to focus the session.

PlayMobil figures are an alternative to finger puppets, but have less character and flexibility. Finger puppets can be given different accessories, so that you protect them with shields, helmets or hats. With small masks, one can also illustrate that some emotions or modes are also used for deception and, for example, show a sad face while they are actually angry.

Figure 12.8: Angry child mode with deceptive sad face

Using positions to depict important aspects of modes is helpful. (Variants of finger puppet work are also described in 12.3.1.) The power of a mode can be illustrated by using a throne or a position of height. Relationships between modes can be expressed in the collective appearance and how close the dolls are. Based on the 'Family Board' with wooden figures (Ludewig & Wilken, 2000), another variant is suitable. The first question in this method is 'Who belongs to me and my family?' Real conflicts and relationships are represented on the board, with characters for family members and other caregivers (including friends) selected and named by the child. Then alternative arrangements are considered. Using these kinds of materials enables the patients themselves (and also the parents) to have a new, often deeper level of understanding of the emotional conflict. They are then able to name and find a solution. At the beginning of therapy the figures also provide some optimism for change and motivation by providing a new way of seeing the conflict. Modes allow a child to begin to let go of the ego-syntonic experience of symptoms (experiencing themselves as 'a failure', 'evil' or 'weak'). This is often created and reinforced by the social environment ('you're evil, you can't do anything'), but the experience of externalising difficult aspects of self allows a child to see that aspect as only one part of their selves. In spite of the lack of differentiation of the Family Board figures, it is easy for younger children to attribute individual figures with very specific characteristics. Many children show surprising creativity and determination. Because the Family Board figures lack structure, they are generally acceptable for older children and youths. A strong rejection of this material is unusual (Eckardt, 2012, p1).

Wooden figures can be given attributes to illustrate schemas (e.g. minor injuries drawn with a pencil). Conflicts and dialogues between different modes can be played out with wooden figures and small objects. A change in material can be useful to distinguish between modes and the whole person. The modes could also, for example, be designed as putty, clay or threaded figures. Once the modes have been defined, the child can use a 'detective thinking' process to find other parts, such as the Clever and Wise mode: 'What are you good at? What do you like doing? What do your friends like about you? What positive things would your teacher tell me about you?' Homework gathering 'evidence' for Clever and Wise Child mode can support this strengths-based work at a micro level. These reports can be depicted on the Family Board in the therapy session with parents, e.g. in the form of new characters or other accessories.

Figure 12.9: At the front the teenage patient is shown in Self-Aggrandizer mode on the pedestal (figure with pedestal), next to the Vulnerable Child mode, hiding from the father who is in Punitive Parent mode. The parent's Vulnerable Child modes stand next to the parents.

Complex or difficult therapy situations

In mode work with finger puppets, you can suddenly encounter traumatic experiences, which are activated by certain modes. This allows an opportunity to process the trauma by rewriting it, using the Schema Therapy concept of re-scripting. The child replays the traumatic scene with the dolls, but at the crucial point a Healthy Adult enters the scene and provides what the child needed, e.g. comfort, protection, validation. This provides a corrective emotional experience, reducing previously experienced feelings of shock and increasing feelings of protection.

Case example

While selecting dolls in therapy 10-year-old Katie remembered her father being repeatedly bitten by his former drug-addicted partner. The dialogue with Frightened Katie had evoked these memories. She re-enacted this experience using dolls as parent figures spontaneously, demonstrating high levels of fear and distress. The therapist validated Katie's feelings (Therapist: 'That must have been terrible, not to be able to do anything about it and crying by yourself in the room, and with no one comforting you?') and addressed Katie's needs ('What did you need? Your real mum to come and help, or the police to be called?'). However, Katie wanted to re-script the scene differently. Katie wanted to have a serious talk with the violent stepmother, surrounded by all her dolls (her modes) in a corner of the room on the floor, and vigorously put her in her place. Over the course of further sessions Katie wanted to 'play' this scene with several variations. Encouraging these very lively, creative re-scriptings enabled her to gain mastery over the earlier traumatic scene imaginatively (for more information on reprocessing and re-scripting, see Arntz & Jacob, 2012).

In working out how to deal with distressing modes, children often want to play out a fantasy of killing, banishing or imprisoning them. Children who have a difficult time with managing impulsivity or anger often want to be instantly free of those modes. They suggest that 'Evil modes' can be tied up or magically disappear forever. In such cases, we need to therapeutically challenge these simplistic approaches and highlight positive features of these repudiated parts: 'However, Evil Frank cannot simply be gotten rid of like that, he belongs to you. He still thinks he has to defend you if someone disagrees with you. He needs to be convinced that he is not the boss and he is only allowed to come out when Clever [child's name] wants him to. Unless Clever Frank says he can act, he needs to have a holiday from bossing everyone around.' If the child is insistent on getting rid of a Child or Coping mode, the child needs clear direction on how to disempower this mode in everyday life, or how to have parents help manage the mode: 'If Evil Frank starts kicking again, what should your mother do, hold him or tell him to go to his room?' The child can be made aware that Angry Child modes or even Aggressive Coping modes have to be limited, rather than eliminated. All parts have a meaning and a function, so integration, not exclusion or destruction of modes, is the goal.

Hyperactive children like to use the puppets to express their wild impulses and, in doing so, throw them around or even destroy them (usually accidentally). Or they flip (mode flipping) from one doll to another with erratic attention so that any reflection or emotional processing is not possible. Puppet play can therefore be a stage for expressing aggressive actions without a therapeutic benefit. The therapist needs to consider whether there is a deeper meaning underlying the apparently chaotic sequence, which can be explored therapeutically. Otherwise, the therapist takes an instructional role and provides limited re-parenting by not only protecting the puppets, but also modelling speaking up for their own needs: 'I can't allow that. The dolls need to be safe. This is becoming too wild and chaotic for me; we need to take a break and decide what we want to happen in this room. I do not just want to be a spectator in a destructive game. If you want to fight with me or just want to jump around, let's choose something else instead of dolls.' A script that the child and therapist re-enact can helpfully guide the process.

12.3 Schema Therapy using chairs

Chairs have been used in gestalt therapy (Moreno, 1946; Perls, 1943) as a way of externalising and projecting certain persons or parts. In gestalt therapy patients were able to enact conversations with their own parents and dialogue with them in order to express unresolved or unspoken concerns and feelings. Even for adults this can be an intimidating and scary experience. For example, if a very dominant father is 'placed' in front of them, the childhood memory is activated, making the father feel much bigger and intimidating to the patient. Therefore care is needed to provide adequate support and 'protection' for a child.

The use of chairs helps people imagine an absent person more effectively than an imaginary empty space does. In Schema Therapy, chairs are used to externalise modes or emotional states and thus encourage perspective taking and the growth of the healthy modes. This technique can be used with adults and adolescents (who are engaged and have sufficient imagination or creativity) as well as children from the age of about 9 years (depending on the level of cognitive and emotional development).

Opposite is a description of Schema Therapy using chairs, incorporating the elements listed in section 10.2. The formulation discussed is typical when working with 9- to 12-year-old children and should be adjusted for work with adolescents.

Figure 12.10 shows a typical chair set-up, in which the Demanding Parent/Critic mode sits on the right chair, the Vulnerable Child sits on the left and the Clever and Wise mode sits in the middle.

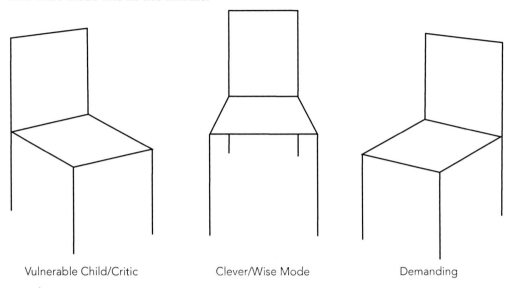

Vulnerable Child/Critic   Clever/Wise Mode   Demanding

Figure 12.10: Typical chair positioning for mode dialogues

Chairs can be used to explore modes early in therapy as well as once a child has a good understanding of their modes.

1. Identify the presenting modes

First, the child ascribes each mode to a different chair. Ideally, to assist in visually representing the modes, different sized chairs should be availa ble. To introduce the concept, the therapist can say: 'We have noticed that you have different parts (feeling states/feelings) inside you. Not all of them come up at once. If you're happy, you might just feel one. Sometimes they alternate. Sometimes only one is in charge. I imagine it like this, for example, the Boss inside you sits on a chair, crosses his arms and says what he wants and what he does not want; he doesn't care about the other's views.' The therapist checks this idea and asks the child whether the chair suits them or if they want to change. The child is asked to write the name of the mode on a piece of paper and to attach it to the back of the chair. Now the therapist asks which modes will sit in the other chairs. Mode names are attached to the other chairs. We recommend putting the most important modes in the centre, such as the dominant Coping mode (e.g. Angry or Detached Protector), the Vulnerable/Lonely/Abused Child (e.g. Sad Lisa, Lonely Tom) and the Clever and Wise mode (Clever Sam, Wise Lin Mae). Also, a Punitive/Demanding Critic mode (the Strict Leigh or The Dictator) should have a chair. However, the number of chairs needs to be manageable.

In the second step, the child is encouraged to identify and empathise with each mode, and alternately sits on the various chairs with the appropriate posture (e.g. in Detached Protector mode, leaning back with folded arms). 'Would you like to sit down on this chair in Boss mode and show how you feel about that? [Conceptually, the 'Boss' mode is the Spoiled Child mode]. What does he say, then, for example, if your mom wants you to clean your room?' The therapist offers the child time to sit in the chair and experience the mode. For elementary school children, sitting on chairs may be too restrictive. In order to help activate the mode, they may need to move from the chair and to 'play the mode'. The Angry Child mode can be expressed with foam bats, for example. The mode that tends to inhibit impulses (Demanding/Criticizing Critic mode) can then be represented by playing a police officer ('Attention, attention, this is the police: you can never react like that!'). The Dominator mode is encouraged to act and speak in the aggressive way that the child has used previously. A real life experience can be re-enacted. The Detached Protector mode can wear a helmet, headphones or cool sunglasses (see section 9.3.4), while the Self-Aggrandizer mode can wear a crown; the Clever/Wise mode can wear glasses as a symbol of wisdom and the ability to stand up for him/herself in a helpful way.

2. Access the Vulnerable/Lonely/Abused Child mode

The therapist begins the dialogue (see the online material for a mode interview) with the parts of the child and asks the Boss what they think, feel, and do.

'Hello, lovely [mode-name], I am pleased to be able to get to know you. I've heard a lot about you; [child's name] has already told me about you. How long have you belonged to Frank? And what is your job? When do you appear?' The interview with this mode is now completed and is followed by a new interview: 'Frank, would you like to sit down on the other chair now? [Vulnerable Child mode] How long have you known Frank? And what is your job? What do you think or feel, Sad Frank? What would you like? What do you think about the Boss Frank? What do you, Little Frank, need so that you can feel better? Who can help you?'

Sad Frank gets special attention and support. He needs comfort, protection and people to support him. He is asked frequently about needs, feelings, safety and wishes. Each interview goes into detail, including the accompanying body sensations and behaviours. However, children tend toward fast mode changes, which the therapist should follow. If the therapist notices a child 'flipping' into a different mode, the child can be guided to that chair to express the current state.

3. Determine each mode's functionality (in dialogue)

'Clever Frank can sit here now; do you want to come over?' In the interview: 'So you're smart Frank. What happens inside you, when Frank's mom demands that he clean up? What do you think? What do you think of the other two? Is there another

way to respond to Mum? I also know this Cool Frank [Detached Protector mode], *who does not respond and acts as if nothing matters. I would like to talk to him as well some time.'* (Initiate chair change.)

The therapist shows a non-committal attitude toward difficult modes, thanks them for the statements and asks the child to go back to the original, neutral chair. The neutral chair is the one on which the child normally sits outside of the mode work. This chair represents an observer status, from which the events are watched and reflected upon. From here, the child is asked to evaluate the pros and cons, strengths and weaknesses of the various modes and estimate their impact on life. The therapist can encourage this process by asking: 'Who talks the most or plays the leading role, and who is probably overlooked?' A dialogue between the parts may also be possible.

The goal is to strengthen the Clever Child mode. The therapist also needs to nurture and support the Vulnerable/Lonely/Abused Child mode and bring ideas about how to meet the needs of this part, with healthy coping strategies. The Clever/Wise Child mode can get its own chair – separate from the neutral chair of the child – that is just as big or even identical to the observer's.

4. Strengthen adaptive modes and weaken dysfunctional modes

In the observer chair, the child is asked what they would like to do with all the modes (a kind of second Clever/Wise mode of a higher order). The child's ability to manage these two perspectives, the Clever/Wise mode and the observer role, needs to be assessed. If a child does not have the cognitive sophistication needed, just stick with the Clever and Wise mode. This wise part should be encouraged to find age and situation-appropriate solutions for dealing with distressing events (e.g. parents, teachers, peer group, etc) and to identify which basic needs were not met: *'Now that we have found out what Little Frank was feeling and needing, who could best help to meet those needs? Can the Boss maybe step aside? Can Clever Frank put in a good word for Little Frank?'*

Dialogues between modes assist with both strengthening positive modes and weakening dysfunctional modes. In Arntz and van Genderen (2011), different chair work techniques with borderline patients are described, which are (with some modifications) also appropriate for youths: for example, if the Punitive Parent (Critic) mode shows up in a teenager, the therapist should begin a dialogue with that mode. The teenager moves to a separate chair for the Punisher mode. The adolescent's original chair (observer or Clever Child) now remains free and can be moved back to after hearing from the dysfunctional mode. Therapist:

'I want to talk to Punishing Frank again by myself. Just sit on the chair and speak for him. I just heard the punishing part inside you say that Little Frank was stupid and dumb ... Please explain that to me in more detail!'

The therapist then encourages the teenager to express, in the Punisher mode, the typical criticisms that the child often says to him/herself. Once the mode has expressed those ideas the child moves back to the original chair. The therapist faces the Punisher mode chair and defends Little Frank. Therapist (speaking to the empty chair): 'I do not think that Frank is stupid at all. I do not want you, Punishing Frank, to put Little Frank down, insult, or punish him; you have no right to do that and it does not help him. He needs love and encouraging words and not those insults!' Now, the therapist asks what Punishing Frank would probably say at this point. The client moves back into Punisher mode (by sitting on the particular chair and repeating the thoughts) before moving back to the observer chair. The therapist says, for example, 'I want these insults to stop now. Little Frank is no different from anyone else, he has got good reasons why...' The therapist gives examples and explains that all children make mistakes and that they do not deserve such criticism or punishment. The therapist leads the dialogue until the child in observer role thinks that Punisher Frank has given in or would probably give in. The therapist can also move the Punisher Frank chair, rotating it, distancing it or putting it out of the room completely. If the therapist has the impression that other parts of the child are strong and confident enough, they can encourage the Vulnerable Child or Clever Frank to speak up and to face Punisher Frank, with the therapist also providing moral support (e.g. 'Leave Frank alone, we are really tired of these insults!').

After the mode dialogue the therapist can use the ideas from the dialogue to develop a role play, where the client practises expressing their needs in an appropriate and authentic way, without using deprecating, insulting or destructive behaviour patterns.

As progress is made in therapy, the therapist needs to help the client negotiate changes in their family system. The therapist needs to prepare the teenager for possible difficulties that might occur when they change the way they speak to their parents. Discussions about managing relationships with parents need to be done mindful of the possibility of triangulating, resulting in conflicted loyalties. One way to prevent the child feeling unhelpfully conflicted is for the therapist to act as if the parents were sitting in the therapy room at all times, being conscious of their perspectives and not trying to vie for the client's trust in a way that undermines the parent–child relationship. Developing new skills and assistance to implement them helps to minimise unhelpful modes, particularly Coping modes. The therapist helps develop plans for the patient to stay safe without needing to resort to overcompensation. One way to do that is to use the Detached Protector mode briefly, to assist the child to get some space or protection (e.g. stop listening for a while). However, this can only be a short-term solution. The activation and growth of the Clever and Wise mode is indispensable. Developing a Clever/Wise mode includes helping the patient express needs in a socially acceptable manner and defending against unhelpful criticism or humiliation.

5. Generalise therapeutic gains to everyday life

The more playful and experiential work is rounded out with reflection and planning, if possible in the same session. Clearly identify mode triggers (see www. pavpub.com/resource-374CoCr for Worksheet: Mode Flashcard) and create a Clever and Wise mode plan for those moments. These action plans provide a healthy way to manage each mode and can be tested in specific situations as homework. Flash cards are also a helpful way of reinforcing the experiential learning that takes place in therapy sessions (see box and section 14.2). One way of helping a child have more awareness of typical mode activations is setting an observation task in which the child notices which modes occur, in which situation or in what time period (see the online material for worksheets for mode observation).

Finally the therapist discusses how other members of the system (parents/siblings/teachers/peers) can be involved. They ask the child what the parents can do differently so that the Clever and Wise mode is supported and the Vulnerable Child is cared for. The therapist offers to communicate the new approach to the parents for the child, or find compromises between parent and child interests.

Mode flash card example

When my mother gets angry at home again and tells me to clean up,

- I use Clever Frank and say, for example: 'Mum, you don't need to get upset, I can handle it … I'll take care of it myself.'
- I catch Boss Frank before he starts yelling and send him on a mini holiday. He would usually say 'Leave me alone' or 'I won't do that.'
- Temporary solution: If Mum is really upset, I can still use the Detached Protector to turn down her volume and wait until she is finished, and then say 'okay'. The following trick helps me: I imagine wearing headphones and listening to my favourite music.
- Or I (or the Clever one) listen to Sad Frank and let him speak. He then says...

When the teacher tells me off for not doing my homework or rushing...

Of course, these suggestions should be discussed with the teachers and parents/caregivers, and possibly also with grandparents or coaches.

Variants of chair work

The child can choose stuffed animals or other figures as a symbol of their modes and put those onto the appropriate chairs. Any of the different techniques already discussed can be combined; for example, finger puppets, pictures or cards can be put onto the chairs. The 'occupation' of a chair with real objects can facilitate the anchoring and 'handling' of modes in everyday life. The child may want to take one character home from therapy and carry it as a reminder. Photographs or video recordings of the mode work are also useful both as 'transition objects' from the therapist and as reminders for the child, between sessions, of the current therapy work.

Tips for chair work

When shifting between modes it is important to notice the idiosyncratic body language of each mode. Ideally, the child is encouraged to sit in the chair in that mode's typical posture. This makes the unconscious, physical reinforcers (e.g. gestures, facial expressions, body posture) of the mode more conscious, allowing effective correction. For example, in order to help the Clever and Wise mode replace a problematic mode, the child needs to get to know the gesture variations and facial expressions for those modes and practice shifting from the problematic mode to the healthier mode. One way to build awareness is to photograph mode-typical gestures, facial expressions and body postures. This increases a child's ability to observe and recognise a mode in everyday life. It also increases the child's empathy with the mode (we often say to clients: 'Don't think about it, just be the mode!'). Video recordings allow even more fine tuning of the Clever and Wise mode, including paraverbal mode characteristics such as tone of voice, intonation and speech behaviour (articulation, volume, rate of speech and intonation), including pauses and silences.

Case example

14-year-old Eddy comes to the second session as part of his inpatient treatment. He sits down with his legs apart (an indication of the Spoiled Child mode), and says that before we begin he wants to tell the therapists what's wrong with the programme. He doesn't understand why he is not allowed to go into the staff kitchen, and he also demands a different kind of juice. In addition, he needs an orthopaedic surgeon, physical therapy and a massage for his neck. Eddy wants the therapist to enter the complaints immediately in the computer because he has to take them seriously and document them. The therapist then asks him about his neck, and how he feels about it exactly (addressing of the needs of the subjectively neglected and probably Vulnerable Eddy). Eddy changes his body language (less tense, folded arms untighten), softens his voice, rubs his neck and describes his discomfort with the stiff and tic-plagued neck. The therapist takes a seat in front of his computer and requests a physiotherapy consult for Eddy. Eddy is surprised and wants to check whether the therapist is really sending the message. He returns to his demanding and challenging behaviour, continues with his complaints list and asks for the orthopaedic consult also. Therapist: 'I noticed something interesting about you spoke just now. It sounds like a king talking, giving instructions to his subjects about what to bring him.' (Eddy smiles a little, irritated and embarrassed). 'This seems to be how you usually deal with difficult situations. It must be hard to always have to demand things. But if you let me know how you actually feel, I can be more helpful to you. What do you think about my King idea, can you see some of that in yourself?' Eddy agrees, somewhat embarrassed. This often happens at home as well. 'I would like to set up a chair for this version of you, a throne with a back rest, which you can sit on to help with feeling high up and give others instructions.' (The therapist immediately takes a chair and sets it up. 'This can be "King Eddy" then, is that OK?' (Eddy nods, grinning.) 'But there is also another part of you, a side in which you express quite calmly what you wish for or need. I will put this part here on a smaller chair. What could we call that?' Eddy: 'Little Eddy?' Therapist: 'Great, tell me something about Little Eddy. Would you like to sit down over there and fill me in?' Eddy is reluctant to move into expressing the mode, and instead prefers talking about Little Eddy.

In the later stage, the therapist asks about the impact of the modes on the relationships with others. 'What effect do you think these two modes have on other people?' Eddy describes quite accurately the consequences of both feeling overwhelmed and dominating others, and says (a little too readily, in the therapist's estimation): 'So I have to put away the King!' The therapist pauses, saying that it does not work that easily. 'First you need to talk about where he came from and what important task the King had in your life story.' Eddy immediately suggests that it is connected to his bullying experiences. As a King he wouldn't have 'to give a shit' about others. This suggests that 'the King' represents a mixture of Spoiled Child mode and an Overcompensation mode – narcissistic self-aggrandisement. The therapist suggests that this probably gave Eddy a feeling of strength and superiority, and draws a mode picture in which the Mistrust schema is symbolised as a sore point and the King as a coping strategy.

In the same session, a third, alternative mode, 'Wise, Reasonable Eddy', is placed on a chair. Eddy is asked to summarise what they have now found out: 'Well, I have different personalities, and the King will have to go.' The therapist asks him if he would be willing to work on figuring out how the King could step aside, so that he (Eddy) can get along with other people better, and ultimately reach his career goal of becoming a professional golfer. He could start this work by not immediately putting the King away, but instead watching when he appears. Eddy says that this is too difficult, so the therapist offers help by enlisting caregivers (nurses and other staff in the inpatient unit). They could call his attention to the King, by using a code word ('Hakuna Matata'). This allows Eddy to avoid embarrassment and creates a collaborative relationship with staff, beginning the process of seeing the King as ego-dystonic. He could then decide whether the King mode is helpful or whether he might need a different mode to express his needs.

References

Arntz A & Jacob G (2012) *Schema Therapy in Practice: An Introductory Guide to the Schema Mode Approach*. Chichester: Wiley.

Arntz A & van Genderen H (2011) *Schema Therapy for Borderline Personality Disorder*. Chichester: Wiley.

Biermann G, Kos M & Haub G (1975) The graphic test, the enchanted family, and its application in educational counselling and paediatric clinics (author's transl). *Padiatrie und Padologie* **10** (1) 19–31.

Berbalk H (2009) 'Behandlungskonzept mit der MAP.' Unveröffentlichtes Manuskript.

Eckardt U (2012) 'Schematherapeutische Arbeit mit dem Familienbrett.' Unveröffentlichtes Skript.

Jordan K (2004) The color-coded timeline trauma genogram. *Brief Treatment and Crisis Intervention* **4** (1) 57.

Ludewig K & Wilken U (2000) *Das Familienbrett*. Göttingen: Hogrefe.

Moreno JL (1946) Psychodrama and group psychotherapy. *Sociometry* **9** (2/3) 249–253.

Oaklander V (1988) *Windows to Our Children*. New York: Center for Gestalt Development.

Perls FS (1943) *Ego, Hunger, and Aggression*. London: Allen & Unwin.

Rosenbusch K (2010) *Alternative Verfahren zur Erhebung von Schemamodi*. Vergleich von Fragebogenverfahren und MAP (Modusarbeit mit Puppen), Diplomarbeit am Fachbereich Psychologie der Universität Hamburg.

Wöller W, Leichsenring F, Leweke F & Kruse J (2012) Psychodynamic psychotherapy for posttraumatic stress disorder related to childhood abuse – Principles for a treatment manual. *Bulletin of the Menninger Clinic* **76** (1) 69–93.

Chapter 13: Schema Therapy – Using Inner House and Imagery

Christof Loose, Peter Graaf and Ruth A. Holt

13.1 Working on the 'inner house'

Work on the inner house is a psychoeducation technique developed for older children and adolescents in order to provide a mechanism for understanding the background to their emotions and behaviour. It helps to establish an ego-dystonic attitude toward the problem behaviour, which is necessary to reduce this behaviour in the long term. Each house is individually designed and built for the child. Once built, therapy can begin on the mode level (see 13.1.4).

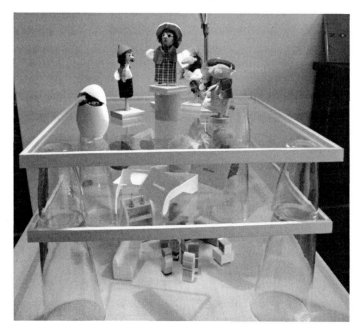

Mode-level

Schema-level

Experience-level

Figure 13.1: Shows three levels of an inner house, explained below.

13.1.1 Mode level

The mode level is the top floor of the inner house and is set up first. It represents conscious experiencing and behaviour in the here and now. In Schema Therapy, as explained in 10.2 and in greater depth in sections 9.2, 12.1, 12.2 and 12.3, the child's 'inner states' are explored and ascribed to finger puppets who then represent these inner states or modes. The therapist makes sure that at least the main modes (such as Vulnerable, Angry, Happy Child modes, Demanding or Punitive Critic modes, Dysfunctional Coping mode and Clever and Wise mode) are represented as 'something everyone has inside them' (psychoeducational element).

To understand how a child views the modes and which ones they accept or approve of, the child lines up the chosen finger puppets with these instruction: 'Which mode do you like the most, what state do you feel most comfortable in? Place the appropriate finger puppet on the far left please, in the first place. And who comes next?' etc. 'And what mode do you dislike the most?' A photograph of this line-up is recommended, as it will be needed later (see 13.1.4).

Side note: On a practical note, we recommend that the finger puppets be placed on a shelf (e.g. glass of a picture frame) which – when more floors are added – can be easily lifted without having to change the line-up of finger puppets. When buying a frame, make sure that the glass is fixed to the frame in order to avoid contact with sharp edges.

Depending on age and the child's ability to deal with abstract concepts, a total of three dimensions can be defined (proximity, power, contact); nonetheless, not all dimensions have to be processed in the standard procedure (see below). It should be noted that the procedure presented here slightly differs from the procedure in 12.2, in order to make the reader familiar with an additional variant of the mode-finger puppet line-up.

Proximity

From the age of 6 a child can understand that the modes that occur at the same time can be depicted by their proximity to each other. In the standard procedure, the proximity of the finger puppets reflects how commonly occurring those modes are in everyday life. For example, if the child has a 'Slightly Irritable mode' (the child's own phrase) and this Irritable mode increasingly appears with the 'Angry mode' ('First I'm only irritable and then I'm angry!'), the finger puppets that represent these modes should stand close to each other. Even though it is not clear whether these modes are child modes or coping modes yet (child mode: see Table 2.7, coping mode: see Table 2.9 to 2.11), the therapist uses the child's terms and continues working with it. Neighbouring finger puppets form a kind of 'gang' or 'clan', or, in the terminology of therapists, a subgroup or a mode cluster.

Power

The power of each mode is also represented by finding out which mode speaks up or is dominant in a given situation. The prevailing mode finger puppet is placed on a 'throne' (building brick, etc.). The physical aggrandisement indicates that this particular mode dominates how the child feels, thinks and acts in a situation ('Who is the boss in this situation?'). At the beginning, mapping many everyday situations is recommended ('Who sits on the throne the most?', 'How do the other modes feel about that?'). Here ambivalences or inner conflicts can be displayed playfully and visually for the child as an 'argument'. If in doubt, the therapist should check whether 'rivalry' exists among the modes ('I have the impression that x as well as y want to sit up on the throne, is that true? And how does that work then? And what do you think about that yourself?' etc).

Since different modes/finger puppets can occupy the 'throne' over the course of a day, it is advisable, for assessment and playful reasons, to discuss typical positive and negative situations. Let's start with a positive situation. It is important to discuss positive situations to orient the child to the house image and to provide some evidence for its usefulness if later problem areas are to be addressed, which raises the possibility that the child may threaten to exit the conversation.

Once the description of problematic interactions has been developed, the next stage can be attempted. The therapist can ask what needs to happen to transform the image from the unhelpful mode constellation (e.g. Irritable mode is on the throne) into a more helpful representation: 'Who could push the Irritable mode off the throne? Are there any tricks or do you have any ideas what the others could do? Should maybe several finger puppets interact together?' etc). On this level, the child's problems can be represented visually, playfully and in a solution-oriented manner, thus making the situation more approachable for the child.

Contact

For older children (from 10 years) and teenagers, the third dimension, contact, can be added. Contact refers to the qualitative communication each mode has with another mode and is indicated by the line of sight of the finger puppets: if a finger puppet looks at another puppet, the mode that is represented by this finger puppet is in contact with the other mode; it appears ready to communicate. If the finger puppet receiving the communication looks back, the two finger puppets/modes are in a mutual exchange, i.e. they influence each other. If a finger puppet looks at another, but the watched one is turned away, there is a blockage of communication. This provides diagnostically valuable information, which can be processed therapeutically. The Contact dimension is sometimes difficult to reflect with finger puppets, since the modes are in very complex relationships (cf. mode dynamic in Zarbock & Zens, 2010).

Dimension	Illustrated by	Meaning
Proximity (Basic, from 6 years)	Spatial distance between the finger puppets	Co-occurs in everyday life (producing an alliance of modes)
Power (Basic, from 8 years)	Height of the finger puppets	Dominance of modes (Reflecting mode assertiveness)
Contact (Advanced, from 10 years)	Line of sight of the finger puppets	Qualitative contact (willingness to communicate)

In the next step, we ask the child what mode interests them the most or which they would like to get to know better. Often a child chooses a positively viewed mode, which is helpful for introducing the concepts. 'Let's become detectives and find out when this mode first appeared. Where does it come from? What is it doing to you?' (For further guidance see www.pavpub.com/resource-374CoCr for the Mode interview.) These questions directly focus our attention on a level that has not been discussed yet, but has a central role for understanding the mode level: the experience level.

13.1.2 Experience level

Work on the experience level requires lifting up the first level and putting it on approximately 5- to 7-inch columns (for example, glasses, vases, blocks, etc.), one for each corner. In the resulting space under the mode level, typical experiences from the past can be restaged. Begin with a positive mode – for example, with Happy Felix. 'When did you first notice Happy Felix?' The child might talk about a friend's birthday, or a trip, or seeing Mum or Dad, or an encounter after which other people said that they were really happy. In order to make this memory more vivid, it is worth introducing additional characters, such as those from the Storytelling card game (such as 'Dr Gardner's Story Telling Card Game'; 24 figures with 30 scenery cards). Of course the child and therapist can create characters or original scenery pictures. The children re-enact this remembered scene with the material on the experience level, from their own perspective.

'From this wonderful experience you have a great memory that has stayed with you. I think it has become a kind of pattern or programme inside you, an inner film, which you can replay and it makes you really happy. No wonder you like remembering it – what a positive experience! Let's find an object that reminds you of this lovely experience. We will come back to this later.'

This item is placed to one side for now and later activated when working on the schema level again. 'Should we look for another story from a different finger puppet?

What story comes to your mind thinking about this mode? Let's re-enact this. And what object would be suitable for this story?' The therapist continues to restage and represent experiences with the child, and encourages them to talk about many beautiful things from childhood and to mark them with symbols. When the therapist feels that the child has experienced sufficient positive experiences and felt supported in telling their story, a problematic mode can be addressed. 'Shall we have a closer look at the story of Sad Felix?' The therapist begins in a similar way, asking about situations the child connects to the origins of the mode and what images come to mind from the past. 'When did you notice Sad Felix for the first time and what happened back then?' The process resembles an imagery exercise (see section 13.2), in which the child is asked to describe the scene in as much detail as possible (often the story comes from kindergarten or primary school). It is important that the child imagines the scene as vividly as possible in their mind, which is more easily done with closed eyes. Given that children in therapy often do not want to close their eyes, the therapist can close their own eyes and ask the child to describe everything as accurately as possible, so that the therapist can reconstruct an image or film in their own head. The goal is to guide the child to enter into the thoughts, feelings, body feelings and experiences of the earlier event as richly as possible. While this is occurring, the therapist can begin to feel what the child may have felt at that time through empathic attunement. The therapist can provide validation for the emotions felt at the time, a way to understand the situation and build language around the experience and also provide support for the child, a form of limited re-parenting. In a positive experience, the therapist can be happy for/with the child (as if they had been with the child in the situation); in a negative experience, the end of the story can be re-scripted (reprocessing and re-scripting; see section 13.2). This approach allows the therapist to affirm and meet the needs of the Vulnerable Child ('What? No one helped you? That's not OK. I wish I could have been there and gone through that together with you. Who else could we get to come and help?').

In summary, the goal of the experience level is to provide biographical context. The more concrete, vivid and – within therapeutic limits – emotional the representation is, the better (see also remarks on optimal window of tolerance in Roediger *et al.*, 2018, p. 17). The inner house needs to be filled with life and personal experiences. Feel free to replay more than one situation: it is important that the child understands why each mode has developed, i.e. there needs to be a connection between the experience and the mode level. Once enough examples of the development of a mode have been found and all major modes understood (usually this is done after 3–5 stories), the third level should be opened.

In order to create the third level, the top (mode) level must be lifted with the finger puppets in place and a second plate (frame) placed on the already existing columns (above the experience level). On this newly added plate, four new columns (e.g.

glasses) are put on, which can carry the mode level: the inner house is completely 'built' now. However, the middle level, the schema level, must be set up.

13.1.3 Schema level

Now the child is asked to choose objects (such as a hedgehog, ball, animal, softball, star, etc) to represent schemas derived from memories. They should be objects that stand for the positive and negative schemas and represent a link between what was learned back then (lowest level) and the behaviour of today (top level). It is essential that there be some good experiences that have led to the development of useful and positive schemas. These objects are placed in the middle level, in order not to confront the child with his past too strongly. A helpful rule is to always begin with a positive schema (e.g. confidence of performance, emotional warmth, social acceptance, justice, honesty, bravery, courage, etc) before the more difficult topics or maladaptive schemas can be approached. The therapist's role is to keep a positive tone, which is only possible if significantly more positive than negative schemas are discussed. The ratio of 4:1 (positive: negative) is helpful to keep in mind. Ideally, the child leaves the therapy session feeling that they have had a happy childhood, but probably needing to work on a problematic schema. Under no circumstances should the inner house be set up to display, for example, four negatives next to just one positive schema.

If desired, a thread from level to level can be used (e.g. red lace, yarn) to make clear how the early experience (on the experience level) led to the formation of a pattern (schema level) and how the pattern plays out in everyday life in modes, 'because only the top level can be seen from the outside, without a closer look', which again represents an educative element. We recommend taking a photograph of this image, which can be referred to in later sessions, without the inner house having to be rebuilt. The inner house moves abstract ideas to concrete shapes and symbols. These objects can be touched and make visible the history and causes of both positive and negative issues in everyday life. These consequences or effects (e.g. current problem behaviour in school or family) should be attributed again and again to schemas (represented in objects), in order to clarify the effect of the pattern (schema) on the problem behaviour.

13.1.4 Using the inner house in therapy

Each level can now be processed. On the mode level for example, the modes can be integrated ('to become a team') by placing all finger puppets in a circle, with the most popular mode standing beside the most unpopular, ensuring its integration. The unoccupied throne (block) can be moved to the middle. Now the child coordinates a kind of huddle with the help of the therapist. In huddling the modes the patient becomes a 'leader' (cf. Schulz von Thun, 1997), assigning each finger puppet arguments and together comes up with solutions. ('Which mode is appropriate, for example when your mother tells you to clean up your room?') Several thrones can also be set up if it is helpful in finding the solution. An example: a typical school situation is reenacted on the lowest level (level of experience), or – if the structure of the inner house is too complicated or time consuming – imagined (e.g. 'My classmates start teasing me'). This usually leads to an automatic schema activation (*Defectiveness / Shame*), which has previously activated certain modes (Bully/Attack mode automatically places himself onto the throne and the child behaves aggressively). 'Stop, Felix. Now give the whole team time to think about the situation.' Each finger puppet could now 'speak' for itself (eliciting four characteristics for each mode: thought, emotion, body feeling, behaviour) and give its perspective. The mode team can then consider (i.e. the therapist helps the child to listen to each) which mode would provide the best solution for Felix (possibly the Clever and Wise mode).

A lot of flexibility on the part of the therapist is necessary, so that the ideas of the child can be recognised and integrated into the game. Strict rules are unhelpfully constraining and reduce the child's sense of competence while playing. If the previous method of collaborating with the child's ideas has not been fun enough, gummy bears or other incentives can be given for each mode of self-expression with its four facets (see above). This exercise is helpful because it shows the child what modes are on their team and what emotional, cognitive, physiological and behavioural components they contain. If a symptom (e.g. stomach pain) occurs in session, this gives the child a hint that, for example, 'Impulsive Felix' has snuck onto the throne, because he is the only mode that produces that particular body feeling (stomach pain). This helps the child to become an expert on their own mental state and learn to anticipate the negative and positive consequences of their behaviour.

When working with the inner house as it stands, reference should also be made, again and again, to positive schemas or their symbols. 'What could your positive schemas contribute now? Which modes might want to put these onto the throne and why?' The therapist can then decide together with the child how the transfer of this knowledge might look in everyday life, such as when C was an exclusively problematic behaviour within a ABC model and so far no attractive alternative behaviour C has been available. It is important to remind the child of the positive schemas as valuable resources in supporting the adaptive modes ('Use your great experiences!'). Another way of strengthening the adaptive modes is to play out, on the experience level, positive experiences the child could have had to build a useful schema (e.g. self-confidence). This creates a foundation for future experiential and behavioural interventions (e.g. imagery exercises, role plays and in vivo exposure or similar). Also, from these therapeutically initiated experiences, first steps toward solidifying positive schemas are taken.

For the first construction of the inner house we recommend scheduling a double session; subsequent constructions are quite feasible in a 50-minute therapy session (including tidying up). The experiences of setting up and playing in the inner house are generally very positive. For the therapist, insight into relationships becomes clear when viewing the inner house. Children also get a much better understanding of their problem behaviour and have a safe way of exploring their own behaviour playfully.

The child should be at least 6 to be able to engage in the mode level, at least 8 for the next level (experience level) and at least 10 for the entire inner house. When working with children with psychomotor challenges (e.g. children with ADHD problems), we recommend raising the age limit, although this also greatly depends on introspective ability and emotional sophistication. We recommend the mode level be done first, and then decide whether and to what extent the child is receptive or willing to complete other levels.

13.2 Imagery in Schema Therapy

Before we begin the next section we invite you to do an exercise.

- How many people were at your last birthday? Stop.
- Think about it before you keep on reading.
- How many checkout lines are in your favourite supermarket? Stop.
- How did your child dress this morning? Stop.

Please reflect on how you proceeded in answering. Usually people recall memories visually, as if they have a kind of film running, or they visualise a picture of the scene in their mind's eye. Maybe they walk up and down through the locations of events in the mind's eye again in order to get an answer. Imagery can be a great help to remembering past events, it can help us to anticipate future situations. We can play future events out in imagination in order to practise an action.

When working with children, working with internal imagery and external images is very important. When children can't write, read or listen for long it is helpful for to have visual cues and anchors. It is also helpful for teenagers, as therapeutic concepts and new information can be stored figuratively in imagination. The human brain is responsible for two-thirds of the processing of visual information and eye movements. Thus, the visual system is the most represented sensory system in the brain. Visual memories are stored in the same cortex areas where the original visual stimuli was previously processed and integrated. The brain areas that are active when imagining an object or a scene are the same as those that are active when experiencing that image or object in reality (cf. Grawe, 2017). That makes the visual system a very helpful way to process both difficult past and predicted future experiences as well as reparative experiences. When a positive or distressing image is recalled it often activates already built, associated emotions. Just think of looking at old holiday photos: if these images reflect a great holiday, positive feelings come up, no matter how poor the image quality or the situation in which you are looking at the picture. The opposite is also true: a high-definition, colourful image set in a beautiful location can cause highly aversive feelings if the photograph reminds us of an unpleasant or negative stimulus. Thus, visual memories are closely connected with the corresponding set of emotional impressions that were present in that situation. This brings hazards and risks (e.g. intrusions or flashbacks within PTSD), but also opportunities for providing corrective emotional experiences for injuries that occurred in an earlier phase of life (e.g. situations that produced feelings of abandonment and defectiveness) (Holmes *et al*, 2007).

Imagery work is found in the cognitive behavioural tradition and has increasingly gained an evidence base (Holmes et al., 2007). Over the past 20 years the inclusion of emotionally rich imagery experiences has provided a turning point from the CBT of the 1960s and 1970s (Roediger, 2009). Using imagery and re-scripting of imagery provides a rich emotional complement to traditional cognitive therapy. Within Ellis' Rational Emotive Behavior Therapy (REBT) there are also techniques for using imagery with children (e.g. Petermann's Captain Nemo stories, discussed in Klott, 2013 and Ellis & Dryden, 1987). Imagery allows a way to modify intense emotions (e.g. transferring rage into appropriate anger; Waters, 1982).

As yet, there is no diagnosis-specific evidence for the use of imagery with children from a Schema Therapy approach. We also do not know exactly what types of imagery are suitable at each cognitive developmental age. Imaginative ability increases with age, beginning in the second year of life as the child's ability to reproduce human activity in imagination increases. As the child moves toward school age thinking becomes less concrete and by adolescence abstract thinking is possible. Throughout the teenage years there is also an increased ability to 'think about thinking' – metacognition. The precondition for doing imagery work with children is that the young person needs to have sufficient emotional stability so that they can regulate excessively activated emotions when needed. In general, emotional activation in children should first be done using chair dialogues (see above), which allows the therapist to supervise the child's emotional processes and allows more interaction between the therapist and patient.

13.2.1 Contraindication and negative experiences with imagery

According to Kirn and colleagues (2009, pp. 28 f) there is no empirical study that has methodically dealt with contraindications for imagery. However, their experiences suggest caution when working with cases of intense fear of lack of control, excessively health-focused anxiety, highly anxious self-perception, histrionic presentations, post-traumatic stress disorder, intense depression, borderline personality disorder with a high level of dissociative symptoms, psychosis, dissociative disorders, substance abuse and dependency and mental retardation. Zarbock (2011) also warns of patients who have difficulty re-orienting to time, person and place or who experience a strong disorganisation and disorientation as a result of an imagery exercise ('I'm quite confused now'). Zarbock recommends using the 'Sunflowers test' (see below) to understand a patient's capacity to engage in imagery and its effect on the patient, prior to other imagery exercises.

13.2.2 Requirements for imagery exercises

Since imagery exercises can provoke intense confrontations with negative experiences, the therapist must be trained (e.g. by certified Schema Therapy trainers; see the ISST webpage for details, https://schematherapysociety.org) and proceed carefully. The therapist needs to be competent in stabilisation and distancing techniques, and to have practised them with the client. In general, it is also advisable to inform the parents in advance about the approach ('we will be doing work on some of the more difficult experiences your child has gone through') and to obtain consent for the imagery exercise. This also provides an opportunity to again explore possible negative or traumatic experiences, which parents often avoid or forget to mention in the assessment sessions ('[I] thought it was not important'). The following case illustrates the necessity.

Case example

Steven presented with oppositional behaviour. As a 5-year-old child, while his mother was being treated in a psychiatric hospital for depression, Steven's stepfather punched him repeatedly. She stayed three months, and when she came home Steven repeatedly told his mother about the abuse. However, his mother didn't believe him. Some years later, when Steven was in outpatient treatment for ADHD, he suddenly 'saw' the abusive situation with his stepfather while using a relaxation exercise (safe place; see below). During assessment, Steven's mother had not reported this trauma. At the end of the therapy session, Steven was completely overwhelmed. He had flipped into Vulnerable Child mode, staying in a helplessness state for days, which the therapist had not expected. At this time his mother was not able to comfort Steven because she was annoyed about the new issue that had just presented. It was difficult to engage Steven's mother, who was quite 'busy' at that time. Only later, in a telephone call and the next therapy session, was it possible to go over the events again with the mother and Steven: 'Steven, you were very upset in the last therapy session, can you explain to your mother now what made you so sad?' Finally the Vulnerable Child, Little Steven, was able – with the help of the therapist – to reach the nurturing side of his mother and be comforted.

This example shows the need for a thorough medical history and shows the need to practise effective distancing techniques (see below) before an experiential exercise or a potentially triggering therapeutic activity.

Sunflower test

In the sunflower test, the child is asked to imagine a sunflower (or a tree, or a chocolate cake, or an equally sensual concrete object) as realistically as possible and to touch it in imagery, if the child wants to. It is helpful to have closed eyes, but the child can also focus on a point in the room with open eyes. After 30 to 60 seconds, the child is asked to describe in detail their perceptions. Important questions for the therapist to ask are:

- Can the child engage with the exercise?

- Is the child open to this type of direction, or are there possible loss of control fears?

- Are the child's needs for orientation, protection or self-determination threatened?

- In addition to visual perception, tactile and olfactory perceptual ability is required. How much detail can the child describe (white hairs on the stem, etc.)?

- Very important: Is the child able to follow the therapist's lead during imagery, i.e. the therapist might instruct the child to zoom into the sunflower and to pull back again (screen-observer technique).

- Are there any other images/perceptions that intrude into the imagery?

- Is the child able to engage without becoming overwhelmed emotionally (flooding), which of course should be avoided?

- If there is confusion (or disorientation) after such an exercise, the therapist needs to change to other techniques.

To familiarise a child with imagery work, games or fantasy tasks are helpful (Plummer, 2007). For example, 'Imagine that you are talking to your pet cat (hamster/dog). Talk to it about how school was today. Now imagine you could put yourself in the cat's position and respond'. Or: 'We will imagine that we have become cats and tell the humans what it's like to be a cat' (as an aid, the cat's qualities can be named, such as warm, gentle, happy, tired, sleepy, hungry, needy and cuddly, snappy). 'Close your eyes and begin to stretch and move as if you were a cat. I'm writing down what comes to your mind. Begin to talk like a cat, e.g. to say how that feels right now. My name is...'

Safe place

Another way to assist children to obtain distance from a difficult image, in addition to the screen technique mentioned previously, is to introduce a 'safe place' where a child can feel secure and relaxed (Irblich, 2010). Before the Schema Therapy imagery exercise (see below) the therapist and child always visit the safe place image. From this safe place, the 'journey' into the past begins. The safe place is visited again after the imagery work and then the child can enter the real world (see the online material for imagery exercises including the Fantasy trip to the Clever & Wise mode).

Build a safe exercise

The therapist helps the child to build a 'safe' in imagery as a storage area for images/events that are too distressing to deal with currently. This provides another way to reduce upsetting thoughts or memories or to store for later processing. The child can choose if they would like to have the key /combination to the safe, or the therapist can manage that aspect.

Zapping

Children also like to imagine a kind of 'channel change', in which they can easily switch or change the programme, like on TV at home.

More relaxation and distancing techniques can be found in Cohen and colleagues (2016). In any case, it is important to carry out a thorough assessment and listing of possible trauma (e.g. The Trauma Symptom Checklist for Children; Briere, 1997). Having a full understanding of a child's trauma history reduces the risk of negative emotional flooding and allows for graded 'exposure' to trauma images.

13.2.3 Imagery re-scripting

In Schema Therapy with adults, imagery re-scripting is, alongside mode dialogues, one of the two major experiential interventions (Arntz & van Genderen, 2011; Arntz & Jacob, 2012; Roediger *et al*, 2018; cf. Young *et al*, 2003). Imagery re-scripting techniques have proven to be a particularly intensive and successful method of treating traumatic experiences in developmental history. By providing a space to experience and reframe difficult events that have contributed to maladaptive schemas re-scripting has great potential for therapeutic change. In imagery, the therapist is able to meet the needs of the child and confront the abuser or distressing event, providing a corrective emotional experience. This is a powerful way to reduce the maladaptive emotional schemas and dysfunctional modes. In order to be able to process emotional problems, an 'emotional language' must be developed (cf. affective and cognitive representation code; Sachse *et al*, 2008, pp21f).

The imagery re-scripting method (imagery reprocessing and re-scripting, IRRT; Smucker & Dancu, 2005) deals with a particular kind of imagination exercise, in which past stressful memories are rewritten imaginarily. This procedure is also used with other clinical problems; Imagery Rehearsal Therapy identifies threatening elements of recurring nightmares and replaces them with positive elements using imagery. This process, with appropriate practice, leads to a significant decrease in nightmare frequency and subjective distress (e.g. Krakow *et al*,1995).

In Schema Therapy the goal of imagery re-scripting is to not just reduce distress but to create experiences of a child having their needs met, experiencing 'the Vulnerable Child being looked after'. Imagery re-scripting creates experiential learning that can be built on within the therapeutic relationship (through limited re-parenting) and by increased experiences of nurture outside of therapy. A memory or scene, which has led to feelings of guilt and shame, is chosen from the child's history. This young person is guided to 'enter' the memory and experience in sensory detail the experience up until the point at which intervention was needed (importantly, the client is not rehearsing the whole event, only the point where intervention was required. This point is chosen by the young person.) A 'healthy adult' enters the scene and provides protection, nurture, validation, limit setting and so on, which the young person experiences as a very positive experience. Although the past cannot be undone, the patient can still experience considerable need satisfaction through imagery re-scripting. Young *et al* (2003) provide more detail about the process when working with adults.

Limited clinical experience and research on imagery re-scripting in Schema Therapy with children and teenagers is currently available. This is partly due to limitations in cognitive capacity with younger children. It is probably not until adolescence that the children are able to observe themselves thoroughly from the Clever/Wise mode perspective, let alone confront experiences of lack of care from this mode. More research is required to ascertain at which developmental age a child is able to see things from the Clever/Wise mode perspective. Nonetheless, even small children tend to re-enact stories of their own volition, which closely resembles a conversion of a traumatic situation. Presumably they are looking for alternative endings to a terrible experience without therapeutic support. Imagery re-scripting could therefore be seen as a guided form of positive compensation, even in young children.

If, however, there is evidence of de-compensation in the child, trauma-specific approaches such as psychodynamic imaginative trauma therapy for children and adolescents (PITT-KID; Irblich, 2010) can offer valuable assistance. Schema Therapy developments in this area include Smucker's IRRT (imagery reprocessing and re-scripting therapy) for type II traumas, which can be adapted to the child's age (Roediger, 2011, p263 with respect to Smucker *et al*, 2008).

13.2.4 Process for imagery re-scripting

The process of imagery re-scripting is outlined here. First, it is important to orient the client to imagination exercises. A detailed, but also age appropriate, description of the process helps to meet the control and security needs of the client. However, it is also important not to detail every element of the process. Here, trust is necessary. If the client is open to trying imagery work and there is sufficient trust, begin by getting the child sitting comfortably, or possibly reclining. Some children prefer to lay their head on a pillow or on folded arms, sitting at a table. They can close their eyes more easily and have control of the seating position. A comfortable room temperature and calm atmosphere are important.

a. The child discusses a distressing event and describes the situation in as much detail as possible. What body feelings come up (headaches, stomach pressure, etc)?

b. The therapist then guides the child to the safe place image that has been developed. From there, the child is instructed to place him or herself in the previously described conflict or distressing situation.

c. The therapist attunes to the activated emotions, thoughts and body sensations, supporting the child to experience them.

d. The therapist then uses an affect bridge: the client is instructed to 'wipe' the current image but hold onto the emotions and body sensations and scan back to when they were younger and felt the same emotions and body sensations (e.g. mixture of anger, sadness and shame; tight chest, etc.).

e. This earlier scene should be described with as much detail as possible using all sensory modalities. Particular attention is focused on the activated feelings.

f. In the following step, needs satisfaction is introduced: the client describes what they would have needed in this situation (e.g. encouragement, support, help in limiting an aggressor, etc), or the therapist makes suggestions if the client is not sure.

g. Now the re-scripting begins. The client brings their 'Clever and Wise mode' (in adults, the 'Healthy Adult') into the imagery and looks after the small, Vulnerable Child. The client may also help their Vulnerable Child by giving the Vulnerable Child insight they have gained that the little part didn't have ('It wasn't your fault, you were just trying your best'). Other helper figures (e.g. relatives, friends, and/or even figures like Batman) can be brought into the scene to provide help. The therapist can also be brought into the scene if desired by the child. Ultimately, it is all about supporting the small wounded, Vulnerable Child from the child's history and fulfilling the basic emotional needs. The central question is: what does the child in the imagery need right now in this situation? After the child's needs have been met in imagery (e.g. restricting the aggressor – for instance in the case of a violent parent or the need for an escape from the situation, possibly with the police being called in cases of abuse) and the Vulnerable Child in imagery has been soothed, the therapist asks about the body feelings ('how is your stomach feeling/chest feeling?'). These should have subsided by now.

h. The imagery is completed with the Vulnerable Child placed in a safe environment (e.g. at home, in a relative's house, in a park to play, etc). After this work, the client is instructed to exit from the image and then come back into the therapy room via the safe place. The scope for using imagery to create safety and nurture is wide. The child should receive maximum support and security in imagery.

13.2.5 Strengths-based imagery work

A less confronting way to conduct imagery (without needing to revisit traumatic scenes) is to use strengths-based imagery work to activate Caring Parent or Helper modes. Indeed, when children begin to re-experience terrible situations from the past, they often switch to 'another film' involuntarily. This child-typical behaviour, called zapping, can be supported therapeutically by imagery journeys that develop the strengths that the original scenes required. For example, a child's history of neglect, resulting in an *Emotional Deprivation* schema, suggests that the child will need help with the idea of being cared for. Going on imagery journeys can develop this capacity as the Clever and Wise mode can learn to accept nurture and bring along Vulnerable Child in her pocket.

In the literature (e.g. from the field of hypnotherapy), a variety of strengths-based exercises can be found. We can use them to strengthen certain internal modes. We are currently gathering more experience and aim to publish this research after evaluation. (However, the reader can find concrete exercises in the online materials, with imagination exercises to activate healthy modes, e.g. 'A trip to my own strengths', based on Portmann, 2008; 'My house', based on Irblich, 2010.)

Also, mode dialogues can be designed as a conversation in imagery between, for example, the Furious Child and the father, or an inner dialogue between modes (analogous to chair work). Imagery is also useful for preparing concrete action steps and behavioural experiments. For example, an anxious child refusing to go to school can use imagery to rehearse arriving at school and using the strategies developed to reduce anxiety.

Summary

Imagery in Schema Therapy for children and adolescents is an advanced method that should only be used by experienced and trained therapists. Emotionally engaging with past experiences can overwhelm a child (e.g. in the case of a serious trauma). Therefore, distancing and relaxation techniques should always be practised in advance. Techniques such as chair, schema and mode work with pictures and drawings, as well as stem stories, are preferable initially because they allow better control of the child's inner processes. More experience and research is required to develop understanding and guidelines around imagery re-scripting with children.

References

Arntz A & Jacob G (2012) *Schema Therapy in Practice: An Introductory Guide to the Schema Mode Approach*. Chichester: Wiley.

Arntz A & Van Genderen H (2011) *Schema Therapy for Borderline Personality Disorder*. Chichester: Wiley.

Briere J (1996) Trauma symptom checklist for children. *Odessa, FL: Psychological Assessment Resources*, 00253-8.

Cohen JA, Mannarino AP & Deblinger E (2016) *Treating Trauma and Traumatic Grief in Children and Adolescents*. New York: Guilford Press.

Ellis A & Dryden W (1987) *The Practice of Rational-Emotive Therapy (RET)*. New York: Springer Publishing Co.

Grawe K (2017) *Neuropsychotherapy: How the Neurosciences Inform Effective Psychotherapy*. London: Routledge.

Holmes EA, Arntz A & Smucker MA (2007) Imagery rescripting in cognitive behaviour therapy: images, treatment techniques and outcomes. *Journal of Behaviour Therapy and Experimental Psychiatry* **38** 297–305.

Irblich D (2010) *Psychodynamic Imaginative Trauma Therapy for Children and Adolescents*. PITT-KID-The Manual.

Kirn T, Echelmeyer L & Engberding M (2009) *Imagination in der Verhaltenstherapie*. Heidelberg: Springer.

Klott O (2013) Autogenic training – a self-help technique for children with emotional and behavioural problems. *Therapeutic Communities: The International Journal of Therapeutic Communities* **34** (4) 152–158.

Krakow B, Kellner R, Pathak D & Lambert L (1995) Imagery rehearsal treatment for chronic nightmares. *Behaviour Research & Therapy* **33** 837–843.

Plummer D (2007) *Self-Esteem Games for Children.* London: Jessica Kingsley Publishers.

Portmann R (2008) *Spiele für mehr Sozialkompetenz* (6. Aufl.) München: Don Bosco.

Roediger E (2009) *Die innere Botschaft. Einführung in die Schematherapie.* Seminar auf den 59. Lindauer Psychotherapiewochen 2009. MP3-Format: Auditorium Netzwerk.

Roediger E (2011) *Praxis der Schematherapie: Lehrbuch zu Grundlagen, Modell und Anwendung* (2. Aufl.) Stuttgart: Schattauer.

Roediger, E. Stevens, B.A., & Brockman, R. (2018). Contextual Schema Therapy. An Integrative Approach to Personality Disorder, Emotional Dysregulation & Interpersonal Functioning. Oakland, CA: Context Press.

Sachse R, Püschel O, Fasbender J & Breil J (2008) *Klärungsorientierte Schemabearbeitung: Dysfunktionale Schemata effektiv verändern.* Göttingen: Hogrefe.

Schulz von Thun, F (1998) *Miteinander reden 3 – Das innere Team und situationsgerechte Kommunikation.* Hamburg: Rowohlt.

Smucker M, Reschke K & Kögel B (2008) *Imagery Rescripting and Reprocessing Therapy: Behandlungsmanual für Typ-I-Trauma.* Aachen: Shaker.

Smucker MR & Dancu C (1999/2005) *Cognitive-Behavioral Treatment for Adult Survivors of Childhood Trauma: Imagery Rescripting and Reprocessing.* Lanham, MD: Rowman & Littlefield.

Waters V (1982) Therapies for children: Rational-emotive therapy. In: CR Reynolds and TB Gutkin (Eds) *Handbook of School Psychology.* New York: Wiley.

Young JE, Klosko JS & Weishaar ME (2003) *Schema Therapy: A Practitioner's Guide.* New York: Guilford Press.

Zarbock G (2011) *Praxisbuch Verhaltenstherapie. Grundlagen und Anwendungen biografisch-systemischer Verhaltenstherapie* (3. Aufl.) Lengerich: Pabst.

Zarbock G & Zens C (2010) Bedürfnis- und Emotionsdynamik – Handlungsleitende Konzepte für die Schematherapiepraxis. In: E Roediger and G Jacob (Eds) *Fortschritte der Schematherapie.* Hogrefe: Göttingen.

Chapter 14: Homework, Flashcards and Diaries

Christof Loose, Peter Graaf and Ruth A. Holt

14.1 Homework

Homework has a special role in Schema Therapy, which we want to address in this section.

In general, if the child is in weekly outpatient psychotherapy (and assuming about 10 hours of sleep a day), a child spends about 98 hours awake per week, only one of which is spent with the therapist. Figure 14.1 represents this graphically. The time in therapy is very small relative to the rest of their life. Therefore it is not surprising when children and adolescents forget the content of a therapy session until the next session, especially when they did not start therapy voluntarily or are unmotivated for other reasons.

What actually happens in the remaining 97 hours between the therapy sessions? Zeek and colleagues (2004) describe this time frame as a 'neglected area of research', which is astonishing considering the ratio of actual therapy time to the remaining hours of the child's life. Nevertheless, it is generally agreed that homework is essential in CBT work (Blagys & Hilsenroth, 2002), with nearly every textbook about CBT mentioning the necessity and importance of homework in the therapeutic context.

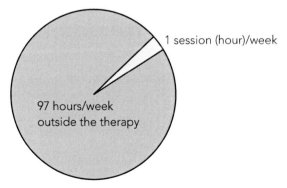

1 session (hour)/week

97 hours/week
outside the therapy

Figure 14.1 Ratio of treatment time to remaining hours spent awake for a child in outpatient weekly psychotherapy.

In work with preschoolers and even younger children, the parents are the focus of the homework. It is important to keep checking how the parents are getting on with homework and how they are incorporating it into everyday life in order to see changes in the problem behaviour. A typical difficulty is that children and adolescents (or, with younger children, the parents) do these tasks only partially or halfheartedly at home, if at all. It can feel burdensome to be getting homework from the therapist as well as from school or work. Zandt and Barrett (2017) suggest using other terms, e.g. behavioural exercise, behaviour experiment, therapy task, practice or training task agreement, (therapeutic) agreement and/or daily test. From our own experience, we don't recommend using the terms 'treatment', 'homework' or 'therapeutic tasks' in child and adolescent psychotherapy; instead we speak of doing experiments, running tests, challenges, detective work, exploring, training exercises, and so on.

However, children and adolescents often have difficulty completing home-based exercises (or whatever the therapist calls them). This of course undermines progress: after all, it's all about (in whatever form) recording, practising and consolidating the new behaviour or experience, generalising to everyday life and being able to apply the skills in an emergency. As in any therapy, then, the question of how to make therapy transferable is very important, so that therapeutic gains can be displayed in the classroom setting, at home and with the peer group, not just in session. Of course, new behaviour must be practised for a significant change to be expected. Therefore, help and support for the completion of homework is required (e.g. parents should pay attention) or incentives created (e.g. behaviour plans).

Other issues can also develop with homework, such as the caregiver taking over the client's task. If this happens the child is often too passive, and more of an observer than the director in their life. Not infrequently, therapists, parents or teachers become resigned because it's difficult to keep on motivating or attempting to force a child to do something they seem unwilling to do.

In Schema Therapy, not-doing and/or forgetting homework is a 'welcome behaviour' that gives a reason to talk about therapy motivation and other factors that will undermine the planned behaviour change. Forgetting homework can mean 'I don't want to change anything' or 'it's not that important to me' or 'that's too much work, I can't do that'. Of course, it could also be a symptom of attention and concentration problems (e.g. in the context of ADHD issues) or a general absentmindedness (e.g. excessive demands at school). The therapist can start to determine which issue is being presented by noticing whether the child is really sorry about missing homework or whether they are angry about their own forgetfulness. Most children and adolescents give the impression that they do not care, which may be more of an expression of not wanting to have additional responsibilities whose meaning they do not understand or do not want to understand. ('I go there once a week, that's got to be enough!')

Schema Therapy sees a lack of compliance as crucial information about the presenting schemas and ways of dealing with those schemas. The resistance of children ('I don't want to do my homework') is actively taken up and becomes the issue for conversation. The aim is that the children see the benefit of the exercises and consequently also want to show the therapist that they have come closer to their goal. The difficult part is building up this desire in the young, mostly externally motivated patient. The young client requires special attention and special effort (see psychoeducation in children, 9.3). Children sometimes forget what the benefits or aims of therapy even are, which means that the child and adolescent psychotherapist must regularly show the child the goals and emphasise the advantages.

14.1.1 Homework behavior

Schema Therapists see the 'forgetting' of homework as an indication that they have not put forward the central goal of treatment and maintained motivation to change. As the therapist reflects on this 'useful feedback' from the client, the therapist needs to return to relationship-building and check exactly where the client has lost touch with the therapy objectives. It is also helpful to determine which schemas were responsible for the lack of motivation. For example, not doing homework can indicate *Dependence / Incompetence* schemas ('I'm just going to stay with Mum because I'll never be able to do it; I'm just too stupid for this') or *Social Isolation / Alienation* ('I'm different to other kids, one day others will also realise that; I'm simply being authentic'). The therapist is advised to explore empathetically the feelings and cognitions of the child with obvious compassion: 'Look, Felix, I know how it is when you have to do things you don't want to do at all, and perhaps you don't even know why they have to be done. As a child and later as a teenager, I was always annoyed about that, and sometimes I simply did not do these things. For example, sometimes I thought, man, that's exhausting. Another time, I wanted to stand up to the teacher. "Screw him", I said to myself. And another time I didn't understand what they wanted from me; so I just forgot about it on purpose. Somehow I was too embarrassed to ask again how to do it. You can see I had several reasons for not doing things. That's quite normal, Felix. I'm not angry with you. I'm sure you have your reasons for forgetting as well! So now I'm really curious about your reasons?'

Hopefully, the child or adolescent notices that this is not a lecture on the virtues of homework or the usual talk of rights and responsibilities or violations of agreements: this is just about the child and what kind of thoughts or feelings come up, which images and memories arise when the homework exercises (or more generally, duties and expectations) are not achieved. If the child is silent and/or cannot identify their thoughts themselves (for whatever reason), the therapist can offer the child cognitions from Tables 2.2 to 2.5 for the 18 schemas so the child only needs to nod agreement or deny. 'Oh, you know, Felix, even adults sometimes have trouble noticing and expressing their thoughts and feelings. It is really difficult. I think it's still important that we try to find out what's going through your head. Would it be okay with you if I just read out a few thoughts that children have when things are not going so well in their everyday lives?'

Now the therapist can – depending on the complexity or motivation of the child – ask for a dichotomous or scaled response to each schema (yes or no, scale 0–10 for true to not true at all, or similar). When the child agrees with the thought, the above-mentioned table provides further opportunity for analysis: does the indicated parent or caregiver behaviour fit the child's parents? Do the coping strategies fit the child's behaviour as well?

'Look, Felix, I know that children who have these thoughts often have problems in … areas. However these children do not all behave equally: some get through the situation by … (representing surrender). Others make sure they never face such a situation (avoidance), and others are trying to convince their friends that the exact opposite is true, which is of course not the case (explain overcompensation). Do you recognise yourself anywhere? What is your strategy when thoughts like (repeat child cognition) come up?'

When working with adolescent clients the underlying schemas can be discussed more fully in a therapy session: 'Your thoughts and behaviour could indicate the … schema which can be characterized by … (brief description of the schema). If so, in which areas of life – except homework – could the schema be active and cause trouble?' The coping strategies can also be discussed in more detail (e.g. in order to reduce feelings of guilt or a need for explaining).

If, despite your best efforts and empathic explanations, the child or adolescent still refuses to do any homework, additional methods such as cognitive restructuring, exposure treatment and relaxation exercises should not be used. According to the Schema Therapy perspective, the patient's non-compliance comes from maladaptive schemas or the activation of dysfunctional modes. Therefore the therapist has a good reason to assume (as evidenced in the homework denial) that they have found one of the key causes of the presenting problem behaviour. Ignoring this hint, for example by accepting that this patient is not capable of doing homework, would possibly lead to the ineffective use of otherwise proven techniques and methods. The 'failure' of these techniques would further entrench chronic problem behaviour ('Even the proven techniques did not help me') and an intensification of an ego-syntonic understanding of schemas/modes ('See, that's just me, there is nothing that can be done; I'm a hopeless case!').

One way to motivate a client towards participation in this process is to play games or do activities that only work with two people participating: for example, in a game of table tennis one person could serve all the time, while the other one barely tries to return the ball. Other examples are cycling with only one leg, cutting meat with only one hand, watching a 3D movie with only one eye, grabbing without thumbs, and so on. The therapist and client could also rent a rowing boat and see what happens when only one person uses their paddle. Using novel approaches helps the child to understand that cooperation is extremely important and essential for the therapeutic progress. The therapist needs not to accept an overly passive attitude in the patient. If reasonable homework is not done, that might be indicating the core of the problem, the reason why the child started the therapy in the first place. Here calmness and patience is required by the therapist to transition the client into being ready for therapy, not prematurely moving on to different methods or strategies.

The homework that is given of course depends on the motivation of the child and the current state of the therapeutic process. Fehm and Mrose (2008) point out that tasks that are too difficult or extensive can be overwhelming and frustrating, and can ultimately lead to a termination of therapy. In particular, 'obedient' clients (e.g. clients with *Shame/Defectiveness*, *Self-Sacrifice*, *Failure* or *Subjugation* schemas) can build up enormous pressure on themselves, which the therapist needs to be aware of and manage therapeutically. One way to deal with this is to 'forget' the therapeutic homework on purpose or address empathetically why the patient does everything the therapist tells them to do (addressing the coping mode, Compliant Surrenderer or Currying Favour mode). However, this needs to be embedded in the context of the therapy and not be applied randomly.

In order to save space, we won't discuss homework in more detail here. However, you can find helpful worksheets in the online material that can be used for homework (e.g. mode-week protocol, flash cards and diary). The use of these worksheets is described in the corresponding information within the book (cf. Chapter 10).

In summary, homework is just as essential in Schema Therapy as in CBT, with the additional bonus of having a way to formulate non-compliance and address that issue within the mode model.

14.2 Flash cards and diaries

In this short section, we present various ways in which children and adolescents can transfer the knowledge gained in therapy to everyday life and record progress. When working with young clients, material is created during the therapy sessions that they are able to carry around or hang up at home. Images or characters can be used to remind the child of the experiences and ideas from session. The client, for example, can hang a copy of the mode image or a photo of his finger puppets up in his room, in order to remember which modes get activated. Pictures and sentences from the mode work in session can be used to remind the client to show or activate important modes (e.g. Vulnerable Child or Clever and Wise mode). The following materials are helpful:

- Mode images
- Photos of finger puppets, preferably with speech balloons (with positive notes to self)
- Photos of the inner house
- Photos from a mode dialogue session

Many clients ask their mother or another caregiver to carry laminated mode images as a reminder (Figure 14.2). With the child's permission, in a triggering situation, the mother can then hold up this card as a reminder of which mode might be being activated and a prompt to bring in Clever and Wise mode, to use the solutions discussed in therapy.

Figure 14.2: Section from the mode image as a signal card for the child

Mode pictures can also be used for self-monitoring tasks. The child acts as a schema or mode detective in daily life to discover hidden modes in appropriate moments (see the online material for image cards for mode work).

For older children and adolescents, typical schema or mode activations can be drawn on a map and then the alternative thoughts and feelings that the Clever/Wise mode has can also be written down. (In the online material the reader will find a blank card to fill in.

Figure 14.3: Visual Mode Flash-card or Mode map (see online materials)

14.3 Summary and process for combining individual techniques

The techniques described in this book show how to work therapeutically with both schemas and modes in young clients. The underlying patterns behind the symptoms and problem behaviour are explored in a way that is accessible to children and provides rich possibilities for change. Schema Therapy provides a framework for vividly understanding how patients see themselves and respond to their environment, for both children and adolescents. The therapist is then able to engage in a playful dialogue with the modes of the client. As therapy progresses, as the role of each mode is respected and understood, the therapist helps to integrate rejected or unloved parts and to disempower overwhelming modes. These therapeutic insights are then transferred into concrete behavioural changes and exercises in everyday life.

The authors combine several techniques in order to stimulate the creative potential of the child. When working with children from the age of 6–7 years, it is best to start with mode drawings. The mode image then becomes more vivid in the form of finger puppets, as modes are allocated to chairs, in the imagination, or in games. As a child begins to understand and experience their modes, heightened emotional processing occurs. The charm of the image interacts with the power of the vivid game. Transferring the mode model into everyday life is more easily done once chair work/mode dialogue or puppets have been used, rather than just drawings. One way to combine therapeutic elements (psychoeducation, cognitive and experiential techniques) is to use the large Folkmanis® puppets (also indicated when working with children under the age of 6). Modes can be brought to life as speaking and acting parts. As the mode dialogue progresses the child experience mode changes, reflected in changing puppets as mode flips occur, providing valuable progress in building the Clever and Wise (no child) mode. This can then be reflected in a drawing for the child to take home. The techniques described in this book can be very easily combined, allowing the therapist to better adjust to the needs and abilities of the child and take the child's own strengths into account. Figures 14.4 and 14.5 provide a summary of the different techniques and combination possibilities.

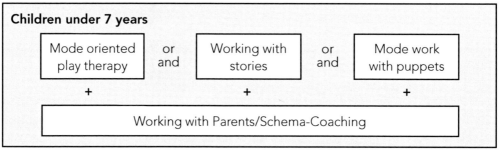

Figure 14.4: Mode and Schema Therapy elements when working with children under 7 years

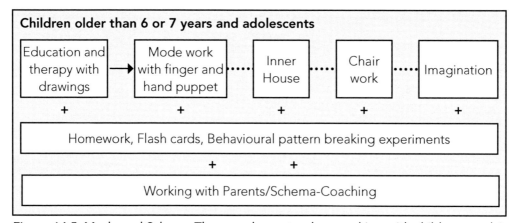

Figure 14.5: Mode and Schema Therapy elements when working with children aged 6 or 7 years through to adolescents

The foundation of Schema Therapy work is the therapeutic relationship. We want to stress once again that good therapy is not based on excellent techniques, but on the relationship (see 9.1). Part of that relationship is having a mode-focused formulation (visual case conceptualization (or step by step procedure for case conceptualization; online material)) that guides the use of the techniques, rather than being driven by trying techniques without a framework. Within the relationship, and providing there is a sound Schema Therapy framework, there are limitless possibilities for creative ideas and implementation! The determining factor is not necessarily the methods, but the attitude of the therapist in applying methods. A genuine understanding of the client and looking beyond the symptoms to focus on meeting the needs of the child characterise this attitude. The limited re-parenting role of the therapist always provides the context for intervention.

References

Blagys MD & Hilsenroth MJ (2002) Distinctive activities of cognitive-behavioral therapy: A review of the comparative psychotherapy process literature. *Clinical Psychology Review* **22** 671–706.

Fehm L & Mrose J (2008) Patients' perspective on homework assignments in cognitive-behavioural therapy. *Clinical Psychology and Psychotherapy* **15** (5) 320. Retrieved from https://search.proquest.com/docview/213888986?accountid=178506

Zandt F & Barrett S (2017) *Creative Ways to Help Children Manage BIG Feelings: A Therapist's Guide to Working with Preschool and Primary Children*. London: Jessica Kingsley Publishers.

Zeek A, Hartmann A & Orlinsky D (2004) Intersession processes: A neglected area of psychotherapy research. *Psychotherapie Psychosomatik Medizinische Psychologie* **54** (6) 236–242.

Chapter 15: Parents and the Family System from a Schema Therapy Perspective

Peter Graaf and Ruth Holt

Working with parents is very important in Schema Therapy for children and adolescents. When children are the patients, parents play a major role in many ways, including a role in the development of symptoms, often unconsciously modelling or interacting in ways that perpetuate issues. Therefore Schema Therapy involves 'coaching' the parents so that they can support the therapeutic process in session and between sessions.

15.1 Schema Therapy parent work

15.1.1 Schema Theory and CBT, family systems and narrative therapy

Schema Therapy parent work aims to complement current CBT approaches to working with parents, 'guiding parents to provide their children with a relationship that stabilizes their self-worth by providing a consistent parenting style' (Borg-Laufs, 2005, s. 7). In addition to building parenting skills, CBT approaches aim to improve the parent–child relationship and communication within the family, and to develop skills in expressing feelings and needs as well as handling conflict. At the same time, the parents' history is also taken into account in order to understand the origin of parenting behaviours. Schema Therapy, however, provides a much more nuanced understanding of the relationship between parent and child and how it has developed.

In this chapter, principles and ideas from systems theory are integrated into Schema Therapy for children and adolescents. Although a systemic approach to Schema Therapy is beyond the scope of this book, this chapter aims to present Schema Therapy with children and their parents from a systemic perspective. Bringing a systemic perspective to Schema Therapy provides scope to understand and intervene in the rules and patterns of the family or system (Bitter, 2013). Therefore, the interplay between the actions, perceptions, thoughts and feelings of each person and the interactional structures need to be examined. In line with Kriz's (1991, 2008, 2013) person-centred systems theory, the Schema Therapy approach considers the interactions between the family members as expressions of the personalities of the individuals involved. However, we also suggest that the patterns of behaviour and perceptions are influenced by the patterns of the system.

In order to see the patient as part of their system, the Schema Therapist assesses the role of circular causality within the structure of family interactions. The therapist analyses how the behaviour of the patient is part of the self-organising feedback system and how the 'symptoms' have a meaning and coherence within the overall system (Bitter, 2013). The schemas and modes of the individual are ultimately part of the 'relationship dance' (Minuchin & Fishman, 1981) and the constructions of reality formed by his/her surrounding system as a consensus of how things are supposed to be.

Similar to systemic approaches, Schema Therapy aims to change the way people talk within their family – about themselves, each other and their problems. Understanding schemas and mode interactions makes it easier for family members to get a new perspective. It gives them a clear terminology and thereby a linguistic method of disconnecting the problem from the person. As White suggests, the person who has the problem is not *the problem* (White, 1991). Experience has shown that children and parents are much more likely to cooperate if they are not identified with the problem. Unlike in other systemic approaches, however, in Schema Therapy the problem is not externalised (White & Epstein, 2004) and given negative connotations, but is introduced as a way of expressing a part of the person, often with good intentions.

15.1.1 Schema coaching for educators and parents

Schema Therapy parent coaching (Schema coaching) involves counselling and parent work to accompany the child-focused therapy. Schema coaching extends the skills of the individual members of the system while also focusing on their basic needs, schemas and modes. In contrast to the behaviourally focused term 'parent training', the term 'parent coaching' underlines the complexity of the help that Schema Therapists provide to assist parents to see their children with new eyes and to build new, creative ways of handling the family interactions. This is a process of instruction, education and assisting with self-help and self-discovery. Schema coaching helps parents to solve the problems and symptoms independently, helping them learn how to meet their own needs. Schema coaching also helps avoid schema clashes by guiding parents to identify and change their own unhelpful patterns.

Parents and caregivers are supported to notice unconscious multi-generational schemas in their families of origin. The child's problem behaviour is then also recognised as a symptom of family schemas and modes. As the therapist reveals these connections and softens the family rigidity they make room for the question: 'Why should the child have to fight this schema all by themselves, when the schema and behavioural patterns are deeply embedded in the family schemas?' Teachers and child care professionals can also be given Schema coaching to provide understanding of the treatment approach and to assist the child to implement strategies in a range of environments.

15.1.2 Elements of Schema Therapy parent coaching

What follows is an overview of parent coaching, with specific procedures and best practice more thoroughly illustrated later in the chapter. Parent coaching is more helpful the more the therapist understands the family system. Therefore, in order to make a thorough assessment of the family system, the following steps are helpful:

- Assess the parent's resources (see questionnaire on family resources).
- Evaluate how core emotional needs are met in the family (parent questionnaire about the need balance as a checklist for therapists).
- Educate about schemas and modes in the parent–child interaction.
- Develop a Schema Therapy formulation, including:
  - Understand family rules, boundaries, roles, coalitions and delegations in the family by using questionnaires for diagnosing family structures (as checklists for therapists), family sculptures and family boards.
  - Hypothesise the function of the symptoms in the family interaction patterns.
  - Identify parent schemas and modes. Explore parent's childhood (using the YSQ), schema genograms (ideally over three generations), and 'projective' techniques. Identify which modes/schemas are activated (the 'emotional buttons' of the parents) and by which trigger (e.g. child's behaviour).
  - Create a schema and mode landscape to illustrate the complex family interactions: vicious cycles, mode escalations.

■ Address parent schemas and modes that are particularly harmful to the parent–child relationship: for example, if a parent has a *Defectiveness/Shame* schema there can be a high level of guilt, seemingly related to the child's behaviour. As the therapist understands the origin of the parent's schemas, the therapist can help untangle the guilt and increase the parent's Healthy Adult mode. Likewise, if parents themselves have experienced gross neglect or abuse it is important to assist them with these issues first, otherwise their schemas will impact on their ability to engage in their child's treatment.

■ Conduct mode work using experiential techniques (chairs, dolls, imagery): first to identify a parent's dysfunctional Coping modes, then to assist with accessing and supporting their Vulnerable Child mode, identifying existing Healthy Adult/Caring and Guidance strengths, building Healthy Adult functioning (for example self-care) where there are deficits, and also disempowering Punitive and Demanding Critic modes in the parent.

■ 'Go back' to the parent's childhood (if necessary) in order to clarify which core emotional needs were met or remain unmet (for example, using mode dialogues or imagery).

■ Raise awareness about the needs of their own parents (the grandparents of the child/patient), which were met or went unmet, forming an intergenerational narrative.

■ Identify the legacy of schemas on each generation with questions such as 'What impact did this schema have on that family, and how does it impact on your family now? What is the impact of that schema on your children?' and so on.

■ Provide practical guidance to the parents in how to deal with their child's modes, for example, through therapist modelling in role-play or by monitoring homework (e.g. noticing when parents are not able to use strategies because they are avoiding triggering their own schemas; assisting with establishing Caring and Guiding Parent modes).

■ Establish positive activities and rituals in order to strengthen adaptive modes in the child.

■ Determine whether further interventions are needed, such as developing parenting skills, couple therapy, case management and other services from community welfare organisations, individual therapy for one parent, occupational therapy, video feedback, social competence/ skills training or other interventions to assist the child (therapy focused on learning, homework help and so on).

The limits and contraindications for Schema Therapy with parents will be addressed in Chapter 17.

15.1.3 Parent training from a Schema Therapy perspective

■ Traditional parent training approaches are primarily oriented towards changes in behaviour or attitudes. This is effective for prevention and with parents who are unsure how to deal with difficult situations. Parent training provides an understanding of the modelling that was passed on in former generations, even when it was problematic. Parent training, such as Triple P (an evidence-based intervention for prevention and development of positive parenting skills; see e.g. Nowak & Heinrichs, 2008), is in our clinical experience not sufficient for complex psychological disorders and schema-based family interactions. Parents can be overwhelmed by the challenging nature of children with complex or chronic problems. They can then experience strong feelings of failure or inadequacy, which are then associated with the child and/or the therapist. This is partly because, in parent training, there is not enough attention paid to the deeply ingrained maladaptive schemas and emotional processes.

Even if the 'parent trainer' notices a parent's maladaptive schema, the setting does not provide the opportunity to address the individual's schema within a group. If a parent's schema is activated, they can take the suggestions for dealing with their children the wrong way and misuse an otherwise good idea. For example, a parent with *Unrelenting Standards* and/or a *Punitiveness* schema can harshly implement a 'sticker chart' approach, resulting in more distress for the child and increased acting out. The parent's experience then suggests that the strategy 'doesn't work'. 'Natural consequences' can also become a punitive experience when parents act based on their own 'sore points', out of their own distress. The assumption of many of the parent training approaches is that the parent is able to remain in Healthy Adult/Caring and Guidance mode whilst implementing strategies. But if a parent's Demanding Parent mode is activated, the usual guidance (for example, 'Be consistent! Give natural consequences – if the child takes too much time finishing their task, they will miss out on the family activity') can be perceived as unhelpful permission to devalue a child. Suggesting parents say 'Stop shouting/crying, talk in a calm voice' can partially enforce Demanding Parent modes and promote escalation processes for parents whose own schemas are getting triggered.

Parents with a *Punitiveness* schema and a deeply ingrained Punitive or Demanding Parent mode often set limits and boundaries with an unhelpful negative undertone that is intimidating to their child. However, because they do not understand their schemas and modes, they believe that they are acting according to professional advice. They may even experience short-term success (at first the child responds with obedience, but later with more avoidance).

However, in the long term they are building distress in the parent–child relationship. This pattern can reinforce the child's negative schemas and coping modes (Detached Protector mode and Defiant-Oppositional mode) and solidify vicious cycles. Often parents then complain to the therapist that his/her recommendations didn't work. Ultimately, good recommendations will become unhelpful if the parents' emotional needs are not met or when the advice does not take into account a family mode formulation.

Another reason why parent training approaches may flounder is related to unconscious parental 'resistance', such as avoidance of painful feelings. Schemas and modes that interfere in therapy need to be addressed. Many CBT therapists are aware of these challenges; however, Schema Therapy provides parents with a more in-depth understanding of their own responses and ways to address these issues more effectively. This can be done in individual as well as group settings.

15.2 Systemic perspectives on Schema Therapy

15.2.1 Preliminary observations on systems approaches

More than 30 years ago, the family systems perspective found its way into psychological treatments such as CBT, depth psychology and psychoanalysis. As a result it is now accepted practice to understand and assess a child in the context of the family and their environment.

Most therapists do not think in simple causalities anymore. However, when searching for the precipitating and main factors of a problem, an individualistic culture can often look for an individual's mistakes or failures. When working with children, symptoms are oftentimes reduced to a 'product' or result of the parent's problems or inappropriate parenting practices. This point of view can be tempting because it (seemingly) diminishes the feelings of helplessness caused by the complexity of looking at a system. On the other hand, this point of view makes it harder for parents to seek help because it assigns blame, resulting in feelings of shame and guilt (see 17.1.1). As a result, many parents who bring their child to therapy are worried about being exposed as the guilty party. A *truly* systemic approach has to consider the interactions of the members of a system as well as the individuals in a system. In this book, we assume that the reader has an understanding of the basic ideas and concepts of systems theory and therapy (holism, shifting the locus of the problem to the system, subsystems, homeostasis, circular causality and so on; see Cowan & Cowan, 2006).

What follows is an overview of the characteristics of a family system and how they relate to Schema Therapy with children and parents. The following sections describe interdependent characteristics, building a picture of how a family system functions in terms of system boundaries, role assignments, system rules, functionality and vicious cycles.

15.2.2 Boundaries of systems and subsystems

Boundaries define the relationship between a part and the whole (Minuchin & Fishman, 1981). For example, within a family with two children, there are different subsystems: first, the parents exist as individuals (meaning they are people sharing a living space); second, they exist as a married couple and lovers (couple level); third, they exist as father and mother (parent level). Another subsystem would be the whole family with the assigned roles father, mother, daughter and son. The siblings also make up a subsystem and then there are also two sets of grandparents, couples in their own subsystem. A family can be understood as being made up of many different subsystems.

Therapists should examine the system or subsystem boundaries: Do system boundaries exist? If so, are they flexible and appropriate or unhelpfully open or rigid? Are the parents able to deal with their couple conflicts without impinging on or diverting the distress to the child level, or do disputes 'spill over' to the children ('triangulating' or conflict detouring)? Are there coalitions between the generations (e.g. mother and daughter against father)? Are the parents enmeshed with their children or sufficiently individuated? When working with divorced or separated parents, it is important to identify if there are coalitions between parents and children against other subsystems, and to look at interactional patterns that are reflecting high levels of distress that are not being adequately contained. For example, the child could take on the role of a witness for the prosecution against the ex-partner to repay injuries from the marriage.

Case example

A boy develops encopresis following his parent's separation. Starting with a strain-induced constipation, a vicious cycle develops into faecal soiling behaviour. Each parent uses this 'problem' as an opportunity to blame the other for causing too much stress for the child. The boy, in an effort to alleviate his feelings of shame and guilt, aligns with whichever parent is present and complains about his/her bad treatment. In this situation the *aim of therapy* is to restore damaged or blurred subsystem boundaries and to change dysfunctional coalitions (see overleaf).

15.2.3 Role assignments and role induction

Pathogenic role assignment

Parents and other caregivers can actively assign roles to their children that are (mostly unconsciously) about meeting their own needs (Zarbock, 2011). Here, the term 'role' is defined as the sum of conscious and unconscious expectations directed to the other. Richter's (1974) concept of pathogenic role assignment is a helpful way to approach this issue. Typical role assignments are:

- child as a substitute partner for a single parent

- child as idealised self (the child needs to achieve everything that the parents are not achieving/doing in their own lives)

- child as scapegoat (anything and everything negative is attributed to the child, so that the rest of the family is held together by a common enemy)

- child as 'whipping boy' (anger is not expressed toward the perpetrator, but diverted to the child as a weaker member of the system)

- child as parent substitute (a reversal of roles or 'parentification', where children assume parental emotional or other responsibilities). For example, a child who has to care for an alcoholic parent, or a very needy mother who is childlike herself

These roles are selectively reinforced and create a perception within the system (and the individual) that is then acted on, which produces group expectations that become 'self-fulfilling prophecies'. For example, if the child has been placed in the role of 'scapegoat', schemas are being formed such as *Defectiveness/Shame* and *Mistrust/Abuse*, triggered by the parent's ostracising behaviour. As the child internalises these experiences, cognitions and feelings, they then behave 'in role', which relieves more tension from the system, cementing the family perceptions. In the case of children as substitute partner role, schemas such as *Enmeshment/Undeveloped Self* and *Self-Sacrifice* develop. If a child is given the role of the parent's idealised self, schemas such *Entitlement/Grandiosity* or *Unrelenting Standards* may form.

Interpersonal delegation as a variation on role assignment

Delegating within a system refers to the process by which people in a group delegate certain parts (feelings and emotions, but also behaviours) to other people in the group (often externalising those parts). Delegation is traditionally an efficient way of dealing with a complex task, used widely in working groups (hunter/gatherer divisions or 'housewife' and 'breadwinner' divisions). However, within families, depth psychologists have described delegation as an interpersonal defensive process (e.g. Mentzos, 1990, cited in Cierpka *et al*, 2005); systemic authors, meanwhile, describe it as intra-familial transference (e.g. Stierlin, 1975, cited in Cierpka *et al*, 2005). Schema Therapy helpfully provides a way of understanding these processes through a mode model, suggesting that the roles that are assigned become modes. For example, in a family, a father may take on the role of 'Caring Parent', essential for the group's functioning, while a mother who may have ongoing health issues may take on the Vulnerable Child mode (or in a situation with a drug-addicted parent who is most often in Impulsive/Undisciplined Child mode, a parentified child takes on the Caring Parent mode).

Young people can also express the impact of these family systems in other systems that they are a part of. For example, a child may restore the inner balance of these unhelpful modes (roles) by using their peer group to explore and express disavowed aspects of self, as in a child from a very strict and emotionally repressed home exhibiting a strong Impulsive or Angry Child mode with friends. Within a family, difficult, unpleasant or disliked parts (or those that do not fit a person's temperament) are 'passed on' to other group members but are still available to that person. So there is often a 'loud' or 'angry' child, who expresses what other family members are not permitted to express themselves. While each family member has their own role or specialisation, collectively the members take care of the functionality of the family and, as a group, meet their emotional needs. For a short time, this can be seen as 'interplay' of complementary roles that strengthen the group and each group member. Yet, in the long run, it also weakens the group. When these roles become rigid and interfere with individuals developing Healthy Adult/Caring and Guidance abilities to meet emotional needs internally, the family system creates dependencies (skills deficit as a result of poor practice, routine or practical knowledge) or even conflict. This leads to polarisation between people, as participants exaggerate certain attitudes or values in an attempt to force change.

Care example

Eight-year-old Michael's mother complains about his aggression and dominance. He regularly hits her arm or back with his fist when his wishes are not fulfilled (Michael is displaying Angry/Spoiled Child mode with a potential Intimidator mode). Her husband does not take this behaviour seriously; he jokes around and plays a lot with his son (the Father is often in Happy Child mode). The mother, on the other hand, tries to respond to each family member and show consideration for all of them (she is attempting to be in Caring Parent mode mixed with Compliant Surrenderer mode). She cares a lot about her young daughter, Anna, who is frequently sad and very needy (Anna is in Vulnerable Child mode). Each member of the family appears to be stuck in rigid roles/modes within the family.

In earlier years, Michael's mother was proud to have such an assertive son, because that contrasted with her experience of being fearful as a child. She also appreciated how Michael's father had so much fun and connection with Michael, and would have liked to be in Happy Child mode with Michael herself. Michael's mother identified most with her daughter Anna, but she didn't dare show her own Vulnerable Child mode, because she did not want to be seen as the wet blanket or 'sad sack', compared to her husband. All four family members mutually fulfil a function, because they express something that is underdeveloped in the others or is not appreciated adequately. However, over time these modes will solidify and lead to more tensions and chronic frustration of needs.

Schema Therapy approaches

Balancing emotional needs

The Schema Therapy approach to dealing with dysfunctional family roles aims to help caregivers to be able to balance their emotional needs with their child's needs. We believe that ideally parents are in the Healthy Adult/Caring and Guidance mode when they are dealing with their child and are therefore able to act with care toward their child, to meet emotional needs, but also to set boundaries and provide guidance when the child expresses frustration intolerance. The Schema Therapist then takes on a systemic viewpoint and examines how or why the parents are 'kicked out' of the Healthy Adult mode or why, in the worst case, they are not able to access Healthy Adult/Caring and Guidance mode at all.

A good place to start is with each different subsystem in the family, beginning with the couple system. Are the partners in Healthy Adult mode or in Happy Child mode (even adults can be childlike, carefree, open to experience and 'in the moment') when relating to each other? Or is the couple dynamic characterised by clashing modes (for example one partner is often in Vulnerable Child and the other in Punitive Parent mode)? The couple relationship needs to be stable in order to support the child in achieving normal emotional development. As the couple's unhelpful mode interactions become clear, the therapist is able to understand how the child is impacted. The pathogenic role assignments given to children depend on whether and which aspects of Healthy Adult/Caring and Guidance mode the parents display. The parent's ability to stay in Healthy Adult/Caring and Guidance mode depends on whether his or her own core emotional needs are met.

Need orientation: Basic needs can infringe on the parent's ability and willingness to be responsive to their child. In addition to the most basic needs (food and shelter), these include sleep, rest, recreation, health, vitality, physical integrity, safety and financial security. Typically, the birth of a child takes a heavy toll on all of these realms. There is a similar connection between a parent's emotional needs and their ability to be present and emotionally available for their child (see 1.2.1). The core emotional needs are the needs for autonomy, relationship/ belonging, pleasure, structure/orientation or self-esteem. These needs are also challenged by the birth of a child. For example, if the parent has taken leave from work, there are fewer external sources of structure and self-esteem.

New parents experience less opportunity for self-expression in their other roles, which may have been significant to parents' sense of self, individually or as a couple (Shapiro *et al*, 2000). Am I still seen as a wife or husband, or lover? As a competent worker, colleague or co-worker? As a friend, or am I 'only a mother/father'? Even the temporary pause in career or leisure can cause great dissatisfaction as a new parent re-negotiates their identity. If these important roles are neglected further and emotional needs are not met in other ways, there is a risk of chronic needs frustration and an activation of dysfunctional modes. If parents remain 'stuck' in these modes they can literally 'forget themselves' and assign the child a role (whipping boy, partner substitute, etc. – see above).

The focus on meeting core emotional needs in Schema Therapy is a high priority also when it comes to parent work. The fact that a parent's everyday stresses restrict their capacity to meet their own needs, sometimes even violating their emotional needs, is often underestimated – especially the impact that has on the parent–child relationship. These pressures leave too little time for carefree play with a child and can render it impossible for the parent to respond to the child's needs. Parents can then get into a conflict between their goals of being a 'good parent' and their own emotional needs.

One of the realities of family life is that not all members' needs can be met at the same time. It is necessary for parents with young babies to temporarily put aside their own needs and focus on the child. Parents need to be attuned, mindful and 'present' when they are with their child, so that they feel the child's moods and needs and meet them. However, when a parent's needs begin competing with the child's, tensions surface.

Meeting a child's needs can also be a complex balance of seemingly 'competing' requirements. Parents ideally are mindful of the changing/oscillating needs of the child for closeness and distance, autonomy and bonding and reasonable boundaries, balancing between care (sympathy, compassion, appreciation, child-directed play) on the one side, and guidance/instruction (leading, protecting and setting boundaries) on the other (also see Baumrind's 1971 parenting styles in Chapter 5).

This balancing act is particularly difficult when the needs of the parents have been neglected in their own childhood (e.g. if there is an *Emotional Deprivation* schema). If these schemas are triggered, conflicts are more likely to arise between the parent's own Vulnerable Child mode (e.g. Neglected Child) and the actual/real child (which may then be experienced as demanding). Only when a parent's Vulnerable Child mode is satisfied, or at least comforted and consoled, is the parent able to make room for the actual child and respond to that child's needs; otherwise, both compete with each other (see Figure 15.1). These issues are elaborated on in attachment theory (e.g. Cowan & Cowan, 2001), which describes the impact of a parent's attachment injuries, resulting in a lack of sensitivity toward one's own child.

Demanding real child

Vulnerable inner child

Figure 15.1: Conflict between the real child and the parent's inner child (injured Vulnerable Child) who sees the real child as demanding

One final word on the subject of role assignments: the therapeutic interventions listed below are designed to protect the child against pathogenic role assignments. However, this requires that parents are able to take on the Healthy Adult/Caring and Guidance mode. If parents are unable to make the transition to the parent role they will need therapeutic support. As a diagnostic aid and basis for discussion with the parents, again we refer to the parent questionnaires (Family needs questionnaire, family relationships questionnaire, questionnaire for the diagnosis of family structures as a checklist for therapists).

Therapeutic interventions to strengthen Healthy Adult/Caring-and-Guidance mode and reduce dysfunctional roles in the family

- Limited re-parenting of the parents by the therapist in order to help them understand and meet their own physical needs (for example, challenging a parent's *Unrelenting Standards* schema that may be interfering with their ability to rest when the baby sleeps).

- Limited re-parenting of the parents by the therapist in order to help them understand and meet their own psychological needs; the need for autonomy, bonding/ belonging, pleasure, structure/ orientation and self-worth. The therapist can support the parents to maintain or to develop ways to meet their basic emotional needs, so that they do not have to unhelpfully sacrifice too much of their own self in their parenting role.

- Address typical conflicts that arise within the parenting role (e.g. conflict between the Healthy Adult/Caring and Guidance mode and the parent's Vulnerable or Angry Child mode). With support to balance those modes, the parent is able to contain their distress, rather than have the tension unhelpfully flow to the child. Children are sensitive to feeling the underlying anger of their parents. Impulsive children will then react with defiance, or even with provocation, setting up a vicious cycle.

- Activating external support from extended family or from service providers (e.g. assistance from the school), building a sense of 'team' around the parents, collaborating and empowering them to use their strengths.

- Empathic confrontation of parents about pathological role assignment (see 15.2.3).

- Guiding the parents in managing the task of appropriately delaying gratification of needs in order to fully concentrate on the child. Helping them to identify times when the needs of all family members cannot be realised/ fulfilled simultaneously.

- Guiding the parents in being aware of their child's needs, balancing between care (such as sympathy, compassion, appreciation, child-directed play) on the one hand and instruction/ guidance (such as leading, protecting and setting boundaries) on the other.

- Activation of 'Good Parent' mode through memories of positive experiences with safe caregivers in their history or provided by imagery re-scripting when needed.

■ Mode experiments in order to explore and practice the development of healthy modes in the parents. Example: If a father has been uninvolved and the mother goes out of town for the weekend, assisting the father to take care of the child. Given the roles that the couple have adopted this 'experiment' provides an opportunity to activate the Caring Parent mode in the father, which the mother has not expected. The therapist is able to then elaborate on this experiment with further behavioural pattern breaking.

It is important to make sure that in addition to cognitive approaches and psychoeducation (schema and mode pictures/maps) there is experiential work (e.g. imagery work, mode dialogues or family sculptures) to further transform rigid mode dynamics, and to make sure the family work goes beyond a one-off moment in therapy.

The interventions discussed above are intended for sessions with both parents or one parent alone. Schema Therapy techniques for working in a family setting are still in development. In addition to the sculpture work (see 16.1), we would like to test the extent to which finger puppets, dolls, animal figures, chairs, foam pillows (e.g. for building caves and 'walls'), masks and other similar media are suitable to illustrate and experience mode flipping or interrupt unhelpful modes in a playful way. For example, the family members could use their finger puppets (see mode work with finger puppets in 12.2) to experientially develop goals, such as which modes they would like to place more importance on, which parts they would like to take better advantage of and which modes they want to manage differently.

15.2.4 Family system rules

'Family system rules' describe principles, family traditions, norms, values and emotional styles that are internalised and determine the relationship between the family members. Family taboos describe unchallenged rules of what can be talked about. In every family, but also in larger systems (e.g. a national community), one can identify a culture of how feelings are to be dealt with. These system rules serve to orient the respective system and help the system to sustain itself both internally and externally.

Internal working models can also be part of the system rules of a family (such as a woman's self-image, including how she wants to be as a mother in the family). These working models contain representations or images of specific bonding experiences passed on from generation to generation (intergenerational transmission). These working models have the ability to significantly influence parental sensitivity (Cowan & Cowan, 2001). Mental representations also influence the child's development of a sense of self and the building of relationships (Grossmann & Grossmann, 2007).

The values of a family are also reflected in the parent's visions of the future. When there is a clear vision for the future, parents can view their child's symptoms as a threat to this vision. For example, distractibility can be seen as a threat to future career achievement. There can be concerns regarding the development of the child, which can lead to considerable tension when the child is not achieving. The parents may also deny any symptoms in their child because their vision for the future of their child colours their perception of their child's abilities.

An important aspect of assessment, then, is asking about family values, norms and visions for the future. In therapy those family rules (and the schemas that they are expressing) may need to be questioned. As schemas are weakened and mode triggering is reduced (for example the Punitive or Demanding Parent mode; see below), Healthy Adult/Caring and Guidance values are developed. Psychoeducation about a child's normal development can reduce unsubstantiated worries.

Suitable questions for exploring values and norms include the following: 'What do you wish for your child's future? Do you have specific ideas about your child's life, what relationships or career they might have? What kind of behaviour or conduct do you expect from your child at the moment? What were the unwritten rules from your family of origin or other important caregivers? Which of these do you find important for your own family? What was your vision for being a young mother or a young father? What values did you want to keep from your parents and your experience of being parented? And what did you want to do completely differently? What is your idea of an ideal mother or father? What kind of behaviour do you expect from your children? Are there certain rituals or customs that used to be, or are now, important for the family? For example, what's the daily routine, weekly pattern or important family events? Is there a life motto, an attitude to life or a way of life that you have for your family?' Questions to elaborate on these can also be found in the Adult Attachment interview (Main *et al*, 1985).

Another way to elicit family rules is to present a list of statements, starting with the question: 'These are statements many other families agree with; which ones apply to your family?' For example: 'We do not talk at the table', 'We should all stick together', 'Boys do not cry', 'For girls, education is not that important', 'All siblings fight, so a punch up every once in a while is normal', 'Parents should be like friends to their children', 'Parents should never leave their children alone', 'A few slaps on the butt have never hurt anybody', 'If you are lazy at school, you will not amount to anything', 'Children should be seen and not heard'.

15.2.5 Functionality

From a behavioural therapy perspective, the function of a symptom or behaviour is identified using functional behaviour analysis (see for example Sturmey, 1996). The function of problematic behaviour for the patient or their caregivers is understood in the context of the psychological impact of situational variables (internal/external stimuli), endogenous variables and maintaining consequences. Incorporating a systems perspective, the role of the presenting problem behaviour in the system or subsystems needs to be examined in detail. The symptoms of one family member can be seen to be 'functional' for the whole family as well as for the person. With a symptom a patient can either achieve something for themselves and the system, or avoid something. The behaviour of one member serves the other and vice versa. Thereby, each member helps to hold the system together in 'homeostasis' (Jackson, 1981). Systems approaches refer to the dual nature of symptomatic behaviour. Even though the presenting problem is difficult, it is also a solution at the same time. It causes grief, but prevents distress that could be worse. For example, a child who refuses to go to school uses abdominal pain (Complaining Protector mode) in order to avoid failure or rejection by classmates, but at the same time his behaviour leads him to be an outsider, which in turn will eventually hurt him. Boeckhorst (1988) differentiates four ways in which symptoms can be expressed in a family (when symptoms have no organic basis, e.g. tic disorders, enuresis due to urinary tract infection or as a result of trauma:

1. The symptom is an ineffective solution to a problem (for example abdominal pain, as described above).

2. The symptom has a protective function and stabilises family relationships, for example by intercepting a conflict or diverting attention from another family member.

3. The symptom gives power. The patient can control the interactions in the family.

4. The symptom may symbolically and metaphorically point to other problems in the family.

Zarbock suggests that the way to understand the functional meaning of the symptom is through the lens of the inner experience of the patient (2011). For example, the goal of the behaviour may be to maintain self-esteem, confirm identity or avoid distress. Schema Therapists would say that the symptom is an attempt to cope with schema triggers – namely, by activating unhelpful coping modes.

Hand (2015) describes several examples of *dual functionality*. For example, a child's phobia of butter helps the child avoid being confronted with the death of his grandmother who always had this butter at home. At the same time, the phobia also serves as an expression of anger at his parents, who haven't shown the child much affection (Hand, 2008, p. 135). A child may develop compulsions (an over-compensation such as Over-Controller mode) to cope with a fear of change within the family (conflict, fighting parents or an imminent parental separation) and to bring the parents together again out of concern for the child, or to make the parents start therapy.

These examples demonstrate how one individual's symptoms can dominate not only their own emotions, but the whole family. The family literally revolves around the symptoms as they surrender to demanding behaviour or power struggles.

Implications for therapeutic work: symptoms as an attempt to solve a problem

A Schema Therapy approach sees symptomatic behaviour or coping modes as an attempt to solve a problem or deal with distress given limited other skills. Coping modes have both an interactional and an interpersonal function in the micro and macro systems. Therefore a systems perspective is important to understanding how to intervene with a maladaptive mode, as any changes in the behaviour of a person will always have repercussions on their environment.

This perspective suggests caution, not 'jumping the gun' and giving a hasty response to parent's requests for change. If the therapist acts too quickly the functionality of the symptoms may be overlooked, which will reduce the patient's motivation and the system's willingness to adapt (Hand, 2008, p117). Therefore, when drawing up a treatment plan, care should be taken to not buy in to the narrative of the 'identified patient', that the symptomatic family member is necessarily the cause of the 'problem'. Also, the initial symptom carrier is not always the main fault in the system (Hand, 2008, p257). The symptomatic behaviour of the child may even have a function for other 'systems', such as the child's school class or circle of friends.

In the literature you can find several cases in which discovering the functionality of a symptom alone results in a reduction of the symptoms (ibid.; Lang, 2007). However, in the majority of cases, especially with chronic presentations and young patients, the unconscious functionality of certain symptoms is less accessible, because the symptoms have precisely the function of masking painful feelings. Therefore, attempts to discover the function of the symptoms triggers resistance, unless the child can expect immediate relief.

Reviewing the motivation for change

Given that the current symptoms may serve a 'function', the therapist needs to assess the motivation for change. Could it be that the parents want a space to express their distress without really wanting to initiate change? Are they seeking an 'expert' who will affirm that no change is possible? As goals are being defined, it is helpful for the therapist to assess whether the verbalised motivation is real or perhaps a feigned self-motivation or external motivation. Considering the patient's present life and relationship situation, what is the motivation to reduce symptoms (Hand, 2008, p69)? Is it even possible within the family rules for a parent to have permission to want change?

Motivation for change is difficult when the symptoms are maintained by negative or positive reinforcement and when they serve as a protective mechanism for the patient or family members (Hand, 2008, p67). Without clarifying the motivation of the overall system, no individual therapy will be useful. Therefore it is important that all members of the system be asked about possibly differing objectives and motivations. If the child or young person lacks the motivation to participate, there needs to be an intervention in the system. For example, the therapist can begin by increasing the family member's resistance and reducing or preventing the benefit that comes from the destructive behaviour of the 'unmotivated' patient. This can be achieved by strengthening the parents' ability to assert boundaries and not 'give in' to the behaviour (see 17.1.4).

Mission clarification and statement

Before initiating an elaborate intervention, an assessment needs to be made about whether the family members can endure the change. This can be done using well-known questions from systemic approaches (Bitter, 2013).

Questions about motivation for change

- Who in the family wants anything to change?

- Who wants what from whom and for what purpose or why?

- Is the family only here because someone else wants change? What is the referrer's position and expectation? Is he/she a member of the problematic system, e.g. a teacher or another family member?

Questions about the problem context

- Who would say that there's no problem at all?

- Who reacts to the problem behaviour/mode the most?

- Who feels more or less disturbed/bothered by the problem?

- What has changed in the relationships since the problem has begun/since your child has started to show this side of him/her?

- What would change in the relationship if the problem was to stop/if your child no longer showed this side of him?

Solution-oriented questions, including miracle questions

- What if the problem/this mode disappeared overnight? Is there anything or any side of your child you might miss then? Is there any reason why it would be good to keep/maintain the problem or mode for a while? Would it be helpful to have the problem/mode come back from time to time?

'Absent' fathers should also be strongly encouraged to cooperate and play an active part in clarifying the goals of therapy, even if they appear to be unwilling at first. One way to do that is to call the parent concerned and offer a chance to talk about the issues before making a commitment to therapy.

Prioritizing problem areas

To prioritise where to start (Hand, 2008, p119), when there is sufficient motivation, the primary system problem should be treated first. Helpful questions to ask in this instance are; What aspects of the problem are related in what way? What area should the treatment start with first? What should be prioritised? For example, a child's aggression could have four aspects: a high level of couple conflict, a mother's self-doubts, the child's aggressive behaviour and the child's lack of social skills.

Depending on the priority, different intervention foci may be suggested. The choice of intervention should be made in collaboration with the family and should be focused on questions such as: Which intervention will have the most impact? Is the cost of the intervention worth the benefits? Content-related questions are also helpful: What is the most distressing aspect of this issue? What is easy to change and most impactful? What is a foundational aspect that opens up other areas for change? (See also Sturmey, 1996, p154.)

Treatment options following prioritising

- If there is an impending family break-up, where the child fears losing access to a parent or being exposed to one parent criticising the other, couple therapy (Schema Therapy; see 4.4.3) would be helpful. The focus would be on assisting the parents to clarify roles and to provide communication training (Hand, 2008, p230) and coaching in meeting the emotional needs of the child. The child then can be relieved of the weight of their parents' distress, knowing that the parents will remain in Healthy Adult/Caring and Guidance mode even in the event of a separation.

- If there is ongoing conflict following a separation (e.g. very abusive parents), it may be helpful to bring in a mediator backed up by the youth welfare office to function as a referee, allowing the family system to have a more functional adult within.

- In the absence of parenting skills, such as not being able to set proper limits, lacking authority and appropriate assertiveness when there is uncertainty about handling practical issues, parent training may be useful – to build adequate parental behaviour (such as reinforcing of non-symptomatic behaviour, less attention on symptomatic behaviour).

- Psychoeducation on developmental processes (see Chapter 4).

- (Video-based) communication instructions (see Chapter 4).

- Parent-focused therapy when there are high levels of Child modes evident.

- Child-focused therapy with parental involvement.

- Social skills training (in a group setting) for the child with support for parents.

- Sibling conflict training and parent training.

- Family therapy with involvement of the grandparents or the step-family.

- Other specific functional therapies (learning therapy, occupational therapy, physiotherapy) as to assist with motor, educational, physical issues.

- Involving youth welfare office (e.g. to provide additional support).

The therapist as a part of the system

The systemic perspective also includes looking at the role that the therapist is playing. The therapist will inevitably, directly or indirectly, be involved in the system. How a therapist behaves toward one person has repercussions for the other people involved. As early as the initial meeting, family members (especially children) are looking at 'whose side' the therapist is on.

The therapist initially follows a systems approach by joining with the system and temporarily strengthening individual system members. Therapists need to notice and manage their own schema and mode activations, relying on their own training, self-therapy and supervision. Without appropriate training, therapists can unconsciously enter coalitions with specific family members (e.g. aligning with the child against his 'evil' parents). They can also develop interventions which, while being technically well executed and justified, are carried out in the 'wrong' mode, which can hinder therapy processes.

In his book on Schema Therapy (2003) Young wrote a long chapter on the effects of the therapist's own schemas, to which we refer the reader.

15.2.6 Connecting vicious cycles to mode escalations within a system

In some disorders an individual psychological perspective focuses on intra-individual models, such as the fear–avoidance cycle (Zarbock, 2011, p134). A disorder can be maintained after its first occurrence based on the consequences resulting from the disorder itself. For example, agoraphobia is reinforced when a patient avoids certain places because their negative expectations are generalising. From a systemic perspective, there is a particular focus on interpersonal vicious cycles. Let's start with a relatively simple cycle. For a depressed client, low mood and lack of motivation can result in increased caring and nurturing behaviour from the family. This reinforces the passivity and thus the social skill deficits of the 'suffering individual' (the Regressive Child mode). However, the Regressive Child mode in turn leads to a further loss of motivation and energy.

Or in the case of a shy child, the Avoidant Protector mode can trigger loss of friendship or peer rejection. This reinforces the feelings of shame and strangeness, further fuelling the avoidance. Zarbock (ibid.) points out that symptom-specific vicious cycles exist for ADHD/ADD patients also (p. 138f), as in the following examples. A primary attention deficiency can cause forgetfulness and volatility, which can lead to failure and negative outcomes. Many patients respond to this experience of failure with defiance or carelessness (appearing resigned – Detached Protector; or avoiding further 'failure' by day dreaming – Detached Self-Soother mode), resulting in a reactive attention deficit. A child with a primarily neuro-biological hyperactivity with psychomotor restlessness and distractibility can be frequently in trouble, criticised and excluded in class. The resulting distress leads to hyper-vigilance and reactive anxiety as a way to channel the tension or deflect negative feelings (Hyperactive Protector). A child with impulsivity often acts with hasty, inappropriate behaviour which leads to rejection or blame. The child can then 'play to their strengths' and use impulsive or reactive defences to avoid negative emotions (Dramatist mode or Dominator mode).

When families have been stuck in a dysfunctional system for a long time, dysfunctional modes can 'take hold' of the family member(s). The over-compensation modes are particularly volatile, clashing more frequently and destructively – like a well-rehearsed play involving the personality traits of those involved. Parents can 'gang up' on the over-compensating child, characterising the interaction as a 'fight'. However, when the battle lines are drawn in this way, both parties take up defensive modes like armour, while the Vulnerable Child modes remain 'protected' and invisible to everyone. Families under external stress (financial constraints, poverty, illness, social isolation or divorce) are particularly susceptible to such vicious cycles. Parents might be so exhausted that they want to 'buy' peace. Tolerating adverse child behaviour patterns (Compliant Surrenderer mode) can activate a circuit of mutual negative influence between parents and their child. Patterson (1982) describes the following classic cycle: a mother asks a child to do something; the child responds with aggression or whining. There is a high probability that an exhausted mother will give up because she wants to conserve energy or wants to end the incident as quickly as possible. With each repetition of this cycle the mutual behaviour is reinforced; the child's behaviour (Complaining Protector or Bully Attack mode) is reinforced by the mother's withdrawal (in Compliant Surrenderer mode), just as the mother's behaviour is reinforced by the peace and quiet. The child is then more likely to respond with aggression or whining and the mother is more likely to give in again. Gradually, both will believe that the mother is no match in the 'tug of war' and cannot cope with the situation.

Occasionally, the mother may try to stand up to the behaviour. However, the child's behaviour will then escalate, because there has been success in the past with that behaviour. Nagging turns into screaming; threats turn into hitting. In the end, the mother will often give in. And again, the cycle will escalate. Gradually, the mother will get accustomed to the attacks or whining; perhaps she will even stop hearing it (Detached Protector mode), as a kind of survival mechanism: 'If you can't stop it, then don't notice it.' Therefore the Detached Protector mode saves her from painful feelings, with the longer-term impact that the mother detaches from the child. The author calls this 'blindness' (as in blindness to dangers or injuries) that can spread to other areas, such as not knowing who the child is hanging out with or what they are doing outside of the home. The Detached Protector mode can become so pervasive that the mother is absent from the child's life. If then the father is also unavailable, the child in effect becomes parentless (Patterson, 1982). Within the vicious cycle, parent and child mutually react to each other in more punitive ways. On both sides there is less and less positive affect and self-esteem. Both sides develop an ever more negative image of each other. Both sides feel unfairly treated and take revenge on each other.

The vicious cycle can develop a momentum of its own, reinforcing distorted perceptions. The family members polarise into good/evil and friend/enemy. Both sides perceive each other through a stereotype; the other (the culprit) is evil, stupid or at best, sick. On the other hand, they see themselves as only good and simply as a victim of the other. There is only victory or defeat. In the back and forth of the power struggle there is mutual humiliation when the opportunity presents. As parents lose grasp of their authority they often demand compliance in such an offensive manner (using irritation and sarcasm, in Bully/Attack mode) that the child experiences them as a threat to their integrity and self-worth (Vulnerable Child mode is activated). Because the child feels backed into a corner, they strike back in Bully/Attack mode. Humiliated parents fall back on their only remaining instrument of power: harsh or draconian punishments. Seeing this cycle as a clash of modes helps each person in the cycle to understand, step back from their coping modes and develop healthy ways of dealing with the situation.

The therapeutic goal is to interrupt the vicious cycle by using interventions that go beyond the classic instruments of established therapies. In presenting these techniques we are borrowing from the concepts of nonviolent resistance and parental presence (see 17.1.4).

15.2.7 Resources and strengths

In considering contextual factors, the strengths and resources of a patient and their environment can be included in the assessment process (see Rudolph & Epstein, 2000; Borg- Laufs, 2011). The environment, with its ecological (living conditions), economic and social resources (network, family, caregiver resources) is part of this assessment. Borg-Laufs (2011) suggest using circle diagrams to complete a network analysis. The child as well as the parents can fill out the inner and outer circles with names of people they are connected to and who are important in the context of family, friends and others. Information about their interests can be entered into the pie chart: Response to statements such as 'What I like' are entered into the 'interest pie', with the sectors divided into 'with the family', 'with friends' and 'by myself'. Another method of mapping a child's resources is an 'Eco-map', developed by Hartman (1978) and described in detail by McCormick *et al* (2008). (The online materials also contain a list of questions for parents to reflect on their strengths and resources.)

Schema Therapy simultaneously focuses on reducing unhelpful modes and increasing strengths by increasing the nurture and care of the Child modes (for both parents and children), building healthy coping (e.g. to tolerate discomfort) and particularly increasing the Clever/Wise Child or Healthy Adult/Caring and Guidance modes. Together with the parents, Schema Therapists explore when and in which situations children have experiences of self-confidence and self-efficacy (Tedeshi & Kilmer, 2005). Therapists should also seek precise details about the parents' positive experiences and states and ultimately seek to evoke these modes: 'Tell me about moments when you have felt confident and competent in your role as a father/mother? Create an image of that scene in detail again. How are you feeling physically? What feelings and thoughts are you having? What helps build that feeling? What does your body feel like? What posture fits this feeling? Could you adopt that same body posture again and see if the feeling comes back?'

When the therapist observes that the parents show positive attitudes and nurturing instincts, appropriately set boundaries, and so on, they draw the parent's attention to that moment ('You did a great job here when you ... That's your Healthy Adult/Caring and Guidance mode').

15.3 Mode clashes and mode activation in the system

In the case of complex interaction cycles with mutual entanglement, Schema Therapy models provide a way to illustrate the intricate dynamics to the family in an understandable and non-judgmental way; schemas and dysfunctional Coping modes lead to negative reactions, which in turn reinforces the patient's schema as a self-fulfilling prophecy. The partner's 'attempt to find a solution' triggers the other's schemas, which in turn reinforces the schemas of the partner.

Case example

In a couple relationship a man compensates for his *Emotional Deprivation* schema by compulsive controlling behaviour (Over-controller mode). This in turn activates the *Subjugation* schema of his partner, who then reacts with avoidance (Avoidant Protector mode), which in turn reinforces his *Emotional Deprivation* schema, and so on. When this couple has children, they may try to meet those emotional needs with their children. The child can become a substitute parent (cf. Richter, 1974; see Fig. 15.2) and, given that a child is not able to (and should not be required to) meet a parent's needs for emotional nurture, the cycle continues.

Parents often try to fulfil their own unfulfilled needs through children. They use the child as a parent substitute (see Richter, 1974).

A common vicious cycle occurs when a mother who has experienced violence develops a *Mistrust/Abuse* schema. An impulsive and angry son can trigger the schema, resulting in the mother's Vulnerable Child mode being activated. The mother then flips into Detached Protector mode and distances herself from her son. This in turn triggers the boy's *Emotional Deprivation* schema and an over-compensatory Controller mode or Bully/Attack mode, escalating the 'threat' to the mother, which in turn fuels the mother's Detached Protector – which may also alternate with a pacifying Compliant Surrenderer mode. Aggressive boys

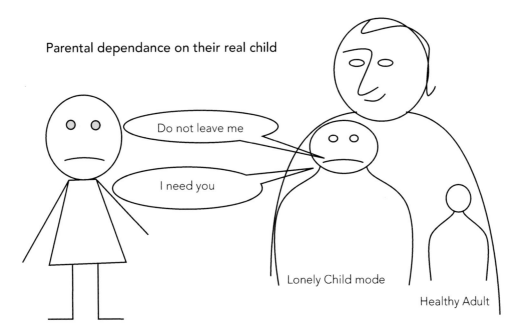

Figure 15.2: A typical mode clash where the mother's Lonely Child mode creates dependency on the real child: 'Do not leave me. I need you.'

can very easily reactivate traumatic memories in mothers with experiences of violence in their history. In the case of these traumatised people, we often observe dissociative reactions.

Detaching from the triggering behaviour results in repressing and neglecting to challenge the aggressive impulses of their child. This can appear as 'tolerating and putting up with' the violence of their own child. As a result of these mode clashes the parent has lost contact with their Healthy Adult mode. They then avoid healthy self-assertion in order to protect themselves from being victimised by their child's attacks (see Fig. 15.3). The lack of appropriate limits on behaviour increases the child's violence. These escalations can occur regardless of the intention behind the aggression, whether it is an attachment-related desire for connection or aggression based on impulsivity. Therefore, therapeutic interventions need to be mindful of the parent's schemas in order to address relational patterns.

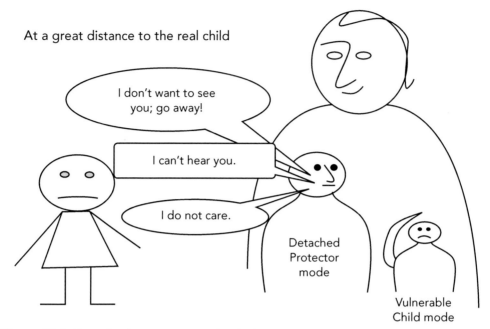

Figure 15.3: Detached protector mode clash

In Chapter 4 of this book, typical parent–infant modes clashes were described. In the next section, we contrast 4.1.3 with how the Healthy Adult/Caring and Guidance mode responds to a child's expression of needs, dealing with schema triggering and the unhealthy mode activation that can occur. For common patterns in the father–child dynamic, refer to 4.2.

15.3.1 The development of the dysfunctional parent modes

We all draw on different experiences when dealing with our own children or the children entrusted to us. Most people have a biologically based, genetically predisposed intuition to nurture a young child (Perry, 2001). Babies trigger a parental impulse to protect and provide, through the activation of the bonding system. Parents take pleasure in helping a child discover the world and grow. In the millions of interactions between parents and child, parents pass on deeply rooted patterns of behaviour that every child needs in order to be able to deal with the challenges of life.

Yet, over the centuries, parents' ways of dealing with their child have been influenced by the environment and cultural values. Thus shifting societal norms and the values of the current social network impact on child rearing. Children internalise both loving and harsh interactions – *introjections*, in psychoanalytic terms. Caring or punitive interactions that are repeated become a part of the self. These response patterns become unconsciously memorised. Internalisations of harsh or demanding parent–child interactions are referred to in adults as Punitive or Demanding Parent or Critic modes.

Parents can find when under stress, even (or especially) if they have decided to do things differently from their own parents, that they often fall back on the old methods, finding themselves saying the very words that their parents said to them. For example, in a moment of anger, you may speak in exactly the way you hated as a child. So certain schemas or coping modes can be passed on from generation to generation – modified perhaps by the current zeitgeist and other diverse influences. Recommendations from self-help books or new knowledge can help to set new standards in dealing with your child and get rid of 'old habits'. However, the experiences that exert greatest 'power' under distress are the unconscious processes that remain unexamined.

Case example

As a child, Mrs Mueller was grounded for days whenever she received bad grades. She has pledged not to use such punishments with her own son because she still remembers these as sad and painful moments. Instead, she follows the advice of a self-help book and imposes a three-day TV ban for her son as a natural consequence and tries to teach him study skills. Even though she has modified her behaviour, Mrs Mueller repeats the father's pattern of punishment – a different version of Punitive Parent mode. The words and interaction may be more nuanced, but the attitude that the mother displays is still punitive. After her son has failed several exams, she becomes more distressed and the Punitive Parent mode becomes stronger; she gives her son the fierce look she often experienced from her own father.

When working with parents, the Schema Therapist is always looking for mode activation, evident in excessive, rigid, particularly stressed and emotionally arousing response patterns. When the child evokes a parent's schemas, powerful emotional reactions occur in parents and their reactions are less flexible. These 'automatic' responses are rooted in deeper layers of their memory and biographical history. Thus, a Punitive Parent mode might gain the upper hand (see Figure 15.4) in directing a parent's reaction. This often happens in the case of aggressive and impulsive children. Those children often trigger the parent's Punitive mode and family disputes quickly escalate; the child feels rejected (the Vulnerable Child mode) and behaves aggressively (the Angry Child mode) in response. In the worst cases, the child has already developed schemas such as *Defectiveness/Shame*, which can lead to a strengthening of the above-mentioned modes.

Figure 15.4: Typical mode clash: Detached Protector mode, hiding the parent's Vulnerable Child mode; Demanding Parent mode then activates the Detached/Dissociated Protector mode in the child

In Schema Therapy there is a focus on noticing and naming the typical mode clashes in the family; and, together with the family, creating a mode model that illustrates the relevant schemas and mode-escalation cycles. This provides a road map for working on the unhelpful modes and schemas.

15.3.2 Schema avoidance in parents: dysfunctional defences against Negative Parent modes

Many parents report that they want to treat their children very differently from the way their parents treated them, not wanting to inflict on their children the same negative experiences.

In striving to provide the opposite experience they develop an idealistic model of a good mother or a good father. One of the difficulties these parents encounter. is that they are clear about what kind of parent they *don't* want to be, but not clear on how to be the kind of parent they *do* want to be. In particular, when trying to find what Healthy Adult parenting looks like, they have difficulty developing a confident and self-assured way to be a mother/father and nurture their children. One of the reasons why this is so difficult is that this parent is missing a first-hand experience of good parenting. They have images based on childhood wishes or positive experiences with other caregivers. However, because there has not been exposure to daily experiences of healthy parenting, the Healthy Adult/Caring and Guidance mode is not internalised.

Therefore, in times of acute stress, it is difficult to access the Healthy Adult/Caring and Guidance mode. When an adult is relying on their 'gut instincts' they will often revert to experiential learning rather than the more abstract 'ideal parenting' model. From a Schema Therapy perspective, the following mode flips occur:

- Children's age-appropriate behaviour activates the parent's internalised modes.

- In stressful situations unhelpful modes are often stronger than Healthy Adult/ Caring and Guidance mode because they are deeply ingrained and activation is automatic in distress.

- Furthermore, mode flips are connected to a negative trigger. For example, a father might get angry and feel the impulse to scold his son. However, anger triggers memories of being scolded and schemas are activated (e.g. the *Subjugation* schema). Because the father wants to avoid schema activation when dealing with his real child, he tries to relate to his child in a way that avoids getting angry. The result is the creation of a 'no go zone' of schema avoidance. The father is not able to rely on 'natural' impulses triggered by slight annoyance to correct his child's behaviour (developing Clever/Wise mode). Instead, he believes his impulses are harmful to the child and holds them back as long as possible or flips into Detached Protector mode.

- Oppositional modes activated by conflict can also produce a Compliant Surrenderer mode or quick mode flipping. Parents feel conflicted and torn between different modes, as if they had 'two or more people fighting inside'.

- Typically these mode conflicts either resolve by one of the two modes being restrained for a longer period of time (using the dissociative process: see section 1), until the mode re-appears with stronger force, or parents vacillate between the modes – mode flipping. The mode flipping that is triggered by schema activation leaves the parent unable to provide a clear, unambiguous stance, impairing their ability to meet the need for orientation and predictability for the child.

Case example

A father is annoyed by his son's messy room. He has already asked him several times to tidy up the floor and clear the desk so he can do his homework without being distracted. One day when he comes home and sees the messy room again, he starts to get angry. His dominant, demanding father's words come to his mind. Yet, the sight of his son activates his *Subjugation* schema. His own Vulnerable Child mode mirrors his (real) son: 'I always felt horrible when my father told me what to do.' Because the father's Vulnerable Child mode is activated he finds himself paralysed, not wanting to give in to his Demanding Parent mode (internalised father). So he restrains himself from correcting his son, only reminding his son to tidy up in a half-hearted and ineffectual way, until later he comes back angry and demanding. Or he goes back and forth between a stern voice and relaxed tone (mode flipping).

Schema Therapists instruct parents to seek rather than avoid situations in which schemas are activated. This can be gradually achieved by practising with role plays or homework tasks – in difficult cases, direct coaching can be helpful (in-patient or home-based support). Ideally, this coaching happens after the parents understand their relevant schemas in the context of their biographical origins. As parents confront their schemas and learn to stay in Healthy Adult/Caring and Guidance Mode they provide a stabilising impact on the system.

Another common issue when working with parents is the need to help in distinguishing between Healthy Adult and Punitive/Demanding Parent modes, particularly when expressing anger and setting limits. Helping parents to understand how to experience justified anger and stay in Healthy Adult/Caring and Guidance mode is an important focus for therapy. Imagery re-scripting is very helpful for parents. It helps to both understand dysfunctional parent modes and internalise Healthy Adult/Caring and Guidance mode. For example, by going back to experiences that were instrumental in developing dysfunctional parent modes, a mother or father can 'see' the origin of their mode through Healthy Adult eyes. Confronting or banishing maladaptive parent modes helps to de-power these modes. Also, as that figure is challenged and a corrective emotional experience provided, the mother or father is able to experience what Healthy Adult/Caring and Guidance mode feels like.

15.4 Therapist stance when working with parents

The therapeutic relationship contains elements of consulting, coaching, mentoring and therapy. When working with the parents, Schema Therapists use limited re-parenting to serve as a corrective to the parent's existing schemas and modes. As described in Chapter 4 of this book, the therapist's role is also defined as 'Limited Grandparenting' or 'Limited Co-Parenting' (depending on the what dynamic fits best for the parent), where the therapist takes on the role of the helpful grandparent or co-parent. This role enables the therapist to coach parents and at the same time support the child patient by being on hand with help, advice and guidance. Work with parents may also include therapeutic sequences, in which the origins of schemas are explored with the parents in the framework of individual sessions. Here, deep pain, anger or shame can surface and be processed therapeutically. Schema Therapy with parents should focus on the needs, schemas and dominant modes. Each parent/ family will need very different therapeutic approaches, from very precise instructions and guidance for some to a less 'hands-on' approach that encourages the existing strengths of the parents for others.

15.4.1 Aspects of the role of the therapist

■ Guiding parents on how to instruct their children (capacity building), for example through specific suggestions, role-plays and modelling behavior (the therapist as a role model for the parent's Healthy Adult/Caring and Guidance Mode).

■ Providing insight so that parents understand their, often confusing, situation.

■ Assisting parents to manage violent or abusive behaviours through practical strategies and strengthening of the parents' Healthy Adult/Caring and Guidance mode presence.

■ Information about causal and maintaining factors.

■ Psychoeducation about normal development and pathological developmental paths.

■ Selective self-disclosure, with parents providing personal examples to model overcoming difficulties, as well as the therapist's experience with other parents.

■ Displaying respect for the parents (so they don't feel like the 'objects' of therapeutic techniques) by treating them as equals.

■ Providing information about treatment approaches so that therapy is transparent. Presenting hypotheses to the family members so they can review/ check them for themselves as well as modify them if necessary.

■ Emphasising parental involvement as crucial for the child's recovery.

■ Confronting injustice when parents use violence.

■ Challenging unhelpfully high standards and addressing feelings of shame and guilt.

■ Focusing on the values and good intentions underpinning failed 'experiments/ attempts at change'.

■ Showing respect for the effort and recognising the distress and helplessness parents can feel in the face of their child's difficult temperament and modes.

- Strengthening the Healthy Adult/Caring and Guidance modes by:

  - providing information, instructing parents on normal developmental stages and basic needs (what children need at what age, what you can expect from them at what age, what requirements are appropriate, how the tasks of the parents change according to the age of the child)

  - recognising the parents' own child modes and acknowledging the personal needs of the parents as individuals and as a couple (including a satisfying sexual relationship)

  - encouraging the use of supports in helping with child care, assisting with time management and other organisational issues.

References

Baumrind D (1971) Current patterns of parental authority. *Developmental Psychology Monograph*, Part 2 (4) 1–103.

Bitter JR (2013) *Theory and Practice of Family Therapy and Counselling*. Cengage Learning.

Boeckhorst F (1988) *Strategische Familientherapie*. Dortmund: Modernes Lernen.

Borg-Laufs M (2005) Bindungsorientierte Verhaltenstherapie – eine Erweiterung der Perspektive. In: J Junglas (Ed) *Geschlechtergerechte Psychotherapie und Psychiatrie*, pp127–136. Bonn: DPV.

Borg-Laufs M (2011) *Störungsübergreifendes Diagnostik-System für die Kinder- und Jugendlichenpsychotherapie (SDS-KJ): Manual für die Therapieplanung* (2. Aufl.) Tübingen: Dgvt-Verlag.

Cierpka M, Sprenkle D & Thomas V (2005) *Family Assessment*. Cambridge, MA: Hogrefe.

Cowan PA & Cowan BC (2001) A couple perspective on the transmission of attachment patterns. In: C Clulow (Ed) *Adult Attachment and Couple Psychotherapy*, pp62–82. Hove: Brunner-Routledge.

Cowan PA & Cowan CP (2006) Developmental psychopathology from family systems and family risk factors perspectives: Implications for family research, practice, and policy. In: D Cicchetti & DJ Cohen (Eds), *Developmental Psychopathology* Vol 1 (2nd ed.) (pp.530–587). New York: Wiley.

Grossmann K & Grossmann KE (2007) *The impact of attachment to mother and father at an early age on children's psychosocial development through young adulthood*. Rev. ed. In Tremblay, R.E.,

Hand I (2015) Obsessive-compulsive patients and their families. In Ian R.H. Falloon (Ed) *Handbook of Behavioural Family Therapy* (2nd ed) pp231–256. New York: Routledge.

Hand I (2008) *Strategisch, systemische Aspekte der Verhaltenstherapie*. Wien: Springer.

Hartman A (1978) Diagrammatic assessment of family relationships. *Social Casework*.

Jackson DD (1981) The question of family homeostasis. *International Journal of Family Therapy* **3** (1) 5–15.

Kriz J (1991) Mental health: its conception in systems theory. An outline of the person-centered system approach. In MJ Pelaez (Ed) *Comparative Sociology of Family, Health and Education* (Vol. XX, pp6061–6083). Espania: University of Malaga.

Kriz J (2008) *Self-Actualization: Person-Centred Approach and Systems Theory*. Ross-on-Wye: PCCS Books.

Kriz J (2013) Person-centered approach and systems theory. In: J Cornelius-White, R Motschnig-Pitrik and M Lux (Eds) *Interdisciplinary Handbook of the Person-Centered Approach*. New York: Springer.

Lang M (2007) *Resilience: Timeless Stories of a Family Therapist*. Kew, Australia: Psychoz.

Main M & Goldwyn R (1985) *Adult Attachment Scoring and Classification System*. Unpublished manuscript, University of California, Berkeley.

McCormick KM, Stricklin S, Nowak TM, & Rous B (2008) Using eco-mapping to understand family strengths and resources. *Young Exceptional Children* **11** 17. Available online at: doi: 10.1177/1096250607311932

Macpherson HA, Cheavens JS & Fristad MA (2013) Dialectical behavior therapy for adolescents: theory, treatment adaptations, and empirical outcomes. *Clinical Child and Family Psychology Review* **16** (1) 59–80. Available online at: doi:http://dx.doi.org/10.1007/s10567-012-0126-7

Minuchin S & Fishman HC (1981) *Family Therapy Techniques*. Cambridge, MA: Harvard University Press.

Nowak C & Heinrichs N (2008) A comprehensive meta-analysis of Triple P – Positive Parenting Program using hierarchical linear modeling: effectiveness and moderating variables. *Clinical Child and Family Psychology Review* **11** 114–144.

Patterson GR (1982) *Coercive Family Process*. Eugene: Castalia.

Perry BD (2001) Bonding and attachment in maltreated children. *The Child Trauma Center* **3** 1–17.

Richter H (1974) *The Family as Patient*. New York: Farrar, Straus & Girous.

Rudolph SM & Epstein MH (2000) Empowering children and families through strength-based assessment. *Reclaiming Children and Youth* **8** (4) 207.

Shapiro AF, Gottman JM and Carrère S (2000) The baby and the marriage: identifying factors that buffer against decline in marital satisfaction after the first baby arrives. *Journal of Family Psychology* **14** 59–70.

Stierlin H (1975) *Von der Psychoanalyse zur Familientherapie*. Stuttgart: Klett.

Sturmey P (1996) *Functional Analysis in Clinical Psychology*. Chichester: John Wiley and Sons.

Tedeshi & Kilmer, 2005

White M (1991) *Deconstruction and therapy*. Dulwich Centre Newsletter, No.2.

White M & Epstein D (2004) Externalizing the problems. In: C Malone, L Forbat, M Robb & J Seden (Eds) *Relating Experience: Stories from Health and Social Care*. London: Routledge.

Young JE, Klosko, JS & Weishaar ME (2003) *Schema Therapy: A Practitioner's Guide*. New York: Guilford Press.

Zarbock G (2011) *Praxisbuch Verhaltenstherapie, Grundlagen und Anwendungen biografisch-systemischer Verhaltenstherapie* (3. Aufl.) Lengerich: Pabst.

Chapter 16: Assessing Parent Schemas and Modes

Peter Graaf and Ruth Holt

16.1 Assessment of parent schemas and modes

In order to assess parent schemas, techniques and materials can be used that are described in other chapters (see e.g. Figure 16.1). Schema Therapists can form hypotheses about patterns and modes relatively easily based on observation; they can then name them in the assessment process and review together with the parents.

16.1.1 Direct survey

The simplest and most obvious way to detect schemas is the direct questioning of parents about their own 'sore points' (see formulations in 16.2). Therapists who have built good rapport and affirm that it is normal for parents to have strong feelings triggered by children who show difficult behaviour do find parents receptive to exploring their own schemas. A personal example shared by the therapist (using judicious self-disclosure) can be helpful, so that parents don't begin to feel defensive. Parents can appreciate that if they understand their own reactions they can help their child more effectively.

16.1.2 Family board

The family board (Ludewig & Wilken, 1983) or similar wooden figures are not only suitable for representing closeness/proximity and distance, or coalitions, but also for the formation of hypotheses about patterns and modes which can be symbolised and represented, for example, in the form of figures which are particularly small or which stand apart from each other (see 12.2 for more details). The family board consists of a board and a number of differently sized, round and rectangular wooden figures that feature faces that are merely hinted at. Guided by the therapist, family members can use the figures to represent

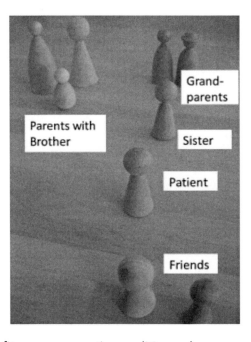

Figure 16.1: Wooden figures representing coalitions, closeness and distance. Used to form hypotheses about the formation of schemas and modes

different family or inner structures and illustrate their relationships. Thereby, family structures and conflict dynamics that have never been verbalised, but which often work across generations, become apparent. This allows a non-blaming approach to understanding the development of symptoms.

The family board shows the emotional needs of the family members, opening up new ways of expressing emotional states. It is an opportunity to practice 'meta-communication on emotional issues. It offers the possibility to bring out the innermost, and to turn the inside out as well as to permanently change it, in connection with the experience of being able to influence something' (Eckardt, 2012, p2).

16.1.3 Family map in circles

Drawing a family map in circles (Arnold *et al*, 2008 or McCormick *et al*, 2008) provides a similar representation of the different connections in a family. Through drawing different types of lines, limits/borders can be illustrated. For example, parents can draw partially broken/dotted/dashed or interlocking lines between family members. Even though schemas cannot be directly deduced from this method, hypotheses may derive from the family map circle; for example, if the circles of a parent and a child are very much interlocking, this can point to *Enmeshment* or *Dependence/Incompetence* schemas. Very remote or separated circles hint at a *Social Isolation* schema, very small circles against dominant large circles indicate a *Subjugation* schema, and so on.

How to

Instruct the parents to 'imagine each family member is a circle drawn on this sheet of paper – as a snapshot of your relationships. You can determine the size, colour and shape. Also, you can draw the borders/confines of the circles differently (dotted/dashed lines, translucent or thick) and illustrate the proximity and distance between the circles. You can also draw the circles so that they merge or blend into each other or so that they touch, or they can be completely separate. Now let the picture impact on you! What do you notice? What comes to your mind? How is this or that circle going with this arrangement? Is there anything you would like to change or be different? Would you like to draw a second image, how you envision it to look in the future? What steps would be needed to get to that ideal?'

Home visits

Home visits/in vivo observational studies at home are useful if during therapeutic interviews insufficient information about relevant influences was gathered. Sometimes it is only during a home visit that hidden schemas can come to light – for example, significant chaos or disorder in the home (showing a parent's Undisciplined Child mode) or creepy decorations with monsters or violent videogames/inappropriate material around the house (reflecting a child or parent's *Mistrust/Abuse* schema). For example, one might observe that the boy of a single mother sleeps in a dark solitary room, while the little sister sleeps in the mother's own room (an *Emotional Deprivation* schema potentially developing in the older child). These observations alone are obviously insufficient to interpret as schemas, but can suggest further helpful lines of enquiry.

Questioning of other people who are closely related to the family

Although at first the questioning of grandparents or other acquaintances/ relatives of the family seems elaborate, time consuming or laborious, it often helps quickly to clarify factors and aspects that the parents and children may hide. Even friends of the parents often provide striking insights into crucial systemic factors that may be more easily accepted than hypotheses made by the therapist. People who are closely related to the child or the parents are not only experts on the family system and its pattern, but often also significant supporters or critics of it. Grandparents can powerfully activate feelings of failure and inadequacy in parents, especially in the case of children displaying behavioural problems.

Video-based exploration

Videoing certain tasks in the family (parent and child playing together, doing homework, planning weekend activities that may trigger familiar family conflicts) can assist with joint evaluation of previously unconscious patterns and modes.

Family sculptures

Sculptures (see Von Schlippe & Schweitzer, 2015) allow an experiential representation of the relationship dynamics with their underpinning schemas. A family member is in charge of creating the 'sculpture', moving bodies and body parts to form how they see and experience their family. One after the other, each family member arranges the other members, so that proximity and distance as well as power relationships are represented. If only part of the family is able to participate, chairs can substitute in the sculpture. Afterwards an 'ideal sculpture' can be created.

Case example

A parent couple set up a sculpture of chairs to represent the relationship to their child without their son being present (see Figure 16.2). In this sculpture they put their child on a small chair, but the son's chair was put on a table, to emphasise that 'everything' was about him – everything revolved around the son, as he was the centre of their attention. The parents put their chairs in front of the table. At the end of the assessment process schemas such as *Entitlement* and *Admiration/Recognition Seeking* were evident, along with a narrative of the need 'to be special'. These issues were the triggers of the son's Defiant Oppositional mode and Self-Aggrandizer mode.

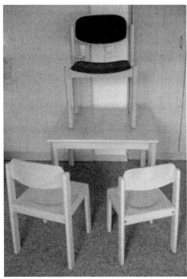

Figure 16.2: Sculpture work with chairs. The parents sit on small chairs in front of their child – an expression of their *Entitlement and Approval/Recognition Seeking* schemas

Another sculpture method is to create a mode sculpture in which each family member expresses how mode clashes occur by assuming a certain posture. For example, when a father shows a demanding posture by pointing his finger and looking powerful (Demanding Parent mode), his teenage daughter freezes him out by showing him the cold shoulder (Detached Protector mode). Healthy Adult/Caring and Guidance Mode can be developed by asking: 'What posture would result in change?' and playing out a different dynamic. Objects or props could further illustrate what happens when schemas (e.g. illustrated by glasses, burdens) or modes (illustrated by hats, masks or suitcases) are activated. Elastic bands or ropes can illustrate borders around people or define bonds or barriers. With the help of these objects, changes may be explored playfully: 'What would be different if your father could take these sunglasses off (representing his *Mistrust/Abuse* schema)?'

16.1.4 Observing behaviour

Of course, parent behaviour during family sessions often provides enough 'material' for formulating hypotheses about schemas. But sometimes, in these 'clinical' situations, parents and children are on their 'best behaviour', making it difficult to experience the drama of domestic conflict within the therapy setting. At times these dynamics can become apparent before or after the therapy sessions, for example when family members say goodbye or parents start to ask their children to do something in the waiting room.

Staged provocation

Oftentimes a staged provocation of typical conflict is helpful. For example, a short role play or drama with large puppets can help to trigger the response patterns that usually occur in stressful situations. The therapist can heighten the experiential component of the play, using the arms of the doll or putting sentences into the mouth of the doll to bring 'to life' an overly cognitive analysis. Just a few words or gestures can trigger spontaneous emotions or impulses to act and express modes before they are filtered by the 'censorship' of Healthy Adult mode.

Miracle questions

Miracle questions not only reveal the functionality of a symptom and explore solutions in systemic work, but also shed light on the needs or schemas that are being maintained by the symptom. For example: 'If, all of a sudden, my child was able to fall asleep without constantly coming out of their room, I could finally spend cosy evenings with my husband' (suggesting that the mother's needs for connection are being impacted by the child's bedtime behaviour, possibly maintaining an *Emotional Deprivation* schema). It may also be plausible that, if there is an *Emotional Deprivation* schema, the 'interruptions' may be playing a role in the mother's avoidance of situations where her husband may reject her emotionally, so she may be unconsciously encouraging interruptions, rather than face possible rejection and schema activation.

Circular questioning

Circular questioning in the tradition of systemic work can also be used to diagnose mode activations and their functionality within the family system. Family members are encouraged to adopt an external perspective and to recognise modes as part of a relationship pattern: 'What mode does your husband flip into when your son goes into Angry Child mode? Then which mode does your son flip into?'

Visions of the future

Questions about future visions help to highlight overcompensation by parents when schemas are activated (e.g. *Unrelenting Standards*, *Enmeshment*, *Dependency/Incompetence*, etc.): for a parent with an Enmeshment schema, the question 'How do you think you are going to feel when your child becomes an adult and moves out of home?' can highlight the underlying trigger for overprotective behaviour. Even retrospective questions about the future can reveal covert schemas: 'What vision for your child did you have before your son was born?' An answer such as 'one day, he will be a powerful person who is not afraid of anyone' could indicate that the father expects his son to compensate for his own *Subjugation* or *Defectiveness/Shame* schema. In other words, he is using his son to cope with his own schema.

Genogram

A genogram should not solely be used to graphically illustrate the family tree, but should be expanded as an exploration of typical family messages and values. Asking additional questions often reveals unexpected depth in the biographical patterns which make schemas more obvious. 'What kinds of messages, expressions or gestures do you remember this person using/giving?' 'Can you think of an important story about this person?'

Questionnaires

The use of questionnaires such as the Young Schema Questionnaire (YSQ-S3) with 90 questions is relatively complex for child-centred therapy. For children aged 8–14 we use the Schema Questionnaire for Children (DISC – Loose *et al*, 2018). However, the YSQ-S3 can be useful for parents if extensive parental work is required (including mode and coping questionnaires).

YSQ-S3 R	Young Schema Questionnaire	90 questions
SMI	Schema Mode Inventory	118 questions
YPI	Young Parenting Inventory	72 questions
YCI - 1	Young Compensation Inventory	48 questions
YRAI -1	Young–Raigh Avoidance Inventory	40 questions
DISC	Schema Questionnaire for Children	36 questions

Schema Therapists and accredited mental health clinicians have access to these questionnaires at www.schematherapy.org.

16.2 Education using formulation aids and drawings

Based on suggestions from Berbalk, therapists can explain schema and mode concepts to parents using the following examples with everyday language.

16.2.1 Describing 'schemas' in everyday language

'All people have sore spots or vulnerabilities, based on difficult life situations. Often, these developed early in a person's life and usually had an impact on how life was experienced. The sore spots are like a part of us. Because we have not always been treated well or may not have received what we needed, we have developed protective mechanisms around those sore spots. So, even as adults, we are sensitive to certain situations or triggers that remind us of the pain, disappointment and hurt of that earlier time.

When those triggers happen we react the same way as back then, when we were a hurting child who couldn't fix or stop it. The sore spot may now be a part of the situation that you came to me to get help with. When the sore spot is activated, we overreact to normal events, as if someone has pressed a button. We call that 'schema activation'. But sore spots can be soothed or, ideally, healed. Can you think of your own sore spot, where you don't feel confident or like a grown-up, but more like a child? Is there anything you are particularly sensitive to?'

16.2.2 Describing 'modes' in everyday language

'Only a few people feel, think and act exactly the same in every situation. Our moods may vary a lot in everyday life. After such mood changes we can even feel like a different person. Most people can clearly feel when they switch from one state or mood to another. Sometimes, a particular "mode" dominates all of your feelings, all your thinking and your actions, but after that a different "part" takes over and dominates your mood. All people have different "modes or parts" of themselves and it can be very helpful to know which of these parts are helpful and how to deal with the unhelpful modes. Some "parts" of yourself make your life difficult. Can you relate to what I am saying?'

Now the 'mode work' can begin with these kinds of questions: 'What are your main or most important modes/parts of yourself? It is good if you can give these modes names. Through naming them, you can, not only recognise them better, but you can also identify them and ultimately influence them if they are unhelpful. Are there any other modes that are weaker or might only rarely appear?' Another approach is to identify a mode that has already been evident in the discussion: 'I noticed that when you talk about Sam you shift posture, get teary and talk in a quiet voice. We would call that your Vulnerable Child mode. Does it feel like being little person, who doesn't know what to do? Then I also hear a more harsh, dominating part of you that is sick of Sam taking over your household – that's sometimes called a Punitive or Demanding Parent mode; it's very tough and angry ... let's see what that mode is about.' As the modes are identified, helpful Schema Therapy approaches include:

- **Cost–benefit question:** 'What did the mode help you with, back when you were little? When did you use the mode and what for? Is it still the same today? Are there any drawbacks/ negative consequences when you are in that mode? Is there a connection between your current difficulties and that mode?'

- **Change question:** 'If the mode could soften or get weaker, or if you could even give it up, what would be the consequences? What would be the impact on your life? Is that also true for other modes as well?'

A very useful educational method is the 'schema and mode drawing' or 'map' which is described in the previous chapter (and in Chapter 3). When working with parents the map can be made more complex and tailored to the family. During the assessment phase, the therapist can draw a visual representation of the family relationship patterns for the parents. Then the therapist can note key words or phrases that the parents relate to or report. This helps the therapist to provide a picture of what happens when all the relevant schemas and modes interact. This map then can serve as an orientation and guideline for therapy with parents so that 'sore points' can be gradually worked on. Visually, this might look like Figure 16.3.

Old Scenes/Childhood experiences behaviour schemas modes core emotional needs

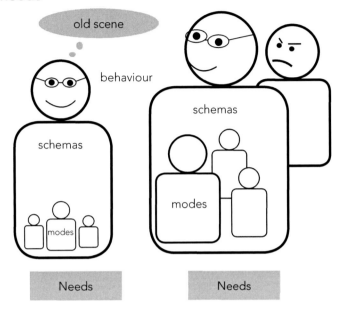

Figure 16.3: Schema and mode map

Siblings or other relevant people can also be included and drawn on the map. Childhood experiences that still have an effect in the present, can be represented in the form of thought clouds. Typical beliefs or family 'rules' can also be represented in the form of balloons.

The vicious cycles can be illustrated using this map, with arrows indicating which modes or schemas mutually activate each other.

References

Berbalk H (2012) *Arbeit mit Handpuppen in der Schematherapie*. Vortrag in Hamburg am 25.4.2012.

Ludewig K & Wilken U (1983) *Das Familienbrett. Hinweis zur Benutzung*. Hamburg: Eigenverlag.

Loose, C., Meyer, F. & Pietrowsky, R. (2018). The Dusseldorf Illustrated Schema Questionnaire for Children (DISC). Psicologia: Reflexão e Crítica, 31, 7.

McCormick KM, Stricklin S, Nowak TM & Rous B (2008) Using eco-mapping to understand family strengths and resources. *Young Exceptional Children* **11** 17. Available online at: doi: 10.1177/10962506 07311932

Von Schlippe A & Schweitzer J (2015) *Systemic Interventions*. Vandenhoeck & Ruprecht.

White M (1988) The process of questioning: A therapy of literary merit. *Dulwich Centre*

White M (1991) Deconstruction and therapy. *Dulwich Centre Newsletter*, No.2.

Young JE, Klosko JS & Weishaar ME (2003) *Schema Therapy: A Practitioner's Guide*. London: Guilford Press.

Chapter 17: Interventions with Parents

Peter Graaf and Ruth Holt

17.1 Interventions for schema and mode work with parents

The aim of the work with parents is to help them be able to recognise their own schemas that are typically triggered by their child or other important family members. Once the origins of the schemas are identified, the impact on parenting can then be examined. When parents can see the influence of their own life experiences on their children, they are less likely to feel they are being made into 'the patients' or seen as the guilty culprits. This understanding helps parents feel that their perspective of the child is being taken seriously. We explain to parents that they can help their child best when they are aware of their own reaction patterns and are able to manage those feelings better. They are then able to be the calm and supportive parents that they want to be. In mode work, the focus is on the parent recognising their Child modes and the response patterns that get triggered. As the parents become less reactive, by caring for their own Vulnerable or Angry Child mode, they can deal with their actual child more effectively. Parents are also assisted to recognise how their own emotional states interact with those of their child. The mode work aims at strengthening the parents' Healthy Adult/Caring and Guidance Mode (through a lot of recognition and respect).

The goal of Schema Therapy work with dysfunctional modes (e.g. Detached Protector) is to weaken them, or even to banish the abusive modes (e.g. Punitive Parent modes). Sometimes parents feel these 'modes' are a vital part of themselves and that they serve a protective function ('When I am in Punitive mode my child doesn't mess with me'). In these situations, parents will be reluctant to give up these 'parts', particularly if they don't experience any other, more healthy types of strength and power. Therefore it is important to work on developing a strong and powerful Healthy Adult/Caring and Guidance Mode. It is the mode strengthened in experiential interventions and is frequently called upon: 'Imagine you are in Healthy Adult. How would a confident and calm person think when/ if ...'. The Healthy Adult/Caring and Guidance Mode is able to manage the self-care of the parents, and also pay attention to and recognise their (actual) child's needs. Punitive Parent modes are disempowered and banished as they serve no healthy function. The Angry Child mode is guided to express feelings and needs appropriately. In the end, the parents' Healthy Adult/Caring and Guidance Mode is responsible for integrating the various modes into a functional whole and managing them, so that their own needs and that of the child are taken into account.

17.1.1 Dealing with guilt in parental work

Guilt is an important aspect to parent work as it can potentially cause a lot of resistance in therapy. Many parents agonise over what they have done wrong and how their mistakes have contributed to their child's symptoms. Parents always find shortcomings and mistakes in the way that they have related to their, often very challenging, child. Sometimes others blame them for the problems of the child as a way to take the pressure off themselves.

There are three main ways that guilt can play out in parental mode flips. One way is to trigger the Vulnerable Child mode and then an overcompensating mode. I know countless parents who become very distressed by constant complaints coming from their child's school because the child, for example, has difficulty paying attention during class or get along with other children. Guilt is hard to bear and must be warded off in the long run, but initially parents switch from the Vulnerable Child mode (who is being attacked because of 'bad' parenting) to the Bully/Attack or Angry Protector mode. When this happens the parents form a coalition with their child ('The school is making him into a scapegoat, but the teachers are to blame! It is their fault that our boy is so violent. Therapists can't help, they are incompetent').

Another way that guilt can play out in parents is for the parent to flip into Detached Protector mode and no longer let the concerns of others impact them. From the outside (and from the inside) they seem to be indifferent, as if they do not care, which usually escalates accusations in a vicious cycle. In the end parents and teachers are on opposing sides of the 'struggle' and the family creates a bulwark against the 'hostile' outside world. A third possible way in which parents cope with the guilt of the situation is to blame the child, who then gets punished by the parent or overwhelmed with reproaches. Over the long term this then triggers a *Defectiveness/Shame* or *Failure* schema, which in turn must be responded to by the child in Defiant Child mode or Bully/Attack mode.

Therapists can also trigger parents' guilt. They can trigger guilt because they are looking for causative factors in the parents' behaviour and find causal connections in their biography. Parents, understandably, are afraid of that, even if at the same time the therapist relativises the question of guilt. The dilemma of the therapist's situation is to see the parents as contributors and causes of the problem and at the same time to validate and esteem them for the challenge of the situation. This balance is difficult and often results in therapists reassuring the parents without actually dealing with the issue of guilt. Furthermore, the therapist's remarks often confirm what other friends or relatives have already said. It is also not helpful if therapist 'beats around the bush' by softening their formulations or hiding hypotheses that they are constructing, in order to not aggravate the parent's guilt. It gets even more complicated for everyone involved when therapists overly identify with the child's distress because of their own biographical history and their own schemas (e.g. *Subjugation*, *Mistrust/Abuse*, *Emotional Deprivation*), and as a result form a coalition with the child against the parents. Parents (and children) can be highly sensitive to a therapist's triggering (sometimes more so than therapists themselves). For example, patients or parents can feel a peculiar distance being kept by the therapist, or certain hints being dropped by him or her. All of these examples demonstrate that parental guilt is an important and difficult area to address.

In addition, many psychological models meant to explain some developmental disorders provide a wealth of unilateral causal attributions for symptoms that land on fertile ground when some parents hear them. For example, in analytical tradition, if an ADHD symptomatology is seen as caused by early traumatisation, such a diagnosis can reinforce parental despair. If, then, a medication plan to manage impulsivity is rejected, the parents may be given the impression their only option is years of therapy (which often is still quite ineffective), while vicious cycles continue to go on. The parents can become absolutely helpless and left with their feelings of guilt and inadequacy.

The question of guilt gets even more difficult when grandparents start to apportion blame and try to give advice: 'It's no wonder that the boy acts out like this, you need to be more consistent', or 'You're way too strict! It is only natural that your child reacts that way.' Quite often I have heard quotes from grandmothers who – back when they were helpless mothers themselves – have put some kind of hex on their daughters – 'I hope one day you will have a baby that is just like you are!' – setting up a narrative of helplessness in the face of a 'devilish child'. The eerie 'magic' of such curses can be explained as introjection and identification (contained within the Punitive Parent mode). When the mother's child starts to display the same difficult temperament (oftentimes as early as infancy when they become the 'colicky baby'), the prophecy seems to be coming true, and the self-accusation begins. The Punitive Parent mode condemns, blames and accuses the mother and undermines her feelings of competence. When the child later rubs salt in the wound ('you're so stupid, mum'), the mother runs the risk of losing all her confidence. Even when babies scream or simply look away, it might trigger the mother's schemas and can be experienced as a reproach.

Parents with schemas such as *Failure*, *Defectiveness/Shame* or *Dependency/Incompetence* have it particularly hard when trying to manage guilt. Because their schemas are being frequently triggered they flip between different modes frequently: the Vulnerable, Rejected child mode is activated and then quickly protected by a dysfunctional Coping mode (e.g. Angry or Detached Protector), which then quickly activates the internal critic modes (e.g. Punitive Parent mode: 'You really are a bad mother'). In this rollercoaster of modes, it is difficult to find the mother's Healthy Adult/Caring and Guidance Mode.

However, the schemas listed above may not necessarily have been established since childhood. Just as with a child, events can trigger a *Failure* schema-inducing guilt in parents. Accidents, birth complications, disabilities or a child's disease can have a schema-developing impact in less psychologically afflicted parents, not just trauma survivors. Many people's way of coping with this difficult situation involves assuming responsibility and therefore guilt. A fateful event is reconstructed incorrectly in retrospect ('If only I had taken more care of/paid more attention to ...") in order to manage the unbearable helplessness creating an unconscious motto: rather guilty than powerless.

Addressing parental guilt

We will outline below the key elements in dealing with parental feelings of guilt, although there is not sufficient space to fully cover the methods in their entirety. Parents often need help to overcome their feelings of guilt (even in the context of a child-focused therapy). Through careful exploration and questioning, the various facets of parental guilt can be identified. Parents can then learn to distinguish:

1. Which part of my guilt is based on objective facts (was there something that I missed or did wrong that a 'good enough' parent would have done differently)?

2. Which part of the guilt was externally imposed (which part of the feeling possibly serves to relieve or take pressure off others)?

3. Which part of my guilt did I construct so that I didn't have to feel my own helplessness?

4. What part of my guilt was learned and fits my typical schemas or modes (is there a strong Demanding Parent mode, *Unrelenting Standards* or *Defectiveness/Shame* schema that was triggered)?

Each individual component of guilt needs a different therapeutic response. For the fourth element, schema work is helpful (see below). In the third element, insights about how dysfunctional feelings of guilt have developed and the role of guilt as a protection from helplessness need to be explored, allowing the parent a safe way to process helplessness, rather than sublimate it.

The second and fourth elements require the therapist to provide 'protection' from external judgement and encourage the parent's Healthy Adult/Caring and Guidance mode to become a stronger 'voice'. The therapist can provide their expertise and question everyday theories and common beliefs as well as correct distorted perceptions. The therapist can guide the parents to find arguments to help them to stand up to unjustified blame. Here, helpful methods are role plays, scripted responses (e.g. phrases for dealing with people in public) or even a written position that may be passed on, for example, to neighbours: 'Dear neighbours, we – Sam's parents – would like to inform you that we are trying a new approach to dealing with Sam's behaviour. In this context, Sam is to learn to recognise certain limits and be able to cope with his frustrations. Therefore over the next few weeks there will be some loud protests coming from Sam, but it should subside after that. We ask for your understanding and patience as we work through this issue.' The therapist can also encourage others in the wider system (e.g. grandparents) to discuss the situation and the question of guilt (if these people have the capacity to be safe and respectful). These methods are aimed at strengthening the parents' competence and determination (Healthy Adult/Caring and Guidance Mode).

The first element, the question of whether actual mistakes or failures occurred, should be addressed directly by the therapist, so that parents can courageously face this part of the truth. Finding support from others is also helpful. Attending a parent support group or finding solidarity with other people who are also affected may reduce the burden of this guilt. In an inpatient setting, often times parents find it immensely comforting to hear that others have similar problems and feel the same way ('I am not alone'). Friendships between families can be established, which helps to overcome social isolation. Guided outpatient parent groups can serve a similar function. Single parents in particular will need extra support to be able to deal with the guilt by themselves. Especially when they feel attacked by or unsupported by an ex-partner, a community can be very comforting. In private and professional discussions, parents need benevolent listeners and the encouragement from merciful people to overcome their mistakes and to let go of their guilt (Cohen-Filipic & Bentley, 2015).

Another intervention that is helpful in dealing with guilt is an experiential exercise called the 'inner court'. This exercise involves placing the prosecutors and defenders on chairs (these could be based on actual people, or, for example,

Punitive Parent mode, or *Unrelenting Standards* or *Failure* schemas). In the presence of the therapist, 'the accused' can adopt different perspectives and listen to other voices. In the course of this therapeutic trial, mitigating circumstances that help explain the actions of the culprit/defendant can be recognised and put forward against the *Unrelenting Standards* schema, so that the defendant has an opportunity to be heard and understood. The joint responsibility of other parties is also addressed, as well as the question of a penalty. In addition, possible remedies and ways to make up for mistakes can be discussed. The latter should carefully thought through (and not be an excuse for ongoing appeasement of *Self-Sacrifice* or *Subjugation* schemas), but should involve specific, therapeutically well-justified compensatory impact.

Often the parents need to be able to express their guilt and be understood from a compassionate perspective, provided by the therapist: the therapist can explain to the guilt-ridden parent (or the court) how a lack of parenting skill came about, by providing psychoeducation. For example, a parent may be hindered from being caring, loving and attentive toward their child as a result of traumatic experiences. An explanation of the effects of traumatic experiences, such as, for example, flashbacks when Vulnerable Child mode is triggered, may very well help the parents to understand themselves and their own behaviour better, and ultimately to see themselves with more compassion (Healthy Adult/Caring and Guidance Mode).

To relieve feelings of guilt, it is also essential that the parents talk with their child and express what they feel sorry for. In apologising for the misdeed (e.g. a lack of skill or attention) the parents should apologise from Healthy Adult/Caring and Guidance mode, not Vulnerable Child mode, and be careful not to manipulate or 'parentify' the child. Parents should be encouraged to not torment themselves with a bad conscience for years, but to take opportunities (e.g. in a therapy session with the child) to ask their child for forgiveness – even for events that may have taken place a long time ago. If done with care, the child's distress can be recognised and understood (as long as the child is not overloaded with an excess of parental feelings, as in parentification). For young children, however, such a dialogue is too much. In this case, it is better to conduct a dialogue in imagery. The mother/father can visualise the child at an older and more understanding age. The therapist can verbalise the accusations that the parents imagine or fantasise. The parents look for answers or confess their sorrow to the child. Then, the therapist or the parents themselves can take the child's position and react, by accepting the apology and expressing appropriate positive affect. For additional information on a specific apology ritual see 17.1.4.

There are also parents who need to be sensitised and made aware of their responsibility for their child's development. In this case, the therapist should not be afraid to openly address the involvement of parents in their child's problem, using empathic confrontation (see 15.4).

17.1.2 Cognitive techniques

Once schemas and modes are identified, they can be challenged using cognitive behavioural therapy methods (see Jacob & Arntz, 2011). Cognitive techniques can also be used to help the parent understand their strong reactions to their child; their response is a result of their Vulnerable Child mode being triggered. They can then be coached in how to switch to Healthy Adult/Caring and Guidance Mode. Cognitive methods include the following.

Reframing
The child's behaviour is placed in a different context and reinterpreted by a greater understanding of children's needs (e.g. when the therapist educates the parents about the developmental psychology of children, this helps them to understand the typical behavioural patterns and underlying needs of children. For example, when a child is crying from hunger in a supermarket, the parent can reframe that behaviour as expressing an appropriate need, rather than as a desire to embarrass them).

Making pro and con lists
Identifying the advantages and disadvantages of or asking about the impact of certain thoughts or behaviours.

Cognitive restructuring of irrational beliefs
Restructuring irrational beliefs ('My child will reject me if I say no'), e.g. through making lists of possible alternative thoughts or reminding the parents of counter-examples from their own experience.

Psychoeducation
It is helpful for parents to hear how normal it is to experience distress and even childlike feelings as parents. It is comforting and normalising to know that making mistakes is part of learning to be a parent. It also challenges the idea that their children's behaviour is proof of their failure as a mother or father.

Written aids for common triggers
The schema or mode flashcard/memo can help parents to better understand typical reactions and to connect back with their Healthy Adult in those moments. Parents can use the flashcard to see their problems from a mode perspective and put everyday reactions in the context of the mode model, with instructions for emotional regulation/healthy adult behaviour.

Flashcard for parents

Recognising the current emotion
If my child is (common trigger) ... I'm feeling ... in this moment.

Recognising my schema
I know that this is probably my ... schema, that I learned through ...
Because of this schema, I'm exaggerating the extent to which I ...

Reality check
Although I think that (negative thoughts) ..., the reality is (Healthy Adult/Caring and Guidance perspective) ... The evidence for that, which supports the healthy point of view, from my own life, includes (specific examples): ...

Instructions on what to do and how to act
That is why, although I feel like (negative behaviour) ..., instead I could (Healthy Adult/Caring and Guidance Mode) ...

17.1.3 Emotional approaches and methods

Imagery

The use of imaginative techniques can help parents to separate themselves from their automatic negative reactions to their child. Imagery can also help parents to develop new 'visions' for a positive approach to handling difficult situations, Healthy Adult/Caring and Guidance Mode. In imagery the parent is taken to a recent triggering event and identifies the schemas or modes that were triggered. The parent then moves back to a childhood memory connected to the recent event by the same emotions or body sensations. The events that connect to the current distress help the therapist identify the roots of the parents' schemas and the needs that were not met at that time. The more apparent and clear these needs become in imagery, the more likely the parents will be to connect with the needs of their own child. In imagery the parents' young selves are cared for and nurtured, providing a corrective emotional experience. After an imagery session, parents can often think of softer, gentler solutions for the recent conflict and transfer these to everyday life with their child.

How to use imagery with parents

- Imagine a current situation with your child that triggers a strong negative feeling or a strong reaction.

- Describe your body reactions and feelings (deepening of emotion) to this situation. What is your need/What do you desire or want in that moment? What happens in your mind?

- Go back to a situation from your past that connects to that feeling or body sensation (link with biographical images and memories from the past).

- Which body reactions and feelings come up? What do you need? (possible re-scripting of the situation by introducing a 'healthy adult/good parent' into the scene to meet needs and address the schema).

(Returning to the original situation with the parent and child)

- What happens? What ideas come to your mind? What do you do? During imagery, new emotional patterns can be established (as in adult Schema Therapy) (see Jacob & Arntz, 2011).

In the imagination, fear or shame-inducing situations are changeable. 'Negative emotions (fear, shame, guilt, and disgust) can be replaced by feelings such as safety, security, perhaps even joy and pleasure' (*ibid*, p130). Grief is validated and requires comfort (by the process of 'imaginative overwriting': ibid.) The sequences of the intervention steps detailed in 9.12.3 are relevant to working with parents. Therapeutic interventions of this kind can quickly exceed the scope of accompanying parent work, but they do not have to. Parents who have a level of emotional stability can benefit from individual imagery re-scripting when there is enough trust with the child therapist. The therapist should inform and prepare the parents that painful memories may be evoked and that these can linger on after a session. If the therapist is aware of experiences of violence or abuse (including sexual abuse) in a parent's family history, traumatic scenes must not be elicited without being embedded in a more comprehensive parent therapy. The parent should then be strongly encouraged to seek such therapeutic support.

Chair work

As an introduction to the method of working with chairs, especially for parents with a certain fear of role-playing games, it is a good idea to start with a model sculpture with chairs. After exploring the parents' modes, the therapist gives the parents some chairs to arrange into a sculpture. Other props (small tables, blankets, pillows, coats and suitcases or ropes) are suitable to depict and symbolise the modes and to activate emotions. Small chairs can symbolise child modes. The small chairs can be put underneath larger chairs and 'hide' there. Parents can also, for example, use a suitcase to build a 'wall' between themselves and the chair of their child to symbolise a Detached Protector.

Example

'I would like to illustrate the picture I have in my mind about the modes and emotions that your son triggers. Sometimes you manage to be confident and stay calm. That is what this big chair here stands for. [Therapist could possibly sit down on that chair for a moment and repeat a few sentences he has heard from the parent or sentences that express the Healthy Adult/Caring and Guidance Mode of the parent.] Here you are very determined, but you are still nurturing. Yet, sometimes you "slip" into a position that feels helpless or shaky to you. This feeling is represented by the little chair here, because you sometimes feel small, like a child. But if it gets too much, you sometimes get very angry, in a helpless rage. In those moments you don't feel confident or strong but explosive. Let's use this other chair to symbolise that feeling. Our goal is to help you stay in that calm confident mother space more and more, even if your boy tries to attack or annoy you.' During the arrangement of the chairs, the therapist should check in regarding whether the mother or the father is following the idea, agreeing with it, or if they look irritated. He should then encourage them to correct the choice or arrangement of the chair. It would be even better if the parents – and not the therapist – freely designed and arranged the chairs by themselves. 'Would you like to try and illustrate all the different emotional states you go through, by assigning different chairs to those emotions? Let's choose a single chair for your son. Which one would fit? Then choose another chair and arrange it so that it fits how you feel when he attacks you. Then, you can select other chairs and arrange them in a certain position, close or further away from each other, opposing or facing each other etc.' The next step is to encourage the parent to take a seat on each different chair in order to enter the state in an emotionally deeper way. The therapist gives the parent time to feel the states/emotions and asks how they feel. It is helpful to draw attention to the different postures connected to the different emotions/ chairs. The third step is about bringing 'movement' to the current mode configuration. So far, the parent has been guided to get a more detailed image of the internal dynamics of their feelings by setting up the chairs and begin to notice the, often unconscious, processes by giving them an outer shape. Now the parents are invited to 'physically' identify with the different sides of themselves by successively sitting on different chairs and ultimately entering into a dialogue. 'I would now like to invite you to try a little experiment with me. Let's pick a chair and sit down on it. Now open yourself to the scene from this perspective. How do you feel here? What thoughts and words come to your mind? Speak from that place on your chair. Take time to empathise with the situation and perspective. If possible, change the chair and go to a different position. So here, for example, now sits the mode connected to your strict father. Can you speak from his perspective – what does he think? Let's have a dialogue between your Healthy Adult and your Demanding Parent side.'

The therapist now helps create a dialogue between the parent's different modes (Child mode, Parent mode, Coping mode and Healthy Adult/Caring and Guidance Mode). Encourage the parent to find the right words for each mode. For example, the therapist might also suggest words or statements and heighten the emotional experience of each mode's approach. The therapist can also temporarily take a seat on one of the chairs and take on the role of one of the modes ('May I sit on the chair and make a few suggestions?'). This is especially important if the Healthy Adult/Caring and Guidance Mode is very uncertain or seems weak and needs a model. The therapist reinforces this part of the parent by, for example, contributing arguments. The therapist helps to protect the Healthy Adult against unjustified attacks while helping the parent to develop adequate self-assurance and self-confidence. The 'healthy' viewpoint is reinforced, encouraged and given room to grow. At the same time, the therapist deals sensitively with the parent's Vulnerable Child mode by acknowledging and validating their feelings and respectfully mirroring them. He may also comfort the Vulnerable Child directly – for example, by comforting them with caring words ('May I again speak directly to Little Susanne ... This has often hurt you, yet you're a very likable girl and you do not deserve punishments from your parents. I think it is important that the Big Susanne/Healthy Adult speaks up for you and cares for you'). In that way, even a spoiled child may have their say and get meaningful answers from a Healthy Adult/Caring and Guidance mode.

Punitive Parents are 'disempowered or banished' as a matter of principle. When working with a Punitive Parent mode it is important to make a distinction between negative consequences for misbehaviour and Punitive penalties. The therapist responds to Punitive modes respectfully, but challenges them with a confident stance and clear arguments. In these moments when the therapist argues against these 'Punitive modes', the real parents should not sit on the chair of the 'Punitive Parent' for too long. This can weaken the Healthy Adult/Caring and Guidance Mode and lead to a stronger identification with the internalized Punitive parts.

Starting a dialogue with a Punitive Parent could be phrased as: 'May I interfere here and have a word with your father? Do you want to take on your father's role and talk for him? You switch into the Punitive Parent and out of this side so you can speak from that part of you. What do you say to your daughter, Mr Smith?'

[After listening to the reply, the therapist may answer in return:] 'You are wrong. I will not allow you to criticise and punish Little Susanne in this way. She is just a little girl, trying her best and making mistakes which is what all children do. Could you step aside and see how tough your punishment is and how much it hurts her?'

Parents are further encouraged to experiment with the chairs – for example, by putting distances between the chairs. Parents can try out 'putting down the wall', an image of the Detached Protector. This intervention helps the parents develop a sense of strength and inner clarity. It also helps parents distance themselves from problematic modes and develop a Healthy Adult/Caring and Guidance mode observer role.

One variant of the chair work that fits well with systemic approaches (Von Schlippe & Schweitzer, 2015) is to introduce the parent's schema into the dialogue as its own entity: a schema-based 'adviser chair' is placed right next to or to the side of the respective parent chair. The essence of this schema-adviser is written on a large sheet of paper. An example of *Subjugation* schema would be: 'Everyone walks all over me. I am not listened to.' An example of *Emotional Deprivation* schema would be: 'I never get what I need.' This essential message is now repeated by the therapist, sitting on the adviser's chair, as a sort of chorus or double voice. The parents let these voices impact on them, noticing how it makes them feel, think and respond. They are asked how the relationship with their child could develop, in a better way without these advisers and their statements. It is helpful to notice if there is any resistance to the statements (an expression of Healthy Adult/Caring and Guidance) or if the parent needs support to challenge this schema. In the case of a couple that are hopelessly at odds, the therapist may also confront them as follows: 'The schema has you under full control. What damage does the schema do to your lives? What would you do if you could free your relationship from the tyranny of this pattern?' (Von Schlippe & Schweitzer, 2015).

Working with finger puppets

Even with parents, this material is a good way to deal with emotions in a deeper way. It sometimes takes a little bit more time, but it has several other advantages. With the finger puppets, the interaction between the parents' modes and the child's modes can be illustrated more directly. The parents can take photos with them as a reminder (if not the finger puppet as a gift) to help integrate their understanding into everyday life. With this in mind, Berbalk (2012) starts by asking parents to arrange the different modes of their child as puppets in a commonly occurring situation. Here, the first step is to learn to distinguish between the parents' Child modes, maladaptive Coping modes and Healthy Adult/Caring and Guidance mode. Then as a next step, the parents are instructed to select which of their own modes work well to connect with their real child's Vulnerable Child mode. They are then encouraged to put aside their dysfunctional modes (e.g. their own Angry Child) in favour of Healthy Adult/Caring and Guidance Mode.

One way to build Healthy Adult/Caring and Guidance Mode is the following imagery exercise: in imagery, parents are instructed to go back to a time before the birth of their child, when they felt the Healthy Adult/Caring and Guidance

Mode strongly. As they have more contact with that mode in imagery, they will be able to connect to it in the present more effectively.

Berbalk points out that puppets can be used in lively chair work. When puppets that have been attributed feelings, experiences and thoughts are placed on the chairs, the experiential work is given more emotional charge, which is necessary for change. The mother then sits down on one of the chairs, takes the doll on her lap and talks for each mode. Sometimes it is even easier at first to use the doll and speak for it, in a more conscious distance to 'yourself'. To anchor the mode work in the everyday life of the parents they can create visual memos, such as photographs showing the posture/attitude of Healthy Adult/Caring and Guidance Mode, a photo of a specific finger puppet, photos of a particularly successful interaction/game scene (from the video feedback) or a mode diary.

Physical body processes

The authors of this book start from the premise that effective interventions induce a change at all 'levels' of a patient. Not only their behaviour, cognition and emotions but also their physical processes should be affected when parents develop a different way of dealing with their child. Work with parents can be more effective if it not only aims at changing attitudes or behaviours, but also directly addresses the maintaining physiological processes. Using the mode concept, therapists can address the posture, gestures and facial expressions of the parents, which are so profoundly important for the children. For example, if parents can identify their own gestures, facial expressions and body sensations as expressions of a particular mode, it is easier for them to permanently change them. If parents are advised that they should smile at their child more often or physically express their attention more, these suggestions have a longer lasting effect when they are linked to developing Healthy Adult/Caring and Guidance Mode. As parents are able to understand their own body signals more deeply, they become more open to feedback about their physiology and increase their ability to access Healthy Adult/Caring and Guidance Mode. Schema Therapy interventions try to shift whole mode patterns, not just 'cosmetic' facial expressions correction. When a parent has a solid understanding of modes, education about their origins and a solid diagnostic groundwork a body-related mode intervention can be simple, yet very touching.

Example

T = *therapist*
M = *mother*

T: It strikes me that just now your voice has changed in a certain way. When you talk about the conflict, your voice sounds like ... I am still looking for a word to describe it the right way ... do you also notice that?

M: You mean this strict derogatory tone. That was exactly the tone in which my father always talked to us if we had done something wrong.

T: And so in a way this voice surfaces in you and in your own voice if your daughter behaves like that?

M: Yes, exactly, but I had not noticed it before.

T: How did you feel as a child [here the therapist induces the switch from the Punitive Parent mode into the Vulnerable Child mode] as your father spoke to you like that? Go back in time to one of these moments and hear your father's voice. [The therapist may briefly repeat the words of the mother again by using or just hinting at the strict tone.]

M: I have always got scared and wanted to run away.

T: [gives enough time to give room to the words and emotions] What would you have actually needed or wanted from your father?

M: He should have sat down with me and explained to me in calm words what had bothered him or had made him angry and what I should do differently next time.

T: [validating and generalising] That's right, as a child, you need clear guidance and instruction, even with a serious voice, but without these harsh words.

M: Yes, that was what I needed. I mean, it was true, I did something wrong so my father had to say something.

T: Let's go back to the situation with your daughter [The therapist gives some time and begins the change to Healthy Adult/Caring and Guidance mode, prompting the mother about her daughter's recent behaviour.] What kind of tone of voice and what kind of words now come to your mind as an alternative to the voice of your father?

M: [now manages to use a very different variation and voice]

T: How does that sound to you now? How do you feel as you say that?

M: With this voice I don't feel so mean, but clear and determined. It is still an unfamiliar voice and way of talking, but I might try it more often.

After this, the intervention could be rounded out, and better anchored in the parents' behaviour, by using a role play. The mother comes out of the Punitive Parent mode and practices the role of the Healthy Adult/Caring and Guidance Mode. Alternatively or as an addition, she could experiment with her voice, so that she can recognise it better in everyday life. Homework could focus on self-observation of the voice as a specific aspect of a mode diary. It would be possible (when the mother shows appropriate acceptance) to include the partner or even the child in this (self-) observation.

It can be helpful to agree on a specific sign or symbol (e.g. threatening finger) as a prompt for the mother that she is in Punitive Parent mode. This feedback is to be given from a playful or gentle perspective, as a hint, rather than a criticism. The mother can choose her response to the hint, and has the therapist's permission to continue to speak in Punitive Parent mode or choose to try a different approach. If the family 'tells' her to stop that tends to take some of the 'power' away from her, reducing her opportunity to choose her confident Healthy Adult/Caring and Guidance Mode.

Just like the example above, mode-related body language can be addressed as part of family work. Turning away a head (avoiding eye contact) or crossing arms is a possible indication of a Detached Protector or Punitive mode. When the family becomes more aware of these indicators, they can begin to talk in mode terms at home. Also, it allows the therapist to empathetically confront parents about inappropriate body language, gestures and facial expressions, raising awareness of hidden modes and opening up other avenues for work.

Working on stress-triggered mode activation

In Schema Therapy work, parents can be assisted to manage stress in everyday situations. Stress responses are part of the evolutionary processes to avert danger and to maintain access to basic needs. This feeling of high tension as a protective reaction is often an adaptive process. However, when stress triggers schema activation there is an escalation in dysfunctional reactions. Parents whose schemas are being triggered react with one or more versions of the classic 'Fight, Flight, Freeze' responses (Coping modes). When parents react with threatening and attacking (overcompensation) responses, or escaping (avoidance) or paralysing (freeze) reactions with a child, an inevitable escalation occurs.

A goal in this area is to assist the family to develop awareness and intervene earlier, building awareness of how tension grows in family relationships and how everyday stresses lay the groundwork for dysfunctional mode activation. Often parents do not notice everyday stressors, so this awareness is crucial. If parents have Impulsive Child modes they will need therapeutic interventions aimed at helping them perceive and manage their body tension. Dialectical behavioural therapy techniques can provide concrete skills for managing Impulsive Child modes (Macpherson *et al*, 2013). These skills need to be embedded in the mode conceptualisation and used to both reduce unhelpful modes and increase Healthy Adult/Caring and Guidance mode. Other techniques, such as Jacobson's progressive muscle relaxation or other relaxation approaches, also assist parents in managing every stressor and mode activation.

17.1.4 Behavioural techniques

Deconstructing parental schema avoidance

In order to interrupt dysfunctional patterns of behaviour and to build a new child-oriented Healthy Adult/Caring and Guidance mode, it is often crucial for the parents to reduce well-practised schema avoidance, as this is a necessary precondition for overcoming schemas. Many parents have developed everyday habits, which they are not aware of, that help them to avoid conflicts or distressing encounters with their own child. In this stage of treatment, parents will be assisted to begin to set limits and require healthy responses, which they may have avoided doing previously. For example, a parent may have acquiesced with a child for fear of being rejected by the child (successfully avoiding triggering of their *Abandonment*, *Incompetence* or *Subjugation* schemas).

Once the interaction patterns are understood in the context of schema triggering, the therapist can alert the parent to the significant role they are playing in the family dance. For example, the parent can see how they have avoided contact for fear of rejection (*Abandonment* schema). As the parent develops more of the Healthy Adult/Caring and Guidance mode, they can ask the child to take on age-appropriate responsibilities, rather than easing the child's workload (preventing the child from experiencing 'failure', which is seen as intolerable by a parent with a *Failure* schema). Giving up on schema avoidance can also mean that parents are more able to tolerate a child's distress and provide comfort in those moments, rather than detach from the child in order to avoid triggering their own *Emotional Deprivation* schema.

Therapist modelling to build parental skills

Parents need practice and support to build their parenting skills and stay in Healthy Adult/Caring and Guidance mode. The therapist can model these approaches, tell exemplary stories, provide the parents with the language they need and reflect with the parents upon how the therapist displays the Healthy Adult/Caring and Guidance mode in their presence, strength and attitude toward the child. Role plays are useful to practice competence and can assist with embedding more healthy behavioural patterns as treatment progresses.

Instructions for dealing with specific modes in the child

Parents also need guidance in dealing with specific modes in their child. Here therapists can tend to hold back and leave the parents to work it out, outside of therapy. However, this sets the parent up to be helpless when, for example, they have to deal with violent or abusive behaviour or when their child distances from them and they can't seem to reach the child.

As a therapist it is important to remember that certain modes can occur at home differently and more strongly than how they are experienced in therapy sessions. As therapists, we are then asking parents to not only try out new 'dance' steps (by managing their own triggering), but also nurture and manage their frightened or aggressive child. This will require significant support from the therapist. The mode conceptualisation helps the parent to have a road map for their role. Mode pictures with finger puppets or chairs also help the parent understand how they can deal with each of the child's various modes in a useful and productive way. These ways are outlined below.

Dealing with Vulnerable Child mode

The Vulnerable Child mode needs care, attention and nurture. Parents are asked to identify moments when they might have done this in the past (e.g. the classic 'exception' question). They then suggest gestures, words and situations that are appropriate for meeting the needs of the Vulnerable Child mode. In role-playing games, these ideas are tried out and changed until they feel right for the parents. One hurdle is a parent being reluctant to provide an overly needy child with nurture if the child appears to be 'acting like a baby'. One way to manage this situation is with psychoeducation about how children often will regress when in distress. The parents are then also helped to determine if setting some limits on this nurture is helpful, so that it doesn't 'get out of hand' (this can help the parent to learn to tolerate providing nurture). The parents can set specific times or rituals in which they can and should 'pamper' the child.

Dealing with Angry Child mode

Therapists can guide parents in taking the child seriously but also finding appropriate ways to deal with anger. For example, the child can be encouraged to say what it is that is making them angry. Before saying 'yes, but', parents should reflect what they have heard from their child and what need they see behind it, the reason for the anger. ('You are really angry because your feelings were hurt'). They then provide a possible solution, with limits (channelling of the anger) to how anger gets expressed ('You do not need to shout so loudly, we have understood you').

Dealing with Clever/Wise mode

Parents should practice noticing and addressing the Clever/Wise child when that mode appears. For example, when the Vulnerable Child mode has been comforted or when the Angry Child has calmed down, the parents can praise the Clever Child for being able to soothe or calm. The parents can then discuss and negotiate boundaries with the child by exchanging perspectives. Negotiating, however, is not appropriate with the Undisciplined or Impulsive Child mode (see below) and should not be used if it is going to reinforce aggressive behaviour. Discussions should also not be conducted with the Defiant-Oppositional or Dominator modes. Parents need to learn to get around unhelpful Coping modes and encourage the Clever/Wise mode to come back to the negotiation table (such a table may actually become a ritual) and to talk about what the child needs in an age-appropriate way ('If you can talk in a calm and reasonable way, maybe we can find a solution together').

Dealing with the Undisciplined and Impulsive Child or Bully/Attack mode

Therapists can help parents feel secure and confident about limiting the excessive aggressive impulses of their child (again being mindful of not avoiding their own schema trigger). Using calm words is the first step ('I understand that you're angry, but this is not OK. You can tell me what makes you angry without breaking the furniture or attacking me'). In the event of escalating aggression, parents should also be able to physically stand up to their child to prevent themselves from becoming the victim.

Sometimes it's necessary for parents to physically hold the child so that the child feels safe (physically stable) and to provide the child physical boundaries and support (see Figure 17.1).

Figure 17.1: Therapeutic holding for the sake of the child's safety

Depending on body size, this method can be used for children up to 12 years. For older children, we refer to the methods of parental presence (Omer & Lebowitz, 2016; Omer *et al*, 2013). The use of a 'time out' room in some cases also requires physically assertive guidance to bring the child to the room. From the author's experience it can be unhelpful to use a time out approach as some children perceive 'time out' as a punitive act (loss of contact to the caring person), and for highly aggressive children there is too much scope for damaging property (rioting in the room), or even a chance of injury in trying to get the child to the time out room. Yet this method works for some parents because it gives them a calming distance from the overacting child.

On the other hand, it can be helpful to teach parents how to physically hold their child, if the therapist can trust that the parents can stay in Healthy Adult/Caring and Guidance mode while having their child under physical control. Injured parents tend to flip into Punitive mode and to punishment while holding the child, which is threatening for the child and escalates the situation.

When the parents can stay in Healthy Adult/Caring and Guidance mode, holding the Angry Child has a stabilising and reassuring function, even though the child resists at first. The parents calmly remind the child that they will only physically hold the child when they attack the mother/father.

Parents should provide opportunities for the child to self-manage and self-monitor, by, for example, regularly counting from 1 to 10, then releasing the child to give the child an opportunity to self-manage. If then the child hits or kicks again, they will again be held until they stop being violent. The 'time out' alternative, in the child's own or another small room, is better for some parents (and children) because it provides them with a safety distance and thus helps them to calm down. This was clearly the case with the father of Astrid Lindgren's fictional character Emil of Lönneberga (Lindgren, 1988), who often gave his son a time out in the shed, where he was safe from the even more violent anger of the father. With such consequences it is not only crucial that the parents follow clear behavioural therapy rules (Erford, 1999). But it is equally important to stay in Healthy Adult/Caring and Guidance mode in this stressful situation. Time-outs and physically holding the child can cause significant damage when parents lose control and, for example, flip into the Vulnerable Child mode or Detached Protector mode. Parents can remain in Healthy Adult/Caring and Guidance mode more easily when they can follow very clear guidelines and have repeated practice at using physical strength so that they can use the appropriate grips calmly.

When trying out physical techniques, and after the therapist has thoroughly defined the method as well as practised with the parents by themselves, the child is to be directly involved too: 'Felix, I invited you to this session because we are talking about what your parents can do when you get very angry again. We have lots of ideas of what you and your parents can do to solve the conflict with words. But when that does not work, it's the parent's job to protect themselves and their children from violence. If it is necessary, they may also need to restrain their child physically. Or do you have a different idea? What would you prefer them to do, for example, put you into a different room? If you don't have a better idea, then I will show you and your parents again how they can hold you. Shall we try it? You can always say stop, if you want them to stop.'

After the therapist has shown how the holding works, the parents practice it. When the child is in a good mood, the therapist conducts a role play where the child tests the parents' limits. They practice the hold and saying when the grip starts to hurt. The child could suggest what the parents might do differently. Thus the child, while in a very calm, Clever/Wise mode, is rehearsing for a possible scenario. The therapist uses these moments to form a coalition with the child's Clever/Wise mode. The 'team' strategise how to limit 'Furious Felix' as a way of beginning the process of Clever Felix 'staying awake' when Felix's temper blows up, and assist in self-control.

In my experience, most children (aged 5–10 years) can accept and integrate such an exercise well. But it is sometimes more difficult for parents, when these holding techniques make them feel uncomfortable or when they activate underlying schemas. Especially when a child starts to complain in between the counting ('You're hurting me') or even if they just sit there quietly, many parents think they are being too rough and hard on their child and feel guilty. In other words, they begin identifying with the child and projecting their own experiences of powerlessness and impotence (*Mistrust/Abuse* schema) on the child. They get into a bind: either they are being victimised by the child, resulting in Vulnerable Child mode, or (in their own imagination) they turn into the abuser (the mode of the punitive father/mother). It helps to discuss the idea that this is a therapeutic intervention that has been very well rehearsed and is a last resort until more healthy behaviours are developed. When they practise they will develop a new memory of holding, rather than tap into an old memory of powerlessness.

Afterwards it is crucial to discuss and reflect, with only the parents present, on what the experience was like. Parents may have difficult experiences that come up after this intervention. Those feelings that come need to be validated and contextualised in the parent's history. The therapist then checks whether the parents are able to stay in Healthy Adult/Caring and Guidance mode. Sometimes it is helpful to practise such scenarios in a therapy session so that the intervention doesn't run the risk of getting out of hand or of ending up in a re-traumatising power struggle.

Case example

Before being taken into emergency care, 8-year-old Jonas tended to show violent outbursts of anger and rage triggered by everyday requests from his parents. For example, if his parents wanted him to remove his homemade 'caves' from the living room before bedtime, he went to the open window and threatened to jump out. The neighbours had called the police, who in turn called the youth emergency service. In the course of his inpatient stay at a parent–child clinic, the boy appeared well adjusted and complied with his mother's rules.

Therapists had suspected Jonas may have Obsessive-Compulsive Disorder because he was often ordering and organising. In a session, the therapist suggested to the mother that next time he had an outburst of anger and rage she could try restraining him. The mother thought that the idea of physically holding the boy was unreasonable and would not work because she thought her son was too strong. The therapist offered an experiment when Jonas was in the session, so the therapist demonstrated holding him sitting on the ground. The boy seemed happy and playfully tried to get the upper hand. When he gave up resisting, he said mischievously that he would think of a way out for the next day. After saying goodbye to the boy, the therapist asked the mother how she felt when watching him holding the child.

The therapist had intentionally not invited the mother to try it out herself, as she was very uncertain. Then she confessed how terrible it was for her to watch the scene, because her boy had seemed so powerless and so humiliated. The therapist and the mother then worked on the causes and origins of those feelings and thoughts, starting with 'why is this feeling familiar?' It turned out that the situation had activated her experiences of humiliation and powerlessness (*Mistrust/Abuse* schema, activating her Vulnerable Child mode). This seemed to block her from staying in Healthy Adult/Caring and Guidance mode and distorted the perception of her own child.

In another case, a mother practised the holding techniques with her highly aggressive 7-year-old boy. After she initially claimed that she did not have enough strength to hold him, in preliminary exercises the mother clearly experienced that she did have enough strength. The therapist invited her son into the practice session. As soon as the mother held her boy in her arms, the son complained, 'you're hurting me'. The mother instantly let go of him and gave him the opportunity to mischievously escape from her grip. The therapist addressed his behaviour spontaneously: 'What was going on here ... that was a good trick?!' The son just grinned. "You're a trickster!" He confessed and confirmed that the mother's grip did not really hurt, but by saying that it hurt, he knew he would be released. In the boy's presence, the therapist told the mother: 'You think you are seeing a wounded child in front of you, but instead, you are dealing with a trickster.' The practice helped to give the mother a chance to practise appropriate body control (holding technique: see above). At the same time, however, the therapist helped the mother identify the schema avoidance and correct her perception of the situation. She then became more and more confident and more secure and could use the holding grip to prevent her son from attacking her by biting.

We only recommend physically holding a child in very specific circumstances and when in Healthy Adult mode. Also, parents should only physically hold a child when all other approaches fail, and should use the hold only in a controlled way and only for as long as necessary. For older children, the situation can escalate if the child breaks the hold with greater force. From a Schema Therapy perspective the therapist, and later the parents, use the holding grip to cope with an out of control Angry Child mode or a Bully/Attack Coping mode, when those modes cannot be managed with other techniques.

A helpful exercise for parents who are dealing with physically abusive children may also be a 'provocation' exercise with large puppets. The therapist uses the arms of the doll and behaves similarly to the child (e.g. sticking out his tongue, or holding his fist in front of the mother's face or slapping her arms, etc). In this type of experiential exercise the parent's hidden modes may come to light, providing invaluable understanding of the parent which might otherwise have been unavailable.

Experiential exercises involving body contact to train the parents' assertiveness are particularly useful when the parents tend to react too indulgently and defensively when their child crosses lines. The therapist could, for example, act out the Bully/Attack mode and confront the parents, getting too close to them with clenched fists. The parent can then try out different gestures and tones of voice to set limits on this behaviour. For example, they can practise using techniques such as a stop signal until they and the therapist feel like they are in Healthy Adult/ Caring and Guidance mode (e.g. there is a firm but calm tone and clear body language). After physically or verbally setting limits with the child, the child can be asked to express themselves without attacking and with appropriate words.

Homework

Trying out and practising skills as homework is essential not only to successfully implementing these skills, but also for reviewing and checking the hypotheses and therapeutic approach. Parent skills can be broken down into steps similar to 'exposure' (although in this case it is an experiential technique), to prevent the technique 'failing' without adequate guidance and instruction. If parents are not adequately equipped or if their schemas have not been sufficiently addressed on an emotional level, Vulnerable Child mode could be triggered, resulting in a 'relapse' where the parents fall back into their Coping modes. It can be helpful to begin by asking parents to 'simply' endure certain terrifying behaviours from their children, and their own distress with it. Healthy Adult/Caring and Guidance mode in this instance is about distress tolerance. When parents repeatedly learn to endure a conflict without going back to the old fight or flight modes, they can develop a new quality in their relationship to their child.

Instructions for parental presence

Nonviolent resistance techniques focus on helping parents increase their 'parental presence' (Omer & Lebowitz, 2016; Omer *et al*, 2013). In Schema Therapy this means that the parents are instructed to stay in Healthy Adult/Caring and Guidance mode even when their child is aggressive or rude, and to express messages of calm and care. They are very carefully prepared for possible reactions from their child, and can use 'sit ins' or provide an 'announcement' rather than continue patterns of mutual escalation. Perseverance without flipping into Punitive mode or wrestling for power builds confident parenting skills and provides an exit from the usual vicious cycle. Experience shows that children and adolescents may initially react with escalating Coping modes, but only for a short time. When the parents continue to stay in Healthy Adult/Caring and Guidance mode, however, the child will cease to respond in such a negative manner.

An important principle of parental presence is perseverance. The parents should be encouraged to be persistent in spite of their fear that the child will ignore or reject them.

Case example

The importance of parents persisting is illustrated by this story, told to me by a father, from his own childhood. One evening when he was 6 years old he desperately wanted his mother's comfort and help with his bad conscience over his behaviour. He also needed her reassurance about his fear of the next school day. But because he was stuck in Detached Protector he rejected her three times, giving her the cold shoulder. His Clever Child mode had started to appear, saying he would speak out and open himself up when she came back the fourth time. But she gave up and unintentionally reinforced his *Emotional Deprivation* schema.

Video feedback

Video feedback is a very powerful technique because it allows the therapist to observe the parents in short, real-life moments (despite the camera effect). When used in the right way, video feedback is an excellent way to reinforce positive and confident parent behaviour. Through a skilful use of questions, the parents' self-reflection (Healthy Adult/Caring and Guidance mode) can be initiated and expanded. For example, parents can be made aware of new aspects of their child and schema activation can be interrupted ('You can see here that your child does not in fact want to hurt you').

Yet parents often feel easily criticised when they are being observed via video monitoring and therefore easily feel judged. Therapists who have their own Demanding Parent mode can easily find something to gripe about and catch parents 'red-handed'. Therefore we would like to emphasise here (based on Süß, 2011) that the therapist must calibrate their expectations based on normal, 'good enough' parenting. Therapists may need to watch 'normal' parent–child interactions in a non-clinical setting, where many short episodes of suboptimal interaction may be observed. Otherwise, therapists set and apply a standard that is too high for parents. Süß also emphasises the importance of being aware of our own experiences of parenting and being parented and reflecting on our own relationship patterns, as they have a significant impact on our ability to help clients develop Healthy Adult/Caring and Guidance mode.

Establishing positive parent–child activities is another important part of Schema Therapy with parents, encouraging more Happy Child. You can call it 'fun and play time' or 'quality time'. For Süß (2011) the reinforcement and empowerment that comes from a child's joy is as important as the development of parental sensitivity. Without joy, other skills or learned competencies will not be kept and maintained. These activities do not necessarily have to be time-consuming and they do not have to cost anything either. Therapists should look for the little everyday pleasures, such as 'rumbling' or 'building something' between father and son, or the cosy browsing through magazines between mother and daughter. Small targets like this are more easily integrated into everyday life or weekly schedules and therefore run less risk of leading to disappointments or conflicts over limited time. Recurring positive interactions have a longer lasting positive impact than big but rare events (e.g. Gottman's bids for connection, 2011).

Everyday rituals

Everyday rituals are part of the behavioural methods used in working with parents. They often work well to activate Happy Child mode or to correct schemas. Families often have established habits that children hold on to emphatically. These include bedtime stories, cuddle times, falling asleep side by side with their mum, watching a particular TV series together or possibly even 'acts of caring' (e.g. preparing the child's clothes for the next day, a bathing time in the evening with the mother for little children), group singing or listening to music. For some families, sharing meals, regular treats or fun rituals are ways to create an atmosphere of joy and pleasure and show care. The therapist, as part of the assessment process, can find out about these rituals and then value and praise them as a precious resource or family culture. The parents can be advised not to use these rituals as means of punishment (no homework, no bedtime story). Instead, after conflict, they are important moments and give time and room for the positive modes: Happy Child and Healthy Adult/Caring and Guidance mode.

Parents are also encouraged to make more room for Vulnerable Child mode and to look for ways to provide nurturing that has been missing. For example, parents should be careful to not expect too much autonomy from the child too early. This is different, of course, in the case of the Spoiled Child mode. Here the child's entitlement in 'having everything done for them' needs to be challenged and over-functioning behaviour should become an exception (a special 'day of pampering'). We often recommend parents have a daily emotional check-in at the end of the day as a family ritual, with opportunities to catch up on the events of the day. Parents can model talking about their own feelings (with age-appropriate disclosure) based on the incidents from the day, even if the child is finding it difficult to open up, e.g. is not talking about school. Persistence pays off here as it encourages the child to open up, as long as the parents don't use the opportunity as a means of controlling the child. A similar ritual is to practise daily appreciation or gratitude, which helps both child and parents see their positive modes. The parents and children can take on the task of giving and receiving compliments at dinner, or at least talk about a positive experience with the family.

Apology rituals

Apology rituals require special instructions. Many families (and even bigger systems, such as companies) are missing a culture of dealing with guilt and blame. As a result parents are often uncertain as to whether and how they should talk about their own inadequacies and mistakes. The absence of this modelling means that children don't know how to repair a relationship and the parents can be unsure how to help a child take responsibility for wrongdoing. The therapist Ben Furman provides a good model of how to apologise with his 'steps of responsibility' (Furman, n.d.). The website kidsskills.org provides information and pictures and a manual for a sequence of steps which can be recommended to both children and for parents. (In the online material there is an adaptation of Furman's steps, simplified and with additional suggestions for restoration, see www.pavpub.com/resource-374CoCr). By using this ritual, the parent's Healthy Adult/Caring and Guidance mode can be developed, and a contrast to the destructive Punitive and Demanding Parent modes is provided.

If the child is unwilling to participate in this ritual, the caregivers should gently persist and work toward developing an ability to apologise on following occasions. It can be helpful for the child to miss out on an attractive activity (or have some other restriction) until there is some progress on the steps. In the case of repeat offences, additional witnesses or caregivers should be involved in the ritual.

Self-care

One task of parenthood is to develop skills in meeting one's own needs, with appropriate self-care, independent of the parental role. It can be helpful to routinely ask parents whether they themselves experience closeness, love and nurture; if they get enough rest. From experience we know that if parents are not doing well, the child will not be doing well, or they will not be doing well with the child. When therapists encourage self-care that involves making concrete plans and involving the larger support system. At other times, the therapist will need to request that the parents put aside their own needs in favour of the child. The ideal of uninterrupted time is difficult to achieve for many parents who are single parents or have young children, especially when they also have to fulfil work obligations in addition to bringing up their children (a double workload). Yet, some household activities allow parents to simultaneously show loving care for their child and self-compassion (e.g. having a special box of toys that only come out when mum needs a rest, or having a break at a café after grocery shopping).

It is also important that the therapist addresses perfectionism (*Unrelenting Standards* schema) in parents because parents often expect that in the therapy they have to do more for their child to become better parents. Schemas such as *Unrelenting Standards*, *Punitiveness*, *Defectiveness/Shame* or the already existing feelings of guilt should be challenged. Here, again, some appropriate self-disclosure by the therapist might help. It helps the parents see that perfect parents are not necessary for healthy child development. Experienced in 'small doses', negative events can have quite a resilience-building and empowering effect on children. Furthermore, negative events give parents the opportunity to model how to apologise or take responsibility (see above). It's fine for parents to make mistakes if the child gets the opportunity to articulate their feelings about it. Mistakes are not harmful to the child *per se*, but if nobody talks about those mistakes, the child is left alone with their feelings.

17.2 Case study, 'Ron', to illustrate different interventions

Ron's mother, Tina, started with the question 'How should I deal with the tears?' Her 9-year-old son was experiencing depressive symptoms and social anxiety, with somatising features. When questioned, she says she means her son's tears, although she herself had been in tears already following remarks from her husband. Following the assessment process, the therapist draws his formulation of the child's and the parents' schemas on a 'mode map' (*Self-Sacrifice, Dependence/Incompetence, Mistrust/Abuse* and *Vulnerability to Harm* schemas). During the session the mother describes and displays strong body reactions when remembering the difficult birth and the time after giving birth (sweating, trembling at the mention of the intensive care unit and her fear for the life of her infant). She said she had worried 'for months … just worried, worried and worried'. The parents explain that they have tried to stop their overprotective behaviour toward Ron, but that they sometimes fail.

In the second session, the mother describes a recent situation in which she met her crying boy at school because he found the noise of his classmates unbearable. She describes her typical reaction to it: first she rushes to him and tries to comfort him. If then he continues to cry longer, she gets annoyed and starts to rebuke him. The father confirms this 'roller coaster of emotions' and adds that they still argue about whether Ron was really deeply unhappy or just putting on a show.

The therapist illustrates Ron's different modes in the image and also matches the modes of the parent (for example, the 'tearful distress' of the mother's Vulnerable Child mode and, on the other hand, the Healthy Adult/Caring and Guidance mode). The therapist interprets the conflict between the parents as an expression of Ron's different modes: both modes are a part of him, but each parent focuses on a different side.

The therapist initiates a role play, asking the mother to take on the role of her son. In this situation the therapist models a sympathetic and guiding response to 'Ron'. The parents say that they have already tried to deal with Ron in a similar way. So the therapist switches roles. The mother takes on Clever/Wise Child mode, on the same level with the child. In the next step, the therapist and the mother switch roles again, so that the therapist can mirror the gestures and responses that the mother used, which she instantly identifies as her own response to Ron. Then she would normally switch into Angry Child mode.

The therapist then proceeds to a mode dialogue. He takes two chairs and places them next to the mother: 'Now I would like to "place" your different modes on these different chairs. The little chair stands for your sympathy and compassion, your rather childlike feeling of sadness. Right next to it is the chair representing the annoyed side that is tired of Ron's dramatic mood. Now you sit on the chair of the self-assured/confident mother (Healthy Adult/Caring and Guidance mode). Across from your chair we will put little Ron.' The mother spontaneously engages in the set up of the chairs and says that she always goes back and forth between the two chairs. She thoughtfully looks at the little chair, saying: 'Because I do not want to be like my mother. I do not want to do what my mother always did to me when I was a child. When I cried, she slapped me and told me, "See, now you have a reason to cry".' While the mother is switching into this mode, the therapist looks at her sympathetically and tells her that the scene is touching him: 'Now, little Tina is sitting on this chair and feels just like back when her mother was so unfair and unjust to her.' He waits a little, and after having had a good moment of eye contact with the mother, he opts to go deeper into this mode, addressing the adult mother and initiating another role play: 'And you know that there is still a third way – apart from going back and forth between sympathy and angry ranting like your mother. When "sitting on this chair" (Healthy Adult/Caring and Guidance mode) you can show sympathy and understanding for your son, but also give him guidance and instructions. He doesn't need just your sympathy but also guidance about what is going to happen next. Do you want to try to deal with Ron's whiny mood like a self-assured/confident mother – with a mixture of sympathy, but not too much care (as earlier in the role play)? Also pay attention to your posture and check which posture and body language fits best to this chair.'

The mother spontaneously sits up straight and puts on a clear, confident look, and then acts in decisive Healthy Adult/Caring and Guidance mode. Afterwards the therapist gives her feedback and asks her how she feels about how the situation ended. The mother replies that she did not feel good about the ending of the situation, because she felt like she had just abandoned Ron and left him in the lurch. The therapist could interpret this as a re-activation of the Vulnerable Child mode. Instead, he interprets and reinforces this impulse as a caring thought, and gives the mother instructions as to how to use it an opportunity to reframe: 'You do not need to let him down or abandon him. You can bring him something to drink and tell him that you will come back in five minutes. You are offering a chance to practise a new way of coping. Plus, you have already comforted him, just not sitting with him and being sad with him for too long. He needs a mother who has loving compassion, but who doesn't get stuck in misery or sadness herself, and who can also set boundaries for her son. Otherwise, he will worry about you, and then you will worry about him, and then both feel bad again.' The mother is relieved that now there is a solution to her dilemma.

In a third session, the therapist shows Ron's 'mode model', developed in session without her, which has a big impact on Tina. Her tears express her joy, but also her sympathy with Ron's underlying worries. The parents are ready to discuss the question of what it is that keeps them from feeling genuine joy for their son. The therapist encourages them to be completely forthcoming with any feelings of anger and negative thoughts about their son – to put it on the table. Tina says her son's weepiness is hard for her to bear because it seems too 'girlish and weak'. The father talks about his impatience with Ron's anxieties. He describes how difficult it is for him to comfort his son and to feel sympathy for him.

With the help of the parent's mode model, the therapist can explain which modes are being activated within them. Ron's behaviour activates a Demanding Parent voice which criticises crying and demands that he pull himself together. Ron activates his father's anxious Vulnerable Child mode – a mode that had obviously been denied by the father for a long time.

As a next step, the therapist uses a big hand puppet (for mode work) to represent Ron and sits him on a small chair. Then he asks the father how he feels when Ron is upset by a comment from his sports teacher. When imagining this situation the father starts to get angry and he describes the strong frustration he feels toward the teacher. The therapist validates the father's feeling and tells him that he can understand the anger at the teacher, but he refers back to what Ron needs now. The father sits still and stiff and confirms the assumption that when he was a young boy he had never experienced comfort and loving encouragement. As nobody had ever showed sympathy toward him, it was hard for him to show it toward his own son by, for example, giving him a hug. The therapist hands him the hand puppet and asks him to try it out once.

17.3 Summary

The family's interaction and communication patterns play a central and essential role in parental work in Schema Therapy for children and adolescents. It is crucial to understand the family structures, without blaming the parents for their child's development of symptoms. In successful therapy the boundaries of the sub-systems should be strengthened, but also remain permeable. Schema activating role assignments should be detected and, for the parents, a satisfactory division of responsibilities should be reinforced. Parental work does not only orient itself to the needs of the child but also considers the basic needs of the parents as individuals and as a couple. Positive experiences of nurturing (Caring Parent modes) should be activated, whereas Punitive and Demanding Parent modes should be disempowered, e.g. through conducting dialogues between the therapist and these modes.

Systemically oriented Schema Therapists consider the functionality of childhood symptoms both in terms of the emotional distress of the patient and from the perspective of family systems: What is the function of the symptom? Whom does it serve and for what purpose? What purpose does the symptom and its associated mode serve in the entire system? Could the changing of the child's symptoms possibly cause and endanger the internal balance of another family member?

Schema Therapists pay special attention to vicious cycles, negative interaction cycles and mode escalations – a mutual escalation of dysfunctional modes in the parents and the child. For diagnosis and therapy, Schema Therapists can choose between a variety of mediums. These include visually representing schema and mode maps especially for information purposes, creating mode diaries and schema memos/flashcards, mode work with dolls or chairs or imagery work. Classic systemic or behavioural therapy techniques may also be integrated and used to meet the goals of Schema Therapy: questioning techniques, family board, family circles, video-based feedback, sculpture work, reframing, cognitive restructuring and creating genograms to explore schemas.

17.3.1 The limits and contraindications of Schema Therapy work with parents

Schema Therapy mode work does not present any special intellectual challenges for the parents of patients. Even less able parents can benefit from the mode work. Experience has shown that, because of its illustrative and visual nature, the mode work is not too complex for most clients. The techniques are well received if the parents are given a choice between different approaches (for example, preferring dolls over chairs). The parental work described in this chapter may exceed the normal scope of typical family consultation, yet, depending on the complexity of the case, it may still be successful within usual time constraints. However, at the beginning of the child's therapy sessions it is advisable to schedule sessions at close intervals in order to facilitate a deeper process with parents and to establish a good basis for the treatment of the child. The presented approaches have all been tried and tested with parents in distress and parents who have received mental health diagnoses. So far, no specific contraindications are known. For traumatised parents, on the other hand, it is advisable to treat them in their own personal therapeutic framework.

References

Berbalk H (2012) *Arbeit mit Handpuppen in der Schematherapie*. Vortrag in Hamburg am 25.4.2012.

Cohen-Filipic K & Bentley KJ (2015) From every direction: guilt, shame, and blame among parents of adolescents with co-occurring challenges. *Child & Adolescent Social Work Journal* **32** (5) 443–454. Available at: doi:http://dx.doi.org/10.1007/s10560-015-0381-9

Erford BT (1999) A modified time-out procedure for children with noncompliant or defiant behaviors. *Professional School Counseling* **2** (3) 205. Retrieved from https://search.proquest.com/docview/2132648 65?accountid=178506

Furman B (nd) *The Steps of Responsibility: How to deal with the wrongdoings of children and adolescents in a way that builds their sense of responsibility*. Kidsskills.org Retrieved 22 September 2017, from http://www.kidsskills.org/english/responsibility/

Gottman JM (2011) *The Science of Trust: Emotional Attunement for Couples*. New York: WW Norton & Company.

Lindgren A (1988) *Immer dieser Michel*. Hamburg: Oetinger.

Macpherson HA, Cheavens JS & Fristad MA (2013) Dialectical behavior therapy for adolescents: Theory, treatment adaptations, and empirical outcomes. *Clinical Child and Family Psychology Review* **16** (1) 59-80. Available at: doi:http://dx.doi.org/10.1007/s10567-012-0126-7

Omer H & Lebowitz ER (2016) Nonviolent resistance: helping caregivers reduce problematic behaviors in children and adolescents. *Journal of Marital and Family Therapy* **42** (4) 688–700. Available at: doi:http://dx.doi.org/10.1111/jmft.12168

Omer H, Steinmetz SG, Carthy T & von Schlippe A (2013) The anchoring function: parental authority and the parent–child bond. *Family Process* **52** (2) 193. Retrieved from https://search.proquest.com/docview/1424667979?accountid=178506

Süß GJ (2011) *Bindungsqualität bei Helfern.* Vortrag SPZ Psychologen- und Forschungstag am SPZ Lübeck am 17.6.2011.

Von Schlippe A & Schweitzer J (2015) *Systemic Interventions.* Vandenhoeck & Ruprecht.

White M (1988) The process of questioning: a therapy of literary merit. *Dulwich Centre Newsletter,* Winter.

Chapter 18: Group Schema Therapy with Children and Adolescents (GST-CA)

Maria Galimzyanova and Elena Romanova

Group work with children and adolescents can be a very helpful addition to individual work. According to Gardner (1999a), group work is considered as important as individual psychotherapy, and even more important in some situations.

18.1 Benefits of group therapy for children

Group work helps children to connect, developing necessary social skills that will help them at school and in other social environments.

Group work counteracts alienation, and reduces feelings of isolation. Children benefit from listening to others when they discuss similar problems. In encouraging children to share their problems, feelings of isolation and alienation often decrease. A Schema Therapy (ST) group represents both family and the society in miniature. A friendly, accepting environment is created in the group, enabling children to express their feelings with peers and therapists. GST-CA allows children to explore their modes in a safe atmosphere where they can receive feedback and modify their behaviour. The group provides its members with understanding, confrontation and identification with more than one person.

Having two therapists increases the opportunity to work on family issues. GST-CA also gives the children a chance to see and analyse their own behaviour and the behaviour of others in a safe and comfortable space (where they are protected by the rules and can be sure that nothing terrible will happen).

The group helps children to find better ways of dealing with the life problems that are at the foundation of most forms of psychogenic psychopathology (Gardner, 1999a). The group provides new models for identification – the therapists and other group members. In the ST group the identifications are healthier than those that the child may have utilised previously when they have had to deal with difficult situations. The group helps children to develop metacognitive skills, which can be useful in managing both intrapsychic and interpersonal problems. The group facilitates open expression of thoughts and feelings in order to develop healthy processing of distress and more adaptive skills in managing emotions. Groups help children develop their problem-solving skills, consolidate positive experiences and develop resources and functional relationship habits.

18.2 Benefits of group therapy for adolescents

Grouping behaviour is natural for adolescents – they gravitate toward groups in order to meet their needs for belonging, connection, companionship and socialisation and to compensate for feelings of inadequacy. Socialisation is one of the important tasks of adolescence – it is essential for young people to become a significant part of a group. Adolescents can feel that the group has far greater strength then the sum of the individuals within it, which is why they feel more confident being a recognised member of a group. Among their peers they are able to have therapeutic social experiences. Adolescents are very dependent on their peers and this dependency can be utilised in group therapy. Peers are viewed as those whose opinions are more worthy of respect than the opinion of an adult.

Group work provides a natural opportunity for a therapist to observe an adolescent's social interactions, rather than relying on their own reporting of how they respond in relationships. Possibly one of the greatest benefits of group psychotherapy is the opportunity for the therapist to gain accurate data about the patient's interpersonal style. Also, in a group, a young person can experience a corrective therapeutic social experience. The group experience can also be useful for adolescents as an opportunity to develop new relationships, which is very therapeutic.

18.3 Indications/contraindications for GST-CA

GST can be carried out with a wide range of child/adolescent problems, but certain areas may particularly benefit from a group dynamic. They are:

- anxiety and fears
- depression
- low school performance

- low levels of impulse control

- trauma processing

- psychosomatic problems

- low self-esteem

- eating disorders (at a sub-acute/medically stable weight range)

- obsessive compulsive disorder

- relationship difficulties

- self-harm

- rigid behaviours and attitudes

- interpersonal problems, conflicts with family members, peers, teachers, and so on

- antisocial behaviour (according to Gardner (1999b), children/adolescents exhibiting antisocial behaviour may benefit from the psychotherapeutic group if they are in the minority in a group). We also add that it's best to include the antisocial adolescents in a ST group if they already have received or are receiving individual Schema Therapy before the group or, ideally, concurrently with the group. This allows the therapist to provide safety for the group members and support the adolescent

- ADHD (if the symptoms are manageable in a group setting and the children with ADHD are in the minority in the group)

- lack of goals and direction

- lack of resources or awareness of own resources

- 'treatment resistant' issues

Ideally, the group age difference is no larger than two years. The younger the children, the smaller the age range of children within one group.

Exclusion criteria:
- substance abuse and addictions (unless the group is specially devoted to this theme, it is held in a facility that provides containment and all the other members have the same issue)

- psychosis

- acute disorders

- organic brain disorders

- antisocial personality disorder
- pervasive developmental disorders
- acute or severe suicidality where individual attention is required
- low intelligence
- siblings or close relatives in one group.

When organising a group, consideration needs to be given to the combination of children, especially adolescents who may be the same chronological age but at significantly different cognitive and social developmental levels. Not taking these differences into consideration while forming a group may lead to peer rejection and feelings of inadequacy and frustration that may hinder the group growth and personal development of the group members.

18.4 Collaboration with the family

Collaboration with the family is an essential part of GST-CA. The details (what kind of sessions are used for the parents, how many hours of parent and family therapy are implemented, how much psychoeducation is given, etc) depend on the clinic and its structure.

18.4.1 First meeting with the parents before the group

We meet with each set of parents before the group to get detailed information about the family history, prenatal period, birth and early stages of development: infancy, early childhood, preschool period, primary school, and so on. It is important to understand the parents' concept of the origins of the child's problems, and to reduce the guilty feelings that the majority of the parents have in regard to the child's upbringing. It is very important to establish a good connection with the parents, as usually they are the ones who bring children to the group and, if the group is held in a private psychological centre/clinic, they are also the ones who pay for the group therapy.

18.4.2 Anticipatory socialisation

Ideally, we have some time before the group for anticipatory socialisation. It's necessary to have at least one or two individual sessions with the child and at least one session with their parents. It is much better to have even more individual sessions with the child before the group, to provide much needed information about the child, the problems, schemas and schema modes.

Preliminary individual sessions with the child help to:

- establish rapport with the child
- help the child understand why the group will be helpful
- explain what group work is, the advantages and possibilities, what they can expect from the group and what will never happen in a group
- increase the child's motivation
- validate the child's feelings and express their belonging in the group even if they are angry, sad or lonely
- emphasise how much support a group may give and how other members may increase this validation
- reduce fear and anxiety by showing the child the group space (an excursion around all the rooms explaining what will take place in each room usually significantly lowers tension)
- explain and discuss the ground rules (it is important to stress that the rules are to increase safety).

Goals of GST-CA

1. Create an atmosphere where the core needs of the children can be met, and the Vulnerable Child is taken care of, heard and healed
2. Develop basic emotional awareness and emotional regulation
3. Identify the modes and explore their origin, their effect on everyday life and current problems and any mode triggers
4. Weaken and replace the Detached Protector mode and/or other maladaptive coping modes (if they are present in the group) that may impede connection and block access to the Vulnerable Child, creating an atmosphere where it is safe to express feelings, connect with other people and express needs. Replace the Coping modes with healthy coping skills
5. Listen to the Angry Child mode and teach the Angry Child appropriate ways to express anger (in an assertive, but polite manner) and express needs
6. Validate the feelings of the Vulnerable Child, explore their needs, provide consolation and protection
7. Weaken and disempower other dysfunctional modes: Demanding and Punishing Critic modes; impulsive, Undisciplined Child modes; other dysfunctional Coping modes (surrender, avoidance, overcompensation)
8. Free the Happy Child mode – help children to express their creativity and enjoy the process of learning and development
9. Strengthen the Wise/Clever mode. Schema mode change allows changes in dysfunctional life patterns and enables meeting child's core needs
10. Help children to generalise therapy results in their everyday lives

18.5 Setting the stage for GST-CA

18.5.1 Group size

It's best for GST-CA to have groups of 8–10 participants. In the bigger groups, awkward, withdrawn and introverted children can be overlooked, and not receive sufficient attention. In the smaller groups the psychological load on each child increases. For some children it is not only difficult to share feelings; even speaking in front of other people is challenging, especially being the centre of attention. Smaller groups also provide a way to manage social dynamics, reducing the variability of reactions and behaviour escalating. Another factor influencing group size is the range and severity of the children's symptomatology.

18.5.2 Age range and the duration of group sessions

In our psychological centre, Anima, in St Petersburg, Russia we work in GST-CA with children of all ages, starting with the first school year and covering the whole school period, from 6 or 7 years old up to 17. There are also groups for children of preschool age that help to prepare children for school education and facilitate school adaptation.

We prefer a format of groups lasting three months, with group meetings once a week. Each meeting lasts for 120–240 minutes according to the age of children. The length of the sessions allows most problematic behaviours and Coping modes to become visible after the first hour, when self-control decreases. During the sessions, children experience a variety of activities – games, exercises, art work, and so on – so the group meetings become intensive and very dynamic, and provide opportunity for in-session changes in children.

18.5.3 Our experience with group combinations

- First school year (6–7 years old): 120 minutes with a 20-minute break. It is better to have children in their first school year in one group and not mix them with older children, as (especially at the beginning of the school year) they are experiencing adaptation stress and are extremely sensitive about their school performance. The presence of older children that have more skills may increase tension, competition and feelings of inadequacy. At this age children can concentrate on group work for no longer than an hour without a break, which is why the optimal duration of the group session is 120 minutes with a 20-minute break in the middle. It's also possible to mix children in the first school year with those who are going to school the next year. For the first year school children this provides an opportunity to feel successful (meeting their need for achievement) and be experts for smaller children, while at the same they can prolong their playing period (many children are not ready for rather strict school rules yet). For the preschool children it is good psychological preparation for school.

- Second and third school years (7–9 years old) – 'primary school' group: 120–150 minutes with a 20 minute break.

- Fourth to sixth school years (9–12 years old) – 'early adolescence' group: 150 minutes with a 30 minute break. At 9 some changes have already begun and many parents and teachers notice the first features of adolescent behaviour. The changes that occur in children at this age are really tremendous and the group work is very powerful.

- 12–15 year olds: 180 minutes with a 30 minute break. During these years peer connections become crucial, so group work is indispensable. It coincides with the development of introspection and self-reflection, which is why the group sessions may become longer.

- 14–17 year olds: 240 minutes with a 40 minute break.

- Every course is 3–4 months long, running September–December and February–May with a one month break in winter and a three month break in summer. Such a format allows a focus on one theme at a time, as every three month Schema Therapy course has a focus: for example, Feelings, Conflict Resolution, Communication, Self-Knowledge, Confidence, etc. It helps the therapists to be prepared in advance for the psychoeducational part and for children to have a feeling of novelty every time they enter a new aspect of the group. Groups cover all ages during the school period and they accompany children throughout all the stages of development. Every child has an opportunity to visit all the groups, from their first school year till the last, or to choose groups that are more interesting to them.

18.6 Limited re-parenting

Limited re-parenting is a keystone to successful treatment in GST-CA. Therapists are the mediators between the adult world and the child/adolescent world. Very often we hear the parents of the children/adolescents say: 'I said that a thousand times, but when they heard it from you it was like a new discovery. Why didn't they hear me when I have been saying it for so many years and yet they heard you so easily?' Therapists become people whom a child/adolescent trusts. Being a good parent to the children's Vulnerable Child mode, therapists find ways to acknowledge and accept the feelings and needs of different modes. Therapist interventions match the developmental level and the modes the children are in. The therapist's task is to help the children to find ways to get their needs met outside the group, establishing healthy relationships with their parents, teachers, peers and others. Therapists do what a good parent of a child/adolescent would do: meet the needs of that child (within professional boundaries). In meeting core emotional needs, the main goal is to help the children develop their Wise/Clever mode. The therapists take different stances according to the different modes: they are very warm and empathise with the Vulnerable Child mode; are very firm with the Inner Critic and Demanding mode; challenge the Coping modes; and are very respectful to the Wise/Clever mode.

Group work increases the possibilities to meet the needs of children, as they are met both by the therapists and the group members. The group represents a family with two 'parents' – the therapists, and 'sibling' group members. It helps children to learn how to communicate effectively with their parents, teachers and other 'members' of the adult world, and with peers (achieving one of the main developmental tasks of adolescence).

18.7 Relating the therapist's own personal experiences to the group

Many children enjoy hearing about their parents' childhoods. When parents share the details of their lives with children they improve their relationships with them. Children love this kind of intimacy – a spirit of mutual confidence in the relationship. Therapists can also use appropriate self-disclosure, being open and sensitive, which creates mutual trust and facilitates self-revelation in children and adolescents. It is difficult to overestimate the therapeutic benefits of the therapist's self-disclosure. These stories, told with the purpose of helping the children in their treatment and with direct relevance to the problems of the group members, provide useful therapeutic communication and bring the children and the therapist closer to one another. The therapist's own experience serves as a metaphor for the children's experience. Obviously not all the details have to be revealed, and the therapists need to select specific aspects useful for the given group members.

Just knowing that the therapists have had similar experiences may be helpful as it can lessen the children's burden. Knowing that the therapist, whom the child may regard as perfect, has also had these experiences makes the therapist more real.

18.8 Sequencing of activities during the session

All sessions are planned using the principle 'from simple to complex'. First, easy tasks are given to the children; as new knowledge and skills develop, the material, exercises and tasks become harder.

The beginning of the session

We begin every session with a discussion about the children's emotional state.

For the beginning of each session it is helpful to express feelings as colours, weather, music, movement, sport, animals, and so on. This format helps children to understand and analyse their emotions, because at first they don't notice their feelings. We ask them to describe their emotional state with a colour, for example, and as the group progresses they come to understand how they actually feel as they can talk about it. It helps to sneak around the C modes that can be triggered by a difficult question such as 'What are you feeling now?' There is less stress using a metaphor than asking directly.

It is very useful to start the sessions with a weather report. The therapist reads the weather report: 'Today is sunny with a gentle breeze. I don't remember the last time I felt a gentle breeze on my face. And I sure don't feel sunny. How do you feel?' Children may say, for example, 'I feel like a big thunderstorm coming in'. This is good exercise to help children express feelings in a safe way and be validated.

Safety image

It is good to start every session with a safety image (Safety Bubble, Safe Place Image, etc) that may change over time. In the early sessions it's better to use the images provided by therapists. That is especially true for groups of highly traumatised children who haven't experienced much safety in their life. An image of a safety bubble (around each child and around the group) is the best one to start with. It usually becomes a favourite activity of preschoolers and younger schoolchildren. Later we help children to develop their own Safe Place Images.

Good Parent messages

It is very important to start the group work with supportive phrases of a Good Parent to reassure the children that they are warmly welcomed, safe and protected by the therapists and the group, and to encourage them for good and helpful work.

Early working period

'Welcome' games

It is good to begin with a quick 'Welcome' game that will help children to communicate with every member of the group and the therapists. It usually takes 3–7 min and helps children to feel a connection with the group as a whole and with the different participants personally. There are a lot of variants that the therapists may introduce. For example, children are asked to walk around the room and greet everyone by shaking hands or touching the ears of each person with their own ears; to greet everyone as people of different professions (named by the therapists) would greet each other; to touch each other with three parts of the body; to develop a greeting ritual; to whisper compliments or encouraging messages in the ears of other members, and so on.

Warming-up quick active game

A quick active game in the beginning helps children to warm up, collaborate and better concentrate on the further group work.

Middle working period

Early middle working period

During the early middle working period it is better to do the main exercise of the session, which requires maximum concentration, at the beginning. It is good to start with some theoretical material that is discussed in the group and later is assimilated with the help of the worksheets, exercises and games.

Theory

It's very important to present theoretical material to children in a simple, age appropriate and interactive form. Different metaphors, patterns and outlines are used to illustrate the material. Any theory studied during the group sessions is immediately worked out in practice in the form of exercises. Handouts and worksheets for the personal workbooks with the main theoretical ideas are elaborated beforehand and are given to children during the group sessions.

The break

Around the middle of a session there is a break, which itself becomes a very important part of the therapeutic process. It's time that the group spends together sitting around the big table in the dining room, discussing various topics and playing different games. It's time that is unconsciously seen as 'not serious', where the children can relax and be spontaneous (even if they feel very comfortable in the group, they enjoy the coffee break). Therapists are an important part of the break. Children often ask the therapists questions about their life and it's a special time for sharing different stories, jokes, anecdotes, and so on. For some smaller children it may become their first successful social experience, when they gain authority within their peers, becoming a storyteller, telling jokes and becoming a game leader during a coffee break.

Late middle working period

After the break it is best to do an experiential exercise, creative work/art therapy exercises and/or to play games that don't require much concentration and cognitive work, as closer to the end of the session it becomes harder for children to concentrate. Just after the break it is important to propose a quick warming-up exercise to help the children concentrate and switch back to group work focus again.

Wrap up, grounding and feedback

We wrap up the sessions asking the children what they are taking with them from this session, what their most vivid impressions were, what they remember most, what was most important for them during the session, and so on. The discussion becomes more dynamic if we use a ball. If there is a lack of time or the children are very tired we ask them to express their impressions about the session using just one word that can best describe their feelings/experience/impressions.

It is also important to monitor children's emotional state using the same metaphor as in the beginning of the session. So we can ask: 'What colour is your mood now?', 'What is the weather like now for every member of our group?', 'What movement is it now?', and so on.

'For whom has it remained the same and for whom has it changed? What is it like now?' It is essential to ask the children again about their feelings at the end of the session as the emotional state of children and especially adolescents may change dramatically within a couple of seconds and it's very significant for the therapists to be aware of the children's emotional state to be able to help the child immediately if it's needed. It is always possible to speak to the child after the session if the therapist suspects that the child is not well or is struggling with something.

Feedback

Also at the end of the session, you can ask the participants to fill in a special feedback worksheet. It gives the children an opportunity to reflect upon the process, to summarise the results of the work. It also gives an idea of how comfortable participants feel in the group, how interested they are, what was important and useful for them and what, on the contrary, they did not like.

Also, completing this form allows the therapists to respond quickly to the possible and unpredictable changes of the emotional state of participants (sometimes it is not even connected with the process itself, and may be a response to some actions or words of other participants).

Member name: _____

Date: _____

1. On a rating scale of 1 to 10 how interesting was today's group meeting for you?

   1 2 3 4 5 6 7 8 9 10

2. Have you learned something new today? If so, what was it? _____

   _____

3. On a rating scale of 1 to 10 how comfortable did you feel in the group today?

   1 2 3 4 5 6 7 8 9 10

4. What topics, exercises, games were most important for you today?

   _____

5. What did you like most in the group meeting?_____
_____

6. What didn't you like in the group meeting today? _____
_____

7. What topics would you like to discuss during the next group meetings?
_____

8. What were the goals that you've worked on today?_____

9. If there is something that you want to ask the therapists about, please write
it down._____

_____

It is good to create group rituals for ending the session. We usually use the
'Finding a common rhythm' exercise and the 'Orchestra conductor' game
(a game that helps to establish eye contact with everyone, to create a good
mood and enjoy interaction with others).

18.9 Cognitive interventions

Cognitive interventions help the children to understand, recognise and learn to
distinguish their schema modes and engage their rational part in preventing the
formation of early maladaptive schemas, or fighting them.

Cognitive work in a group helps children to build a verbal framework for later
experiential work and understand some of the distortions their schemas and
modes bring into their everyday life.

Main cognitive interventions

- Educational material on Schema modes, needs, feelings. Handouts are collected
  during each course and collated in a personal workbook together with the
  worksheets, drawings and other creative material obtained during the group.
- Learning to distinguish thoughts, feelings and behavior
- Working with negative and positive beliefs
- Pros and cons exercises
- Audio flashcards

18.10 Experiential interventions

Experiential interventions involve the children's feelings and provide corrective emotional experiences.

Main experiential interventions

Imagery (Safety Bubble, Safe Place, etc)
Mode roleplays
Transitional objects (identity bracelet, Vulnerable Child treasure box)
Various games and exercises

18.11 Behavioral interventions

Behavioral interventions typically come later in Schema Therapy, as there is greater awareness of modes and as the Wise/Clever Child mode is developed, enabling the child to generalise group learning to everyday situations.

Behavioral pattern breaking interventions

Role-play practice
Mode management plans

In what follows we will discuss interventions, techniques and exercises that are used in GST-CA. Also, we will provide (as an example) some exercises, developed by us for work with children and adolescent groups.

18.12 Stages of GST-CA

The stages of GST-CA are the same as in GST with adults, and are described in the works of Farrell and Shaw (2012, 2014), but there are some changes in the content of the stages in accordance with the age of children/adolescents.

18.12.1 Stage 1: Bonding and emotional regulation

As in GST with adults (Farrell & Shaw, 2012), the first stage of the group work in ST-CA is aimed at facilitating connection, establishing a group 'family'. The therapists facilitate bonding and cohesion between the 'family members' and help the children to feel safety, have a sense of belonging and be accepted. An atmosphere in which the core needs of the children can be met and the Vulnerable Child is taken care of is carefully created by the therapists and is crucial for the group's success.

A key goal is the development of the basic emotional awareness and emotional regulation as these skills are usually very scarcely developed at the preschool and primary school age, and very often are still underdeveloped in adolescence. Emotional awareness and emotional regulation involves helping children become aware of their feelings and triggers, practise self-soothing techniques and reach out for support. Learning these processes strengthens the connection between the group members and builds safety in the group.

Components of this stage are:

- Learning the group ground rules, setting personal goals and getting to know what to expect from the group. This stage prepares the way for the mode change work.

- Facilitating connection using experiential exercises, such as the 'Connecting web' exercise" (Farrell & Shaw, 2012), 'Getting to know you' games and other games that establish contact with others (both verbally and non-verbally).

- Developing the imagery skills widely used during GST-CA, especially safety images: safe place image, safety bubble (Farrell & Shaw, 2012, 2014), and so on.

- Providing transitional objects such as resource bracelets/identity bracelets, small toys, a group toy (children take turns taking the toy home with them and taking care of it for the week), stickers, pieces of fleece, different transitional objects developed in the group, and so on.

- Increasing emotional awareness by learning to label emotions; to associate feelings with colours, weather, and so on; to express feelings with facial expressions, intonation, movements, pantomime, and so on; writing group stories about feelings; making an iceberg of feelings.

- Imagery re-scripting may also be used where there is a past traumatic event. Generally we give preference to role play and behavioural pattern breaking given that most of the problems and difficulties are happening in the present. Therefore participants need to understand and practise new behaviours to be able to solve the current problems and difficulties that they have, both in and outside the group.

The main psychoeducational component in this first stage is education about needs and feelings. Theoretical material is focused on the mode model and provided in the second stage of group work.

18.12.2 Stage 2 – Schema mode change

Stage two consists of two parts, mode awareness and mode change.

1. Mode awareness

We begin by presenting the Schema Therapy mode model to the group and helping the children learn to be aware of their modes in their everyday lives. The goal of mode awareness is that children learn to identify their modes and explore their origin and impact on everyday life and current problems.

Presenting the mode model in group settings

Sometimes it is a challenge to present a mode model in child/adolescent groups. Children and adolescents don't generally sit and listen to lectures, so all the theory is presented in an interactive manner; thus children are involved in a game, demonstration, cartoon discussion, and so on. In the group work the same demonstrations and metaphors are used as in the individual ST-CA (e.g. Dolly the sheep, glasses, see 7.3.4), and also we use other ways to illustrate modes – for example, showing clips from cartoons and movies demonstrating certain modes (the clips are shown and discussed with the group).

Using the Matrioshka metaphor

Being Russian child therapists, we could not resist using the Matrioshka metaphor for modes! We use painted matrioshkas (with 10 'dolls'). Each doll represents one mode.

Matrioshka mode drawings

We draw 10 matrioshkas (from the biggest to the smallest) on the sheet of paper (A3). Children are encouraged to imagine each mode and draw one on each matrioshka outline. The mode that appears most often should be drawn on the biggest matrioshka. The mode that appears the least should be drawn on the smallest matrioshka. As a group we hold a 'modes exhibition', where each child plays the role of guide and shows the group their matrioshkas one by one, discussing each mode as much as they are able. The therapists make their own matrioshkas.

Glasses metaphor

We also often use glasses metaphor in GST-CA. The procedure of presenting the glasses can be the same as in individual ST-CA (see 9.3.4).

Making mode glasses

We ask children to design their own glasses, using outlines of glasses made from dotted lines. First, they choose the most frequent modes for them. Children paint the outline of glasses and give them names. We encourage children to draw glasses of any shape and colour, with decorations that fit with the mode, e.g. fiery red glasses for Angry Child mode or dark, heavily tinted glasses for Detached Protector mode.

Using cartoons

The modes can be better described and understood if the children not only discuss them, but also see them in action. One nice way to do this is to discuss the behaviour of cartoon characters. Both children and adolescents enjoy cartoons, but often with older adolescents we use film clips. Cartoons such as 'Inside Out' help children to see how, when modes are triggered, they affect the way a person hears and sees things and how they react. In every country there are cartoons in which different modes are presented very well. Watching those as a group provides a great opportunity for discussion about modes and the behaviour connected to them.

Fairytale therapy and storytelling techniques

We often use fairytale and storytelling techniques in ST-CA. Mode theory and different nuances connected with mode functioning are more understandable for children when they are presented as a fairytale or story. Storytelling is particularly effective when working with children of preschool and primary school age. Fairytales and stories are prepared by the therapist before the meeting and then told to the group with lots of expression. The stories are then discussed in small groups or in a circle. Children make paintings based on the story (fairytale) and can develop roleplays using the characters/modes. Therapists can also develop stories together with the group. In this case the therapist can tell the beginning of a story and the children imagine the continuation and create the end of the story.

One story can be used as a connecting element for each group meeting. One part of the fairytale is told each session (connecting with the theme of the group and the modes discussed). For example, across the 12 sessions we have created, discussed and played an exciting story about different fish and other marine creatures (each of them represented one mode) who live in the Great Barrier Reef.

Making a mode collage

Psychoeducation about modes is more understandable and useful when children are involved in creative activities that express their internal world. For example, making mode collages allows an understanding of modes and an experience of that mode. Creative activities also provide an opportunity to meet a child's need for pleasure and fun.

It is possible to create a collage of all the modes on the one page. Or the group can have a more detailed focus by making a collage of each mode to better understand their functioning (usually child modes) or to activate them (Happy Child and Wise/Clever Child mode).

2. Mode change work

Initial focus of mode work in this stage

Usually in the GST with adults, after the goals of the first stage are achieved (connection/cohesiveness/emotional regulation, etc) we start on the Maladaptive Coping Modes (MCM), as these are what adult patients usually present with in an ST group (Farrell & Shaw, 2012).

As children (especially those of preschool and primary school age) are at a very early stage in their emotional development, schemas and modes are still in development; therefore we tend to speak about schema predispositions, rather than schemas. This developmental factor also means that the Coping modes may not be as pronounced as they tend to be in adult groups. This is also true when working with groups of more healthy adolescents. Additionally, children tend to be more open and react more naturally than adults. Therefore, if the Schema Therapist has done a good job in the first stage of group work, building strong connections and safety between children, the Coping modes won't necessarily impede the work with the Child modes. If the Coping modes aren't blocking access to the Vulnerable Child mode, we suggest starting the mode change work with the Angry Child mode. The goal of this work with the Angry Child mode is to validate, allow for anger venting and assist the child to have healthier ways of expressing anger. When this is achieved, it brings us directly to the Vulnerable Child mode, allowing access to those feelings and needs.

Suggested sequence of GST with preschool and primary school children, if the Coping modes are not impeding connection to the child modes:
1. Angry Child mode
2. Vulnerable Child mode
3. Critic modes (Demanding and Punitive)
4. Impulsive and Undisciplined Child modes
5. Maladaptive Coping modes (if needed)
6. Wise /Clever mode

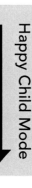

Happy Child Mode

Happy Child mode is addressed throughout the whole GST-CA process. Games, exercises and activities are chosen in order to provide opportunities for Happy Child expression, meeting the child's needs for creativity, fun and self-expression, making the group process enjoyable and memorable.

In the adolescent groups (particularly with those over the age of 12 or 13), there are often Coping modes that can, at times, significantly impede group development, so the same sequence as adult GST is required.

Suggested sequence of GST with adolescents and child groups when coping modes impede the work with child modes:
1. Maladaptive Coping modes (if needed)
2. Vulnerable Child mode
3. Critic modes (Demanding and Punitive)
4. Angry Child mode
5. Impulsive and Undisciplined Child modes
6. Wise/Clever mode

Happy Child Mode

Below, are examples of interventions developed or adapted for ST purposes by the team of St Petersburg Schema Therapists.

ANGRIELLA

Age: 6 and older

Mode: Angry Child

Goal: Understanding what can evoke the angry feelings. Venting anger in the form of a game. Having fun with anger.

Instructions to children:

1. 'Let's think about what it's like when you get angry or mad – your thoughts, feelings and behaviour. If your angry feelings were a creature, what would it look like, and how would it act? Use all the creative material you need and make that creature. Let's call it Angriella. And afterwards you can think of a name for your Angriella and tell us their story.'

2. 'Now I'll give you worksheets, so you can write down the answers to the questions about your Angriella: What does it look like? What character does it have/what is it like? What does it want? When does it become angry? What is it angry at? What and who can make it even angrier? In what situations does it become very powerful? What does it usually say? What does it usually think?'

3. 'Now let's divide into small groups of three and tell each other about your Angriella.'

4. 'Now we can discuss it all together. Please present your Angriella to the group and tell us about it.'

5. 'And now together we'll make an Angriellas concert. Imagine how your Angriella sounds, maybe it roars, barks, cries … How does it move?'

Materials: For this exercise a lot of 'creative material' is needed – coloured paper, scissors, sticky tape, foil, and all kinds of cleaned garbage prepared for recycling will do (you can use empty yogurt cans, egg cases, plastic bottles, wrapping paper, etc).

Recommendations for the therapist: It's important for the therapist to make their own Angriella together with the group. This shows children that everyone may get angry sometimes and there is nothing wrong with anger. It gives the children safety to express their feelings. The therapist becomes a model for expressing feelings in a healthy way. Later the therapist can discuss with children that the most important thing is what do we do with our anger – can we let it out or do we carry it inside us all the time? Do we find an appropriate manner to express our anger, or do we let our uncontrollable anger destroy our relationships? The therapist encourages adolescents to participate in the 'Angriellas' concert, encouraging everyone to interact with each other. (Angriellas may be destroyed or may be taken home according to the wishes of the group members.)

'A WAR WITH PENCILS' and 'SNOWBALLS' GAME
'A WAR WITH PENCILS'

Age: 6 and older

Mode: Angry Child

Goal: Venting anger and having fun with anger in a group, acquisition of new anger management skills

Materials: Lots of recycled paper (A4), quite a large amount of sharpened coloured pencils, chairs, blankets

Instructions: 'We are going to play the war game. Please choose a partner for this game and divide your sheet of paper into two parts. Then each partner will take a pencil of a bright colour – for example, red and green. First each person draws their armoury on their part of the paper. Armoury might include war ships, tanks, artillery, mines, soldiers. Get prepared for the war!

Now you all are well prepared. So please now find in the box at least 10–15 pencils of the same colour that you used, and put them aside for the time being. Now every pair will get a good amount of the sheets of paper. Please don't be afraid to use a lot of paper as it was already recycled and will be recycled again afterwards. Take your pencils and when I count to three the war will start. Your task will be to try to colour the paper in your colour (to cover the biggest space possible) and your partner will try to colour it in their colour. As soon as one sheet of paper is completely coloured or torn, very quickly take another sheet of paper, and then another, and so on until all the sheets of paper I've given to you are finished. If the pencil gets blunt, take another one immediately and continue your battle.' (While you are playing this game you are free to vent all the anger that your Angry Child has.)

During the game the therapist can go round supporting the participants, exclaiming 'Great! You are doing so well!' 'Let go of all the anger that you are feeling, even the anger that you felt last week or anger from a long time ago!'

Afterwards the participants are asked to make snowballs from the sheets of paper they have in front of them and the game may be continued as the 'Snowballs' game.

'SNOWBALLS' GAME

The therapist asks the children to crush the paper very hard, letting go of all the anger that is still left. Afterwards, when each pair is ready, the group is divided into two teams – the pairs go together in the same team and each therapist joins a team. In the middle of the room a barrier is built with the chairs and blankets (so that the children don't throw the snowballs at their peers, but over the barrier). The goal is for each team to get rid of as many snowballs as possible by throwing them quickly to the other side of the room (over the barrier) until the time is up. When the time is finished the snowballs are counted on each side of the room. The winner is the team with the least snowballs left on their side of the room. Usually the group is given 3–5 minutes for the big snowballs game.

It is important to ask the children not to throw the snowballs directly into the faces of the members of the other team.

FRUIT AND VEGETABLE SWEARING (*by Elena Romanova*)

Age: 6 and older

Mode: Angry Child

Goal: Venting anger and having fun with anger in a group, acquisition of new anger management skills

Materials: A list of fruits and vegetables

Instructions: 'When people are mad at each other they very often shout and swear at each other. They do it because they are very angry and they don't have other ways to express their feelings. We want to help you express anger, but without saying bad words and without hurting others. The way we are going to do this is by being angry in this next game but only using the names of the fruit and vegetables. Let's divide into pairs and one of you be the speaker, then the other will respond. So you choose any of the vegetables and say for example "You're a carrot!", expressing anger with your voice, facial expression, posture, etc. Make it like a real quarrel. Your partner answers with another vegetable: "And you are a cabbage!" When you are finished with vegetables, you can use the list of fruit and berries.'

Vegetables	Fruit and berries
Cabbage	Strawberry
Carrot	Cherry
Potato	Plum
Spinach	Cherry

Vegetables	Fruit and berries
Radish	Apple
Turnip	Blueberry
Eggplant	Watermelon
Cucumber	Melon
Tomato	Apricot
Radish	Peach
Broccoli	Nectarine
Pepper	Banana
Zucchini/Courgette	Feijoa
Squash	Avocado
Pumpkin	Guava
Mushroom	Star fruit
Cauliflower	Fig
Corn	Gooseberry
Bean sprout	Cranberry

'YES' AND 'NO' QUARREL (by Elena Romanova)

Age: 6 and older

Mode: Angry Child

Goal: Venting anger and having fun with anger in a group, acquisition of new anger management skills

Materials: Not needed

Instructions: 'Now we'll play a quarrel or argument. Divide into pairs, please; in these pairs you'll be quarrelling but instead of long phrases you'll use only two words, "Yes" and "No". So you'll have only your tone, loudness, facial expressions and body language as instruments to "convince" your partner that "you are right". Start very quietly, then continue louder, and then louder and louder.'

Each pair performs their quarrel in front of the whole group.

BALLOON BATTLE (by Elena Romanova)

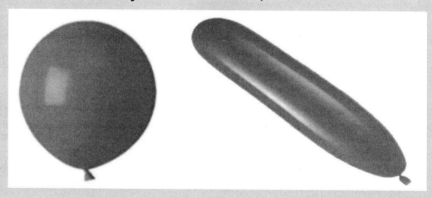

Age: 6 and older

Mode: Angry Child

Goal: Venting anger and having fun with anger in a group, acquisition of new anger management skills

Materials: Long and round balloons

Instructions: 'Now we'll perform a battle, but quite an unusual one. Let's get into pairs: one of you will have a sword (give them long balloons) and will go on the offensive and another will have a shield (give them round balloons) and be on the defensive.' The therapists demonstrate how to do the battle and then encourage the children's joyful anger venting. Afterwards the children change places.

MEAN WORDS MONSTER AND ADDRESSING BULLYING

Age: 6 and older

Mode: Angry Child

Goals: To encourage self-revelation, to provide a cathartic experience of reattribution of 'mean words' and to learn how to deal with mean words

Materials: A 'mean words monster' made of a shoe box and paper, that has a hole in his mouth where we put 'mean words'; small pieces of paper; pens/pencils

Instructions: 'Let me introduce you to my good friend. He is a monster. He is not a regular monster that you've seen on TV, in cartoons or movies, or that children sometimes see in their dreams. He is a very special monster – a 'Mean words monster'. He is called that because he eats mean words. It's his food and he likes it a lot. And he is very hungry now and asked me to help him. So now we'll feed him all together.

We are going to write down the bad, insulting, mean words and phrases that you've heard from people on small pieces of paper. These words have probably hurt you, made you sad or angry, or maybe you didn't have the words to respond and stop people teasing you. On each piece of paper write the words and phrases that you remember and also write in brackets who told you that and in what situation. Later we are going to put all your papers in the monster's mouth to feed him.'

Afterwards the papers are taken from the monster box and as a group, group members and therapists try to find good responses to each word/phrase that are not aggressive or insulting, but funny and assertive. It is very important to tell the children that they can write and say everything that has been said to them in the group, no matter how bad and mean these words are. First the group therapists tell their own stories and give examples of the mean words that they heard in their childhood.

A HEDGEHOG

Age: 6 and older

Modes: Angry Child and Vulnerable Child

Goals: To understand the connection between 'angry' and 'vulnerable' feelings, reflect upon the mode triggers and learn how to talk about feelings and needs in a healthy manner ('I'-messages) and opportunity to practice in the group

Materials: A big apple, toothpicks

Instructions: 'We have spoken before about our modes and you know that the Angry Child mode always defends the Vulnerable Child mode.

So, usually when we get really angry and become mad about some situation/person our "angry" feelings something sitting underneath – the "Vulnerable" feelings – hurt, sadness, guilt, loneliness, disappointment, etc. Those feelings are there because some of our needs were not met.

First of all I want you to think about a situation when you felt really mad and angry and were "thorny" like a hedgehog.

Now we'll make a hedgehog of our feelings. We've brought you an apple and a pack of toothpicks. Now I ask everyone to think of different situations when you were so angry that you were ready to attack the person who made you feel like that. So, when it comes to you, take one of the toothpicks and stick it into your apple. Each toothpick will represent a situation when you got really mad at someone. Please tell us about it and your "Angry" feelings. Then see if you can also say what was sitting under those mad, angry feelings. What was Vulnerable Child feeling? So first name the angry feelings, and then name the "Vulnerable" feelings (sadness, hurt, etc) that are connected with angry feelings. For example: "I am angry when my mother checks my pockets in search of cigarettes, because I feel hurt, not trusted and not understood."' (You may need to refer to a list of Angry Child feelings and Vulnerable Child feelings, or put them up on a board.)

Write all the situations on the blackboard/whiteboard.

'I'll start: When I was 13 I got really mad when my granny entered my room without knocking on the door and interrupted my phone calls, telling my friends off – I felt so angry because my Vulnerable Child was hurt – I felt awkward and ashamed and I was scared that I might lose my friends because of my granny's behaviour! I was angry and shouted at my granny, but she did it again and again and nothing changed. I only expressed my anger but didn't tell her about my vulnerable feelings – fear and shame, and I didn't ask her to meet my needs.

So now we have a thorny apple. This apple is like us – we become as thorny as a hedgehog; that's the anger, fury and irritation. And we push people away. But we see that the other end of the toothpick is inside the apple. And it shows our feelings: insult, pain, injustice, sadness, etc.

Thus, our Angry Child mode covers our Vulnerable Child.'

Part 2 is filling in the table (individual work).

Part 3 is taking the toothpicks out: thinking of a solution, learning to formulate 'I'-messages, asking for the needs to be met.

'Now we need to take all the toothpicks out. For every situation mentioned, we'll try to find a way to talk about your feelings and ask people to meet your needs in a way that won't damage the relationship.

Example: You can tell your mom: "I don't smoke, you can trust me" or explain to your family: "Yes, I smoke. I'm really sorry that it makes you sad, but it's my choice and I am not going to stop it."

Or you can use an 'I'-message:

"When you check my pockets, I feel insulted, because I feel that you do not trust me. And your trust is very important for me. That's why I want to ask you not to check my pockets anymore, because I don't smoke."

"When you check my pockets, I feel offended and hurt, because my private space is very important for me. That's why I want to ask you not to check my pockets anymore. You can ask me if you are worried about something".

So, the goal is to express our feelings in a way that won't damage our relationships and will help us to get our needs met. Let's try it.'

MAKING A "PORTRAIT" OF A VULNERABLE CHILD IN SMALL GROUPS AND MAKING A GROUP LIST OF NEEDS

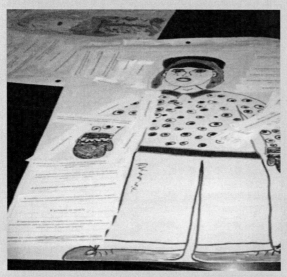

Age: 6 and older

Modes: Vulnerable Child

Goals: Understand the Vulnerable Child mode, explore emotional needs and share those needs with others, collaborate with peers in small groups and make a creative product together

Materials: A flipchart, markers, printed papers with needs, glue

Instructions: 'We spoke about the inner child that lives inside all people, no matter how old they are. Sometimes this child feels sad, lonely and frightened and becomes vulnerable. Now we'll divide into small groups of three and in these groups I'll ask you to imagine what this child looks like, what age, is it a boy or a girl, how is Vulnerable Child feeling at the moment and why. Then we are going to get paper with basic needs written down, choose the ones that are important to you and make a list of needs for everyone in your small group, gluing the paper with the needs on to your picture.'

A LOVE-PATH (*by Elena Romanova*)

Age: 6 and older

Modes: Vulnerable Child, Wise/ Clever/Caring mode

Goals: To heal and take care of the Vulnerable Child by meeting needs for acceptance and love

Materials: No materials are needed

Instructions: First the participants are asked what words they would prefer to hear instead of the Critic's messages and they are written on the blackboard.

'Let's divide our group into two parts and make two rows, so that one person (from the first row) stands facing the other from the second row. Now all together we form a corridor, where you will walk one by one. Now we'll put out our arms in front of us, imagining that our arms are magic antennas sending out attention, love, care, trust, etc. The one who wants to be the first to hear and feel the warm/ caring/loving messages closes their eyes and steps into the corridor. Our antennas will start to send out attention, love and care. You can touch the person, but do it very gently and softly. And while they walk down the corridor – say all the good and nice things that you think and feel about them. You may also use the positive messages that we would prefer to hear, instead of the Critic's messages. The person who will be walking through the corridor will try to do it very slowly, and when they pass you and you say all the nice things you can move to the other end of the corridor in order to extend it a little, and you may say these nice things all over again or say something new.'

MODE-ROLE PLAY WITH THE PUNITIVE CRITIC MODE

Age: 9 and older

Modes: Punitive Critic, Vulnerable Child, Wise/Clever Child modes

Goals: To develop assertiveness, to learn how to give assertive but polite responses to the critical/offensive messages, to support and take care of the Vulnerable Child and to help Wise/Clever mode to take care of and support the Vulnerable Child

Materials:

- Effigy of the Critic (made in a previous group session where participants write critical/offensive messages that they have heard from their parents, relatives, teachers and significant people on the effigy)
- Critic Masks for those who will play this role
- The printed-out phrases – 1. Critical/offensive messages from the effigy 2. Responses to the Critic from the Wise/Clever mode and the Happy Child (assertive and humorous responses). Both sets of messages were produced during the previous sessions.

The process of the role play:

Participants are divided into small groups (usually two participants play the Critics, two participants play Vulnerable Children and all the rest, including therapists, play the Wise/Clever mode). The Wise/ Clever mode group needs to have twice as many participants as the Critic mode.

Those who play the Critics are given the masks and an effigy from one of the previous exercises (if it was not destroyed). It is important for the children playing the Critic to put on masks, to protect them from being later identified with the Critic in the group (transference of negative feelings). This also prevents performers in this role from 'merging' with this mode, and helps to disconnect from it afterwards. The Vulnerable Children are placed in comfortable armchairs, close to each other, situated behind the participants playing Wise/Clever mode. They are given blankets, stuffed animals, etc. The participants playing the Wise/Clever mode are given the lists with the responses to the critical/offensive messages that were prepared in advance during the 'Mean Words Monster' exercise.

1. Each of the Critics chooses one of the critical/offensive phrases from the list and says it.

2. After the first phrase, said by the first Critic, those playing the Wise/Clever mode turn to the Vulnerable Children and (with the therapists' guidance) ask about their feelings, say that they are good, nice, brave, etc., and that they love them as they are, no matter what. They may also add a positive interpretation of the situation ('Dad is probably saying that because he is very angry and hurt and doesn't know another way to express his anger – it's not about you'). The participants playing the Wise/Clever mode then add 'And now we are going to defend you!' and turn back to the Critic.

3. Then the children playing the Wise/Clever mode respond to the Critics. They give assertive/humorous replies/'I'-messages/ etc. with help of the lists of responses, prepared earlier and improvising during the role play. The Critic may answer if he wants to. It continues until the Critic has nothing more to say.

   The therapists provide guidance and help to the children, stopping the action when the children need time to think, before responding to the Critics.

4. Then brief feedback is collected from the Vulnerable Children – they are asked about their feelings and if there are some needs that are not met yet, the children playing the Wise/Clever mode can devote some more time and effort to meeting these needs.

5. The procedure is repeated with Critic no 2 and a critical phrase chosen by them.

6. Feedback is collected from the Critics and Wise/Clever modes.

7. Roles are changed and the procedure is repeated for each Punitive phrase.

8. At the end of the role-play it is important to de-role, saying: 'I am not a critic, I am (name)'.

9. Feedback after the whole exercise. Discuss with participants their feelings and emotions during the game and after it.

10. Afterwards, participants tell the group what words they would have preferred to hear instead of the critical ones.

11. If the group is ready, the therapist tells these positive messages to the entire group at the same time. There is also a more individual variant: the therapists ask the participants to close their eyes, approach each participant, one by one embrace their shoulders and whisper the words in their ear.

12. The participants tell the group how they feel after listening to the supportive messages.

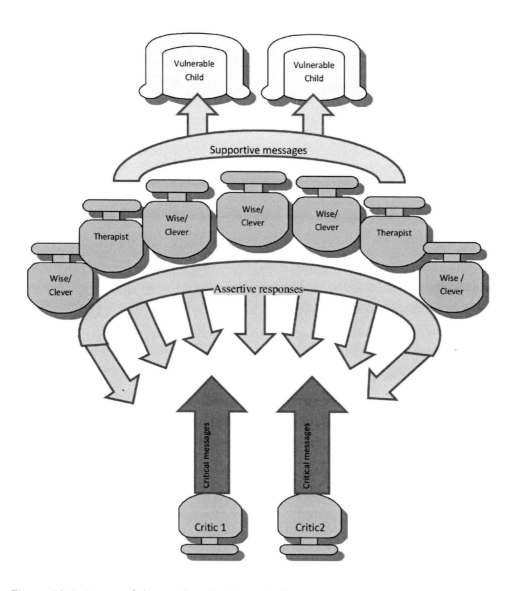

Figure 18.1: A map of the mode-role play with the Punitive Critic mode

'Mode masks'

Age: 12 and older

Modes: Masks can be made for all the modes or only for the Maladaptive Coping modes (it depends on the goals and group)

Goals: To explore the modes and their origins, make a visual representation of the modes and communicate from that mode perspective, giving an opportunity to talk to the mode from a Wise/Clever mode.

Materials: paper, sticky tape, scissors, chopsticks, coloured pencils, felt tip pens, paints, brushes, water, cups

Instructions: 'Today I would like each of you to work with a mode that is important for you now. It can be the most difficult mode for you, or you can choose the mode that you want to develop. First, let's imagine this mode. Then we will draw a draft. After that you will make a mask. I will give all you need: materials, paper, chopsticks. We start by imagining the mode: what creature is it, its facial expression, colour, behaviour. You will have five minutes to make a draft. And then we will make the mask.

Now you have your drafts. Now you can use different art materials: gouache, finger colours, felt-tip pens, pencils, play-dough. To make cuts for eyes you can use knives or scissors. Be as creative as you can. If something goes wrong you can ask for more paper. Please feel free to take anything you want. If you have time you can make a second mask. You have 20 minutes.

So, our works of art are ready. You can put them on the table to let them get dry. In five minutes we will meet our wonderful creatures, our modes. And now you have five minutes to answer the questions about your mode. Here is a list of questions.'

Questions:

■ What mode is it?

■ What is this creature's name?

■ What is the creature like?

- What do they like?
- What don't they like?
- What scares them?
- What do they want most of all?
- What is their attitude to their owner? What does the creature think about the owner?
- What is their function?
- What is their behaviour?
- How do they feel?
- How do they move?
- How do they help their owner? How do they upset their owner?

'Now we are going to introduce our modes to the group. (If there are more than 10 participants, we divide them into two groups.) Please put your mask on and tell us about them.

Now I will turn on the music and we will have a parade of modes. You can feel the mode inside, its behaviour. Please, be careful with other people. It's important to provide safety for yourself and for others. We have 10 minutes.

Now we take our masks off and each of you says: "I am not this mode, I am (Max)".

Now we have 20–30 minutes to work in groups of three. One of you is a person, whose mask (mode) we'll discuss right now; the second and the third will just be themselves (their Wise/Clever mode) and will help the first participant. You as a participant choose which person you want to put your mask on. You can tell your mode about your wishes and suggestions. Choose the type of words that they will accept. The best way is to say "thank you for your work" at the beginning. Than you can explain why this mode limits you (if it does), if this mode is negative for you. If it is a positive mode, you can express your feelings and wishes. Then the Wise/Clever modes can suggest how to meet those needs and express those feelings without the negative outcomes. You can ask for the therapist's support at this point. They can suggest to you what to say or how to say it. The person wearing a mask is trying to feel the mode and to understand the mode's reactions – whether the mode is ready to co-operate or not. If the mode is not ready, the person wearing the mode mask can say what they need in order to be ready to co-operate.

Now discuss this experience in your groups, and then we will discuss it in the whole group.

18.12.3 Stage 3 – Autonomy

Just as in GST with adults (Farrell & Shaw, 2012), the third stage of the group work in ST-CA is aimed at strengthening the Wise/Clever mode. Schema mode change allows changes in dysfunctional life patterns and helps children's core needs get met. One of the main goals at this stage is to help children to implement therapy insights and skills into their everyday lives, remaining in Wise/Clever mode most of the time (see sections in Chapter 10 referring to generalising therapeutic gains to everyday life for more information).

References

Farrell J & Shaw I (2012) *Group Schema Therapy for Borderline Personality Disorder: A Step-by-Step Treatment Manual with Patient Workbook*. Oxford: Wiley-Blackwell.

Farrell J, Reiss N & Shaw I (2014) *The Schema Therapy Clinician's Guide: A Complete Resource for Building and Delivering Individual, Group and Integrated Schema Mode Treatment Programs*. Oxford: Wiley-Blackwell.

Gardner R (1999a) *Individual and Group Therapy and Work with Parents in Adolescent Psychotherapy*. Northvale/New Jersey/London: Jason Aronson Inc.

Gardner R (1999b) *Psychotherapy of Antisocial Behavior and Depression in Adolescence*. Northvale, New Jersey, London: Jason Aronson Inc.,

Holmes DJ (1964) *The Adolescent in Psychotherapy*. Boston: Little, Brown.